P9-EAX-618

DATE DUE

MY 18 '98			
AP 24 '03			
JE 5 '03			

Advocacy in the Classroom

Advocacy in the Classroom

Problems and Possibilities

Edited by Patricia Meyer Spacks

St. Martin's Press
New York

Library of Congress Cataloging-in-Publication Data

Advocacy in the classroom : problems and possibilities / edited by
    Patricia Meyer Spacks.
            p. cm.
    Contains papers presented at a conference held in 1995.
    Includes bibliographical references.
    ISBN 0-312-16127-1
    1. Teaching, Freedom of—United States. 2. Academic freedom-
-United States. 3. Teachers—United States—Political activity.
4. Social advocacy—United States. I. Spacks, Patricia Ann Meyer.
LC72.2.A38 1996
371.1'04—dc20   96-30762
                                           CIP

Design by Acme Art, Inc.

First edition: November, 1996
10 9 8 7 6 5 4 3 2 1

CONTENTS

PART IV: PRACTICE

PART V: RESPONSES

INTRODUCTION

PATRICIA MEYER SPACKS

TEACHERS HAVE THE POWER to change students' minds: that's what makes education possible. Such power holds both promise and danger for a democratic society, its value depending on the specific purposes for which it is used. This collection ponders aspects of the teacher's power, exploring the theory and the practice of classroom advocacy in order to investigate possibilities and limits of responsible pedagogy.

Understandings of advocacy's nature vary from one observer to the next according to political allegiance, disciplinary training, and temperamental predisposition. What some teachers see as their moral and intellectual obligation, others understand as illegitimate intervention. Should the historian trying to engage students in the retrospective perplexities of the Vietnam War feign neutrality in the matter? What about feminists who believe it urgent for students to comprehend their own involvement in issues that have been passionately propounded by writers in the past? Does a gay activist teaching contemporary literature have the right or the duty to argue the activist position? What if that contemporary literature course concerned specifically gay literature? Would it make a difference to the teacher's responsibilities if politics were a course's explicit subject matter? Is it hypocritical to feign neutrality? Which is more dangerous, exerting influence on students' intellectual and moral postures or leading them to discount the urgency of taking stands?

Such questions become increasingly difficult as one contemplates them in detail. At the 1995 conference entitled "The Role of Advocacy in the Classroom" (a conference sponsored by 16 scholarly organizations representing diverse academic disciplines), in which the chapters in this volume originated, debate became heated at times, and differences of opinion abounded—differences reflected in the present volume. Encountering a broad spectrum of disciplinary and personal perspectives enabled some participants to modify their positions; for others, such encounters only sharpened the debate. Virtually everyone appeared to agree, however, about the importance of hearing representations of such a wide range of opinion and about the illumination provided by unexpected convergences of viewpoints as well as by increasingly well-defined differences.

Worry about pedagogical advocacy has a long history, possibly beginning with the execution of Socrates for corrupting the youth of Athens. In chapter 5, Geoffrey R. Stone reviews the early record of attempts to control academic utterance, ending his narrative with World War I. But the history, of course, continues. Many readers of the collection will remember Joseph McCarthy's long reach into the classroom in the 1950s, the era of loyalty oaths, when numerous institutions tried to enforce pedagogical conformity, sometimes against stout resistance but sometimes with abject faculty compliance. The Vietnam years remain vivid: some teachers abandoning their disciplinary responsibilities to participate in "teach-ins" on the war, while colleagues passionately argued the primacy of academic obligation, the continuing necessity that professors should profess the knowledge in which they had been trained. More recently, we have experienced polemics on "political correctness": some thinkers claiming the monolithic politicization of American higher education, with the trinity of race, class, and gender determining every line of investigation. Their opponents argue that knowledge is never neutral, that ways of understanding the past or of grasping a text always further one or another political agenda. They themselves, they would maintain, only make explicit ideological purposes lurking in every classroom. In the meantime, as these extreme positions are debated, thousands of college and university teachers make thoughtful decisions every day about how to present sensitive topics in their classrooms.

The issues these chapters address, in other words, remain immediate and pressing. In Chapter 10, Louis Menand argues that pedagogical passion must always characterize the good teacher, who is by definition an advocate: "It is because we have views about our subjects that we have been hired to teach them." In chapter 8, Gertrude Himmelfarb insists, with equal energy, on the danger of assuming advocacy's omnipresence. She associates the enthusiasm for classroom advocacy with postmodernism and its "denial that there is any such thing as knowledge, truth, reason, or objectivity"—all, in her view, higher ideals than "engagement."

I cite these two chapters to suggest what fundamental disagreements can mark discussions of advocacy: disagreements bearing on pedagogical, moral, social, and political implications of what teachers do in the classroom. Part I, "Themes," establishes many of the complicated issues that in one way or another engage all the writers. The matter of rights versus responsibilities, academic freedom in the context of academic obligation, the difference between representing positions and proselytizing for them, definitions of relevance and irrelevance, intentional as opposed to inadvertent advocacy, ambiguities of power and authority—such polarities and problems preoccupy and vex this group of thinkers. From different disciplinary and personal perspectives, they grapple with intractable difficulties of definition and of recommendation, working out a set of useful—and never dogmatic—principles.

These chapters demonstrate that advocacy as an issue implicates broad questions of academic freedom as well as academic responsibility. The problems connected with it thus touch on some of the most immediately pressing concerns of current academic life. Much is at stake in defining the limits of appropriate classroom advocacy: most urgently, perhaps, the perplexities of how one best seeks and articulates truth. In an eloquent and moving defense of the principle of academic freedom, Ronald Dworkin has demonstrated the weight of meaning attached to the idea that professors in the classroom must suffer no external constraint on their efforts to discover and communicate meaning. He concludes that the profession of university teaching "carries much of the responsibility for maintaining a magnificent ethical tradition."[1] Earlier in his essay, he argues that academic freedom "is an important, structural part of the culture of independence that we need in order to lead the kind of lives that we should," to foster the "ideal of ethical individualism."[2] The chapters collected here substantiate this claim by demonstrating in detail different ways that teachers can express their individual ethical principles. The reader can feel the urgency of ethical discrimination in the struggles of a law professor committed to an anti-abortion position as he tries to leave full freedom for the expression of opposing views in a seminar focused on legal, moral, and rhetorical issues connected with abortion (Chapter 33). The very next chapter conveys the equally compelling passion of a professor of economics who has found satisfaction in teaching Marxian principles to workers. In conjunction, the essentially adversarial positions of a conservative and a radical thinker remind readers of the excitement inherent in the principle of academic freedom, the challenging possibilities of advocacy, and its dangers as well.

Part I defines three broad areas of inquiry: the history of advocacy and of attitudes toward it, principles for separating appropriate from inappropriate advocacy, and classroom practice. The same three categories organize the rest of the volume: Part II, "History," examines issues from 1880 to the 1990s; Part III, "Principles," analyzes everything from the threat of oppression implicit in the principle of political advocacy to the nature of "good" advocacy in art history; and Part IV, "Practice," examines the problems and opportunities of teaching, including relevant legal decisions, the argument for "fight training" in high schools, dilemmas of teaching in public schools, and the special responsibilities of guiding culturally diverse students. The volume concludes with Part V, "Responses," articulating responses to the previous essays.

The disparate chapters generate a powerful cumulative effect by their specificity, their passion, and their sheer variety. They require their readers to ponder legal arguments, principles, and decisions (the case, for instance, of a physical ed teacher who urged his students to tell him if they thought he deviated from the principles of Christian life). They make us reflect about the special kinds of involvement demanded of teachers in traditionally black colleges, the special needs of the student in prison, the pressures of the high school classroom, the implications of teaching Muslim culture in a politically hostile climate, the peculiar requirements of an avowedly religious college.

Each situation imposes a particular set of urgencies. Each narrative and analysis adds new nuances to an understanding of what "advocacy" might imply. Together these accounts make it ever more difficult to assume a simple position for or against classroom advocacy.

Geoffrey Stone concludes his history of academic freedom by observing that

> every form of orthodoxy that has been imposed on the academy—whether religious, political, patriotic, scientific, moral, philosophical, or economic—has been imposed by groups that were fully convinced of the rightness of their positions. And it is equally clear, with the benefit of hindsight and some objectivity, that every one of these groups has later come to be viewed by most thoughtful people as inappropriately intolerant, at best, and as inappropriately intolerant and wrong, at worst. It thus seems clear that . . . we must step back from our own fighting faiths, insist on a less self-righteous stance, and subject our own orthodoxies to ruthless self-criticism.

Our orthodoxies, and our unorthodoxies, as well: we must criticize them and we must value them. Demonstrating diverse manifestations of passionate conviction, this book not only reaffirms conviction's importance, it also implicitly demands tolerance for conviction's many forms. And it dramatizes the many varieties of moral urgency and of pedagogical responsibility that today's teachers bring to their vocation.

The sponsoring organizations for the conference in which the present collection originated were the American Academy of Religion, the American Anthropological Association, the American Association of University Professors, the American Council of Learned Societies, the American Historical Association, the American Philosophical Association, the American Society for Aesthetics, the American Sociological Association, the American Studies Association, the Association of American Geographers, the Association of American Law Schools, the College Art Association, the Middle East Studies Association, the Modern Language Association of America, the Organization of American Historians, and the University of Pittsburgh.

PART I

THEMES

ONE

The Professional Obligations of Classroom Teachers

MYLES BRAND

LET ME BEGIN by briefly describing a skirmish in the recent cultural wars.

At the University of Oregon, where I was then serving as president, an assignment in legal writing for first-year law students was concerned with Supreme Court cases on homosexuality. A part-time writing instructor decided not to follow the prescribed curriculum. He used class time to state that he was gay and to express how he felt about the Court's decisions. He also supplemented his comments with readings from several contemporary literary texts.

A few students felt sufficiently offended by this instructor's actions that they complained to the law dean. The dean concluded that the instructor had overstepped professional propriety and notified him that his contract would not be renewed.

At that point, a firestorm erupted. The local gay and lesbian community, which was not at all fond of this conservative dean, protested strongly. The dean thought that he should publicly explain his actions, and so he called an open meeting for faculty and students. Many attended, including the media. The ensuing meeting was not civil.

Shortly after, my office became involved. I began an investigation by the university's Affirmative Action and Equal Opportunity director. Needless to say, it was difficult to obtain an accurate account of the incident in this highly charged environment.

The director, who was an experienced investigator and attorney, recommended continuing to employ the part-time instructor for an additional year, which would then result in the maximum time a person was able to hold this type of position, according to university regulations. I accepted this recommendation, and the instructor finished his additional year of employment without further incident. However, the dean was scheduled for review the following year, and he was not reappointed. Although this incident did not lead directly to the negative review, it did so indirectly by further eroding the confidence that the law faculty had in him.

During the debate on campus, the subject of professional propriety in the classroom figured prominently. The incident clearly had political overtones, pitting those with a conservative ideology against those with a progressive viewpoint. In particular, it became a significant point of contention between those who publicly argued for the rights of gays, lesbians, and bisexuals and those who desired to inhibit those rights. But with the benefit of hindsight, an intriguing aspect of the debate was the theoretical one. Of course, the political is not wholly separable from the theoretical. But here I want to abstract the theoretical and focus on it in order to explore the relationship between classroom advocacy and the professional obligations of classroom teachers.

Much is said and written about the rights of faculty members. And this is good, since faculty rights are misunderstood, often outside but sometimes also inside the academy. However, professional rights are necessarily accompanied by their complement, professional responsibilities and obligations. In order to understand what is at stake in the theoretical dimension of professional responsibilities, especially with regard to classroom instruction, it is useful to present the major contrary positions in stark form.

The Unbridled Absolutist argues that, no matter the discipline, there is a single, unified set of truths about the subject matter. While we may not know all these truths, our research objective is to identify them, often by working toward closer and closer approximations. It is, then, a faculty member's professional obligation to present to students these truths, and only these truths, as well as the appropriate methods to ascertain them. No other approach in the classroom is acceptable. Thus, advocacy in the classroom—other than in the trivial sense of advocating for the truth—is not permitted.

The Unbounded Relativist argues, to the contrary, that there is no set of truths about any subject matter. He might argue further, though he need not, that truth is a language-bound concept and language cannot in principle mirror the world in a unique way. At best, language can be used to construct a consistent and coherent interpretation or story; but there are indefinitely many such stories, and no designated right one. From this, it is concluded that there can be no professional obligation to present the set of truths to students. And therefore, the classroom teacher is free to advocate for any story he or she prefers, including a highly personal one.

With regard to our part-time instructor, the Unbridled Absolutist would hold that he overstepped professional propriety because he departed from a recitation of the truths embodied in the subject matter, namely the decisions of the Court and the reasoning used to arrive at those decisions. The Unbounded Relativist is committed to the opposite conclusion. Since there are indefinitely many stories about the subject matter, and since no one story has primacy, it was within the professional rights of the instructor to choose the one he preferred.

Of course, these two positions are caricatures and oversimplifications. But they do give us a starting point. My contention is that both the Unbridled Absolutist and Unbounded Relativist are wrong, even when their positions are better articulated and qualified.

Prima facie at least, there is a distinction between normative or value judgments and empirical judgments. In the case of empirical judgments, there is a fact of the matter of which they are about; but in the case of normative judgments, there is no fact of the matter.

These claims are not uncontroversial. Some argue that, at its root, there is no distinction between empirical and normative judgments. I would argue, to the contrary, that there is a distinction to be marked, although likely not in the traditional way of predicating that distinction on certain information, sense data, for example, that is given in some incorrigible manner.

Importantly, even granting that normative judgments are not based on facts of the world, the issue of whether normative judgments are true or false remains open. Some might argue that such judgments are emotive expressions of preferences or attitudes, and hence they have persuasive and rhetorical force but not truth-value. Others might argue that normative judgments reflect a predicted comparison between costs and benefits, or pain and pleasure; and hence they are true or false depending on whether the prediction is accurate for the case at hand or as a general rule.

I side with those who ascribe truth-value to moral and normative judgments, although this is not the place to try to defend a theory of moral judgment or to elucidate a more inclusive theory of normative judgments. The key point here, rather, is that there is a distinction, *prima facie* at least, between empirical and normative judgments.

Now, the Unbounded Relativist argues that there is no purely empirical subject matter; or if there is, it is totally uninteresting intellectually, such as a list of phone numbers, an atlas of place-names, or a compilation of instrument readings. Thus, normative judgments must dominate classroom teaching.

Since there is no fact of the matter in the case of normative judgments, and thus there are indefinitely many consistent stories to tell, the Unbounded Relativist concludes that the classroom teacher is free to present the story he or she most prefers. And if the classroom presentation is based on a faculty member's preferences, then it is impossible for him or her not to be an advocate. That is, a classroom teacher *must* be highly engaged in advocacy.

In response to this line of reasoning, it should be said that the claim that empirical judgments are uninteresting intellectually is controversial at best. While that may be true for pure reports of data, such as lists of instrument readings, it is not the case when we consider generalizations made from empirical information and the conclusions drawn from them. Such generalizations may refer to commonsensical human behavior, for example, when connections are drawn between our attitudes and desires and our actions, or they may be highly systematized, with predictive force, as they are in the physical sciences. Or they may be organized presentations of historical material, as for example in a recitation of Supreme Court decisions. The point is that it is incorrect to claim that normative judgments must, necessarily, dominate in a classroom setting.

However, one should not conclude from this response that classroom teaching is to be limited to empirical judgments. Certainly some normative claims must be part of any learning encounter, if for no other reason than that faculty members must make choices about which material to present and the sequence in which it is to be presented. That is, classroom teaching inevitably involves normative judgments.

Advocacy in the classroom results when normative judgments are conveyed either directly or indirectly through the choice of material and its sequencing. Understood in this way, advocacy in the classroom is inevitable.

It may be objected that the conclusion that advocacy in the classroom is inevitable results from a misinterpretation of the word "advocacy." According to this objection, advocacy involves more than conveying normative judgments. It also contains an element of coercion. When someone advocates a position, within or outside the classroom, he or she is directing you to adopt this position.

This interpretation of "advocacy" is not Webster's, nor is it, I contend, the ordinary, commonsensical interpretation. One way to make this point is to observe that coercion carries with it an implicit threat that there will be some sanction (which can remain un-described) that will be visited upon those who act or believe to the contrary. Thus, it would follow that advocacy itself is tied to the prospect of a sanction. But surely that is not the case. One often advocates for a position, for example, in scholarly exchange, without threat of sanction.

Nonetheless, some persons will want to use "advocacy" in the strong sense in which it implies coercion. This is *not* the sense in which I use it here. To advocate a position is, at the minimum, to state that it is correct and most often additionally to present a defense of the position through the presentation of arguments. In taking sides, as it were, on a position, with or without accompanying argumentation, a person is making a normative judgment. Indeed, every normative judgment is taking sides on some issue.

More to the point, in favoring one position over others, in presenting arguments for this or that position and defending it, the classroom teacher is advocating for it. It is difficult to imagine a successful learning encounter in which the classroom teacher does not present material in this manner. In conveying an interpretation of historical events, the solution to an equation, or a critique of a poem, the teacher is stating a position, and most often giving reasons for it. That is advocacy and it is inevitable in classroom teaching.

Advocacy in the classroom can be either intentional or unintentional. Unintentional advocacy might take the form of unknowingly promulgating the biases of the mainstream of a discipline. Intentional advocacy may reflect a faculty member's favored theoretical approach to the subject matter.

I should think that if advocacy in the classroom is inevitable, in the sense that normative judgments about the subject matter are unavoidably included in the learning encounter, then that advocacy is preferable when it is intentional. Unintentional repetition of disciplinary-based normative judgments runs the risk of perpetuating previous errors and fails to rise to the level of communicated understanding required for good teaching. Certainly a faculty member should understand his or her subject sufficiently deeply to recognize the historical and conceptual context surrounding the mainstream disciplinary approach.

To claim that, if there is advocacy in the classroom, it is better that it be intentional, however, does not yield the conclusion that a faculty member is therefore free to advocate on the basis of his or her personal preferences. There are constraints on advocacy that result from one's professional obligations. To abridge these constraints is to exceed advocacy and undertake proselytizing. There is, I contend, an indefeasible professional obligation not to proselytize.

This obligation is a shared one between the faculty member, on the one hand, and the academic department, school, or perhaps the entire university, on the other hand. The faculty member's part of the obligation is to advocate within the bounds of a *contextualized account;* the institution's part of the obligation is to offer the student a *balanced approach.*

A contextualized account involves at least the following factors. When a position is presented in a classroom setting, it should be located in the context of the dialectic of the field. Subject matter should not be taught as dogma. This point seems obvious in the case of the humanities and the arts. Students, and most certainly students presumed unsophisticated in the subject matter, should not be taught, for example, a psychoanalytic reading of *Macbeth* without also providing either alternative readings or a perspective on the reception that psychoanalytic readings have received. Quite importantly, this point also applies to the sciences, including the physical sciences. To teach physics, for example, as dogma is not to provide a contextualized account. The context of scientific discovery, one that involves false starts, changes of paradigm, active controversy, and social influences, should be included. I suggest that a contextualized approach to teaching physics is appropriate to introductory courses—indeed, it is especially appropriate to introductory courses. Of course, it is not necessary, nor is it desirable, for the classroom teacher to dwell continuously on the context and dialectic of the position advocated. That could well be misleading. Rather, he or she has the obligation to make clear the context of the position and methodology at appropriate times in the course.

A contextual account precludes proselytizing. Proselytizing is not the same as advocacy. Advocacy, in its intentional mode, is the knowing incorporation of normative judgments in classroom presentations. Proselytizing, while it incorporates the use of normative judgments, even knowingly, has an ulterior motive not present in advocacy. The ulterior motive is to persuade, cajole, and in some fashion coerce the listener, who in this case is the captive student, to adopt personally the position advocated. Proselytizing in the classroom refers to the mode of presentation, the intentions and motives of the teacher. It does not refer specifically to the content of what is communicated; on that it is neutral.

We often associate proselytizing with religious activity. The hellfire-and-brimstone preacher is an obvious example, but in general all conversion religions practice the art. However, proselytizing is not restricted to religious activity. One can proselytize about politics, the economy, a specific interpretation of a work of art, a specific physical theory, or indeed about any subject. To proselytize is to attempt to convert the listener to one's position. Except as a tool for that conversion, proselytizing does not include providing a context for the position advocated, nor does it generally attempt to engender understanding of the dialectic leading to the position. The purpose of proselytizing is to convince someone of the rightness of one's position. Leaving aside force, there is little that is precluded for the proselytizer. Again, proselytizing is a mode of presentation whose objective is to convert the listener to one's views. Proselytizing is defined by the intentions with which the case is made as well sometimes as the manner of communication, but not the context of the position advocated.

Sometimes it is easy to determine that the speaker is proselytizing. The social circumstances—a political rally, for example—can be a strong indicator; the speaker's manner of presentation, likewise, can be a signal of proselytizing. But sometimes it can be quite difficult to decide whether the speaker is proselytizing or advocating a position (in the sense of "advocacy" at issue here). The social situation and the manner of presentation—say, a classroom lecture presented with grace—can be deceiving.

Indeed, there is likely a gray area between strong advocacy and proselytizing, in which intentions blur and arguments in context shade into attempts to convert. It is better, then, to think of a continuum between advocacy and proselytizing. Nonetheless, not all cases are blurred. In general, there is a difference between advocacy and proselytizing, and we can discern that difference in the vast majority of situations.

The professional obligation of a teacher is to bring the student to the point of understanding; it is decidedly not to persuade the student, using any and all means available to the instructor, to adopt the position presented. One key goal of a liberal education is to provide students with the information and reasoning facility that will enable them to make decisions on conceptual and practical matters of consequence. Proselytizing attempts to remove this decision from the student; it substitutes the judgment of the teacher for that of the student.

It is not always easy to present a contextual account when one is convinced of a particular position. Often the enthusiasm that a faculty member feels toward a particular approach to the subject matter colors the presentation. I do not intend to suggest that enthusiasm should be stifled, that there is an obligation to be cool and impersonal in the classroom. Clearly, an enthusiastic style invites understanding and improves the learning environment. Rather, the point is that the subject matter should be presented within a dialectic context and without proselytizing. This approach to the subject matter is fully consistent with a style that demonstrates love and enthusiasm for the intellectual endeavor.

A contextual account provides the student with a framework within which to understand and interpret the classroom teacher's position. However, most often it does not provide the student with alternative accounts and approaches. It would be overreaching to maintain that each faculty member should canvass alternative positions and approaches. Faculty members are expected to have a point of view; they are expected to advocate for a position, for an interpretation, for a methodological approach. That trait, it can be argued, is a prerequisite for being a good teacher and scholar. Yet the student ought to have the benefit of learning alternative positions. Some alternatives can be garnered from assigned readings. But that is not sufficient. The student should have available alternatives presented in a manner that permits exploration and debate.

Faculty members' professional obligations do not stop at the doorways to their classrooms. Each faculty member is also part of larger instructional units: the department, the college or school, and the university. It is this larger group that has the obligation to provide a balanced approach. By a balanced approach, I mean access to course work or other instructional opportunities that acquaint students with the major and reasonable positions and methodologies of key subject matter areas. It is the department, or several departments taken together, or even the university as whole that has the obligation to provide this type of intellectual access for students.

Strictly speaking, groups do not have obligations, only persons, the members of the groups. Thus, each faculty member should, as a member of a department, school, and university, assure that every student has access to a balanced approach. A faculty member, then, has a dual obligation: as a classroom teacher, he or she is obliged to present contextualized accounts of the subject matter; and as a member of an academic group, he or she is obliged to assure that there is access to a balanced approach to the subject matter.

To take an example, a contextual account of introductory physics would resist presentation as pure dogma and include a historical context for physical theory. The classroom teacher might, for instance, make reference to the paradigm shift that occurred when relativity replaced Newtonian mechanics, or he or she might discuss some of the present-day controversies in, say, high-energy physics, in order to illustrate the process of discovery. Instruction at this level, which includes but goes beyond a list of equations for problem solving, would yield a good understanding of the nature of our knowledge of the physical world. But this account, although contextualized, would leave out an aspect of physical science that has recently been the subject of significant scholarship, namely the social context of scientific theory. To balance the approach ordinarily taken in physics departments, a student should have access to, say, courses in feminist epistemology or in the history and philosophy of science. It is not that the physicist, in teaching his subject, must include an extensive treatment of feminist epistemology, but rather the student should have access through other courses or means to learn about the social context of science.

One consequence of this perspective is that faculty members have a professional obligation not to be chauvinistic about their subject matter. As citizens of a college and university, physicists have an obligation to ensure—and certainly, not to prevent—that alternative approaches are taught. But similarly, those in, say, women's studies and philosophy departments have an obligation to ensure the continued availability of strong mainstream science instruction.

When describing a balanced approach, I indicated that students should have access to the major and reasonable alternative positions and methodologies. Two points of clarification need to be made.

First, not all alternative positions are reasonable positions. In the study of twentieth-century European history, for instance, a balanced approach decidedly does not include access to courses that argue that the Holocaust did not occur. Similarly, access to courses on astrology is not part of a balanced approach to teaching about the physical world. Astrology and denial of the Holocaust simply are not reasonable positions. Criteria for being a reasonable position are difficult to discern. Such criteria would need to include original and controversial alternative positions, for without them scholarly advances would not occur, but simultaneously exclude approaches that defy empirical confirmation or coherent argumentation. I expect that, in the vast majority of cases, we can distinguish legitimate alternatives from the unreasonable ones, even in the absence of fully specified criteria.

The second point of clarification is that to say a student should have access to such alternatives is not to imply that there is any requirement for students to undertake study of these alternatives. A physics student, like all students, should have the opportunity to study the social context of natural science as well as the history and philosophy of science, but that should not necessarily be part of the mandated curriculum. Similarly, students focusing on feminist critiques of science should have the opportunity to undertake study of mainstream science. It might be presumed that these latter students would automatically have access to regular science courses because they are so readily available in the university. But students lose access if they are strongly discouraged from taking mainstream science by faculty members or advisors. Faculty members in women's studies, philosophy, or other departments that offer alternative approaches to understanding science have a professional obligation to encourage students to explore mainstream approaches. Of course, the converse is also true: faculty members in mainstream science departments have a professional obligation not to discourage students from studying other approaches.

It should be emphasized that a faculty member's obligation to ensure a balanced approach has consequences for constructing the curriculum. Often faculty members conceive of their obligations in curriculum formation as having two primary components. One is to provide a core of courses focusing on skills and competencies, such as writing, critical thinking, foreign language study, basic mathematics, and science. Students often have choices through distribution options in satisfying this part of the curriculum requirements. The other obligation is taken to be development of course work for the major. Usually this part of the curriculum is highly prescribed for students, and the academic department, with some constraints, has autonomy in developing the requirements for the major.

However, there is also a third part of a faculty member's obligations with respect to the curriculum, namely to assure that, taking the curriculum as a whole, students have access to a balanced approach. Through appropriate committees, the entire campus curriculum should be reviewed periodically. My sense is that, for the most part, such reviews rarely occur. The main reason is that developing a balanced approach competes with departmental and disciplinary forces that seek to capture and control segments of the curriculum. The obligation to provide students with access to alternative perspectives overrides the disciplinary inclination to control the curriculum. Here students' needs take precedence. Faculty members should see themselves as members of the university community, not merely as members of departments or schools.

Similarly, departments themselves have some obligation to present a balanced approach to their subject. For instance, a philosophy department that teaches only from the analytic perspective, without providing opportunities for students to study pluralistic or Continental philosophy, fails to provide access to a balanced approach. But in the case of a department's offerings, the lack of a balanced approach can be compensated by other departments' providing appropriate course work. So, the lack of balance in an entirely analytic philosophy department can be compensated by offerings in, say, comparative literature and English. When that occurs, it is incumbent upon members of the primary department, here the philosophy department, not merely to permit such complementary offerings but to encourage them.

To return now to the earlier debate, I part company with the Unbridled Absolutist. He assumes that there is a single, unique set of truths for each subject matter. I make no such assumption. There may be more than one reasonable interpretation of the facts, and most often in complex matters there is more than one.

The requirement that there be a balanced approach is contrary to the Unbridled Absolutist view that there can be only one correct account and that is the one that must be presented. A balanced approach admits of alternative interpretations of the subject matter; it requires that faculty members as a group provide for alternative approaches and methodologies.

The Unbridled Absolutist rejects advocacy in the classroom because, to the extent possible, he eschews normative judgments in classroom presentations. Here the Unbridled Absolutist goes too far. As long as normative judgments are provided within the setting of a contextual account, and not in the service of proselytizing, they fit fully within the scope of professional propriety.

But I also part company with the Unbounded Relativist. He concludes that, since there are indefinitely many stories or interpretations, and since no one of them has claim to be true, all interpretations are equally acceptable. If all interpretations are equally acceptable, then it can only be a matter of personal preference which one the classroom teacher adopts.

From the claim that there may be more than one adequate interpretation, it does not follow that all are equally acceptable. And it certainly does not follow that the classroom teacher is entirely free to follow his or her particular personal preferences. Rather, the professional obligation is to present a thoughtful and reasonable contextual account, and this does place constraints on the classroom teacher.

The teacher who selects for presentation the position that seems most adequate is advocating for this interpretation. In so advocating, the classroom teacher explains why this interpretation is the preferred one, with reference to the history and dialectic of the field.

To recapitulate, a contextual account includes a perspective on the history and dialectic of the subject matter; alternative accounts are primarily the responsibility of faculty members taken as a group. Together, a contextual account conjoined with a balanced approach provides a well-rounded viewpoint but excludes proselytizing. Proselytizing is not identical with advocacy. Advocacy, in its intentional mode, is the knowing use of normative judgments in the presentation of the subject matter. Proselytizing goes well beyond advocacy in attempting to use undue pressure in order to convince students to adopt a certain perspective.

Our goal as teachers in the liberal arts and science tradition is not to persuade and cajole students into adopting one perspective or another, but rather to equip them with background information, abilities to reason, and enthusiasm for the subject matter so that they can develop their own perspective—and, indeed, so that they can change perspectives.

Classroom teachers cannot but be advocates. Advocacy, in this context, means making value judgments in the transference of knowledge. It is hard to imagine a productive classroom learning experience devoid of normative judgments. Proselytizing, by contrast, is intended to persuade through excessive pressure. The professional obligations of a faculty member include the presentation of a contextual account and participation in making available to the student a balanced approach. A contextual account and a balanced approach are not value-free; but they wear their normativity on their sleeves, as it were. Proselytizing does not merely communicate value judgments, it attempts to gain adoption coercively.

Of course, I intend this discussion of the theoretical dispute with which we began to be suggestive, but not conclusive. A more complete argument would develop the key concepts of a contextual account and a balanced approach in much greater detail. So, too, the nature of an appropriate historical or dialectic context needs to be described more fully and accurately. The idea must be articulated that there can be, and often is, more than one interpretation of the facts of the matter, without lapsing into the Unbounded Relativist position that all interpretations are equally acceptable. Additionally, discussion of a balanced approach leads quickly into the issue of curriculum. That, by itself, is a topic of very significant debate, a debate that is ongoing, as it should be.

And what about our part-time legal writing instructor? From the theoretical perspective propounded here, he overstepped his bounds. If the complaining students were accurate in their description of the event, the instructor did not present a contextual account of the material. He went beyond advocacy to proselytizing. He knowingly attempted through undue influence to persuade the students in his class of his perspective. The students complained because—to give them the benefit of the doubt—they felt captive to his presentation. This instructor failed to fulfill his professional obligation.

It might be responded that students in the class had a right to gain a perspective other than that embodied in the Supreme Court cases, and the instructor was providing this alternative. However, the instructor's obligation was to present a contextual account of the Court's decisions on homosexuality, which means providing the framework for the Court's decisions; it does not involve proselytizing for his own viewpoint. It is true that students in the class should have access to perspectives different from the one that the instructor was expected to advocate in the class. But that access should be made possible through other classes in the law school, or more likely other classes in the university, not necessarily in this particular class, with its closely prescribed syllabus. Access, similarly, might also be obtained through visiting speakers, discussion groups, and so forth. To the extent that faculty members in the university have not provided access to the position argued by the instructor (presented, of course, without proselytizing), they are failing to meet *their* obligation to provide a balanced approach to this issue.

Was the instructor's action a firing offense, as the dean believed? Admittedly the instructor's presentation exceeded the limits of a contextual account. But that, by itself, is not usually a firing offense, even for those without the protection of tenure. We would have few classroom teachers remaining if each was terminated for presenting an account that overreached contextual limits and included an element of proselytizing. Repeated failure to meet one's professional obligations when provided with clear and direct criticism would be sufficient for termination, but that is not what occurred here.

Was the community reaction justified by the dean's action, given that there were other means available for reviewing his decision? That is a political question, and I leave for others that topic, including the issue of leveraging classroom disputes into political gains.

The Political Magic of Claims to Neutral Universalisms

Or: How to Appear Fair While Converting Substantive Challenges to Political Advocacy

―――――――――

TROY DUSTER

THE IDEA OF "ADVOCACY IN THE CLASSROOM" is a bit of a Rorschach. Who is doing the categorizing of the advocate, and who is advocating what against whom? Several months after it was announced that I was going to be one of the speakers at the "Role of Advocacy in the Classroom" symposium, I received a letter from a colleague, a professor at another university. In this letter, he asked that I address a particular matter, which he said, was the larger issue. Here is part of what he wrote: "The issue is the nature and source of our professional knowledge and authority. Deborah Bowen raised this issue in the fall 1993 *ADE Bulletin,* when she asked 'How can I teach a reading that allows for difference when by definition I, already endowed with institutional authority in the eyes of both students and self, consider my own reading to be the best?'"

In this formulation of advocacy, the students are characterized as the challengers of professorial authority. "Advocacy" is rendered as a threat to the faculty member's capacity to be authoritative when communicating some important feature of the curriculum. Yet, upon closer inspection, the issue of authoritative voice of the instructor and implied "political" advocacy of the student can be seen through different lenses as anything but a singular truth under attack.

I want to begin by telling four stories—each of them addressing the issue of advocacy and authority in the classroom, from a slightly different angle. I will then shift to provide some interesting social, historical, and demographic data, and finally, return to the main theme.

The first story goes back some twenty-five years, when I was a relatively young, recently appointed instructor. I had one of those nightmarish experiences that one can usually only conjure in the earliest years of one's teaching career. I was invited to the University of British Columbia to teach a course in social anthropology. I was lecturing about the then common wisdom in the field, and all was going along rather well. I was describing the famous "potlatch" ceremony among the Kwakiutl Indians—explaining what it meant to the Kwakiutl—when, all of a sudden, the nightmare came to life. A student raised his hand and said, "Professor Duster, I am a Kwakiutl Indian—and what you say about the ceremony and its meaning just is not so!" He said that Western-trained anthropologists misunderstood the potlatch ceremony—that it was not a purely pathological display of competition. Rather, he said, there was a different kind of symbolic meaning to "giving" that had eluded the anthropologists from an alien culture.

At that moment, I had some choices. I could have treated his statement as a "challenge to my authority," and I could have said summarily, "Young man, what I have reported is printed in the literature of the field, based on observations by the most esteemed of anthropologists. How dare you challenge their interpretation?"

Or I could have listened with an ear to defeating whatever point he was trying to make—a not-untypical debating posture in the academy, when challenged. But something gave me pause. It is my second story:

Recall that at the time, I was still a relatively young instructor, not so far from having received my own graduate training, indeed, not so far from having been an undergraduate. I remembered having taken a course in the history of journalism at Northwestern University when I was an undergraduate. For the whole term, we read about the nineteenth-century giants of the field. But there was no mention of a figure that I knew had been an important force in the history of "investigative reporting." I knew of this figure because I had heard stories at my mother's knee . . . a journalist who, in her time, had been a well-known public figure, and who just happened to be my mother's mother. Had I raised this issue as an undergraduate, I would have been seen as an upstart, challenging the established authority. Now, some 40 years later, my grandmother's story is part of the standard history of American journalism.[1] Sometimes personal experiences make one more receptive to hearing alternative stories from students that challenge the established and conventional wisdom.

The third story is of very recent vintage. I was in Barcelona, Spain, delivering a series of lectures at the university there. One of my colleagues, a well-traveled academic, completely bilingual in English and Spanish, told me a story about his child's educational experience that caught my attention—and that fits perfectly into the theme of this volume.

For several years, he and his wife and young child had lived in England. His son had attended the English schools and had learned of the exploits of Sir Francis Drake. For the English, Drake is a national hero. But the family left England and returned to Spain a few years later. Here the son once again was sitting in a classroom studying history when he heard an account of someone called "El Pirata Drake." The Spanish texts had nothing good to say about "El Pirata Drake."

And so the student raised his hand: "Is this the same Drake who is called 'Sir Francis' in England?"

So, which is he? Sir Francis . . . or El Pirata? Is there a clear and definitive answer? Or are we left with a kind of endless relativism? So far, this is only the student's problem. There are, of course, voices among us that chide those who would say this is a matter of "relativity"—that it depends on one's position—or, as they like to say these days, "positionality." Here is what the *Encyclopedia Britannica* (volume 7) has to say about Drake: "English admiral, the greatest and most famous of Elizabethan seamen. . . . In 1566, he sailed on a slaving voyage from Guinea to South America. [Between 1569 and

1573] he was the most successful of the many corsairs raiding the Spanish main. . . . [In 1578] sailing alone up the coasts of Chile and Peru, he sacked towns and plundered shipping, notably, the 'Cacafuego' treasure ship."[2]

Again, to this point, the problem is simply that of a single student, caught between two versions of an historical figure. So long as all the students in England are sitting in an English classroom listening to an English version of the story, there is no problem of perceived "advocacy." And so long as all the students in Spain are sitting in a Spanish classroom listening to a Spanish version of the story, there is no problem of perceived "advocacy." But what happens when half the students in the classroom are English and half are Spanish? Suppose some have heard version one, of Sir Francis, and the others have heard version two, of El Pirata? Who is the advocate? Now how do we frame "advocacy in the classroom"? What do we do with the presumed authority of the instructor in Deborah Bowen's phrase?

All this is still within Western Europe and refers to some agreed-upon terms such as "piracy at sea." But what do we do when we have Eastern and Western traditions of the world in the same classroom, and we are giving them just the historical facts?

This situation is not just hypothetical. To demonstrate my point Tables 2.1 and 2.2 present the most recent figures from the University of California, Berkeley, indicating proportion of students by race and ethnicity.

At Berkeley, among currently enrolled students, 39 percent are Asian Americans; 32 percent are white Americans; 14 percent are Latino Americans; and 6 percent are African Americans.

The trend continued. In the fall 1995 entering class at Berkeley, just under 40 percent were Asian Americans, whites were at 31 percent of the freshman class, Latinos at 16 percent, and Blacks at about 6 percent.

SET AND SETTING FOR "ADVOCACY"

In San Francisco today, some residents of the North Beach area, which has been predominantly Italian for much of this century, sense

TABLE 2.1

BERKELEY CAMPUS ENROLLMENT BY ETHNICITY, 1995 (%)

	American Indian	Asian American	African American	Hispanic Chicano/Latino	White	Other (& no data)
Enrollment	1	39	6	14	32	8

TABLE 2.2

BERKELEY CAMPUS FRESHMAN ENROLLMENT
BY ETHNICITY, 1995

	American Indian	Asian American	African American	Hispanic Chicano/Latino	White	Other (& no data)
Registered (n)	63	1,268	222	531	1,018	298
Registered (%)	1.9	38.4	6.7	16.1	30.8	6.0

that the community is being "encroached upon" by an expanding Chinese and Asian community.

What is the history of Chinese and Italians in California that might throw this into a larger perspective? Were the Chinese permitted only as immigrants to build the railroads and, later, to do the laundry? Many history books give that impression, and many begin and end there.

What happens when we have a situation paralleling what I described earlier in which the classroom is not just hypothetically half Spanish and half English but rather is actually about one-third Chinese and one-third white, and the instructor tells some version of the following (hi)story?

Historian Sandy Lydon has pointed out how the Chinese were the superior fishermen in the Monterey peninsula—much better than the Italian fisherman. Indeed, they were so much better that the

Italians used political power to establish zones, which ultimately excluded the Chinese. Lydon reports that, by 1878, over half the fish caught in Santa Cruz county were caught by Chinese. The design of the Chinese boats gave them an advantage over the Italians. The coastline at Santa Cruz was shallow and more exposed, and the Italians were using keeled feluccas, not the flat-bottomed boats used by the Chinese. According to Lydon, in 1879 the 139,000 pounds of fresh fish put aboard the railroad in Santa Cruz were joined by the 177,000 pounds of Chinese-caught fish loaded at Capitola and Soquel.

With the coming of the railroad connections to Santa Cruz, several hundreds and then thousands more Italians arrived, hungry for employment. They would compete directly with the Chinese, but not just to see who was best at a meritocratic game. In the late 1870s and early 1880s, the Italians banded together to get politicians to pass regulations to prohibit Chinese from fishing.[3] In 1879 they succeeded in getting a constitutional provision that prohibited the Chinese from fishing in California's coastal waters. In May 1880 this was vigorously enforced, and within eight years the Chinese had been driven out of fishing in the area.

When I tell this story in my class, there is an uncomfortable stirring. Both whites and Asians are listening, indeed both Italians and Chinese are listening, in the same classroom.

Suppose I give the version of the story that the whites like to hear—that through hard work and perseverance, they prevailed? And suppose some Chinese American student, who has been reading about Chinese American history from Ron Takaki or Sucheng Chan across campus, challenges my narrow, singular interpretation?[4] Is that Asian student now an "advocate" guilty of white male bashing? Is it Sir Francis Drake, or is it El Pirata Drake? If I go with the Chinese version, the white students complain that this is just a class in "political correctness." They want their "Sir Francis Drake" and not any disturbing interpretation of El Pirata.

The title of my chapter is cumbersome, but now to the point: The Political Magic of Claims to Neutral Universalisms, Or: How to Appear Fair While Converting Substantive Challenges to Political Advocacy. If I as instructor simply take the position that what I have to say is based on objective truth—that Sir Francis Drake was a great navigator—then, when one of my students raises the question of whether this was El Pirata Drake, I can simply say that the student is being political. Notice that, as instructor, I get to preempt the claim to neutral, technical expertise. I alone possess this control over the curriculum. I get to assert my authority as the holder and upholder of principles of universalisms while the challenge to my assertion is said to be political.

This is what Elizabeth Minnich calls the false claim to universalism that disguises particular interests.[5] Minnich is pointing out that what we often hear in the academy is the preemptive strike of the claim to "universalisms"—which are often little more than unexamined assumptions and unexamined privileges of the group in power. But what do we do? I would be the first to acknowledge that personal experience as the singular source of authority is not the answer—and that there is a danger in taking it down this road! The truth, of course, is that he was both Sir Francis Drake and El Pirata Drake. Those who would deny this truth and claim that they transcend issues of perspective and position would deny the most fundamental truth of all—the role of power in pushing the dominant narrative inside national boundaries.

This is about dialogue, about who gets to come to the table to establish what is the truth: did the Kwakiutl student at the University of British Columbia have a version of the truth—or was he to be dismissed by Lynne Cheney and Dinesh D'Souza and the National Association of Scholars *(sic!)* as simply the purveyor of a victimology, white male bashing, and "political correctness"?[6] Only if I let him speak (advocate?) would I find out. When he did speak, he informed the class with a spellbinding account of the potlatch ceremony that enriched the learning experience—not because he was completely right, or because he brought a single version of the truth, but because he rounded out a picture to help explain why Western-trained anthropologists might see such gift-giving as "excessively competitive, aggressive, and hostile." Meanwhile, the Lynne Cheneys of Spain are insisting that Drake was really El Pirata, and the Lynne Cheneys of England are insisting that he was really Sir Francis—and that those who challenge are "political advocates" in the otherwise neutral classroom.

NOTES

1. Alfreda M. Duster (Ed.), *The Autobiography of Ida B. Wells* (Chicago: University of Chicago Press, 1970).
2. *Encyclopaedia Britannica,* Volume 7, 1965, 626.
3. Sandy Lydon, *Chinese Gold: The Chinese in the Monterey Bay Region* (Capitola, CA: Capitola Book Company, 1985), 49, 51.
4. Ronald T. Takaki, *A Different Mirror: A History of Multicultural America* (Boston: Little, Brown & Co., 1993); Sucheng Chan, *Asian Americans: An Interpretive History* (Boston: Twayne Publishers, 1991).
5. Elizabeth Minnich, "Liberal Learning and the Arts of Connection for the New Academy." Scribe for the National Panel on American Commitments: Diversity, Democracy, and Liberal Learning (Washington, DC: Association of American Colleges and Universities, 1995).
6. Lynne V. Cheney, *Telling the Truth: Why Our Culture and Our Country Have Stopped Making Sense—and What We Can Do About It* (New York: Simon and Schuster, 1995); Dinesh D'Souza, *Illiberal Education: The Politics of Race and Sex on Campus* (New York: Random House [Vintage], 1991).

THREE

Fear and Loathing in the Classroom: Faculty and Student Rights in Comparative Context

MICHAEL A. OLIVAS

THIS CHAPTER, LIKE GAUL, IS DIVIDED IN THREE PARTS: a restatement of the law of academic freedom, particularly the "third essential freedom"—how classroom material shall be taught and the implication for student rights[1]; a hurried review of several developing cases that pose new challenges to teachers' autonomy in the classroom; and some unhurried thoughts on the direction this conflict is taking. Several of the examples I draw upon derive from my own, perhaps idiosyncratic, teaching experience; nonetheless, this is not a full-blown exercise in critical race theory,[2] or even in making personal the political. Rather, I attempt to offer guideposts from the emerging case law and to suggest how good practice, derived from professional norms, is highly contextual but also largely intuitive and common sense. It is my experience that very few troubled teachers have pristine records but that their problems have more often been of long-standing concern to colleagues.

But I begin with a more optimistic premise, that, despite the increasing legalization of higher education and a stealthy encroachment by disabilities legislation—which can override pro-fessorial authority in substantial portions in order to accommo-date physically or mentally disabled students[3]—the heart of the learning enterprise is largely undisturbed today, recognizable to its medieval university roots. Today's large labs, high-technology classrooms, and interactive computer-aided instruction are not highly evolved from faculty-student interaction in Oxford, Paris, Bologna, or Salamanca classrooms. It is the legal environment that has changed, not Mark Hopkins on the log.[4]

Thus, I arrive at my formulation of this issue: discussions of academic freedom are a legal discourse; a line of developing cases threatens to politicize and legalize the classroom in ways not envi-sioned before; and only by forging consensus on normative behavior and by self-policing will faculty be able to retain their classroom autonomy. These three elements are essential prerequisites for devel-oping one's own pedagogical style, including how much of an advocate for an ideological/political/partisan position one chooses to be in a given class. But evolving a position and examining that constellation of assumptions is not a theoretical nicety; it is an absolute necessity in undertaking a teaching profession.

While I do not struggle with it daily or let doubts paralyze me, I confess that I teach differently depending on the context of subject matter material, degree of partisanship possible, level of student sophistication, and evolution of the field of study. Thus, when teaching immigration law, I routinely remind myself not to give short shrift to INS viewpoints of the Immigration and Naturalization service on an issue; this remains a constant struggle, given govern-ment perfidy[5] and the developing spirit of nativism sweeping the land, but most important, I struggle with it consciously. On some issues I voice my doubts on both sides, negotiate a discussion in class to elicit polarities, and use the resultant exchanges (usually sharply divided) to gain an appreciation of the legitimate governmental role in this crucial function—the issue of constituting our political community. I have a good colleague, a more conservative Anglo who teaches immigration and nationality law at an elite eastern law school. His major concern is that his ethnic minority students cannot rationally discuss limits upon immigration, legal or undocumented.

As a Mexican American, I am assumed by most students to be pro-immigrant, while he labors under no preconceptions. Issues of advocacy in the classroom often turn upon characteristics ascribed by students to their teachers (such as that women teachers are feminists, favor women, and are "soft on social issues"[6] or that professors of color are "too sensitive" on issues of race, as in Derrick Bell's now-famous case at Stanford Law School[7]), rather than on their professors' actual views, which many of us struggle to control or, at least, not to represent as the only truth.

But I note how little I struggle with these issues of advocacy in teaching legal ethics, even though the opportunity to proselytize is greater in this subject matter where proper behavior is extremely relativistic and uncharted. Here, due to the nonethnic context of the course material, I am not perceived as a reflexively antigovernment partisan. It is little wonder that race, gender, and sexuality provoke the most frequent faculty-student clashes. In legal ethics, I find myself trying to spark student interest, while in immigration law I am always trying to harness it and to channel student beliefs—not well understood but strongly felt—into useful discussions, once the highly technical subject matter has been examined.

ACADEMIC FREEDOM FOR THEE AND ME

In a nutshell, expression of controversial ideas and criticism of the status quo must be protected, even at the risk of discomfort for the teacher or class, when a professor is teaching within her field. Accordingly, a graduate student who wished to discuss men's and women's spatial-reasoning skills in a class he was teaching on comparative animal behavior but who feared prosecution under the university's hate-speech code could convince a federal court that the code endangered his First Amendment rights.[8] But academics still must adhere to professional standards, ones that result from training, developed expertise, and scrupulous care in presenting material. Conversely, a mathematician who insisted that 2 plus 2 equals 5 could be fired for failing to meet professional measures of competence; an English teacher, police file clerk, or telephone operator, on the contrary, could not be fired for holding such a belief.[9] While the calculus grows more complex for interdisciplinary fields, peer-review journals and tenure committees routinely invoke the professional standard of care. Professional standards are common in academic practice.

A necessary corollary, however, is that a heightened core of professional protection need not translate into more protection for "intramural utterances" (nonprofessorial speech) than nonacademics receive. Thus, an art professor who vandalizes rare documents,[10] or a university president who makes an obscene and harassing phone call from campus,[11] should not be able to claim any more or less protection than any member of the community. To broaden protection of such intramural speech, a more principled path would be to exceed the current minimum[12] and expand everyone's political speech rights, rather than to concoct an overbroad conception of academic freedom. Faculty should be entitled to special consideration only in pursuing academic endeavors (hence "academic" freedom), such as in the laboratory, library, or classroom. Extending the protections of academic freedom to extra-academic speech, in this light, is unprincipled.

There should therefore be a permeable border between professorial speech and nonprofessorial speech. Professor David Rabban argues for a similar approach. In distinguishing between "academic freedom" and the general free speech clause, he urges:

> The distinctive professional functions of professors provide the basis for applying a special first amendment concept to them. But what is the first amendment justification for treating the aprofessional speech of professors differently from the speech of anyone else?
>
> The only plausible justification is that the line between professional and aprofessional speech may be controversial, and that protection for clearly aprofessional speech is needed to give "breathing room" to the professional speech that is the special subject of academic freedom. Such a drastic prophylactic rule is unnecessary and would be likely to generate more resentment against the "special pleading" of professors than even a narrow and convincing conception of academic freedom inevitably does.

A generous definition of professional speech is a feasible and better response to this legitimate concern.

There are legitimate first amendment reasons for protecting the political speech of public employees generally. Indeed, the Supreme Court has done so while rejecting the "right/privilege" distinction popularized by [Justice] Holmes. But as the Supreme Court has recognized, it is the free speech clause, not the special first amendment right of academic freedom, that provides the constitutional basis for this protection.[13]

Under Rabban's attractive approach, courts would produce a "coherent and convincing specific conception of constitutional academic freedom,"[14] specifically acknowledging professorial speech by teachers and distinguishing it from other protected speech. This theory harmonizes well with the approach I advocate, where core professorial speech is broadly protected, although still subject to norms of professional practice.

Even if a more fully articulated professorial practice theory were to be accepted by the courts, difficulty might arise in accommodating students' rights in cases in which a professor arguably exceeds professorial authority in classroom instruction. It is to this narrow issue I turn, as the small number of cases in this area directly challenge the broad protection of truly professorial speech advocated earlier. I conclude that students should have breathing room to bring grievances when their rights as learners have been violated, but only when professorial speech is well wide of the mark, such as speech in the context of classroom instruction that is judged by peers as undeserving of protection.

In an earlier article on this subject, I reviewed several important legal cases where faculty and student rights came into direct conflict.[15] One involved prayer in the public college classroom, where the court precluded the practice, finding that the Establishment Clause mandated the college discontinue the practice.[16] Another religion case pitted a public university against an exercise physiology professor who invited students in his class to judge him by Christian standards and to admonish him if he deviated from these tenets. The Appeals Court held that colleges exercise broad authority over pedagogical issues and that "a teacher's speech can be taken as directly and deliberately representative of the school."[17] This troubling logic, which reaches the correct decision to admonish the professor, does so for the wrong reasons and rests upon the erroneous ground that faculty views are those of the institution. The court could have more parsimoniously and persuasively decided the same result but analyzed the peculiar role of religion injected into secular fields of study, especially when the teacher invites a particular religious scrutiny. The closest analogy to my own teaching would be to speak in Spanish half the time and to invite scrutiny and correction from my students on my "ethnic point of view." I am always certain to translate non-English words or ideas rooted in Spanish (*nonrefoulment, bracero,* etc.). In another course, a studio art teacher was dismissed for his habit of not supervising his students; he argued that this technique taught students to act more independently.[18] The court disagreed that his behavior was a protected form of professorial speech, as did a court that considered another professor's extensive use of profanity in the classroom. In a similar vein, a basketball coach dismissed for angrily calling his players "niggers" on the court to inspire them, found an unsympathetic court, which held that the remarks were not a matter of public concern[19] and, therefore, not protected speech. A white professor also lost his position at a black college for making a remark that was interpreted by students as racist and for refusing to go back to teaching until the college administrators removed a student he considered disruptive.[20]

These and other cases made it clear that students had some rights in a classroom, while well-known cases such as *Levin v Harleston*[21] and *Silva v University of New Hampshire*[22] have made it clear that courts will still go a long in protecting professors' ideas—however controversial *(Levin)*—and teaching styles—however offensive *(Silva)*. A proper configuration of professorial academic freedom is one that is normative and resilient enough to resist extremes from without or within, to fend off the New Hampshire legislative inquiry of *Sweezy* and the proselytizing of *Bishop*. In this view, professors have wide ranging discretion to undertake their research and to formulate teaching methods in their classroom and laboratories. However, this autonomy is, within broad limits, highly contingent upon traditional norms of peer review, codes of ethical behavior, and institutional standards. In the most favorable circumstances, these norms will be faculty-driven, subject to administrative guidelines for ensuring requisite due process and fairness. Even the highly optimistic and altruistic 1915 Declaration of Principles of the American Association of University Professors (AAUP) holds that "individual teachers should [not] be exempt from all restraints as to the matter or manner of their utterances, either within or without the university."[23] In short, academic freedom does not give carte blanche to professors, but rather vests faculty with establishing and enforcing standards of behavior to be reasonably and appropriately applied in evaluations.

A DEVELOPING STRAIN OF CASES

Although I have attempted to persuade that the academic common law is highly normative, contextual, and faculty-driven, I have not lost sight of the range of acceptable practices and extraordinary heterogeneity found in classroom styles. Additionally, persuasive research has emerged to show that persons trained in different academic disciplines view pedagogy differently. John Braxton and his colleagues have summarized how these norms operate across disciplines:

> Personal controls that induce individual conformity to teaching norms are internalized to varying degrees through the graduate school socialization process. Graduate school attendance in general and doctoral study in particular are regarded as a powerful socialization experience. The potency of this process lies not only in the development of knowledge, skills, and competencies, but also in the inculcation of norms, attitudes, and values. This socialization process entails the total learning situation . . . through these interpersonal relationships with faculty, values, knowledge, and skills are inculcated.[24]

Moreover, to paraphrase Tolstoy, they are all inculcated differently. To grab a student and put my hands on his chest would be extraordinarily wrong in my immigration law class, but it could happen regularly and appropriately in a voice class, physical education course, or acting workshop. Discussing one's religious views in an exercise physiology class may be inappropriate, but certainly it is kosher to do so in a comparative religion course. Discussions of sexuality, salacious in a legal ethics course, are appropriately central to a seminar in human sexuality. Each academic field has evolved its own norms and conventions.

However, courts are not in the business of contextualizing pedagogical disputes, as is evident from two current cases making their awkward way through the judicial system: *Cohen v San Bernardino Valley College* [25] and *Mincone v Nassau County Community College.* [26] While both of these cases have forbears in other decisions, they form a pair of bookends sufficient to make my points: that if colleges do not police themselves, others will; that disputes between teachers and students are on the rise; and that poor fact patterns and sloppy practices will lead to substantial external control over the classroom. One other thread is that each arose in a two-year community college, making it likely that the results will be taken by subsequent judges as directly pertinent for higher education in a way that K–12 cases (notwithstanding *Hazelwood*'s leaching into postsecondary cases) [27] have not been held. Given the overlap with the mission of senior institutions and their usual transfer function, two-year colleges will not be easily distinguished. If a K–12 case is not in my favor, I can always try to convince a judge to limit it to the elementary/secondary sector; I will not be able to muster such a fine-graded distinction in a post-compulsory world, even though two-year colleges are, on the average, more authoritarian and administrator-driven than are four-year colleges. [28] The widespread use of part-time and non–tenure track faculty makes academic freedom more problematic at community colleges, where faculty do not always have the security or autonomy to develop traditional protections of tenure and academic freedom, particularly the dimension of "how it shall be taught."

COHEN V SAN BERNARDINO VALLEY COLLEGE (SBVC)

Dean Cohen is a tenured English and film studies professor at SBVC, where, in spring 1992, he taught a remedial English class. By his own admission, his teaching style is "confrontational" and aggressive. In order to motivate students, he sometimes uses vulgarities and profanity. He read articles from *Hustler* and *Playboy* magazines in class, and for a class assignment had his students write essays defining pornography. One of his students objected to his style and the pornography assignment, and requested an alternative assignment, which request was refused. The student did not attend Cohen's class after this exchange, and she received a failing grade. After the semester ended she went to Cohen's department chair, complained he had sexually harassed her, and then filed a formal grievance complaint.

The Faculty Grievance Committee took testimony from both parties as well as from other students who had been in the course. The Committee determined that Professor Cohen had created a "hostile learning environment," a form of sexual harassment proscribed by SBVC policy, defined as: "unwelcome sexual advances, requests for sexual favors, and other verbal, written, or physical conduct of a sexual nature. It includes, but is not limited to circumstances in which: . . . Such conduct has the purpose or effect of unreasonably interfering with an individual's academic performance or creating an intimidating, hostile, or offensive learning environment." Under this policy, forms of sexual harassment "include but are not limited to . . . [v]erbal harassment—[d]erogatory comments, jokes or slurs." The SBVC president accepted the Faculty Grievance Committee's findings and determined that Cohen was in violation of the college's sexual harassment policy. This decision was appealed to the board of trustees, who sustained the committee and the president. The board ordered Cohen to:

1. Provide a syllabus concerning his teaching style, purpose, content, and method to his students at the beginning of class and to the department chair by certain deadlines.
2. Attend a sexual harassment seminar within 90 days.

3. Undergo a formal evaluation procedure in accordance with the collective bargaining agreement.

4. Become sensitive to the particular needs and backgrounds of his students and modify his teaching strategy when it becomes apparent that his techniques create a climate that impedes the students' ability to learn.

Cohen then filed a Section 1983 suit, seeking a declaratory judgment, a preliminary and permanent injunction, damages, and attorney fees. In April 1995 Cohen lost on every count: the federal judge denied a declaratory judgment and preliminary injunction, and found the individual defendant to be entitled to qualified immunity; he had already ruled that the entity defendants had Eleventh Amendment immunity.[29]

On the substantive issues, Cohen also lost. The court held that the SBVC sexual harassment policy did not violate the First Amendment but, as had the judge in *Bishop v Aronov*[30] (the case of the proselytizing exercise physiology professor), it cited *Hazelwood*[31] the high-school paper censorship case. Regrettably, the court intermingled other high school curriculum cases with higher education grading and Establishment Clause cases. The court's summary held: "The parameters of academic freedom are not distinct, particularly in relation to the potential conflict with a University's duty to ensure adequate education of its students. What is clear, however, is that invocation of the 'academic freedom' doctrine does not adequately address the complex issues presented by this case. For that reason, this Court declines to hold that SBVC's discipline of Cohen is precluded by general notions of academic freedom under the First Amendment."[32]

The court then reviewed government-as-employer cases, *Connick v Myers*,[33] *Waters v Churchill*,[34] and *U.S. v National Treasury Employees Union*,[35] taken together, these cases will rarely support a faculty member's being punished for classroom behavior, and they did not help Cohen here: "In this case, the record is undisputed as to what speech is at issue: (1) Cohen's use of vulgarities and obscenities in the classroom; and (2) Cohen's curricular focus on sexual topics such as pornography, as well as his classroom comments on sexual subjects."[36] While the court found the speech to be a matter of public concern, necessitating a greater showing of workplace (in this instance, the classroom) disruption, it determined that the college had brought forth "substantial, uncontroverted evidence showing that the educational process was disrupted by Cohen's focus on sexual topics and teaching style."[37]

What the court finds here is so extraordinary that it is important to read in detail the analysis (with all citations omitted):

> There is testimony from the complaining student and from other students in the class that Cohen's sexually suggestive remarks, use of vulgarities and obscenities, and the topics for discussion prevented them from learning.
>
> Furthermore, written evaluations of Cohen by his colleagues done in November of 1992, before [the student] filed her grievance against Cohen, show that while his colleagues respected Cohen as a teacher, several of them entertained doubts as to the efficacy of his confrontational teaching methods. According to one peer evaluator who observed a class in which Cohen discussed and assigned a paper on the topic of consensual sex with children, Cohen's specific focus impedes academic success for some students. . . . "I question whether or not many of our students have the academic preparation and/or emotional maturity (stability) to cope with the nature of Mr. Cohen's assignments."
>
> Another observer stated that Cohen's approach to the topic of "the pros or the cons of consensual sex with children" did not foster unfettered discussion by students but instead "require[d] self-censorship rather than complex analysis of an important issue." The evaluator further wrote that, "[c]ertainly the issue of what in this society is considered to be sexual abuse deserves discussion. But given the student population, it deserves sensitive, complex discussion—not the reductionist approach that Mr. Cohen's assignment requires. Rather than fostering free inquiry, Mr. Cohen's assignment as stated undermines the crucial nature of the issue."

Lastly, Cohen himself concedes that his teaching methods do not work with every student. He has stated that he deliberately uses an "abrasive" teaching style to elicit a response from his students. He admitted during the hearing before the Board that, while his style was effective as to some students, it was not as to others: "[T]here's always a sort of ratio between success and failure. Techniques work with one student and not another . . . ." Moreover, in answer to a question as to whether he considered himself an excellent teacher, Cohen replied, "That would depend on the student. A teacher is good with one student and not so good with another, and that has something to do with the student's perception of the teacher. One cannot be all things to all students."

In fairness, the Court must note that there is evidence in the record that Cohen's teaching style is effective for at least some students. Cohen's colleagues have stated that he is a gifted and enthusiastic teacher. Furthermore, according to the chair of the English Department (who is a defendant in this action), Cohen's teaching style is within the range of acceptable academic practice. The record also contains statements from several students to the effect that Cohen's challenging classroom style contributed to their learning experience. Moreover, the record contains positive student evaluations of Cohen submitted by English 101 and English 105 classes for the Fall 1992 and Fall 1993 semesters. However, this evidence does not controvert the evidence showing that the learning process for a number of students was hampered by the hostile learning environment created by Cohen.

In applying a "hostile environment" prohibition, there is the danger that the most sensitive and the most easy offended students will be given veto power over class content and methodology. Good teaching should challenge students and at times may intimidate students or make them uncomfortable. In a different context, the Supreme Court has previously refused to ban all material which offends the sensibilities of society's most sensitive and vulnerable members. Colleges and universities, as well as the courts, must avoid a tyranny of mediocrity, in which all discourse is made bland enough to suit the tastes of all students.

However, colleges and universities must have the power to require professors to effectively educate all segments of the student population, including those students unused to the rough and tumble of intellectual discussion. If colleges and universities lack this power, each classroom becomes a separate fiefdom in which the educational process is subject to professorial whim. Universities must be able to ensure that the more vulnerable as well as the more sophisticated students receive a suitable education. The Supreme Court has clearly stated that the public employer must be able to achieve its mission and avoid disruption of the workplace. Within the educational context, the university's mission is to effectively educate students, keeping in mind students' varying backgrounds and sensitivities. Furthermore, the university has the right to preclude disruption of this educational mission through the creation of a hostile learning environment. As the *Ynigues* court noted, public employers must have the authority to determine what tasks its employees perform.

The restrictions imposed by Defendants are not onerous. The College has required Cohen to issue a syllabus at the beginning of each semester of his classes. Cohen must attend a sexual harassment seminar. Cohen must be formally evaluated, and he is directed to "be sensitive" to students. These restrictions are tailored and reasonable, in light of the issues involved. The College is not directly censoring Cohen's choice of topics or teaching style. In essence, the College is requiring Cohen to warn students of his teaching style and topics so that those students for whom this approach is ineffective may make an informed choice as to their educations.[38]

Thus, even though Cohen's speech on the topic of pornography was speech on a matter of public interest, the college's interest in effectively educating its students outweighed his interest in focusing on sexual topics in the classroom, to the extent that the university only required Cohen to warn potential students of his teaching style and topics.

As an alternative basis for its ruling, the Court recognizes the constitutional implications of the College's substantial interest in preventing the creation of a hostile, sexually discriminatory environment which would disrupt the educational process. The Supreme Court has found that creating a "hostile environment" based on gender is a form of sexual harassment which violates Title VII. Several circuits, including the Ninth Circuit, have held that sexual harassment is a type of sexual discrimination which violates the Equal Protection Clause of the Fourteenth Amendment.[39]

Thereafter, it only remained for the court to dismiss the issue of fair notice and to distinguish *Cohen* from relevant hate-speech cases that would seem to favor the professor in such an instance. Having covered this terrain, Judge Lew held that,

> under *Connick* and *Waters,* the College has the authority to require Cohen to distribute a syllabus detailing his controversial teaching style, attend an anti-sexual harassment seminar, and to submit to a formal evaluation of his teaching methods. The College is entitled to issue these narrowly tailored requirements because it has shown that its educational mission has been disrupted for some students by Cohen's teaching style. The College's substantial interest in educating all students, not just the thick-skinned ones, warrants the College's requiring Cohen to put potential students on notice of his teaching methods. The College's interest in fulfilling its educational mission is further bolstered by the constitutional implications of sexual harassment.
>
> In so holding, the Court notes that this ruling goes only to the narrow and reasonable discipline which the College seeks to impose. A case in which a professor is terminated or directly censored presents a far different balancing question. Further, the Court notes that the College must avoid restricting creative and engaging teaching, even if some over-sensitive students object to it.[40]

The student had also accused Professor Cohen of making specific and suggestive sexual overtures toward her, claims rejected by both the Faculty Grievance Committee and the board of trustees in their respective hearings. As of summer 1996, Professor Cohen was seeking review in the Ninth Circuit.

MINCONE V NASSAU COUNTY COMMUNITY COLLEGE

This is the second round of a case that began as a request for public records or, in this instance, course materials for Physical Education 251 (PED 251), "Family Life and Human Sexuality."[41] The course is taught in several sections to nearly 3,000 students each year, and in *Mincone,* a senior citizen auditor (enrolled under terms of a free, noncredit program for adults over 65 years of age) who reviewed the course materials before he took the class (to be offered in the summer 1995 term) sued to enjoin the course from using the materials or from using federal funds to "counsel abortion in the PED 251 course materials." Mincone, the representative of a coplaintiff party, the Organization of Senior Citizens and Retailors (OSCAR), filed in May 1995 a lawsuit with eight causes of action: PED 251, under these theories, violates the strict religious neutrality required of public institutions by the New York State Constitution; burdens and violates state law concerning the free exercise clause of the New York State Constitution by "disparagement" of Judeo-Christian faiths and by promoting the religious teaching of Eastern religions with regard to sexuality; violates the federal First Amendment; violates the plaintiffs' civil rights guaranteed under Section 1983; teaches behavior that violates Section 130.00 of the New York State Penal Law (sodomy statutes); violates federal law concerning religious neutrality by singling out one "correct view of human sexuality"; disregards the duty to warn students of course content so they can decide whether to enroll in the course or not; endangers minors who may be enrolled in the course; and violates federal law enjoining abortion counseling.

This broad frontal attack on the course is virtually without precedent, as the plaintiff is not even enrolled in the course for credit and enjoined the course even before the term began and before he took the course as an auditor. While in all likelihood he will be denied standing, in that he has suffered no harm and has no cognizable claim, OSCAR could simply enroll a plaintiff to get over that hurdle. But the wide-ranging claims, particularly those that allege religious bias, are so vague and poorly formulated that it is difficult to believe they will survive.

However, Mincone may have a small point in his objections concerning the materials, if his point were to ridicule. Here, as I am not a health educator or scholar of sexuality, I confess this obvious lack of credentials. But the PED 251 materials do include a home "exercise" to investigate "self-exploration" that includes a picture of a man masturbating and the following instructions:

> Set aside a block of time (at least 1 hour for the entire exercise) when you will have privacy. . . . A good way to begin is with a relaxing bath or shower. You can start the self-exploration while bathing, washing with soap-covered slippery hands in an unhurried manner. . . . You may wish to experiment with using a body lotion, oil or powder. After gentle stroking try firmer, massaging pressures, paying extra attention to areas that are tense. You might like to allow yourself some pleasurable fantasies during this time. For the next step, we recommend that you return to the genital self-examination exercises in Chapters 4 and 5. Once you have completed the exploration, continue experimenting with various kinds of pressure and stroking. Pay attention to what feels good.[42]

Other materials assigned also include films and pictures of persons performing sexual acts, assignments involving cross-dressing, and other exercises in sexuality. At the conference that led to this volume, I read directly from the lawsuit several portions of the PED materials, and I inadvertently elicited substantial laughter at my characterization of the materials; in truth, I was reading only to give the audience the sense of word choices and class assignments to which Mr. Mincone had objected, and I did caution using good judgment.

But when I saw my remarks in the next week's *Chronicle of Higher Education,* they seemed much more prudish and OSCAR-ish than I had meant them to be.[43]

Therefore, I want to elaborate a bit, within the limits of this chapter, so that I not only clarify what I think about classroom materials but convey it clearly. I begin with the premise that faculty members have the absolute right, within the limits of germaneness and institutional practice, to assign whatever text they wish. Thus, subject only to the text being appropriate for the course (for instance, not assigning Updike's *The Centaur* for a math course or a math workbook for a course in legal ethics) and to academic custom (for example, all the freshman composition teachers being required to draw from an approved list of available texts), professors can pick whichever texts seem best for their courses. Sometimes this means a compromise, as in using a central text supplemented by all the extra materials you wish were in the basic text, because not everyone can or is inclined to write his own book. Therefore, there could be materials assigned for purchase that are a compromise as the best available, or even superfluous materials that are not assigned because they are dated, not your style, or otherwise inappropriate. For example, this year I have been pressed into service to teach a new course, so I have recently reviewed over a dozen readers in the subject, not a single one of which is ideal for the class approach I had in mind. However, one (with a good teachers' manual and statutory supplement) had the most updated regulatory materials so I chose it over other texts better suited for a problem-solving approach, which approach I preferred. The one I thought best suited was written in 1989, too ancient a vintage for this fast-moving area of the law. However, the PED 251 syllabus clearly assigns the "self-exploration" exercise, which includes the language I already noted, so this is not an example of superfluous text content.

My objection, if that is the right word, is a little like that of Joycelyn Elders, the former U.S. Surgeon General: I don't believe you can teach college students how to masturbate, inasmuch as they have likely been doing it instinctively well before college credit is awarded for the activity. Again, I stress that this curriculum is not my métier, but I cannot help but wonder if this is a necessary homework assignment. Surely the filmstrips and materials have been chosen carefully for a course that is known to be a lightning rod (by the earlier suit),[44] and if sex education and physiology faculty conscientiously choose these materials, that forms the contextual and professional judgment my theory requires. As AAUP General Counsel, I would have no qualms whatsoever in defending the Nassau County Community College course materials. They were picked by professionals with considerable expertise in this field; the course is widely accepted and regularly fully enrolled; it does what it sets out to do: expose students to wide-ranging issues of sexuality; and the materials clearly put students on notice what the course would cover. Except for the personal and moral objections of the plaintiffs concerning the materials, this course is generically like any course. Context is all, in my formulation, as is professional authority to determine how it shall be taught. This case cannot succeed, or else we are all in trouble. But do we need this trouble?

IMPLICATIONS AND CONCLUSIONS

These cases are fraught with implications for higher education practice, especially for teacher behavior. In *Cohen*, the court could have gone in the opposite direction, as it had for Professors Silva and Levin, by stressing their academic freedom primarily rather than by balancing the competing interests. However, by characterizing the issues as ones of classroom control and students' learning environment, Professor Cohen's interests are trumped, at least with the admonishment. (His orders were to do essentially as Professor Silva was ordered by the University of New Hampshire to do: take counseling, alter his class style, etc.) And the court did suggest that the admonishment was mild: "A case in which a professor is terminated or directly censored presents a far different balancing question."[45] But does it? Can there be any doubt that Cohen considers himself "directly censored" by the formal complaint of one student? Was Levin censored by CUNY's "shadow section"? Is reading *Hustler* letters a good idea for a remedial English class?

While I believe the court went too far in accommodating one "thin-skinned" student, one who dropped the course, two things strike me: an experience from long ago, and the difficulty of a satisfactory solution. When my mother began to attend college on a part-time basis (I am the oldest of ten children) in 1964, I used to go with her to the University of New Mexico for her evening English class. One of the assignments was to attend a movie (I believe it was *Fahrenheit 451*), then showing at Don Pancho's Theater, an art house that has since closed and given way to a Chinese fast food joint. Now in those days, the Legion of Decency pledge, taken annually by all Catholics to promise we would avoid proscribed movies, was a big deal, especially for my mother, who was raised as a Southern Baptist but who converted to Roman Catholicism. My mother, while no fanatic, was pretty strictly observant in Catholic tenets, including this movie prohibition. Mortified that she could not attend the movie (or even go into the theater, a local proscription), she sought advice from Msgr. Joseph Charewicz, our pastor at Our Lady of Fatima Parish— where I was enrolled in eighth grade. I remember my mother taking me with her as she asked Msgr. Charewicz, an imposing, cigar-smoking traditionalist, what she should do. He made it clear that going to Don Pancho's and seeing a forbidden movie was unacceptable. She would just have to quit the course.

My mother, though, was an early advocate of alternative dispute resolution techniques and mediation (very often, between my more disciplinarily minded father and me, so headstrong at 12 or 13 years old). She, like the plaintiff in *Cohen,* offered to write a paper on why she felt she could not complete the assignment. The professor agreed. I remember to this day how hard she worked at her old typewriter on that assignment and that she received a B for the paper. She was very proud on all fronts and even told Msgr. Charewicz how she had negotiated the good faith-compromise. Of course, I was pleased at her achievement (although I had hoped she would also take me to this salacious movie). Professor Cohen, who conceded his style wasn't for everyone, could have been at least as flexible as my mother's UNM English instructor. Faculty do not concede autonomy by reasonable compromise with our students. Rather, we gain cooperation and involve learners otherwise not available to us. I cannot help but contrast the different approaches taken for my mother and Cohen's student.

Finally, there is the issue of a solution to the conundrum of faculty autonomy and sexual harassment jurisprudence. The difficulty is acknowledging that a classroom can be a hostile environment in some instances. In the AAUP, we have hammered out a compromise attempt to preserve faculty autonomy and to acknowledge and deal with an environment so hostile that it can stifle learning opportunities:

Statement Of Policy
It is the policy of this institution that no member of the academic community may sexually harass another. Sexual advances, requests for sexual favors, and other speech or conduct of a sexual nature constitute sexual harassment when:
1. Such advances or requests are made under circumstances implying that one's response might affect academic or personnel decisions that are subject to the influence of the person making the proposal; or
2. Such speech or conduct is directed against another and is either abusive or severely humiliating, or persists despite the objection of the person targeted by the speech or conduct; or
3. Such speech or conduct is reasonably regarded as offensive and substantially impairs the academic or work opportunity of students, colleagues, or co-workers. If it takes place in the teaching context, it must also be persistent, pervasive, and not germane to the subject matter. The academic setting is distinct from the workplace in that wide latitude is required for professional judgment in determining the appropriate content and presentation of academic material.[46]

In our search for the perfect, clarifying epiphany—one that will illuminate once and for all examples that can guide behavior—this proposed policy falls short: what is "severely humiliating"? Is it more than "humiliating"? How much more? How long does harassment have to persist in order to be found "persistent"? Isn't the classroom a "workplace" for faculty? But we are all smart people, highly educated, and experienced in the ways of teaching. To me, in interpreting academic standards, it isn't surprising that things work so badly, but that they work so well.

My own experiences as a student and professor lead me to believe that any comprehensive theory of professorial authority to determine "how it shall be taught" must incorporate a feedback mechanism for students to take issue, voice complaints, and point out remarks or attitudes that may be insensitive or disparaging. At a minimum, faculty should encourage students to speak privately with them to identify uncomfortable situations. Professor Bishop asked his students to point out inconsistencies between his Christian perspectives and his lifestyle. This is excessive, and could itself provoke anxiety on the part of both Christian and non-Christian students. But a modest attempt to avoid stigmatizing words and examples is certainly in order for teachers, and schools should have in place some mechanism to address these issues and resolve problems. I cringe when I see exam questions that consign José, Maria, or Rufus to criminal questions, or when in-class hypotheticals use "illegal aliens" or sexist examples and stereotypes to illustrate important legal points. Such misuse may be especially prevalent in fact patterns involving rape and consent.[47] Our students have a right to expect more thoughtful pedagogical practices.

I can imagine colleagues wincing at the perceived political correctness ax being ground and uttering dismissive remarks concerning self-censoring. I believe in self-censoring, however. Even if it sacrifices the perfect *bon mot* or ideally placed riposte, this seems a modest price to pay to avoid making a hurtful remark or employing an inappropriate example. After all, these prevent understanding and get in the way of learning. Nor does my highly protective notion of professorial academic freedom of necessity flatten the opportunity for self-expression among students or "dumb down" the discussion. Faculty and students have a great amount of autonomy and opportunity for self-expression in class, and a self-imposed code of professorial teaching conduct is no great loss of autonomy or essential authority. Academic freedom is one of the great glories of the higher education tradition as we know it, and we should be vigilant to see that it is not weakened, either by body blows from without or by careless and self-inflicted wounds from within.

NOTES

1. *Sweezy v New Hampshire,* 354 US 234, 262, 77 SCt 1203, 1218 (1957). (Frankfurter, J., concurring) (quoting a statement of a conference of senior scholars from the University of Capetown and the University of Witwatersrand, South Africa): "It is the business of a university to provide that atmosphere which is most conducive to speculation, experiment and creation. It is an atmosphere in which there prevail 'the four essential freedoms' of a university—to determine for itself on academic grounds who may teach, what may be taught, how it shall be taught, and who may be admitted to study."

2. See, for example, Richard Delgado, *The Rodrigo Chronicles* (1995), and Richard Delgado (Ed.) *Critical Race Theory* (1995), for an explanation of this developing field of legal criticism.

3. See, e.g., Laura F. Rothstein, *Students, Staff and Faculty with Disabilities: Current Issues for Colleges and Universities,* 17, Journal of College and University Law 471 (1991).

4. An early president of Williams College, Mark Hopkins, was reputed to be an extremely inspirational teacher: "The ideal college was Mark Hopkins on one end of the log and a student on the other." Frederick Rudolph, *Mark Hopkins and the Log: Williams College, 1836-1872,* (1956), 227.

5. See, for example, Michael A. Olivas, *Unaccompanied Refugee Children in the United States: Detention, Due Process, and Disgrace,* 2 Stanford Law and Policy Review 159 (1990) (review of federal policy on alien children detention).

6. See generally, Kimberle Williams Crenshaw, *Demarginalizing the Intersection of Race and Sex: A Black Feminist Critique of Antidiscrimination Doctrine, Feminist Theory and Antiracist Politics,* University of Chicago Legal Forum 139 (1989); Margaret Montoya, *Mascaras, Trenzas, Grenas: Un/masking the Self While Un/Braiding Latina Stories and Legal Discourse,* 17 Harvard Women's Law Journal 185 (1994).

7. Derrick Bell, "The Price and Pain of Racial Perspective," in Michael A. Olivas (Ed.), *The Law and Higher Education: Cases and Materials on Colleges in Court* (1989), 1038.

8. *Doe v University of Michigan,* 721 F Supp 852 (E.D. Mich. 1989).

9. MIT philosophy professor Judith Thompson makes a similar point concerning belief systems in faculty hiring. In an interesting essay on the appropriate norms for considering scholarly orthodoxies, she considers the candidacy of an astrology expert and rejects the field of study as not sufficiently scientific: "As a member of the committee, I was under a duty precisely to bring my past experience to bear on, among other questions, the question what fields are worth investing in. Given my past experience, I would have failed in that duty if I had refrained from voting against astrology." Judith Jarvis Thompson, *Ideology and Faculty Selection,* Law and Contemporary Problems 155, 160 (Summer 1990).

10. "Ohio Professor Suspected of Theft from Vatican," *Chronicle of Higher Education,* June 9, 1995, A 6 (university professor alleged to have torn out pages from valuable text and to have tried to sell them to private collector).

11. The president of American University, Richard Berendzen, installed a private phone in his desk from which he called women and made harassing and obscene phone calls. See Neil Lewis, "University Chief's Ouster Is Tied to Investigation of Obscene Calls," *New York Times,* April 25, 1990, A19.

12. I would agree that the minimum protection is articulated by *Connick v Myers,* 461 US 138 (1983).

13. David M. Rabban, *A Functional Analysis of 'Individual' and 'Institutional' Academic Freedom Under the First Amendment,* Law and Contemporary Problems 244 (Summer 1990) (footnotes omitted).

14. Ibid., 246.

15. Michael A. Olivas, *Reflections on Professorial Academic Freedom: Second Thoughts on the Third "Essential Freedom,"* Stanford Law Review 1835 (1993). In this chapter, I borrow from the earlier law review article.

16. *Lynch v Indiana State Univ. Bd. of Trustees,* 177 Ind. App 172, 378 NE 2d 900, (Ct App 1978), *cert. denied,* 441 US 946 (1979).

17. *Bishop v Aronov,* 926 F 2d 1066 (11th Cir 1991).

18. 153 Arizona 461, 737 P 2d 1099 (1987).

19. *Dambrot v Cent. Mich. Univ.,* 839 F Supp 477 (E. D. Mich. 1993) (racial epithet was not a matter of concern). As an example of changing norms, a college basketball coach was dismissed for repeatedly berating

his athletes. Debra E. Blum, "Abrupt Dismissal of Berkeley's Coach Stuns the College Basketball World," *Chronicle of Higher Education,* February 24, 1993, A35.

20. *McConnell v Howard Univ.,* Civ A No 85-0298-LFO, 1988 WL 4237 (DDC Jan. 5, 1988).

21. 770 F Supp 895 (SDNY 1991), *aff'd in part, vacated in part,* 966 F 2d 85 (2d Cir 1992).

22. *Silva,* 888 F Supp 293 (D.N.H. 1994).

23. *General Report of the Committee on Academic Freedom and Academic Tenure (1915),* reprinted in Law & Contemporary Problems 293 (Summer 1990).

24. J. Braxton, A. Bayer, and M. Finkelstein, "Teaching Performance Norms in Academia," *Research in Higher Education* 33 (1992), 535-536.

25. *Cohen v San Bernardino Valley College et al.,* 883 F Supp 1407 (C.D. Cal. 1995). After this chapter went to press (August 1996), a three judge panel of the ninth circuit decided this case in Professor Cohen's favor.

26. *Mincone v Nassau County Community College,* 95 F Supp 1879 (E.D. N.Y. 1995); see also "The Eighteenth Alexander Miekeljohn Award," *ACADEME* (July/August 1993), 57-61 (report of AAUP award to president of NCCC, including his analysis of the dispute).

27. 484 US 260 (1988). For example, *Bishop v Aronov* turned upon *Hazelwood,* 926 F 2d 1066, 1073 (11th Cir 1991).

28. See J. Victor Baldridge et al., "The Impact of Institutional Size and Complexity Upon Faculty Autonomy," *Journal of Higher Education* 44 (1973), 532; J. Victor Baldridge et al., *Policy Making and Effective Leadership* (San Fransisco: Jossey-Bass, 1978).

29. *Cohen, supra* note 25, at 1411.

30. 926 F 2d 1066 (11th Cir. 1991).

31. *Hazelwood School District v Kuhlmeier,* 484 US 260 (1988).

32. *Cohen v San Bernardino Valley College et al.,* 1411.

33. 461 US 138 (1983).

34. 114 S Ct 1878 (1994).

35. 115 S Ct 1003 (1995).

36. *Cohen v San Bernardino Valley College et al.,* 1415-16.

37. *Ibid.,* 1418.

38. *Ibid.,* 1418-20.

39. *Ibid.,* 1420.

40. *Ibid.,* 1422.

41. *Russo v Nassau County Community College,* 81 NY 2d 690, 623 NE 2d 15, 603 NYS 2d 294 (1993) (college required to produce course materials).

42. *Mincone v Nassau County Community College.* Unfortunately in April 1996, the federal judge hearing the case refused to dismiss the suit. See Xavier Brand, "Religious Battle Brewing Over College Sex Ed Class," *Education Daily,* May 20, 1996, 4.

43. Robin Wilson. "Teacher or Advocate?" *Chronicle of Higher Education,* June 16, 1995, A17, A18 (report of MLA-sponsored conference on advocacy).

44. *Russo v Nassau County Community College.*

45. *Cohen v San Bernardino Valley College et al.,* 1422.

46. See AAUP Report, "Sexual Harassment: Suggested Policy and Procedures for Handling Complaints," *ACADEME,* (July/August 1995), 62.

47. See James J. Tomkovicz, *On Teaching Rape: Reasons, Risks, and Rewards,* 102 Yale Law Journal 481 (1992). (explaining the difficulty of teaching rape law); see also, Clarence Page, "Where Narrow Minds Stifle Debate," *Chicago Tribune,* December 23, 1990, 3C (citing incident in which New York University Law School withdrew—and later reinstated—a moot court problem involving a lesbian mother's custody battle because students did not want to take the father's side in the case). A new pretrial discovery text includes an entire chapter that constitutes a case study of a woman convicted of petty theft being processed into jail for an outstanding parole violation. Theodore Blumoff, Margaret Johns, and Edward Inwinkelried, *Pretrial Discovery: The Development of Professional Judgment* (1993). There is a graphic scenario involving a strip search, Taser guns, leering guards, and a miscarriage from the Taser shocks. The name of the criminal, the only recognizably ethnic name in evidence, is "Maria Garcia."

FOUR

Choosing Voices

ERNESTINE FRIEDL

THERE IS RARELY A TIME in the academic world when one or another discipline is without controversy over new paradigms, new interpretations, new divisions of knowledge, and the consequences of new connections with related disciplines. Competition for ascendancy among advocates of different points of view is frequently the driving force for change and evolution in all scholarly disciplines. The process is the free enterprise system of the academy and is imbedded in its culture.

On occasion, the advocacy of rival theories, approaches, and topics for scholarly investigation threatens to rend disciplines apart, ravage departments, and come close to destroying the civility of academic discourse. We are now living through one of these times. I have been asked to puzzle over why this should be so; why advocacy, the lifeblood of the intellectual world, has been labeled "political" meant as an epithet and thought somehow improper to pursue. In an effort to answer I shall examine particular conditions that have come together in the second half of the twentieth century. In my judgment, these may account for the heat of contemporary intellectual argument. The conditions are the time-honored nature of the academy and academicians, the advent of postmodern ideas, and the political and social context of the late twentieth century in the

United States. The linguistic codes developed in the debate have also, I believe, exacerbated differences and obfuscated the real intellectual issues. I shall end with brief remarks on the relevance of advocacies to the classroom.

THE NATURE OF THE ACADEMY AND ACADEMICIANS

We academicians should not be surprised at the fervor and power of the controversies that erupt from time to time. Ideally, we enter our profession because we are fascinated and intrigued by a discipline and want to join in unraveling its mysteries. We study and train for many years in poverty, knowing that in most fields our economic rewards will be adequate but relatively modest. We accept a life without a bottom line. There is no profit-and-loss statement that can tell us how we are doing. We must depend on what others think of our work; reputation becomes our currency. Reputations, in turn, are made or unmade by editors, publishers, book reviewers, funding agencies, scholars who invite us to conferences, colleagues on peer review panels and on promotion and tenure committees, not to mention university administrators and the interested lay reader. Our students, undergraduate and graduate, judge us and add or detract from our reputations as mentors and teachers. It is no wonder then that, to live with such uncertainty, we must be passionate about the intellectual positions we espouse. Nor is it surprising that we convey our theories and assumptions to our students with passion. We faculty also help to manage our institutions; we typically make recommendations for appointments, promotions, budget, and curriculum. Without dedication to our ideas and the conviction that what we are doing is important, we could not stay in the academic profession and devote the 50, or 60, or more hours of work a week that are commonly our lot.

In this milieu the stage is set for fireworks when new ideas not only overthrow the precepts of the fathers and mothers of disciplines but, in addition, question the authority to make knowledge claims at all. This is indeed the challenge of postmodernism.

POSTMODERNISM

The root of the postmodern argument is that objectivity in selecting topics for investigation and research, the research itself, and the writing of reports is hardly possible because the entire process is contingent on the power position and ideologies of those who support and conduct the research. Power is defined as the political and economic power of the West traditionally mostly represented by Western white men. Or power rests in academics of great reputation who frequently control jobs, research agenda, and curriculum. Mainstream ideas, it is said, are contingent on the power of the people who accept them but are not intrinsically "correct." The position is that knowledge is not absolute but relative.

My own views on these matters influence my advocacies. Let me mention them briefly. The stance that because scholarly positions are subject to forces that are not always intrinsic to the discipline, knowledge claims are impossible and knowledge is therefore totally relative is, in my opinion, too extreme. It conceptually denies the possibility that there are degrees of objectivity by which the integrity of data and texts can be judged regardless of who produces or promulgates them. Objectivity is not binary, absolutely present, or absolutely absent, but comes in degrees. If someone falls and breaks a leg, in some societies it is called an accident, in others it is viewed as God's punishment for sins, and in still others it is attributed to malevolent witchcraft. But regardless of the imputed cause, to avoid lameness the leg will need to be set. It can also be objectively demonstrated that there are people who believe in accident, in God's punishment, and in witchcraft—all those people and their beliefs can be legitimately studied.

I also consider it self-evident that interpretations of the same data or texts and, indeed, their choice vary in place, time, and circumstance. Further, some interpretations do achieve legitimacy because of the power of governments and prestigious scholars rather than the exclusive properties of the data or text. The Yankee North and the antebellum South did not fight the same Civil War. That there were generals and battles fought is indisputable, but the myriad interpreters of that war, slaves and freemen included, did not necessarily choose the same data to describe and judge the events of that conflict. The particular versions that achieved most prominence were those of whites, northern and southern, who were in powerful positions.

Certainly the plays of Sophocles remain relevant not because they have been interpreted the same way through the centuries but precisely because different generations find in these plays a new kind of beauty or relevance for their times. Scholars in non–English-speaking parts of the world interpret Shakespeare differently. I am reminded of one native German professor who insisted that *Hamlet* could properly be understood only in its German version.

That the evolution of scholarly positions is subject to forces of change both from within and outside a discipline is also self-evident. Paradigms that no longer produce significant new knowledge are replaced by new approaches. Forces from outside, the historical time and place, the technology available, and the points of view of the personnel conducting the research certainly influence how disciplines develop. To use an analogy with skirt lengths in women's fashions: they go up and down in cycles based on the internal needs of the fashion industry for novelty, but a war limiting the availability of fabric shortens skirts whatever the point in the cycle.

THE LATE - TWENTIETH-CENTURY WORLD

In a moderate version, poststructural ideas do not menace scholarship but have forced a fresh look. It is a look undertaken in a twentieth-century world that has seen the end of colonialism and the dissipation and reorganization of political power. No longer does any nation or group of nations exercise decisive control over world political and economic events. The upheavals against the establishment in the United States provoked by the Vietnam War, the coming to self-consciousness and political power of previously disadvantaged individuals and minority groups has brought new voices into scholarship. The voices are those whose traditional lack of equality of opportunity resulted in part from prevailing assumptions that ability and social and economic place are based on gender and ancestry. However, the voices of women, African Americans, Native Americans, Latinos, immigrants, acknowledged gays and lesbians, all of whom are now contributing to the scholarly disciplines, have created a different harmony in the music of scholarship.

Linguists refer to some contrasting terms as "marked" or "unmarked." An analogous example would be the taking for granted in most United States cities that a right turn on a red light is permitted. It is unmarked, no sign is needed. But if, at a crossing, there is no turn on a red light, there must be a sign; it is a marked situation. In similar fashion the new voices have turned the Western tradition and white men (perhaps all men) into marked rather than unmarked categories. Some white men can no longer take for granted that they and their works are the unmarked standards and all others are to be noted as contrast. Or, if we use the analogy of the marketplace, the monopoly of control over the academic and scholarly agenda is fading away and competition is being forced on those who have held the traditional monopoly. Having to defend positions long unquestioned does not come easily.

My own view is that those who have not had an equal opportunity to contribute to scholarship in full measure will provide, as indeed they have already, different insights and renewed intellectual ferment. Some aspects of postmodern ideas and rearrangements of power relationships have already combined to contribute a significant enrichment of thought and scholarship. Judgments about quality will shift and change as they always have. We should support these new voices, not out of guilt for their former exclusion but out of enlightened self-interest.

THE LANGUAGE OF DEBATE

We are currently using the terms, indeed the labels, "diversity" and "multiculturalism" to represent the new voices. Diversity is defined as variation in race, class, and ethnicity as well as gender and sexual orientation. Using these rubrics, scholars and the public alike have labeled such diversity "multiculturalism." As I see it, there are two problems with the implications of these terms. One is the patently false assumption that all Whites, all African Americans, all Native Americans, and similar populations have the same ideas or that their scholarship will be totally influenced by their inclusion in such populations. The second problem is that African American, Latino, Asian, Native American, White, Irish, German, Jew, and the like are not, as popularly conceived, labels for culture. Those of us covered in each collective term obviously vary with respect to our geographic location and the type of community in which we live. Whatever the group, we vary among ourselves in age and gender, in religion, language, and political affiliation. We vary in food habits and tastes in entertainment. Nor are the details of these differences stable; they change with time and place. But most important, from skin tones to the love of noodles, all these traits overlap sometimes more, sometimes less, with those of other peoples. Once labeled as "cultures" as in "multiculturalism," however, the implication is that the designated populations are homogeneous in practice and beliefs, their cultures are encapsulated, and have always been so. This is an essentialist notion of culture resorted to by some populations themselves and by those who so wish to characterize them. It is a notion that conflates culture with ethnic identity and even physical substance.

The anthropology in which I was trained in the early 1940s included evidence that distributions of race (in the sense of some inherited characteristics), culture, and language did not necessarily overlap. Some Whites, Chinese, Japanese, Africans, and African Americans speak English as their first and only language. Northern European Whites embraced Christianity brought by darker-skinned Near Easterners. You can fill in your own examples. I was trained also to think of the capacity for culture as an attribute of humans, all of whom used that capacity to fashion ways of life, elements of which alone or in combination could float free from the people who first practiced them. The term, "multiculturalism" with its implications of essentialism presents the danger of conflating what we think of as race (Whites, African Americans, Asians, Native Americans) with culture, implying that cultural practices are also genetic. This confusion or conflation has no scholarly validity, for both culture and race are, in part, constructed categories that change with time and historical circumstance.

Let us no longer use labels such as multiculturalism and diversity but rather let us explore the inclusion among our faculty and students of individuals whose life experiences differ from those traditionally included in the academy and with these new voices enrich the academy. To be sure it is likely that differences in life experiences will be more pronounced among those we now categorize as African Americans, Asians, Latinos, and Native Americans, just as the recent inclusion of women in larger numbers has conveyed new perspectives. It makes sense to look among all of them for variety. But that is a far cry from assuming that each of these terms represents one uniform, dyed-in-the-wool culture.

We need to remember, nevertheless, that any person asked to join our institutions in an effort to create more variety is an individual whose cultural beliefs and practices may conform not at all or only in part with the beliefs and practices associated with the group. It should not be assumed that individuals are necessarily representatives of their group, and they should not be expected to give group opinions or judgments, unless they themselves wish to do so. Certainly in this day and age, global popular culture and the qualities all humans share create a community of interest underlying the differences.

In my opinion, the term "political correctness" is another linguistic feature that impedes the opportunity for civility in intellectual debates. Values that are as unquestioned as motherhood and apple pie somehow become suspect when labeled "politically correct." Letting nontraditional voices be heard (free speech, equality of opportunity) is now politically correct. Treating those previously almost barred from academia with respect and civility in word and deed (simple good manners) is now politically correct. To advocate the addition of a curriculum or courses that include the works, lives, and histories of those whose experiences have not been traditionally part of the corpus of studies—and, I stress, without supplanting all of those that are part of the tradition (intellectual flexibility and response to a changing world)—is labeled politically correct. To advocate that special efforts be made to include those who have previously not been welcome in the academy (expanding equality of opportunity again) is politically correct.

Because these values and positions have been, on occasion, advocated with vehemence in their support, and because, perhaps more important, some scholars do not approve of what is being advocated, the phrases "political correctness" and "politically correct" have come to have pejorative connotations. When used, the words are often accompanied by a sneer, a snide look, or a condescending air and always appear in mental quotation marks. The advocacy of no change in personnel or texts is just as "politically correct" for those who espouse the status quo but is not so labeled or understood by those who have long enjoyed assignment in unmarked categories. The use of the terms has now come to mask ideas and succeeds in closing off civil debate on genuine scholarly issues and the nature of the academy. Let us banish the label "political correctness." Instead, let us debate the issues of substance the words have masked and maintain a simple respect for opponents.

ADVOCACY IN THE CLASSROOM

The most important purposes of education are to help students acquire knowledge and learn how knowledge is discovered and constructed. Students should become aware that theories and paradigms shift as disciplines develop. What they are expected to learn, they should discover, is contingent on the time and place in which they live and the particular intellectual stance of their teachers. Yet, equally important, they need to be critical and learn what canons of evidence make some information more reliable than others. For such learning to take place, teachers need to make overt the disciplinary points of view they espouse and inform students, without sarcasm, that other positions also exist. Some approaches may have political implications, and these should also be made explicit. Students should understand, however, that while they are free personally to accept or reject a teacher's position, they are nevertheless obligated to learn that position. For example, whenever I taught evolution to those who felt it might undermine their religious beliefs, I explained that no student need personally accept the idea. To be an educated person and to understand the basis of biological knowledge in the twentieth century, however, they needed to know something about evolutionary theory.

CONCLUSION

It is incumbent upon us to recognize that advocacy in the classroom with or without political implications is part of the nature of the academy. Let us eschew the negative campaigning and even hate-filled, emotional, and distorting arguments that have been all too common in recent years. Let us work toward mutual respect and remember that advocacy is our modus operandi and does not preclude civility. Let the current climate of discord over the canon, multiculturalism, and political correctness rapidly become part of our past and let the voice of the turtle once again be heard in the land.

FIVE

A Brief History of Academic Freedom

GEOFFREY R. STONE

ALTHOUGH THE STRUGGLE FOR FREEDOM in teaching can be traced at least as far back as Socrates' eloquent defense of himself against the charge that he corrupted the youth of Athens, the modern history of this struggle, as it has played out in the university context, begins with the advent of universities, as we know them today, in the twelfth century.

In the social structure of the Middle Ages, universities were centers of power and prestige. They were protected, courted, and even deferred to by emperors and popes. In internal matters, medieval universities generally had the prerogative of self-government. They were largely autonomous institutions, conceived in the spirit of the guilds. Their members—whom we today would describe as their faculty—elected their own officials and set their own rules.

There were, however, sharp limits on the scope of scholarly inquiry. There existed a hard core of authoritatively established doctrine that was made obligatory on all scholars and teachers. It was expected that each new accretion of knowledge would be consistent with a single system of truth, anchored in God, and this expectation was often rigidly enforced by the Church, particularly when scholarly inquiry questioned the authority of the Church itself. As Gregory of Heimberg observed in the fifteenth century, "it was safer to discuss the power of God than the power of the popes."

As scholars and teachers gradually became more interested in science and began to question some of the fundamental precepts of religious doctrine, the conflict between scientific inquiry and religious authority grew intense. When Copernicus published his astronomical theories in 1543, he did so very carefully, by cleverly dedicating his work to the pope and by presenting his theories entirely in the guise of hypotheticals. Partly because of these precautions, his heretical publications did not immediately arouse much of a furor.

But by the time Galileo published his telescopic observations some 70 years later, the situation had changed. Galileo immediately was listed as a suspect in the secret books of the Inquisition and was warned that further discussion of the condemned opinion would have its dangers. Despite this warning, Galileo persisted in his work; as a consequence, he was summoned to Rome, threatened with torture, compelled publicly to disavow his views, and imprisoned for the remainder of his life.

Throughout the seventeenth century, university life remained largely bounded by the medieval curriculum. Real freedom of thought was neither practiced nor professed. As one statement of the then prevailing ideal put the point, the teacher was "not to permit any novel opinions . . . to be mooted; nor . . . to teach or suffer to be taught anything contrary to prevalent opinions."[1]

This was the general attitude in America as well as in Europe, and freedom of inquiry and teaching in America was severely limited by the constraints of religious doctrine well into the nineteenth century. In 1654, for example, Harvard's president was forced to resign because he denied the scriptural validity of infant baptism. Harvard explained that it would not keep as teachers persons who had "manifested themselves unsound in the fayth."[2]

Some years later the Harvard Board of Overseers removed a professor from teaching because he had espoused "unsound doctrines." The overseers explained that they had the right "to examine into the principles of all those that are Employed in the instruction of the Students . . . and that no person chosen into such an office shall be accepted or Continued who refuseth . . . to give Satisfaction to this board as to their principles in religion."[3]

This instance of the role of the Harvard Overseers is illustrative of an important and distinctive feature of American higher education—the governance of universities by lay boards of trustees. The essence of trustee governance is that the trustees, rather than the faculty, are the university and that they therefore have the power to hire and to fire faculty and to make all fundamental decisions governing the institution.

The practice of trustee governance is not a law of nature. To the contrary, it grew out of three conditions that distinguished the American situation from that in Europe. First, whereas the European universities had been nurtured for centuries on the medieval guild traditions of faculty self-governance, the American colleges were founded without any connection to those traditions. Second, whereas the European universities evolved out of long-established communities of scholarship and teaching, the first American colleges were created out of whole cloth by communities that had to strain limited resources to support them. As a consequence, they were heavily dependent on the financial support of laypersons, who demanded a measure of control in return. And third, while in Europe a teaching profession existed even before the emergence of the universities, the colleges in America were created before there was any tradition of such a profession. This was important because the very idea of the self-governing university was based on the assumption that teachers are professionals who can manage their own affairs. The first American teachers were predominantly amateurs. It is noteworthy that the power of lay trustees to direct the academic mission of universities, which grew out of this history, has had a significant impact on the evolution of academic freedom in the United States. In any event, returning to my chronology, the latter part of the eighteenth century saw a brief period of relative secularization of the American colleges as part of the Enlightenment. By opening up new fields of study, and by introducing a note of skepticism and inquiry, the trend toward secular learning began gradually to liberate college work. The teacher of science introduced for the first time the discovery rather than the transmission of knowledge into the classroom.

This shift was short-lived, however, for the opening decades of the nineteenth century brought a significant retrogression. This was due both to a rapid increase in the number of colleges and a dramatic growth in sectarian competition.

In 1780 there were only 9 colleges in the United States. By 1800 there were 25. By 1861 there were almost 200. This multiplication of the number of colleges, which was due in part to the expansion of the nation and the difficulty of travel, seriously fragmented higher education. Moreover, the rise of fundamentalism in the early years of the nineteenth century and a growing counterattack against the skepticism of the Enlightenment produced a concerted effort on the part of the Protestant churches to expand their influence and to tighten their control over intellectual and spiritual life. Sectarian pride demanded that every denomination in every locale have its own college, and these colleges were kept under close doctrinal supervision.

As a result of these developments, the American college in the first half of the nineteenth century was deeply centered in tradition. It looked to antiquity for the tools of thought and to Christianity for the laws of living. It was highly paternalistic and authoritarian. Its emphasis on traditional subjects, mechanical drill, and rigid discipline stymied free discussion and squelched creativity.

Two factors in particular stifled academic freedom in this era. First, the college teacher was regarded first and foremost as a teacher. Because academic honors hinged entirely on teaching, there was no incentive or time for original research. Indeed, it was generally agreed that research was positively harmful to teaching. In 1857, for example, a committee of Trustees of Columbia College attributed the low state of the college to the fact that some of its professors "wrote books."[4]

Second, freedom of inquiry and teaching in the colleges was smothered by the prevailing theory of "doctrinal moralism," which assumed that the worth of an idea should be judged by its moral advantages, an attitude that is anathema to scholarly inquiry.

The most important moral problem in America in the first half of the nineteenth century was, of course, slavery. By the 1830s, the mind of the South had closed on this issue. When it became known, for example, that a professor at the University of North Carolina was sympathetic to the 1856 Republican presidential candidate, the faculty repudiated his views, the students burned him in effigy, and the press demanded his resignation. After he refused to resign, he was dismissed by the trustees. There was simply no open discussion of the issue.

The situation in the North was only slightly better. Most northerners distinguished sharply between those who condemned slavery in the abstract and those who supported immediate abolition. The latter often were silenced. A few northern institutions, however, were open centers of abolitionism, but they were no more tolerant than the South of opposing views. At Franklin College, for example, President Joseph Smith lost his post because he was not an abolitionist, and Judge Edward Loring was dismissed from a lectureship at the Harvard Law School because, in his capacity as a federal judge, he had enforced the fugitive slave law.

Between 1870 and 1900 there was a genuine revolution in American higher education. Dramatic reforms, such as the elective system, graduate instruction, and scientific courses, were implemented, and great new universities were established at Cornell, Johns Hopkins, Stanford, and Chicago. New academic goals were embraced. To criticize and augment as well as to preserve the tradition became an accepted function of higher education. This was an extraordinary departure for a system that previously had aimed primarily at cultural conservation. Two forces in particular hastened this shift. The first was the impact of Darwinism. The second was the influence of the German university.

By the early 1870s Darwin's theory of evolution was no longer a disputed hypothesis within the American scientific community. But as scientific doubts subsided, religious opposition rose. Determined efforts were made to hold the line by excluding proponents of Darwinism whenever possible. The disputes were bitter and often very public.

This conflict brought together like-minded teachers, scientists, scholars, and philosophers who believed in evolution and who developed new standards of academic inquiry. In their view, to dissent was not to obstruct but to enlighten. The great debate over Darwinism went far beyond the substantive problem of whether evolution was true. It represented a profound clash among conflicting cultures, intellectual styles, and academic values. It pitted the clerical against the scientific; the sectarian against the secular; the authoritarian against the empiricist; and the doctrinalist against the naturalist. In these conflicts, science and education joined forces to attack both the principle of doctrinal moralism and the authority of the clergy.

A new approach to education and to intellectual discourse grew out of the Darwinian debate. To the evolutionists, all beliefs were tentative and verifiable only through a continuous process of inquiry. The evolutionists held that every claim to truth must submit to open verification, that the process of verification must follow certain rules, and that this process is best understood by those who qualify as experts.

In the attack on clerical control of universities, the most effective weapon was the contention that the clergy were simply incompetent in science. The result of this attack was the almost complete disappearance of the clergy as a serious academic force. In 1860, 39 percent of the members of the boards of 15 private colleges were clergymen; by 1900, the percentage had dropped to 23 percent; by 1930, the percentage had dwindled to only 7 percent.[5]

The Darwinian conflict undermined not only clerical control of universities but the authority of lay boards of trustees as well. Although the prerogative of judging the fitness of professors is formally lodged in the boards of trustees, the debate over Darwinism highlighted the lack of qualification of laypersons to make such judgments. Thus, a secondary consequence of the Darwinian debate was to strengthen the role of faculty and to weaken the control of lay boards of trustees.

The other factor that played a critical role in the transformation of American higher education in the late nineteenth century was the influence of the German university. More than 9,000 Americans studied at German universities in the nineteenth century, and these students enthusiastically transported the methods and ideals of the German university into the United States.

The modern conception of a university as a research institution was in large part a German contribution. The object of the German university was the determined, methodical, and independent search for truth, without regard to practical application. Such a vision of the research university attracted individuals of outstanding abilities rather than mere pedagogues and disciplinarians. The German professor enjoyed freedom of teaching and freedom of inquiry. The German system held that this freedom was the distinctive prerogative of the academic profession and that it was the essential condition of a university.

Although American canons of education were not receptive to this vision of a university in the first half of the nineteenth century, by the end of the century the old assumptions had been cast aside. Before 1860 not a single doctorate had been awarded by an American institution; in 1890, 164 such degrees were conferred; in 1900, more than twice that number.

The single greatest contribution of the German university to the American conception of academic freedom was the assumption that academic freedom defined the true university. As William Rainey Harper, the first president of the University of Chicago, observed in 1892:

> When for any reason . . . the administration of [a university] or the instruction in any . . . of its departments is changed by an influence from without, [or any] effort is made to dislodge an officer or a professor because the political sentiment or the religious sentiment of the majority has undergone a change, at that moment the institution has ceased to be a university. . . . Individuals or the state or the church may found schools for propagating certain special kinds of instruction, but such schools are not universities.[6]

Although American universities borrowed heavily from the German in this era, there evolved two critical differences between the American and German conceptions of academic freedom. First, whereas the German conception permitted the professor to convince his students of the wisdom of his own views, the American conception held that the proper stance for professors in the classroom was one of neutrality on controversial issues. As President Eliot of Harvard declared at the time:

Philosophical subjects should never be taught with authority. They are not established sciences; they are full of disputed matters, open questions, and bottomless speculations. It is not the function of the teacher to settle philosophical and political controversies for the pupil. . . . The notion that education consists in the authoritative inculcation of what the teacher deems true . . . is intolerable in a university.[7]

Second, the German conception of academic freedom distinguished sharply between freedom within and freedom outside the university. Within the walls of the academy, the German conception allowed a wide latitude of utterance. But outside the university, the same degree of freedom was not condoned. Rather, the German view assumed that, as civil servants, professors were obliged to be circumspect and nonpolitical and that participation in partisan issues spoiled the habits of scholarship.

American professors rejected this limitation. Drawing on the more general American conception of freedom of speech, they insisted on participating actively in the arena of social and political action. American professors demanded the right to express their opinions even outside the walls of academia, even on controversial subjects, and even on matters outside their scholarly competence.

This conception of academic freedom has generated considerable friction, for by claiming that professors should be immune not only for what they say in the classroom and in their research but also for what they say in public debate, this expanded conception essentially empowers professors to engage in outside political activities that can and sometimes do inflict serious harm on their universities in the form of disgruntled trustees, alienated alumni, and disaffected donors. Not surprisingly, the demand for such immunity often has strained both the tolerance of trustees and the patience of university administrators.

These issues were brought to a head in the closing years of the nineteenth century, when businessmen who had accumulated vast industrial wealth began to support universities on an unprecedented scale. For at the same time that trusteeship in a prestigious university was increasingly becoming an important symbol of business prominence, a growing concern among scholars about the excesses of commerce and industry generated new forms of research, particularly in the social sciences, that often were sharply critical of the means by which the trustee philanthropists had amassed their wealth.

The moguls and the scholars thus came into direct and serious conflict in the final years of the nineteenth century. A professor was dismissed from Cornell for a pro-labor speech that annoyed a powerful benefactor; an economist was dismissed from the University of Chicago for delivering a speech against the railroads during the Pullman strike; and a prominent scholar at Stanford was dismissed for expressing his views on the silver and immigration issues, to cite just three of many possible examples. This tension continued until the beginning of World War I, when it was dwarfed by an even larger conflict.

During the Great War, patriotic zealots persecuted and even prosecuted those who questioned the war or the draft. Universities faced the almost total collapse of the institutional safeguards that had evolved up to that point to protect academic freedom, for nothing in their prior experience had prepared them to deal with the issue of loyalty at a time of national emergency.

At the University of Nebraska, for example, three professors were discharged because they had "assumed an attitude calculated to encourage . . . a spirit of [indifference] and opposition towards [the] war."[8] At the University of Virginia, a professor was discharged for disloyalty because he had made a speech predicting that the war would not make the world safe for democracy.[9] And at Columbia, the board of trustees launched a general campaign of investigation to determine whether doctrines that tended to encourage a spirit of disloyalty were taught at the university.[10]

This is not, of course, the end of the story, for I have not even touched upon McCarthyism, the tensions of the Vietnam era, or the current controversies over political correctness. But my space is almost at an end, and, in any event, by 1920 the basic contours of the debates over academic freedom already were well defined.

I would like, however, to conclude with a few final observations. First, even a casual review of the history reveals that the real threat to academic freedom comes not from the isolated incident that arises out of a highly particularized dispute but rather from efforts to impose a pall of orthodoxy that is designed broadly to silence all opposition.

Second, a review of the history reveals that every form of orthodoxy that has been imposed on the academy—whether religious, political, patriotic, scientific, moral, philosophical, or economic—has been imposed by groups that were fully convinced of the rightness of their position. And it is equally clear, with the benefit of hindsight and some objectivity, that every one of these groups has later come to be viewed by most thoughtful people as inappropriately intolerant, at best, and as inappropriately intolerant and wrong, at worst. It thus seems clear that if we are to avoid repeating the mistakes of the past, we must step back from our own fighting faiths, insist on a less self-righteous stance, and subject our own orthodoxies to ruthless self-criticism. It is useful in this regard to note that these things do tend to come full circle. It is ironic, for example, that although religious sectarianism once posed the greatest threat to academic freedom, it may now be the case that the most powerful orthodoxy in American universities is the aggressive intolerance of religious ideas and advocacy.

Finally, although trustee governance historically has played an important role in limiting academic freedom, faculty, sad to say, have not been much better. Indeed, in many instances it has been faculty, as much if not more than trustees, who have defined and enforced the dominant orthodoxy. Even in medieval times, when the Church generally was uninterested in purely academic disagreements, it often was drawn into these disputes precisely because one group of scholars forced its attention by accusing another group of scholars of heresy. Some might say that that pattern still is with us.

NOTES

I would like to thank Jeffrey Sharer for his invaluable research assistance. Although I drew on several secondary sources in preparing this chapter, I relied especially on Richard Hofstadter and Walter

Metzger, *The Development of Academic Freedom in the United States* (New York: Colombia University Press, 1955), which I heartily recommend to anyone interested in a much more thorough exploration of this subject.

1. Martha Ornstein, *The Role of Scientific Societies in the Seventeenth Century* (Chicago: University of Chicago Press, 1938), 215.

2. Richard Hofstadter and Walter Metzger, *The Development of Academic Freedom in the United States* (New York: Colombia University Press, 1955), 89.

3. Ibid., 157.

4. Ibid., 286.

5. Ibid., 352.

6. The University of Chicago, *President's Reports, 1892-1902* (Chicago: University of Chicago Press, 1903), xxiii.

7. Hofstadter and Metzger, *The Development of Academic Freedom,* 400.

8. Ibid., 497.

9. Ibid., 497.

10. Ibid., 498.

SIX

First Amendment and Civil Liberties Traditions of Academic Freedom

NADINE STROSSEN

MY ASSIGNMENT, in writing this chapter, was "to discuss the First Amendment and civil liberties traditions of academic freedom" that are relevant to "the role of advocacy in the classroom."

Before I turn to the relevant constitutional and civil liberties principles, I'd like to briefly discuss my personal experience. As a constitutional law professor, I teach my students about issues and cases as to which the American Civil Liberties Union (ACLU) usually has advocated a particular position, which I also personally advocate in many public forums in my other capacity as ACLU president. So I myself constantly confront, very squarely, questions about the appropriate role of advocacy in the classroom in contrast with advocacy in other settings.

Devoted as I am to the ACLU and civil liberties, I consider myself first and foremost a teacher; I think that educating the next generation is the most important contribution I can make and one of the highest callings that anyone can pursue. Consistent with that belief, I have a clear vision of how I should educate my students: I believe that my role is

- not only to inform, but also to inspire
- not only to convey my ideas and those of other people but also to stimulate my students' own thinking
- not only to answer their questions but also to question their answers
- finally, to get them to question all proffered answers—mine, theirs, and everyone else's.

In short, this educational philosophy is intended to promote critical analysis and inquiry.

Consistent with this educational philosophy, here is my answer to the overarching question about the role of advocacy in the classroom:

So long as advocacy is conducted within a classroom context of critical analysis and inquiry, it is completely consistent with constitutional and civil liberties values. But if advocacy is conducted within a classroom context of inculcation or indoctrination, it is inconsistent with those values. In short, the advocacy *content* of particular classroom statements does not determine whether it violates or honors constitutional or civil liberties principles. Rather, one has to consider the overall *context* in which the statements are made.

This point is central to the ACLU policy on classroom advocacy. It stresses the importance of an overall classroom atmosphere of free inquiry and endorses teachers' expression of their own viewpoints within that framework. According to the ACLU Policy Guide:

> In the classroom, a teacher should promote an atmosphere of free inquiry. This should include discussion of controversial issues without the assumption that they are settled in advance or that there is only one "right" answer in matters of dispute. Such discussion should include presentation of divergent opinions and doctrines, past and present, on a given subject. The teacher's own judgment forms a part of this material. If such judgment is clearly stated, students are better able to appraise it and to differ from it on the basis of other materials and views placed at their disposal than they would be if a teacher were to attempt to conceal bias by a claim to "objective" scholarship.[1]

Now that I have laid out my bottom-line conclusion, let me explain how I got there.

First I'll discuss the meaning of some key terms, including that centrally important term, "advocacy." I use this term in the same way that the Supreme Court has used it in some major First Amendment cases: to describe expression that seeks to persuade its listeners of a certain conclusion. Such expression cannot accomplish its goal without appealing to the listeners' reasoning powers; it is designed to trigger their own thought processes.

As such, advocacy is diametrically different from expression that is "inculcating" or "indoctrinating." That kind of expression is designed to preempt the listeners' exercise of their own analytical abilities. Advocacy is intended to open minds; inculcation is intended to close them. Advocacy is intended to spark a dialogue between speaker and listener; indoctrination is intended as a monologue in which the speaker imparts ideas to a passive recipient.

The distinction between constitutionally protected advocacy and constitutionally prohibited indoctrination was well stated in a 1972 decision by the U.S. Court of Appeals for the Second Circuit, in New York. Defending advocacy, the court explained: "It would be foolhardy to shield our children from political debate and issues until the eve of their first venture into the voting booth. Schools must play a central role in preparing students to think, and analyze, and to recognize the demagogue."[2] In contrast, however, the same court condemned indoctrination:

> Although sound discussions of ideas are the beams and the buttresses of the First Amendment, teachers cannot be allowed to patrol the precincts of radical thought with the unrelenting goal of indoctrination, a goal compatible with totalitarianism and not democracy. When a teacher is content only if he persuades his students that his values, and only his values ought to be their values, then it is not unreasonable to expect the state to protect impressionable children from such dogmatism.[3]

The right of teachers to engage in nonindoctrinating advocacy should be protected, even if the teachers succeed in persuading students to adopt their viewpoints. In contrast with all coercion, which is not protected, all persuasion—including effective persuasion—is protected. This point was specifically recognized by the one court case that expressly addressed it. In 1970 the federal court in Connecticut upheld a junior high school teacher's First Amendment right to refuse to recite the Pledge of Allegiance along with her students, despite the fact that some students also refused to recite the pledge and may well have taken this stance because they were persuaded by the teacher's position. The court explained: "It does not matter whether some of [Ms. Hanover's] students, who also refrain from reciting the pledge, were persuaded to do so because of [her] conduct. 'The First Amendment protects successful dissent as well as ineffective protests.'"[4]

With these definitions and distinctions in mind, let's turn to the First Amendment rights at stake in the context of classroom advocacy.

The Supreme Court has not provided specific guidance on the precise questions implicated by classroom advocacy. But we can draw some inferences both from the Court's general pronouncements about academic freedom or First Amendment rights in the classroom setting and from its specific rulings on analogous issues.

These sources indicate that there are several relevant First Amendment rights. First, teachers have the right to express ideas and information. Second, students have the right both to receive and to express ideas and information. Third, students have the right to formulate their own ideas and to be free from a government-imposed orthodoxy in doing so.

How these rights actually apply in particular situations is complicated for several reasons.

First, the precise nature and scope of the rights may well differ depending on the age and educational level of the students. This factor may cut in different ways, depending on the particular right at stake. For example, on the one hand, older students are generally more mature. Therefore, they may well have greater rights to impart and receive information and ideas. On the other hand, though, younger students are in school by virtue of compulsory education laws, and schools are more structured and hierarchical environments than colleges. For these reasons, as well as because of their relative immaturity and impressionability, the younger students may have a greater right to be sheltered from a teacher's expression that is potentially indoctrinating.[5]

A second complicating factor is that none of the rights at stake is absolute, even considered on its own. The Supreme Court made this clear in its landmark 1969 case of *Tinker v Des Moines School District*,[6] in which it first expressly recognized the free speech rights of public school students. In *Tinker*—in which the ACLU successfully represented students who had worn black armbands to protest the Vietnam War—the Court declared: "It can hardly be argued that either students or teachers shed their constitutional rights to freedom of speech or expression at the schoolhouse gate."[7] But the Court did recognize another point at which First Amendment rights *are* shed at school: namely, when the expression "materially disrupts classwork or involves substantial disorder or invasion of the rights of others."[8]

And that latter limitation on students' and teachers' First Amendment rights leads to a third complicating factor when we consider the whole cluster of rights implicated by classroom advocacy. Specifically, all of these rights are to some extent in tension with each other.

For example, the right of teachers to express themselves is curbed by the students' right to learn in a nonindoctrinating environment. This point was made by Duke University law professor William Van Alstyne, a leading expert on academic freedom and longtime leader of the American Association of University Professors (AAUP), as follows: "[T]he use of his classroom by a teacher or professor deliberately to proselytize for a personal cause or knowingly to emphasize only that selection of data best conforming to his own personal biases is far beyond the license granted by the freedom of speech and furnishes precisely the just occasion to question his fitness to teach."[9]

In its seminal 1915 Declaration on Academic Freedom, the American Association of University Professors recognized this same point. The AAUP Declaration states: "[The teacher must avoid] taking unfair advantage of the student's immaturity by indoctrinating him with the teacher's own opinions before the student has had an opportunity fairly to examine other opinions upon matters in question, and before he has sufficient knowledge and ripeness of judgment to be entitled to form any definitive opinion of his own."[10] Likewise, the declaration provides that a professor should "Be a person of fair and judicial mind; he should, in dealing with [controversial] subjects, set forth justly, without suppression or innuendo, the divergent opinions of other investigators; . . . and he should, above all, remember that his business is not to provide his students with ready made conclusions but to train them to think for themselves."[11]

Along with the AAUP, the ACLU also has stressed that teachers' right of expression is limited by their responsibility to respect their students' right to a nonindoctrinating education. This key concept is highlighted by the very title of the ACLU's pertinent policy: "Teachers' Freedom *and Responsibility. . .* in Higher Education." Likewise, the opening sentence of that policy refers to "[a]cademic freedom *and responsibility.*"[12]

Because of the complicating factors I have just enumerated, this discussion is necessarily somewhat oversimplified. Due to space constraints, I have to paint in relatively broad brushstrokes, making generalizations that might not obtain in all classrooms in all circumstances.

I'd now like to sketch the constitutional underpinnings of the three basic sets of rights implicated in classroom advocacy. These rights stem not only from teachers' and students' general First Amendment freedoms as citizens but also from the broad concept of academic freedom that the Supreme Court has repeatedly endorsed.

The Court's paeans to academic freedom have mostly been in "dicta," not essential to its rulings in particular cases. Accordingly, strictly speaking, these edicts are not legally binding. Nonetheless, the Court's repeated, eloquent declarations in this area show its consistent commitment to a robust concept of academic freedom. Therefore, they indicate that if and when the Court were to issue a firm ruling on a specific issue concerning academic freedom, it would likely be predisposed toward a broad concept of that freedom.

The following few statements are typical. The Court itself often quotes these passages, thus underscoring their importance at least in expressing the Court's general attitude toward academic freedom. In the 1957 case of *Sweezy v New Hampshire*,[13] the Court declared:

> The essentiality of freedom in the community of American universities is almost self-evident. . . . To impose any strait jacket on the intellectual leaders in our colleges and universities would imperil the future of our Nation. . . . Scholarship cannot flourish in an atmosphere of suspicion and distrust. Teachers and students must always remain free to inquire, to study and evaluate, to gain new maturity and understanding; otherwise our civilization will stagnate and die.

Ten years later, in *Keyishian v Board of Regents of the University of New York*,[14] the Court echoed this declaration:

> Our nation is deeply committed to safeguarding academic freedom, which is of transcendent value to all of us and not just to the teachers concerned. That freedom is therefore a special concern of the First Amendment, which does not tolerate laws which cast a pall of orthodoxy over the classroom. The classroom is peculiarly the "marketplace of ideas." The nation's future depends upon leaders trained through wider exposure to the robust exchange of ideas which discovers truth "out of a multitude of tongues, rather than through any kind of authoritative selection."

As these statements indicate, the Supreme Court has recognized students' general right to a nonorthodox, nonindoctrinating mode of education. In the *Tinker* case, the Court underscored that right, stating: "In our system students may not be regarded as the closed-circuit recipients of only that which the State chooses to communicate."[15]

It is this right that is most germane to the theme of this volume. Yet neither the Supreme Court nor other courts have precisely defined its contours. Worse yet, far from clarifying the right, the Supreme Court has actually done the opposite, by repudiating it to some extent. Along with its pronouncements about schools' duty not to inculcate their students, the Court has also declared that public schools not only *may* inculcate certain ideas or values in their students but also indeed that they have a *duty* to do so.

In cases involving primary and secondary schools, the Court has said that public schools fulfill a dual role—not only to provide a "marketplace of ideas," stimulating free individual inquiry, but also to instill certain majoritarian views and values. Specifically, the Court has stressed the public schools' "vitally important"[16] role in "inculcating fundamental values necessary to the maintenance of a democratic political system."[17] Likewise, it has said that schools may "promote . . . respect for . . . traditional values, be they social, moral, or political."[18] In one statement that I certainly endorse, the Court said that states may require all students to learn about civil liberties![19]

But how can we reconcile students' general right to a non-indoctrinating education with the schools' mission of inculcating basic constitutional values? Let me outline the Supreme Court cases that have considered this important and difficult question. The most directly relevant case is *Island Trees Union Free School District v Pico*, decided in 1982. In the *Pico* case, the ACLU represented students and parents who challenged the removal of certain books from a public school library at the behest of other parents, who complained that the books were "anti-American, anti-Christian, anti-Semitic, and just plain filthy."[20] Although no five members of the Court could agree upon an opinion, the plurality held that public school students have a free speech right of access to diverse ideas in a school library. They specifically ruled that the removal of library books would violate this right if the reason for the removal was to deny students access to ideas with which school officials disagreed. The justices were seeking to avert "the danger of an official suppression of ideas"[21] in the public educational system.

This is precisely the danger that the ACLU argued against in our brief in the *Pico* case. I reread that brief in preparing this chapter, and was struck by a certain passage because it so directly addresses the volume theme. Review the language in this passage carefully, and you will see how it defends advocacy in the classroom while rejecting indoctrination:

Whether the current orthodoxy is religious . . . or political . . . this Court has consistently invoked both the First Amendment as well as its sense of the proper role of public education in a democratic society to limit the power of the state to inculcate exclusively majoritarian values.

Both the First Amendment and democratic principles . . . still leave school officials with considerable discretion. The . . . schools may teach about the values of the . . . community. Teachers may encourage respect for those values; school officials may promote those values. What they cannot do is to foster community values and ideas by excluding or eliminating conflicting viewpoints.

There is a firm tradition within our First Amendment jurisprudence which holds that school officials cannot advance sectarian or even majoritarian interests to the point of imposing an orthodoxy of ideas or viewpoints within the schoolhouse.

This statement from the ACLU brief in *Pico*—the Supreme Court case most directly on point—refers to other Court cases that are indirectly on point: cases prohibiting public educational institutions from imposing religious or sectarian orthodoxy on their students. Of course, such a prohibition is expressly contained in the First Amendment's clause that bars any government establishment of religion, often described as the "separation of church and state." But constitutional law scholars have argued that the First Amendment's free speech guarantee contains an implied nonestablishment provision. They maintain that this implicit establishment clause should limit the government's influence over our nonreligious beliefs to the same extent that the express establishment clause now limits the government's influence over our religious beliefs. For example, a thoughtful article by Professors Stephen Arons and Charles Lawrence states that "The Supreme Court has eliminated religious indoctrination in public schools but . . . the imposition of secular values may constitute as significant an interference with first amendment values as the imposition of religious beliefs."[22] Accordingly, in a felicitous phrase, they advocate "the separation of school and state"[23] to complement the separation of church and state.

I, too, have written an article explaining why the First Amendment's free speech guarantee implicitly protects against governmentally imposed orthodoxy of any kind, religious or otherwise.[24] Most fundamentally, it is both impractical and illogical to draw any sharp distinction between religious and other beliefs in terms of the constitutional protection they should receive. This is underscored by the fact that the Supreme Court has often equated the two. In many cases, the Court has dealt collectively with freedom of belief, conscience, and thought, treating them as closely interrelated aspects of the individual autonomy that the Constitution insulates from governmental control or influence. Indeed, the Court has equated freedom of thought and conscience with freedom of religious belief specifically in the public school context.

In *West Virginia Board of Education v Barnette*,[25] which held that schools may not compel Jehovah's Witness schoolchildren to salute the American flag, the Court declared that the individual conscience may not be subjected to any state-imposed dogma. The particular reason that the children (who were supported by the ACLU) cited for refraining from the flag salute was their religious belief that the salute constituted idolatry. But the Court's decision did not rely specifically on concepts of religious freedom. Rather, in broad language, it upheld freedom of individual belief or thought on all matters, religious or otherwise, within "the sphere of intellect and spirit."[26]

In one of the most ringing statements in constitutional law, the Court declared: "If there is any fixed star in our constitutional constellation, it is that no official, high or petty, can prescribe what shall be orthodox in politics, nationalism, [or] religion. . . ."[27]

Now that I have outlined the relevant constitutional law and civil liberties principles, I would like to return to, and clarify, a conclusion I stated at the beginning of this chapter, which these principles support: that the critical factor in assessing whether any classroom expression—including advocacy—is protected free speech or prohibited indoctrination depends on the overall classroom atmosphere. Is the classroom an ideological boot camp, or is it a marketplace of ideas?

Let me list some concrete factors that would indicate that the classroom atmosphere is appropriately consistent with free analytical inquiry:

- Any matter that is the subject of reasonable dispute is presented as opinion or theory, rather than as fact or dogma.
- When there are competing opinions or theories regarding a particular subject, with similar degrees of acceptance among the relevant experts, these competing views are presented.
- The students are permitted—or, better yet, encouraged—to ask questions about, and to express disagreement with, points made in assigned materials and in the teacher's presentations.
- Through the assigned reading materials, the teacher's presentations, and class discussion, all theories or beliefs that are presented are subject to critical examination.
- Students are permitted—or, even better, encouraged—to satisfy their class reading requirements, at least in part, by selecting materials from a range of options presenting diverse viewpoints.
- Students' grades do not depend on a rote regurgitation of certain theories or beliefs that are included in assigned reading materials or in a teacher's presentations.
- Instead, students' grades are based on their demonstrated understanding of, and ability to analyze, these ideas.
- Teachers or other school authorities explain to the students that they should not interpret any course material, or any statement by a school official, as indicating the school's approval or disapproval of any theory or belief.

Of course, whether these guidelines are honored depends almost entirely on teachers themselves. As is so often the case, the First Amendment—and Supreme Court decisions interpreting it—are worth only the paper they are written on unless people live by them in practice.

As indicated by the lack of specific judicial rulings involving issues of academic freedom and advocacy in the classroom, courts are reluctant to interfere with the operation of our schools. Moreover, students are not in a good position to challenge what goes on in the classroom. They may well be unaware of their constitutional rights and hesitant to challenge a teacher. Therefore, not only the students themselves but also all of us who are dedicated to academic freedom and sound education depend on teachers' professional dedication and integrity.

Accordingly, I want to close by quoting a particularly germane line from the ACLU's policy on "teachers' freedom and responsibility in higher education." After that policy describes the teacher's responsibility to promote a classroom atmosphere of free inquiry, it concludes as follows: "No set procedures for conduct of a class or for use of materials can guarantee the teacher's own integrity or take its place."

NOTES

1. See *Policy Guide of the American Civil Liberties Union,* at Policy No. 60, (rev. ed. 1994), p. 112. Hereafter *ACLU Policy Guide.*
2. *James v Board of Education of Central School District,* 461 F2d 566, 574 (2d Cir 1972).
3. *Ibid.* at 573.
4. *Hanover v Northrup,* 325 F Supp 170, 173 (D. Conn. 1970), quoting *Frain v Baron,* 307 F Supp 27, 33 (E.D.N.Y. 1969).
5. See Nadine Strossen, *"Secular Humanism" and "Scientific Creationism": Proposed Standards for Reviewing Curricular Decisions Affecting Students' Religious Freedom,* 47 Ohio State Law Journal 333, 369 (1986); William Van Alstyne, *The Constitutional Rights of Teachers and Professors,* 1970 Duke Law Journal 841, 856.
6. 393 US 503 (1969).
7. *Ibid.* at 506.
8. *Ibid.* at 513.
9. Van Alstyne, *The Constitutional Rights of Teachers and Professors,* at 841, 856.
10. Richard Hofstadter and Walter P. Metzger, *The Development of Academic Freedom in the United States* (New York: Columbia University Press, 1955) (hereafter Hofstadter and Metzger, *Academic Freedom*), at

411 citing the American Association of University Professors' 1915 Declaration of Principles at 35.

11. Hofstadter and Metzger, *Academic Freedom,* at 410 citing the AAUP's 1915 Declaration at 31.
12. ACLU Policy Guide, Policy #60. (Emphasis added.)
13. 354 US 234.
14. 385 US 589, 603 (1967)
15. *Tinker v Des Moines School District,* 393 US 503, 511 (1969).
16. *Board of Education, Island Trees Union Free School District No. 26 v Pico,* 457 US 853, 864 (1982)
17. *Ambach v Norwick,* 441 US 68, 76-77 (1979).
18. *Ibid.*
19. *West Virginia Board of Education v Barnette,* 319 US 624, 631 (1943).
20. *Pico,* 457 US at 857.
21. *Ibid.* at 871 & n. 22.
22. Stephen Arons and Charles Lawrence III, *The Manipulation of Consciousness: A First Amendment Critique of Schooling,* 15 Harvard Civil Rights–Civil Liberties Law Review 309, 325 (1980).
23. *Ibid.* at 360.
24. See Strossen, *Proposed Standards,* 375-77.
25. 319 US 624 (1943).
26. *Ibid.* at 642.
27. *Ibid.* at 635.

SEVEN

The Open Classroom and Its Enemies

MICHAEL ROOT

IN 1943 THE PHILOSOPHER OF SCIENCE KARL POPPER published a book entitled *The Open Society and Its Enemies*. An open society, Popper wrote, "rejects the absolute authority of the merely established and the merely traditional while trying to preserve, to develop, and to establish traditions, old and new, that measure up to [the] standards of freedom, of humaneness and of rational criticism."[1] Popper described the enemies of the open society in detail. They are the opponents of individual liberty; they look to the state to define the good life and compel the individual to pursue that life. They are philosophers like Plato who favor the rule of the elites. The friends of the open society, on the other hand, favor a neutral state—one that encourages the individual to develop her own conception of the good and affords her the liberty to pursue it.

Popper's conception of the open society combines two independent ideas: neutrality in contrast to partisanship and free thinking in contrast to dogmatism. These two ideas are often allied. Governments that enforce a religion seldom allow critical thought or discussion of these religious teachings. But the ideas are independent. Free thinking, for religious groups such as the Quakers, goes hand in hand with partisanship. Free and open discussion leads to a conception of the good, and continuing discussion opens the conception to continuing assessment and examination. The Quakers are committed to the second idea, free and open debate, but not to the first, moral or political neutrality.

John Stuart Mill, a friend of Popper's open society, argues that in the public realm, where coercion is the issue, neutrality always protects free thinking.[2] But his reasoning does not extend to the private realm—to the office, the church, the clinic, the family, or the classroom. There the connection between neutrality and free thinking is less clear, and the connection is least clear in the realm of education. Here, I will argue, neutrality can oppose rather than promote standards of freedom, humaneness, and rational criticism.

THE HISTORY OF THE NEUTRAL CLASSROOM

My topic in this chapter is the open classroom and its enemies. I wish to assess the claim that our classrooms are less open now than they used to be because teachers have given up their political neutrality and become advocates. Some of the recent opposition to multiculturalism rests on this claim. The new curriculum, the critics say, replaces neutrality with partisanship. Instead of encouraging students to pursue the truth, teachers advocate a favored political agenda. Multiculturalism is seen as an enemy of the open classroom, as Popper saw communism and fascism as enemies of the open society. These critics of multiculturalism are one-third right; they are right to desire an open classroom but wrong to believe that advocacy is a threat to openness and wrong to think that multiculturalism is the enemy.

The current call for a neutral classroom has a history. Between 1904 and 1917 the German social scientist and reformer Max Weber wrote often of the importance of freeing the university of politics. He called upon his colleagues not to include judgments of moral or political value in their academic teaching and writing. His reasons were two. The first was practical. To prosper, a university must be free to manage its own affairs; only if the work within the university is nonpartisan will those outside be persuaded not to interfere.

Weber's second reason was a point of logic. There was no logical connection, he thought, between fact and value, between what is and what ought to be. Facts and values, he wrote, are "entirely heterogeneous," and honesty requires that we as teachers not pretend that one follows from the other. Moreover, professional and academic wisdom is limited to facts and does not extend to questions of political value. "What is really at issue," Weber wrote, "is the intrinsically simple demand that the investigator and teacher should keep unconditionally separate the establishment of empirical facts . . . and his own political evaluations."[3]

Thus, for Weber, if teachers want academic freedom, they should not preach politics from the podium, and if they are honest, they should preach instead that questions of politics are outside their grasp. Their knowledge and skills equip them to tell others what *is* but not what *ought* to be. Weber's view of academic freedom has deep roots and is tied to the very idea of a university and the work that should go on there.

His view was on my mind when, a few quarters ago, I was reading student evaluations of a course I had taught in moral philosophy. One evaluation in particular stopped me short. "The professor," the student complained, "promoted his own political and moral values in many of his lectures. He should keep them to himself and simply teach the facts." Reading negative student evaluations hurts. Many of us put our souls on the line when we teach, and to learn that our efforts don't measure up is painful, but this complaint was especially unnerving because it seemed to echo a prominent view of the open classroom and to label me the enemy.

Should I take the criticism to heart? Should teachers and scholars give the facts and only the facts? Should they ever allow their own moral or political beliefs to creep into their teaching and research? Should they use the podium to say what is morally or politically right or wrong, or use class time to argue that some public policy, a body of scientific research, a philosophical treatise, a novel, an opera, a painting, or play is evil or unjust? Philosophers love to draw distinctions, and perhaps some need to be drawn here. These questions assume a broad brush: that all departments, disciplines, or classes should be painted the same and that neutrality is an appropriate ideal either for all or for none.

John Stuart Mill painted with a finer brush. On the question of neutrality, he thought that science was different from art. "Science," he wrote, "is a collection of truths, art a body of rules or directions for conduct. The language of science is, This is, or, This is not; This does, or does not, happen. The language of art is, Do this; Avoid that. Science takes cognisance of a phenomenon, and endeavors to discover its law; art proposes to itself an end, and looks for means to effect it."[4] In Mill's view, neutrality is an appropriate ideal for the natural and social sciences—for physics and economics—but not for every sort of inquiry and, in particular, not for the arts. Teaching and writing about the atomic weight of hydrogen, the age of the earth, or the laws of supply and demand should say what is and not what ought to be, but teaching and writing about literature, philosophy, and humanities—courses on Shakespeare's plays, Joseph Conrad's novels, Paul Gauguin's paintings, Puccini's operas, or Plato's dialogues—can include both fact and value. Indeed, it was to his colleagues in economics and sociology and not in literature that Max Weber directed his own pleas for nonpartisanship.

An even finer brush would sharpen the picture further. In philosophy, for example, perhaps teachers of logic and epistemology should remain silent on what morally ought to be but teachers of ethics should speak up. Perhaps the student who faulted my partisanship was half right. Had I been teaching about the nature of knowledge, valid inference, or causality, I should have kept my values to myself, but since my topic was justice and injustice, good and evil, or moral right and moral wrong, I could hardly have been expected to be silent on questions of value.

The critics of multiculturalism and proponents of the traditional curriculum—William Bennett and Allen Bloom—paint with the broader brush.[5] They seem to believe that in the ideal university, all the disciplines and not merely the sciences are above politics. On their view, works of literature and art should not be selected for study or taught on the basis of their political virtues. Though these virtues are important, English departments are not the place to teach them.

In truth, critics like Bennett and Bloom are pleased to have political values taught in the university—as long as they are their own. What they oppose is teaching a politics they disapprove of—the values of multiculturalism or feminism or any of the other "isms" that are alien to the kind of lives they would like all of us to lead. But more about Bennett and Bloom later.

LIBERAL EDUCATION AND LIBERAL GOVERNMENT

During the Renaissance, the term "liberal" was an epithet for an education worthy of free and noble men. These were men whose lives were free from everyday needs and toil. Their education was for the mind rather than the hand—not to serve a vocation, trade, or craft but to discover beauty in the arts, truth in the sciences, and goodness in politics. A liberal education was designed to extend the imagination and sharpen the reason—to promote free and autonomous thought. The topics were general rather than specialized. The aim was to inspire rather than train. Much of this remains in our distinction between liberal and vocational education.

The term "liberal" has another use that also connotes freedom, but here the freedom is from authority rather than narrowmindedness. In the seventeenth century, "liberal" was a label for a particular conception of government. A government is liberal by leaving citizens free to lead their lives according to their own lights. Such a government maintains order without favoring one citizen's ends over another's, without advocating one view of the good over others.

Both a liberal education and a liberal government encourage autonomy, and autonomy, for both, implies neutrality; liberal schooling and governing both encourage individuals to think about beauty, truth, and goodness for themselves—to be free to choose what values to live by. In schooling and governing, liberal contrasts with partisan. Devotion is encouraged but devotion to truth alone.

Weber's ideal of neutrality is a central strand in the larger fabric of liberal thought. Liberal education is to vocational education as a liberal government is to theocracy. While one emphasizes free thinking, the other preserves a body of limited and settled practices.

While one favors a particular form of work or worship, the other favors none.

Why is liberalism so attractive? For some the attraction is autonomy. Many of us who agree on little else agree that autonomy is valuable. For others, the attraction is toleration. By not endorsing one set of values or traditions over others or by equally tolerating all, we avoid a culture war and contribute to the peace. Finally, liberalism is attractive to those who are skeptical on matters of moral value. Weber himself doubted that knowledge of ultimate ends was possible. He thought that men cannot reason but can only fight over basic differences in value.

Mill has a more sanguine view of moral knowledge, but he, too, favors liberal neutrality. Although individuals can learn about ultimate good and evil, neither politics nor science, Mill thinks, are good teachers. Most of my colleagues in the social sciences agree with Mill. The aim of science is truth, but the methods of science, they believe, are not suitable for discovering truths about good and evil. Statements such as the following are common in textbooks in the social sciences.

> Science does not attempt to formulate the ends which social and moral conduct ought to pursue.[6]

> Science, as such, is nonmoral. There is nothing in scientific work, as such, which dictates to what ends the products of science should be used.[7]

> Economics deals with ascertainable facts; ethics with valuations and obligations. The two fields of enquiry are not on the same plane of discourse. Between the generalizations of positive and normative studies there is a logical gulf fixed which no ingenuity can disguise and juxtaposition in space or time bridge over.[8]

The tools of science, these textbooks say, are not designed to diagnose moral wrongs. Scientific methods are suited to discovering what is but not what ought to be. From the point of view of scientific reasoning, morality and politics are seen as inscrutable.

PARTISANSHIP IN TEACHING AND RESEARCH

How, in the face of these arguments, could I want the university to be partisan or for teachers to turn their podiums into pulpits? What reason could I have for not wanting the liberal arts and sciences to be liberal? Do I agree with Bennett and Bloom that our colleges should advance a conservative agenda? According to those authors, the university was once free of politics; the ideals were once truth and beauty; the values were scientific and aesthetic. Now, however, having bowed to pressure from multiculturalists, feminists, racial minorities and tenured radicals, the university rewards lobbying over learning. But Bennett and Bloom are mistaken, for teaching and research at the university always have been guided by more than a love of truth and beauty and always have been pulled by a conception of good and evil. The issue is not whether some conception but *whose* conception.

In my view, the liberal arts and sciences are too liberal when they preach neutrality and encourage the myth that teaching and research are or should be free of politics—silent on disputes concerning justice and injustice, moral right and wrong. Set the myth aside and look carefully at the practice of the arts and sciences, and you see an interplay of fact and value. Careful attention to how decisions are made concerning what texts to publish or preserve, how a canon is constructed, how some works of art come to be heralded and others ignored, shows that ideals of what politically ought to be regulate what academically is.

I study the social sciences, and here the choice and application of research methods—protocols for collecting and sorting data, assessing theories, and devising explanations—are by their nature partisan. The validation of psychological tests and survey question-naires requires that the values of the larger community be passed through to the collecting instrument. An intelligence test is a valid measure of intelligence only if the scores match other measures of who is smart and who is dull, but if these other measures are value-laden, then, in order for the test to be predictively valid, it must be value-laden as well.

According to the ideal of value neutrality, facts and values, science and ethics, are "entirely heterogeneous," and, so, a code of ethics can constrain but not define good science. The ideal haunted a recent conference at the University of Minnesota on biomedical research conducted by Nazi doctors in 1943. The issue before the conference was what to do now with the results of the Nazi "experiments." Is it morally permissible for us today to use the "data" collected by killing and torturing Jews? What every conference participant assumed was that the "data" could be reliable and valid even though they were so horribly ill-gotten. The science was good, on their view, as long as the data were collected under scientifically controlled conditions. The conferees were trying to be liberal and not confuse good science with good ethics. Science, they thought, should be limited by a code of ethics, but a failure to be ethical does not make the science—as science—bad.[9]

Were the arts and sciences open about their partisanship, they would not have to view ethics as an intruder. Ethics could be promoted as a standard by which good teaching and research are to be judged. Definitions of good science or good art could rely openly on a conception of good and evil. Ethics would be seen not as a supplement but a key to the liberal arts and sciences.

But if the arts and sciences are too liberal when they profess and encourage neutrality, they are not liberal enough when they attempt to protect academic freedom. Freedom of speech, on the liberal view, is a value that government and the university should work hard to protect. John Stuart Mill, one of the fathers of liberalism, thought that truth is distinguished from falsehood by allowing both to be heard and to compete for acceptance in a free market of ideas. The First Amendment to our Constitution was designed to prevent government from limiting speech, and policies on academic freedom were designed to prevent schools and universities from silencing speech as well.

An interesting thing happens, however, when policies concerning academic freedom are combined with the liberal ideal of neutrality. Consider, for example, the current University of Minnesota policy on academic freedom. It begins by saying "The University of Minnesota should not impose any limitation upon the teacher's freedom in the exposition of his *[sic]* own subject in the classroom or in addresses and publications." But then the policy reneges a bit. It says "No teacher may claim as his right the privilege of discussion in his classroom [of] controversial topics that are not pertinent to the course of study that is being pursued."[10]

Now, if the ideal of neutrality is used to decide what is pertinent, then a course of study that is politically partisan is not pertinent, and a teacher has no right to teach it. That is, if only scholarly inquiry is protected and the bounds of scholarly inquiry end where partisanship begins, then professors in the arts or sciences who teach what is good and evil or say what ought to be and not merely what is are not protected by our university's policy on academic freedom.

When a social scientist lectures that it is morally wrong to experiment on human subjects without their informed consent, what she says is not neutral and, given the ideal of neutrality, not pertinent to her science and so not protected by academic freedom. Academic freedom protects the teacher as long as she stays within the space of her discipline. Judgments of moral right and wrong are not part of that space and, so, are not protected by academic freedom.

THE ENEMY OF THE OPEN CLASSROOM

How can things be made better? First, we need to be honest and relinquish the myth that the arts and sciences can be neutral. Next, we need to give up neutrality as an ideal for teaching or research in these disciplines. Neutrality might be an appropriate ideal for government because government has the power to compel and not merely tell us what we ought to think or do. A university does not. I have the authority to tell my students that sex discrimination is unjust but not to compel them to think so.

When students are told that they ought not to make sexist remarks in the classroom, their liberty is not limited; were the injunction backed by threats, it would be. Sometimes threats are appropriate and just, but to tell is not itself to threaten. Thus, we are not protecting the liberty or autonomy of our students by encouraging neutrality and enjoining our faculty not to lecture them about what ought to be. Although there is an argument from *autonomy* for the government to be liberal, there is none for the arts and sciences to be.

Once we give up the myth of neutrality, our academic freedom policy becomes more liberal. Partisan research and teaching are protected by the policy. Teachers are free to say what ought to be in addition to what is. They can claim as their right topics that are laden with value even if their course of study is science rather than ethics or political philosophy. The bounds of scholarly standards become more liberal even if their speech becomes more overtly partisan.

My recommendations are not without risk. Imagine a physics professor who spends all of her class time lecturing on the evils of the war in Bosnia or a professor of history who turns her course on medieval European history into a debate about the Republican Contract with America. Allowing teachers to press a political agenda whenever and wherever they please could leave too many facts untaught. Permitting them to be openly partisan in their academic teaching and research could politicize the university. Republican philosophers could teach their agenda and Democrat philosophers theirs, and each could turn the classroom into an attack ad against the other. Instead of teaching Plato, they could accuse colleagues on the other side of the aisle of being too hard or soft on crime or welfare. In short, don't my recommendations invite a campus of acrimony and sound bites?

Obviously, I don't think so. To allow the liberal arts and sciences to be partisan is not to license the worst of politics. Reasonable and responsible debate on political issues is one thing; conducting a mindless campaign is quite another. To remove a prohibition against ever speaking a political word is not to permit only political words in class. To allow that politics can be pertinent to a course of study in physics or psychology is not to maintain that it is always pertinent, and to allow that some forms of partisanship might be pertinent is not to maintain that all might be. Lines have to be drawn, and some of these lines will be hard to draw and even harder to enforce. My brush is broad—political values shape everything—but also fine, for the virtues of partisanship, in my view, are always in the details.

Partisanship is not the real threat to the university. The real threat is an uncritical presentation of either facts or values. The threat is closed classrooms, and classrooms are not closed by opening them up to questions of value. Classrooms, like minds, are closed when they ignore the evidence or arguments—the evidence or arguments against as well as in favor of the teacher's position. Dogmatism rather than partisanship is our enemy.

Some of you might have read one or another of Milton Friedman's books, perhaps *Free to Choose* or *Capitalism and Freedom*.[11] Although these books are intended as a defense of liberty, they are extremely partisan. They advance Friedman's own view of the good life: a libertarian view. Although I don't share his view, I am pleased to have him advance it either in his books or in the classroom. His partisanship does not threaten any ideals I would attach to the arts or sciences. However, the way he presents his view in these books does threaten those ideals. The presentation is not critical but dogmatic. Though Friedman does offer evidence and arguments to support his position, he never suggests that there is evidence or any argument *against* it. Not only doesn't he share and try to rebut contrary evidence or arguments, he writes as if there weren't any. He closes his space—the space between the covers of his books—to dissent. There he doesn't tolerate the many arguments against his libertarian preaching. The way he tries to make his case is, in my view, wrongly illiberal.

CONCLUSION

The open classroom is committed to critical debate but not to value-neutrality. It sets the critical powers of the students free and, to use Popper's words, rejects the merely established and the merely traditional academic authorities while trying to preserve, to develop, and to establish traditions old and new that measure up to the fullest standards of freedom, humaneness, and rational criticism. Such a classroom is the aim of multiculturalism, and today, as a result of our new multicultural curriculum, our classrooms are more open than ever before. Popper wrote in 1943 that "We can never return to the alleged innocence and beauty of the closed society." And I say now, with the same resolution and confidence, that we can never return to the alleged innocence and beauty of the closed classrooms of Bennett and Bloom.

Universities should endorse the academic freedom to say in the classroom what ought to be as well as what is and allow that politics are pertinent to a course of study in science as well as the arts. The teacher should always be critical and never dogmatic. Conservatives such as Bennett and Bloom and libertarians such as Friedman flout these ideals and, as a result, are the real enemies of the open classroom.

NOTES

1. Karl Popper, *The Open Society and Its Enemies,* 2nd ed. (Princeton: Princeton University Press, 1950), ix.
2. John Stuart Mill, *On Liberty,* ed. Elizabeth Rapaport (Indianapolis, IN: Itackett, 1978), 15-32.
3. Max Weber, *The Methodology of the Social Sciences,* trans. and eds. Edward Shils and Henry Finch (Glencoe, IL: Free Press, 1949), 11.
4. John Stuart Mill, *Essays on Some Unsettled Questions of Political Economy* (London: Longmans, Green, Reader and Dyer, 1874), 124.
5. William Bennett, *To Reclaim a Legacy* (Washington, DC: National Endowment for the Humanities, 1984); Allen Bloom, *The Closing of the American Mind* (New York: Simon and Schuster, 1987).
6. George Herbert Mead, *Selected Writings,* ed. A. J. Reck (Chicago: University of Chicago Press, 1964), 256.
7. George Lundberg, *Can Science Save Us?* (New York: Longmans, Green and Co., 1947), 28.
8. Lionel Robbins, *An Essay on the Nature and Significance of Economic Science,* 2nd ed. (London: Macmillan and Co., 1952), 148.
9. Conference on the Meaning of the Holocaust for Bioethics, University of Minnesota May, 17-19, 1989.
10. *Regulations Concerning Faculty Tenure,* University of Minnesota, July 1, 1985.
11. Milton Friedman and Rose Friedman, *Free to Choose* (New York: Harcourt, Brace Jovanovich); and Milton Friedman, *Capitalism and Freedom* (Chicago: University of Chicago Press, 1982).

EIGHT

The New Advocacy
and the Old

GERTRUDE HIMMELFARB

THE IDEA OF ADVOCACY in the university was once readily defined and as readily deprecated. It was, according to the declaration of the American Association of University Professors (AAUP) issued in 1940, the intrusion by the instructor of matter not related to the subject of the course. [1] Although that principle was reaffirmed 50 years later, [2] it has become problematic in ways that could not have been anticipated and that have not yet been fully appreciated. It is not only the attitudes and behavior of professors that have changed, but the idea of advocacy itself. And that idea is intimately related to other ideas that have swept the academy in recent years. Intellectual fashions, we know, come and go, as bold new ideas make way for bolder newer ones. But the old ideas—which is to say, the new of yesteryear—never do go away. Traces of them can be seen on the palimpsest that is the record of academic wisdom—and of academic folly.

In my own discipline, history, one can discern several layers of ideas that have a bearing upon the subject of advocacy. It was only a few decades ago that social history pronounced itself the "new history." (In fact, there were "new" histories before that, but historians, like everyone else, are sometimes lacking in historical perspective.) This latest new history was "history from below," the history of ordinary people in their ordinary lives. The old history—political, diplomatic, intellectual—was dismissed as history from above, elitist history, history written from the vantage point of monarchs and statesmen, thinkers and writers. The class bias of that history, it was said, was concealed behind a facade of objectivity—of documents, footnotes, impersonal rhetoric, and all the other paraphernalia of academic scholarship. The new history, by contrast, was avowedly partisan. Its mission, in the much-quoted phrase of E. P. Thompson, was to rescue the working class, the anonymous masses, from "the enormous condescension of posterity."[3] It prided itself on being "engaged" history—advocacy history, we would now say.

It was not long before this kind of social history, a class-oriented history, was being challenged by the other forms of "engaged" history that derive from race, ethnicity, and gender—black history, feminist history, ethnic history, gay and lesbian history. The purpose was not only to bring each of these groups to the center of history but also to rewrite history from the point of view of that group. There were, to be sure, dissident voices that tried to *dis*engage history, to write about blacks, or women, or gays, in the traditional scholarly manner, as disinterested history rather than as an ideological cause—to be scholars rather than advocates. But that was very much a minority position and could not withstand the passions and pressures of the moment.

What made advocacy seem more than a political ploy and gave it intellectual credibility and respectability was another movement that swept through all the disciplines. This was postmodernism. I am not suggesting that most historians have become postmodernists. I do believe, however, that some of the basic tenets of postmodernism have pervaded the profession to the point where most young historians, and a good many older ones, are accepting those ideas almost unconsciously. Above all they share the radical skepticism and relativism of postmodernism: a denial that there is any such thing as knowledge, truth, reason, or objectivity, and a refusal even to aspire to such ideals, on the ground that they are not only unattainable but undesirable—that they are indeed authoritarian and repressive.

Skepticism and relativism are not, in fact, new among historians; they are as old as history itself. Historians have always been acutely aware of the limitations of their discipline: the deficiency of the historical record, the selectivity inherent in the writing of history, the fallibility and subjectivity of the historian, and thus the imperfect, tentative, and partial (in both senses of the word) nature of every historical work. But professional historians have always made the most strenuous efforts to curb and control these deficiencies, as they see them. This is what used to be meant by the "discipline" of history and why the keystone of every graduate program was a required course on "methodology," instructing students in the proper use of sources, the need for substantiating and countervailing evidence, the conventions of documentation and citation, the means of ascertaining and presenting the facts. Such courses are very nearly obsolete today.

Today the idea of a discipline of history is regarded as disingenuous or hypocritical, just as the idea of facts (the word now appears almost invariably in quotation marks) is derided as naive or presumptuous. All of history, like all of knowledge, is presumed to be a reflection of the power structure, of the "hegemonic" interests of the dominant class. There is no truth, objectivity, or reality in history; there are not even any events—only "texts" to be interpreted in accord with the historian's interest and disposition. "Everything is political," the popular slogan has it.

I have spoken only of history, but much of what I have said is applicable to the other humanities, which have been relativized, subjectified, "problematized" (as the deconstructionist says)—and politicized. Every professor is presumed to be an advocate, and every class, lecture, essay, book, or research project an exercise in advocacy. This is not, to be sure, the first time that advocacy has reared its head in the university. But it is the first time that it has done so with the approval of so many professors in so many disciplines—and not in the name of truth but in a show of disdain for the very idea of truth.

I repeat: This is how it appears to the postmodernist, and not all professors are postmodernists. I suspect that most are not. But many are, including some of our most prominent and distinguished ones, and a great many more accept the precepts of postmodernism almost unwittingly. It is a mode of thought that is especially appealing to the young, who either assume that this is the way things have always been or who are pleased to be at the "cutting edge" of the latest fashion.

But there is a still newer fashion that lends itself to a new and different kind of advocacy. In this new mode, it is not so much a cause or ideology that the professor is advancing as a person, the person of the professor. "Everything is political" is yesterday's slogan. Today's is "Everything is personal." The two slogans are not contradictory. They are complementary; indeed, they have been combined in the feminist motto "The personal is political." Common to all of them is the relativism, skepticism, and subjectivism characteristic of postmodernism itself. It is no accident, as a Marxist would say, that the new "personalism" has emerged most prominently at Duke University, where postmodernism flourishes; nor that so many academic feminists have been attracted to both postmodernism and personalism. The suspicion of reason as "phallocentric," of logic as "logocentric," of objectivity as "patriarchal" or "masculinist" lends itself to a subjectivism that exalts feeling, sensation, emotion, and personal experience.

This trend has been described in articles bearing such provocative titles as "The I's Have It," "Dare We Say 'I'?" and "Don't Leave Out the Juicy Things" (meaning the personal things).[4] The point is not that scholars have taken to writing their autobiographies, but that scholars are being autobiographical in whatever subject they are writing about: Japanese society, primitivism and Western culture, the story of a Mexican peddler, the analysis of a French painter.[5] And the autobiographical mode exhibits itself not in the occasional intrusion of personal reminiscences or reflections, but in the dominating presence of the author in the whole of the work. The personal idiom—the scholar's "nouveau solipsism," it has been called[6]—has been derided by one critic as "the ideology of 'Moi' . . . , [of] Miss Piggy,"[7] and by another as "self-absorbed and confessional."[8] And some of its practitioners recognize that it bears an uneasy relationship to the academy. Yet most have no compunctions about expressing themselves in this personal fashion, in the classroom as well as in their books, taking advantage of the university that permits them to indulge their predilections even while enjoying the perquisites of rank, tenure, and financial security.

The replacement of the "I," the personal voice, for the traditionally impersonal voice of the scholar—the "footnote voice," as it has been derisively called[9]—is congenial to the postmodernist sensibility. It is in keeping with the literary critic who assumes a greater authority in interpreting a poem than that of the author of the poem; or the historian who thinks it a mark of creativity to enliven history with fictional characters and scenes; or the legal scholar who makes "storytelling" part of the analysis and process of the law; or the biographer who identifies herself with the character she is writing about ("George Eliot, *c'est moi*," she announces)[10]; or the philosopher who looks to the novel rather than philosophy for wisdom, because the novel is not inhibited by such archaic ideas as truth and reality; or the feminist who regards courses on women's studies as the occasion for consciousness-raising, therapy, and propaganda. (*Mother Jones,* hardly a magazine hostile to feminism, reports a survey of women's studies programs: "In many classes discussions alternate between the personal and the political, with mere pit stops at the academic.")[11]

The new solipsism, or narcissism, would seem to be far removed from political advocacy. Yet it is itself an invitation to any kind of advocacy, political or otherwise, now sanctioned by the ultimate authority, the sensibility of the professor. It is yet another way of imposing the professor's agenda upon the student, who is once again made hostage to the professor's preoccupations.

As we depart ever more from the traditional conception of the university, it is important to understand the momentum of ideas that have brought us to this point. For these ideas affect not only our views about advocacy—*how* we communicate with our students and with the scholarly community—but also our views about scholarship—*what* we are communicating, what we take to be the nature and substance of the scholarly enterprise.

In the absence of any idea—or ideal—of truth, objectivity, or disinterested knowledge, how can scholarly merit be judged? What safeguards are there against willful ignorance and deception? What is the line between teaching and indoctrination, between academic freedom and academic license? If everything is political, if, indeed, the personal is political, we are truly in the condition depicted by Nietzsche: "Nothing is true; everything is permitted."[12] This is a prescription not for academic freedom but for intellectual nihilism.

Fortunately, we are not yet in that condition. Not all professors subscribe to the new doctrines, and not all who do act upon them.

But there is no doubt that relativism and subjectivism are more pervasive than ever before, that they have been carried to extremes that were once unthinkable, and that they have sanctioned degrees and forms of advocacy that would have been unacceptable only a few years ago. More important, they have had the effect of profoundly altering the nature of academic discourse and of intellectual life.

NOTES

1. American Association of University Professors, *Statement of Principles and Interpretive Comments* (1940).
2. American Association of University Professors, *Policy Documents and Reports* (1990).
3. E. P. Thompson, *The Making of the English Working Class* (New York, 1964), 12.
4. Adam Begley, in *Lingua Franca* (March-April 1994), 54-9; Ruth Behar, in *Chronicle of Higher Education*, June 29, 1994, B1-B2; Liz McMillen, in *Chronicle of Higher Education*, Feb. 9, 1994, A18-A19.
5. Cathy N. Davidson, *36 Views of Mount Fuji* (New York: Dutton, 1993); Marianna Torgovnick, *Gone Primitive: Savage Intellects, Modern Lives* (Chicago, IL: University of Chicago Press, 1990); Ruth Behar, *Translated Woman: Crossing the Border with Esperanza's Story* (Boston: Beacon Press, 1993); Eunice Lipton, *Alias Olympia* (New York: Simon & Schuster, 1992).
6. Daphne Patai, "Sick and Tired of Scholars' Nouveau Solipsism," in *Chronicle of Higher Education*, Feb. 23, 1994, A52.
7. Begley, 57.
8. Clifford Geertz, quoted by Karen J. Winkler, "An Anthropologist of Influence," *Chronicle of Higher Education*, May 5, 1995, A16.
9. McMillen, A18.
10. Phyllis Rose, "Confessions of a Burned-Out Biographer," *Civilization* (Jan.-Feb. 1995), 72.
11. *Mother Jones* (Sept./Oct. 1993), 46.
12. Friedrich Nietzsche, *The Genealogy of Morals*, trans. Francis Golffing (New York, 1956), 287 (sect. xxiv).

NINE

The New Ethicism: Beyond Poststructuralism and Identity Politics

WHITNEY DAVIS

I BELONG, I SUPPOSE, to the generation of *post-* poststructuralists—historians, philosophers, and students of literature, art, and culture who came of age intellectually in the mid- and late 1980s and are now beginning to assert a distinctive point of view in the intellectual landscape of the arts, humanities, and social sciences, partly as a function of the fact that we've now gotten tenure and are publishing the books that solidify and generalize what we've been teaching for five, six, or seven years.

Obviously my initial term for this group and its general perspective—"post-poststructuralism"—is meant to notice that we remain deeply involved with "high" poststructuralism in Europe and North America: for example, with concepts of so-called postmodern sign or cultural production, as schematized in the writing of Baudrillard or Lyotard; with the "deconstruction" of aesthetic, critical, or metaphysical hierarchies, developed most recently by Derrida; with interpretation of the "linguistic" production of the subject offered by Lacan and, to a lesser extent, Foucault; with affirmation of the subject's unruled, nomadic potentiality, à la Deleuze and Guattari; with de Man's treatment of the unstable figurality of literary and perhaps all linguistic meaning.[1]

Most post-poststructuralists earned their first academic jobs by appearing to be able to introduce courses that presented more or less systematically (although often eclectically) all of these products of postwar intellectualization, held to replace such systems as the New Criticism or structuralism itself. If you look into them, our dissertations and first books tend to be almost pure products of applying poststructuralist conceptual tools, often mutually inconsistent, to our own small projects of historical or cultural analysis.[2]

But equally obviously, post-poststructuralism must be the recognition that this whole line of thought, and of personal and academic advance, dead-ended a few years ago. Maybe dead-ended is too strong; most of us continue to suppose that students at the end of the twentieth century cannot and should not escape an extensive and rigorous exposure to poststructuralisms. But several factors strongly separate the generation of older "high" poststructuralists, mostly trained in the 1970s and rooted personally in the political and cultural turmoil of the 1960s, and my own generation, which owes practically everything to the first academic disciples of Derrida, Foucault, et al.—but now finds itself in another world.

These factors are very well known, and I recall two of them only so that I can move to what remains less obvious: what does post-poststructuralism intend to achieve, in its own specific and positive terms, if any? And what might be its pedagogy—its implications, as our theme has it, for "advocacy in the classroom"? First, of course, is the set of global events we now label with the shorthand "1989": seven years later, we know that date marks a decisive shift in global economic, political, and cultural coherences and interactions. Without taking up the transformation in its deepest nature, which only future retrospection will grasp, for my more limited point here 1989, as it now seems to be constructed in the American undergraduate consciousness, is identified as the decisive refutation of Marxism in and through the historical process itself but also apparently fueled by the self-conscious assertion of a successfully generalized popular will, whatever its basis.

Let's be careful here: my point is not, of course, that Marxism is *really* refuted by contemporary history, at some level of general theory or of universal social possibility—both of which will continue to give sustenance to many forms of liberal-through-progressive-to-radical thought. Rather, the ordinary American 19-year-old now thinks that Marxism, like the cult of Osiris, is a defunct species: and if he or she now thinks this, it will, in fact, and as an American culture produced precisely for this young consumer marches across the entire globe, become so—no matter what the professors say. In this context, the one immediate pedagogical agenda of post-poststructuralism must be not so much to *resist* the general advance of this ideology of the historical refutation of Marxism: *that* is irrevocable, and denial has become the knee-jerk dogma of aging unreconstructed pre-'89ers. Instead, it should be to channel its energy in our students—which was always in part just a diffused altruism, at home in all kinds of ethics, not specifically Marxian—into new conceptual pathways and potentially new political structures and moral institutions. I'll take a look at these momentarily.

Note, however, that there's a temporary lack of sync here. Any student with eyes open realizes that a great, though not the whole, portion of "high" poststructuralism was inextricably bound up on the part of its practitioners, in ways personal, political, and professional, with conventional leftist thinking—for some, with the actual coming-of-age in Paris '68 or in the SDS here—and more specifically with established Marxist strategies of ideology-critique or the analysis of culture as epiphenomenon of class; and I'd say that, oddly enough, Louis Althusser, while not a poststructuralist, remains the essentially unquestioned text for many of my grad students—who haven't yet gotten a clear alternative message from their younger teachers.[3] But this Marxian conceptual-political component of poststructuralism—if you try, post-1989, to excise it—leaves an intellectual structure that is mostly the expression of early twentieth-century linguisticisms, sociologisms, and cyberneticisms: and no young intellectual in the late 1990s, in the midst of an information-processing upheaval, can really believe that such de-Marxified structuralism remains sufficiently up to date as an intellectual technology. In sum, without Marx, poststructuralism is a vaguely creaky fossil of what was intellectually high tech about 50 years ago, when *Les Structures Élémentaires* was published[4]; but *with* Marx, it's a creaky fossil of what was once, about six years ago, an active historical possibility. Conclusion: poststructuralism is very to a bit behind the times, and the best students in English or Philosophy 100 shouldn't go to graduate school to do it.

All this, I repeat, is what goes on, I think, among some smarter undergrads today. For their younger teachers, 1989 happened, in fact, as a confirmation of something that had been bubbling since the late 1970s and is probably closer to the self-definition of post-poststructuralists than our sigh of relief that we don't have to join the tired tango, which so worried my own teachers, of Old Left versus anticommie or New Left versus neocon—1989 having re-shuffled all those terms.

This something, my second factor in determining current post-poststructuralism in the classroom, is the emergence of what we now tend to call "identity politics" (or "advocacy," more broadly speaking) in the classroom and in all major intellectual practices—writing, publishing, forming departments and pro-grams, hiring and tenuring. Identity politics has roiled the acad-emy, of course, since the civil rights and feminist movements of the 1960s and early '70s. And in the interest of subtlety, we should remember that many high poststructuralists were and are also avatars of identity politics. Michel Foucault, for example, urged that the identity of the modern homosexual was an artifact of relatively inauthentic and repressive "normalizing" and largely state-derived "discourses" for the self's nature and pathology— you know his claim—and he urged, by implication, that an extraordinary act of self-discovery and self-reconstruction has to be undertaken by contemporary gay people to discover the kernel of authentic human freedom remaining to them, as it does, according to Foucault, for all people, even those socially denied personhood.[5] Here, famously, and setting aside Foucault's histori-cal inaccuracies, poststructuralist models of the self, society, and discourse came together with a liberationist ethics and urgent sense of the existential and communal reality of a particular group's historical experience. But Foucault did not resolve the inconsistency between his ethicist personal commitment—such as his long engagement with prison reform—and his linguisticizing and sociologizing historical and cultural analysis, although in his late work we can watch him moving closer and closer to the true post-poststructuralist position.

This position has been occupied largely by young scholars who got their Ph.D.s from teachers whose own fashioning in the 1960s and '70s led them not just to tolerate but actively to encourage dissertation work overtly based on feminist, gay, African American, or other so-called minority experiences and perspectives. Though not all of this Ph.D. crop of the mid- to late 1980s did this kind of work (much of it was just pseudo-high-poststructuralist cultural and textual analysis), we all went to grad school with friends who *were* doing it; and the post-poststructuralist generation is the first to include scholars whose entire intellectual development—from freshman year up to the postdoc and tenure—occurred in such newly founded practices as women's or gay studies, getting institutionalized—modestly—for the first time on American campuses when we were undergrads in the late 1970s and early '80s.

As the example of Foucault attests, there are notorious tensions between high poststructuralism and any remotely activist identity politics: in the well-worn formula, attention to experiential reality, specificity, variety, and context actively needs concepts such as person, community, meaning, motive, or authenticity that poststructuralist techniques, historicist, semiotic, or deconstructive, seem to undermine. Many teachers of my generation are intellectually determined by this tension; it is the very substance and structure of our teaching: we tend to speak not about persons but "persons," not about meaning but "meaning." There are familiar forms of resolving the tension: despite the hype about PC proselytizing, the real activism of leftist professors of the 1950s and '60s, for instance, has all but disappeared in the academy itself, although not on its peripheries, replaced by forms (as it might look to that old leftist) of ironized, opportunistic self-assertion hooked to abstract, legalistic claims for ever more individualized cultural mandates in the complex demographics of a multiethnic, multinational, multigenerational, economically diverse student population.

More interesting, the challenge of achieving consistency between poststructuralism and what we might call the experientialism of identity politics has been actively taken up by some scholars, such as the so-called queer theorists: here one seeks to show, as one proposal has it, that the instability and indefiniteness of the human person in such fundamental axes of his or her being as his or her gender, sexuality, or race can be "performed": that is, simultaneously inhabited and distanced, occupied and deoccupied.[6]

I do not wish to comment on the plausibility of these perspectives; they seem to me to be ingenious but sometimes more farfetched, less generalizable, than their proponents believe.[7] They still require us to put quotation marks around essences—with the exception of antiessentialism itself. And some post-poststructuralist teachers and scholars are moving toward a more explicit accommodation to the realities of 1989 and contemporary multicultural student demography: the positive content, the active classroom message, beyond poststructuralism and identity politics is what I'd like to call the New Ethicism—an approach that currently makes somewhat strange bedfellows of some traditional (if leftwing) humanists, gay separatists, libertarians, certain philosophers of convention and value, multicultural moralists, and the young post-poststructuralists I identified a moment ago, seeking a route from high theory to practical ethics and public effectivity. Whereas poststructuralism led to the revitalization and generalization of such disciplines as linguistics, semiotics, and rhetoric, the New Ethicism is leading to the generalization of such disciplines as aesthetics, biography, and criticism. Its preferred study, whether carried out in relation to a community's history, an artist's career, the circulation of a metaphor or image, or a general problem of evidence, interpretation, or value is the process of what was once called self-cultivation, anxious, conflicted, often frustrated, always partial, never finished, and continuously changing or moving, in the social field of cultural and aesthetic forms. But it is not culturo*logical,* for it does not insist that the self is determined by culture but rather the other way around; I predict that the New Ethicism will have bones to pick with so-called New Historicism and standard multiculturalism for their continued adherence to the empty abstraction of Culture—that dream of nineteenth-century bacteriology applied, by E. B. Tylor and others,[8] to the description of imperial anthropology—rather than the psychosocial reality of cultivation. And the New Ethicism is not aesthetic*ist,* for it does not focus on the cultural forms for their own sake but on their role in projecting and relaying personhood from one time and place to another throughout an individual history.[9]

The philosophical problems for this New Ethicism are not, as in high poststructuralism, the "arbitrary" relation of language and reality, the demystification of idealism, and the indeterminacy of meaning, but rather the continuity of personal identity, the social basis of aesthetic creation, and the ethics of intersubjectivity. Its moral message—what it offers students—is neither the corrosive skepticism, the cosmopolitan irony, of high poststructuralism nor the celebratory affirmation and what critics like to call the comparative victimology of much identity politics but rather an insistence on personal responsibility for ethical individuation through intersubjectively valid or justifiable aesthetic and cultural production, that is, socially based imaginations of the significance of experience within particular frames of reference. One residue of poststructuralism in the New Ethicism is its reluctance to suppose that moral, aesthetic, and political principles could be objective or universal, as older forms of rationalism, liberalism, or formalism usually required; one might say that identity politics have impinged on the New Ethicism to suggest that such principles are always context-specific. But the universality and objectivity of the principles are really beside the point compared to the more pressing, concrete issue of their intersubjective emergence, circulation, and transformation: we don't care if a form of life is viable everywhere if it is intersubjectively viable and ethically justifiable here in our social fix now.

Operationally, then, the New Ethicism emphasizes the nature of intersubjective or interpersonal ethics and community: if you can get that, you've got everything. The *real* questions are questions such as: How many different subjects, or how much subjective difference, does an ethical or aesthetic principle have to traverse and encompass before it claims our general mutual assent as an intersubjectively validated one? Do some voices in the intersubjective dialogue usefully deserve special status—such as the status of what ACT UP used to call the facilitator—in the interest of the future possibility of the greater intersubjective viability of any convention emergent under such modest regulation? What, in fact, is the social history—what Dan Sperber calls the epidemiology—of convention, defined as the coordination of two agents who do not necessarily preshare a "language" or "culture" or "discourse"?[10] These problems did interest poststructuralism and identity politics; but there they were phrased as questions of metaphysics, of being as such, or of universal moral principle, of right and entitlement or equality, rather than as concrete questions, for instance, of the etiquette and self-coordinating morality of moshing or the Internet. The New Ethicism wants to reflect and interpret *that* social and moral universe—the universe of virtual intersubjectivity in the literal or concrete sense.

Put in the way I've just been doing, you'll notice that the agenda of the New Ethicism must at points resemble, because it must engage, its mirror opposite—namely, an uneducated, philistine Moral Majoritarianism. Thus, for example, the New Ethicism must admit straight off that standards for aesthetic relevance, significance, or idiosyncracy vary by community needs, interests, history, and values; and the logical consequence of admitting this fully generally is simply to acknowledge that highly different and potentially antagonistic forms of individuation and community will emerge in any society that promotes such free ethical cultivation as a general good. Standard liberal policy is often unable to cope with the resulting level of conflict. But that is only to say that liberal thought has probably exhausted itself, compared with emerging libertarian and communitarian ethics.

To take another point, the emphasis in the New Ethicism on the personal labor of ethical cultivation coheres with the increasing call on the part of a number of feminist, gay, and African American intellectuals for *responsibility*—responsibility for the safety, health, and integrity of one's self and community; for the maintenance of its values; for the preservation of its history and tradition. This is not something the value-neutral liberal state can, will, or even should do. And so again, the New Ethicist call can lead both to libertarian and to communitarian politics, in this case of separatism and possibly secessionism—to the formation, for example, of medical, education, or security forces entirely independent of those organized by the state, with all the acknowledged risks of vigilantism or cultish allegiance to useless nostrums. Here the New Ethicism hopes to teach the history and techniques as well as the problems or limits of such active grass-roots responsibility—whether it goes to such unfamiliar lengths or not, at least in the history of the modern liberal nation-state to date.

In the classroom, the interests of the New Ethicism are increasingly visible. At least, it expresses interest in certain texts and problems to which it directs students; hopes to justify certain intellectual and personal virtues, which it can probably do best by example; and phrases the old, grand moral and political questions in a certain distinctive way. The texts that attract the New Ethicism, not surprisingly, are those that systematically reflect on the project of ethical and aesthetic self-construction or stand for a compelling approach to the positioning of a person in his or her intersubjective environment, an environment containing other persons, rules, and artifacts in relation to which the self must project and organize itself. In a course I like to teach, for example, we read Winckelmann, Goethe, and Whitman[11]; and one could equally deal with Montaigne or Spinoza. In an undergraduate classroom these texts require surprisingly little elaborate exegesis; they contain little allegorization—beyond, that is, their obvious allegory of a personal life history—and even their instabilities are, as it were, wholly obvious manifestations of the empirical texture of self-projection. One's labor as teacher is best expended on putting the text into relation with its proximate intersubjective points of reference—for example, the actual or imagined persons addressed, places inhabited or visited, artworks experienced, or social norms observed and evaluated by the writers the students are reading.

Like any real pedagogy, the New Ethicism hopes to validate certain virtues—the virtues it sees as most appropriate for the project of personal ethical responsibility at the end of the twentieth century. Among them I'd certainly include moderation, tolerance, receptivity, communicativeness, and, reviving a useful term, "adhesiveness." Possibly these are merely the qualities that teachers who survived the ice of poststructuralism and the fires of identity politics and who assume multiculturalism as a fact of life would like to see in themselves, although obviously they recall real historical possibilities for ethical individuation in situations of difference from the norm, as in Socrates' temperance or Whitman's homoeroticism.

It hardly interests me to try to map out the New Ethicism in the easy terms of Left versus Right or liberal versus conservative or even—although this would be more relevant—libertarian versus communitarian. Like that common late twentieth century character, the socially liberal and fiscally conservative, the New Ethicist has been drawing from several sources on the conventional political spectrum, although perhaps most strongly shaped by the simultaneous collapse of Marxism abroad and rise of Moral Majoritarianism at home. It's most helpful, I think, to see New Ethicism trying to work out the relations between fraternalism, which pulls one closer and closer intersubjectively to the persons with whom one shares the most historically and emotionally, and federalism, which pulls one closer and closer intersubjectively to the persons with whom one might be very out of touch and out of sympathy. The New Ethicism equally values fraternity and federation, in their most full-blooded, socially and psychologically concrete senses, and wants to discover institutions for their authentic and organic interrelation. At the moment it has no interdisciplinary home of its own, no special-studies program, and only a few prominent representatives—although I venture to say that a large number of exhausted poststructuralists and identity politicians are ready to make the jump.

NOTES

1. For example (to select particularly influential works by the authors named), Jean Baudrillard, *For a Critique of the Political Economy of the Sign* (St. Louis, MO: Telos Press, 1981); Jean-Francois Lyotard, *The Different: Phrases in Dispute,* trans. Georges van den Abbeele (Minneapolis: University of Minnesota Press, 1988); Jacques Derrida, *Of Grammatology,* trans. Gayatri Spivak (Baltimore, MD: Johns Hopkins University Press, 1978), and *Writing and Difference,* trans. Alan Bass (Chicago, IL: University of Chicago Press, 1978); Jacques Lacan,

Ecrits, trans. Alan Sheridan (New York: W. W. Norton, 1977), and *Four Fundamental Concepts of Psychoanalysis,* trans. Alan Sheridan (New York: W. W. Norton, 1978); Michel Foucault, *The Order of Things* (London: Tavistock, 1977); Gilles Deleuze and Felix Guattari, *A Thousand Plateaus: Capitalism and Schizophrenia,* trans. Brian Massumi (Minneapolis, MN: University of Minnesota Press, 1987); Paul de Man, *Allegories of Reading: Figural Language in Rousseau, Nietzsche, Rilke, and Proust* (New Haven, CT: Yale University Press, 1979). Many of these works were published considerably earlier in French. A work as important as Derrida's doctoral thesis on Husserl, for example, was originally published in 1962; see Jacques Derrida, *Edmund Husserl's "Origin of Geometry": An Introduction* (1962), 2nd ed. (1974), trans. John P. Leavey, Jr., David P. Allison (Ed.) (Stony Brook, NY: Nicholas Hays, 1978). The dates of Anglo-American translation and publication, however, are relevant to my historical narrative here.

2. Although partly a function of a purely disciplinary history, perhaps my own case is fairly representative. My dissertation of 1985, based on work begun in 1980, attempted to reorganize the received history of ancient Egyptian official image-making in the light of interpretive models developed by neostructuralist anthropologists and social historians who had inherited the Weberian and Marxist traditions as well as by art historians who were beginning to introduce semiotic and narratological analysis into the discipline, dominated by the stylistic histories preferred by my own professors (see Whitney Davis, *The Canonical Tradition in Ancient Egyptian Art* [New York: Cambridge University Press, 1989]). At the time I felt I could not include what I was encountering in graduate school as high deconstructionist analysis in some branches of literary studies and art history. This approach seemed beyond the pale of what my professors and advisors could accept and what I myself favored, given my relatively traditional education. But after becoming an assistant professor and joining a conversation taking place among other young teachers and graduate students, my next book pushed much further into deconstructionist narratology—although again it focused on a narrow body of empirical materials (Whitney Davis, *Masking the Blow: The Scene of Representation in Late Prehistoric Egyptian Art* [Berkeley and Los Angeles:

University of California Press, 1992]). It was only retrospectively that I realized that much of this book was functioning as allegory—that I was really writing, for example, about the contemporary experience of gay people by way of an historical example drawn from the third millennium B.C. But to develop this recognition was impossible within the terms of the high poststructuralist theory that worked so well for the formulistic—the textual and semiological—analysis of the example as such.

3. Louis Althusser, *For Marx* [1965], trans. Ben Brewster (New York: Vintage, 1970), and *Lenin and Philosophy and Other Essays,* trans. Ben Brewster, Alfred Guzzetti, et al. (New York: Monthly Review Press, 1971); Louis Althusser and E. Balibar, *Reading Capital* [1968], trans. Ben Brewster (London: Verso, 1970).

4. Claude Lévi-Strauss, *The Elementary Structures of Kinship,* rev. ed. [1949], trans. James Harle Bell and John Richard von Sturmer, Rodney Needham (Ed.) (Boston, MA: Beacon Press, 1969).

5. See especially Michel Foucault, "About the Concept of the 'Dangerous Individual' in 19th-Century Legal Psychiatry," *International Journal of Law and Psychiatry* 1 (1978), 1—18, and "The Subject and Power," in Hubert L. Dreyfus and Paul Rabinow (Eds.), *Michel Foucault: Beyond Structuralism and Hermeneutics* (Chicago, IL: University of Chicago Press, 1983), 208—26.

6. See especially Judith Butler, *Gender Trouble: Feminism and the Subversion of Identity* (New York and London: Routledge, 1990). Because of its philosophical insight and sophistication, exegetical accuracy, and rhetorical power, this work can be regarded as a turning point.

7. See further Whitney Davis, "Gender," in Robert Nelson and Richard Schiff (Eds.), *Critical Terms for Art History* (Chicago, IL: University of Chicago Press), forthcoming, and "'Homosexuality,' Gay and Lesbian Studies, and Queer Theory in Art History," in Mark Cheetham, Michael Ann Holly, and Keith Moxey (Eds.), *The Subjects of Art History: Historical Objects in Contemporary Perspective* (New York: Cambridge University Press), forthcoming. Queer theory is currently undergoing active theoretical refinement and political development; it cannot be regarded as a fixed set of proposals. In some of its recent expressions it closely resembles—in fact, it is one kind of exemplification of—the post-poststructuralist attitude considered below; see, for

example, Judith Butler, *Politics at the Scene of Utterance* (New York and London: Routledge), forthcoming.

8. Edward Burnet Taylor, *Primitive Culture: Researches into the Development of Mythology, Philosophy, Religion, Language, Art, and Custom*, 2 vols. (London: John Murray, 1920); see further Christopher Herbert, *Culture and Anomie: Ethnographic Imagination in the Nineteenth Century* (Chicago, IL: University of Chicago Press, 1991).

9. So far few writers who would identify themselves as post-poststructuralist have directly connected the problems of formal and textual configuration (the problems of aesthetics, stylistics, and rhetoric, whether approached in traditional or in poststructuralist ways) and the problems of the definition and history of personal identity—at least at a theoretical level. Needless to say, however, many works of art and literature, major and minor, do just this job as the very substance and texture of their thematic and artistic organization. Thus the substantive and sympathetic criticism of such works is likely to be highly informative. For a philosophical aesthetics that offers, or is, a theory of personhood, see especially Richard Wollheim, *The Thread of Life* (Cambridge, MA: Harvard University Press, 1984) and *Painting as an Art: The A. W. Mellon Lectures in the Fine Arts, 1984* (Princeton, NJ: Princeton University Press, 1987).

10. See Dan Sperber, "Anthropology and Psychology: Towards an Epidemiology of Representations," *Man* 20 (1985), 73-89; for some theoretical considerations, see Whitney Davis, *Replications: Archaeology, Art History, Psychoanalysis* (University Park: Pennsylvania State University Press, 1996).

11. J. J. Winckelmann, *Reflections on the Imitation of Greek Works in Painting and Sculpture* [1755], trans. Elfiede Heyer and Roger C. Norton (La Salle, IL: Open Court Publishing, 1987), and see also *Abhandlung von der Fähigkeit der Empfindung des Schönen in der Kunst, und dem Unterrichte in derselben* [1763], partially translated (although truncating some crucial personal references) as "Essay on the Beautiful in Art" in *Winckelmann: Writings on Art*, David Irwin (Ed.) (London: Phaidon, 1972), 89-103; Johann Wolfgang von Goethe, *Essays on Art and Literature*, trans. Ellen von Nardroff and Ernest H. von Nardroff, John Gearey (Ed.) (Princeton, NJ: Princeton University Press, 1986), and *Italian Journey*, trans. Robert R. Heitner, Thomas P. Saine and

Jeffrey L. Sammons (Eds.) (Princeton, NJ: Princeton University Press, 1989), and see also *J. W. von Goethe: Winckelmann und seine Jahrhundert in Briefen und Aufsätze,* Helmut Holtzauer (Ed.) (Leipzig: Seeman Verlag, 1969); Walt Whitman, *Leaves of Grass* [1855-92], Introduction by John Hollander, Justin Kaplan (Ed.) (New York: Vintage Books/Library of America, 1992). The editions cited form the basic reading list for a course that also includes discussions of paintings and photographs, of buildings and sites, of urban and rural topographies, and of friendship networks and practices of collection, memorialization, and communication.

Culture and Advocacy

LOUIS MENAND

SINCE I RECEIVED MY INVITATION TO CONTRIBUTE to this volume, the first question I have asked myself every day after waking up in the morning has been: What the hell am I going to say in that advocacy book?

For a long time I thought my problem was that I didn't know what my position on advocacy was. Then one morning I had an epistemic breakthrough and realized that my problem was not that I didn't know what my position on advocacy was. My problem was that I didn't know what advocacy was. I subjected my letter of invitation to a variety of exegetical techniques, but the results were not enlightening. I find it extremely peculiar that nowhere in the letter or in any of the other material I have seen announcing this volume is the term "advocacy" ever defined. It turns up, instead, in all kinds of beguiling and suggestive postures, in sentences about cultural relativism, ideological analysis, feminist jurisprudence, critical race studies, changes in student demographics, multicultural curricula, the teaching of evolutionary theory, developments within the disciplines, and the question of whether there can be a single correct interpretation of a literary text.

If what is meant by advocacy is some sort of a departure from what professors have traditionally done in their classrooms, I don't see what any of these things has to do with advocacy, and I am distressed to find them being associated with that term in this highly publicized way. I am supportive of the activities of the various national academic organizations that sponsored the conference that this book grew out of, but I cannot understand how it furthers the interests of American universities to lump these entirely legitimate intellectual issues together under such an alarmist rubric. It is very much my hope that one of the conclusions to be reached by readers of this volume will be that putting together a volume under this title was a bad idea. That will be a useful conclusion to have reached. To put it another way: It will have been a good idea to have put together a volume under this title if it leads us to decide that putting together a volume under this title was a bad idea. This is what we call, in my field, a volume *sous rature.*

I can think of only two hypothetical classroom situations in which what I assume is meant by the term "advocacy" arises as a problem. The first is the situation in which a professor knows that, say, *Heart of Darkness* is not a racist text but teaches it as if it were a racist text because she believes that students should be impressed with the need to combat racism. The second is the situation in which a professor in a math class spends his time lecturing about why we should all emulate the moral life of the Victorians but fails to demonstrate any connection between this idea and the subject matter of mathematics.

Both of these pedagogical practices seem to me wrong, but not for reasons having anything to do with advocacy. The problem in the first case, of the professor who teaches *Heart of Darkness* as a racist text even though she doesn't really believe it is a racist text, isn't advocacy; it's dishonesty. It's also extremely bizarre. I have never heard of anyone doing this, and I cannot imagine why anyone would. The problem in the second case is that the subject matter of the class is not being taught, and it wouldn't matter what the professor was filling the class hour with. It could be his recipe for egg salad. Again, this sort of problem seems to me to be very rare, and I know of no evidence to suggest that it is less rare now than it ever was. It is clearly regulable by the math department or the dean's office when it happens. And it is unrelated to issues about politics, ethics, or academic freedom. It's just unprofessional.

Apart from these virtually nonexistent types of cases, what are we talking about? The various remarks in the agenda for this volume seem to me to boil down to one question: Should professors attempt to put across their own point of view about the material they teach in the classroom? Is this really a serious question? Of course we should. What else could we do? It is because we have views about our subjects that we have been hired to teach them. Our ethical constraint is only that we teach what we honestly believe the significance of the material to be.

When someone teaches *Heart of Darkness* as a racist text, which people certainly do, it's because she really thinks it's a racist text. Another professor may believe that *Heart of Darkness* is an antiracist text and may teach it with that interpretation in mind. The first professor is not obligated to submit to the view of *Heart of Darkness* held by the second professor. That's what academic freedom is all about. If these professors accuse each other of "advocacy," they're just trying to find some high-octane rhetoric to say what professors have always said to other professors, which is: My interpretation is better than your interpretation.

So far as the politics of the matter are concerned, please note that both professors are promoting exactly the same view, which is that racism is bad. No one ever had a problem when *Heart of Darkness* was taught as an antiracist book in order to make that point. Why should there be a professional crisis, why should there suddenly be talk of "advocacy," when the identical point is made by reading it a different way?

Talk about advocacy has emerged from two identifiable camps, and it's worth tracking it back to those origins in the hopes of cornering it there and burying it. The first is the camp of those professors (and nonprofessors) who are concerned about what is referred to as "the politicization of the humanities." These people feel that to teach *Heart of Darkness,* or some other canonical text of literature or philosophy, as racist—or, more generally, as a historically contingent production complicit in the ideologies of its time—is false to both the spirit and the letter of the text.

But the argument about whether a particular text is politically good, politically bad, or politically neutral is an intellectual argument. Nothing is gained substantively by couching that argument as a dispute between advocacy versus some notion of proper scholarly standards. The accusation that professors who emphasize the political implications of the books they teach are not really professors but are "advocates" is an invitation to authorities external to the university to intervene in the university's own legitimate intellectual activity. It is an extremely dangerous rhetorical position to take, and that is why I am so concerned to find it adopted, in however constructive a spirit, by the organizers of this volume.

There seems to be a confusion between teaching texts ideologically, which is one thing, and teaching ideology, which is an entirely different thing. Texts have ideological dimensions. It ought to be possible to talk about those dimensions in class. Doing this does not make one an ideologue. If we can't pursue this line of inquiry and see where it leads, even if it leads nowhere terribly interesting, I don't see how we can have much self-respect as a profession.

It is complained, of course, that the paradigms of contemporary ideological analysis—for instance, race, class, and gender—have come to have a kind of doctrinal status: that they are evoked on every occasion, that they induce, or even coerce, intellectual conformity in students, and that they yield results that have become numbingly predictable. This complaint may be true, but if it is true, the problem is not political. It's institutional. It is the consequence of the way academic disciplines are designed to produce knowledge. Disciplines generate orthodoxies, the heterodox are marginalized or excluded, and along with the interesting and provocative stuff, a lot of mindless, repetitive, and unexamined work gets produced and rewarded until a fresh paradigm arises. Disciplinarity makes us stupid. The degree of dogmatism in academic writing is not a function of the politics of the particular paradigm. Once Cleanth Brooks had decided that all poetry contained paradox and ambiguity, by God, he was going to find paradox and ambiguity in "Tears, Idle Tears" or perish in the attempt.[1]

I have been a little surprised to see it suggested, or implied, in other chapters in this book that the problem with multiculturalism is that it flouts the paradigms of the disciplines. The problem with multiculturalism, at least in literary studies, is that it *is* the paradigm of the discipline and has been for about ten years. A few contributors have evoked the discipline as the basic explanatory and legitimating category for the views we express in the classroom—have argued that the history and context of the discipline is the last turtle, as it were, of our interpretations. I see no reason why we should show the disciplines such respect; there is something, after all, that explains the disciplines. But I also think if you propose to live by the discipline, you have to be prepared to die by the discipline, and in many humanistic fields, multiculturalism and ideological analysis are where it's at. That's what people, in their professional capacity, *do*. There is no other discipline.

The second camp from which talk of advocacy has emerged is the academic Left, for whom advocacy is a term of congratulation. These are the people diagnosed clinically as AAA: Always Already Advocating. It is their view that to teach is inevitably to advocate, and that although other professors may imagine that books teach themselves, or that scholarship can truly be objective, or that knowledge is not political, they, the professors on the Left, are proud to acknowledge, to foreground, as we say, the political assumptions and ambitions of their pedagogy.

This sort of talk seems to me to be mostly an effort by professors on the Left to cheer themselves up. I don't see that calling yourself an advocate, or a citizen professor, or a practitioner of critical pedagogy amounts to anything different from calling yourself a structuralist or a positivist or a Straussian. You are still doing what professors do, which is to present the material to your students in the way you think is most interesting, significant, and useful. If it bolsters your self-esteem to think that professors who teach the material differently are victims of self-deception, or unwitting tools of the powers that be, then think it. Bolster your self-esteem. Everyone else in America does it. But it does not amount to anything more than a way of saying three cheers for our side, and *à bas les autres*.

Most professors who are not on the Left, or who do not believe that being on the Left has any relevance to their classroom practice, do not think that they are in denial about the political implications of what they say in class or that they are teaching the material in some absolutely neutral or objective manner. What they do often think is that they are presenting their views to students in a nondoctrinaire spirit and that they tolerate a diversity of opinions and encourage criticism and debate within the classroom. What these professors suspect about the self-proclaimed "advocate" professors on the Left is that in *their* classrooms, open debate is stifled in the name of a political orthodoxy.

Advocate professors, it's true, tend to hyperventilate about the liberal principles of open debate and free exchange and standpoint neutrality as devices for blocking the road to social change. But when we read those professors' descriptions of their own classroom practice, this is what we find. I am quoting from an essay by Henry A. Giroux. I happen to have read this essay because it refers, very briefly, to me, as follows: "Menand represents the classic liberal retreat into a politics of refusal." Ouch. Having crushed that particular bug, Giroux goes on to address the question of how critical pedagogy ought to be enacted in the classroom. "Making the pedagogical more political," he says,

> . . . suggests that public intellectuals take a stand without "standing still." That is, such intellectuals need to challenge epistemological and social relations that promote reactionary forms of material and symbolic knowledge, but they must also be deeply critical of how their own authority can be made problematic in the service of radical cultural politics. Pedagogically, this suggests that the authority they legitimate in the classroom become [*sic*] both an object of autocritique and critical referent for expressing a more "fundamental dispute with authority itself." [My parents always told me that autocritique gives you warts.] In addition, public intellectuals must move beyond recognizing the partiality of their own narratives, so as to address more concretely the ethical and political consequences of the social relations and cultural practices generated by the forms of authority used in the classroom. . . . It is precisely within the interrelated dynamics of a discourse of commitment, self-critique, and indeterminacy that pedagogy can offer educators, students, and others the possibility for embracing higher education as a critical public sphere while simultaneously guarding

against the paralyzing orthodoxies that close down rather than expand democratic public life.[2]

I could read this stuff forever. I love it. What's more, I agree with it completely. For Professor Giroux is saying exactly what we classic liberals so tragically entombed in our politics of refusal also believe, which is that you should argue your views in a spirit of skepticism and self-questioning. There's an unspeakably reactionary word for the intellectual and pedagogical stance that Professor Giroux and I both endorse, a word I suspect Professor Giroux would not dream of picking up without the sterilizing tongs of quotation marks. The word is "disinterestedness."

The critical pedagogue conducts his class in the spirit of disinterestedness for the same reason the wretched liberal refusenik does: because to do otherwise isn't just bad pedagogy; it's bad advocacy. There is nothing more counterproductive than single-mindedly hammering your own views into the heads of your students. Students' heads have been designed through millions of years of evolutionary development to be impervious to hammering. When you hammer, as everybody does, in desperation, at some point or other in the course of a semester, students tend to go completely rote on you.

Concern about advocacy in the classroom seems to me to underestimate profoundly the good sense of college students. Students know perfectly well when they're being expected to toe somebody's line. They've spent their entire lives reading these kinds of signals from grown-ups, and they figure out pretty quickly that Professor W insists on finding traces of patriarchal discourse in every text under discussion, that Professor Q is extremely keen to uncover evidence of homosocial bonding, that Professor DWEM will give you an A if you mention somewhere in your paper that we cannot know the dancer from the dance. Students know perfectly well what their professor's take on the subject is, and if they find that take disagreeable or uninteresting, they advise their friends to register for someone else's course.

One of the oddest things about the now decade-long assault on the so-called politicization of the humanities is that no one has been able to demonstrate any connection between the supposedly radical ideas that get taught and the subsequent opinions and behavior of college graduates. It's not in the interest of professors to expose the lack of such a connection, because the illusion that they are having a deep and lasting effect on their students' thinking is crucial to their self-esteem. And the people who attack humanities professors always fail to back up their charges with specific examples, because no such link is demonstrable, and I doubt that it ever was. Students aren't quite so spongelike as these debates tend to suggest—or if they are so spongelike, most of what they're soaking up is not coming out of the mouth of a professor. Back in the 1960s, students assiduously took notes while their professors droned on about myths and archetypes and structural functionalism, and then they went out and held a trash-in at the campus ROTC office. In the 1980s and '90s, students assiduously took notes while their professors chattered away about phallologocentrism and the panoptic national security state, and then they showed up during office hours to ask for a letter of recommendation to business school.

The university is, as Henry Giroux, *mon semblable,* would probably put it, a site for the reproduction of culture. I think that what professors say matters less to the culture we are reproducing than many people believe it does, but it matters a little. For professors have a peculiar and special kind of authority, and this authority derives from the perception of their disinterestedness. Of course, the standpoint of disinterestedness is, like any other standpoint, a social construction; but it's one of society's better constructions. Disinterestedness doesn't mean an absence of strongly held views or a willingness to give equal weight to every view. Disinterestedness means that one's views have been arrived at uncoerced—or as uncoerced as possible—by anything but the requirement of honesty.

It is because of our disinterestedness that we can have debates about the political implications of our teaching, or about the possibility of objectivity, or about the relativity of cultural values, or about race or gender bias in the forms of knowledge. These are the kinds of debates universities are designed to enable, and American society would be worse off without them. If conditions change so that it is no longer possible to have them within universities, they are not going to happen anyplace else.

The university's external enemies are real, and they have attained a position of power over us unknown since the 1950s. Those enemies could care less about distinguishing classic liberals and neo-Victorians from critical pedagogues. They loathe the very idea of public subsidy for independent thought, and they would happily put us all out in the cold if they could. We need to defend the right of each of us to express whatever it is he or she believes to be the case. We need to make it clear that in presenting the material we are assigned to teach, each of us, according to his or her own lights, is ultimately trying to enable students gain some measure of control over their own lives. We shouldn't invite more of the damage that is already coming our way by pretending that we don't really believe in empowering our students in this sense, or by pretending that we once all subscribed to some objective understanding of our subjects, or by pretending that our activities are useless unless we do.

The American university has many problems. Advocacy is not one of them.

NOTES

1. See Cleanth Brooks, *The Well Wrought Urn: Studies in the Structure of Poetry* (New York: Harcourt, Brace and World, 1947), 167-77.
2. Henry A. Giroux, "Beyond the Ivory Tower: Public Intellectuals and the Crisis of Higher Education," in Michael Bérubé and Cary Nelson (Eds.), *Higher Education Under Fire: Politics, Economics, and the Crisis of the Humanities* (New York: Routledge, 1995), 253.

PART II

HISTORY

Defining "True" Knowledge: Consensus and the Growing Distrust of Faculty Activism, 1880s-1920s[1]

JULIE A. REUBEN

THIS CHAPTER DISCUSSES the intellectual and institutional context of an important transition in the history of advocacy in the college classroom: the change from the late nineteenth century, when university presidents expected social science faculty to address important moral, social, and political questions of the day, to the early twentieth century, when university officials distrusted and discouraged faculty activism. I explore how contemporary theories of science, which viewed expert agreement as a sign of the validity of knowledge, contributed to the changing attitude of university officials toward faculty activism.

I first discuss how the conception of science that developed in the late nineteenth century relied on consensus to prove the superiority of scientific knowledge. I then examine how some social scientists in the 1910s used the ideal of consensus to critique the moralism of their disciplines. Finally I explore how early academic freedom policies reinforced the notion that consensus was a marker of proper scholarship and refused to protect faculty that provoked controversy. I suggest that the problematic epistemological status of "disagreement" contributes to prohibitions against the teaching of controversial subjects.

Until the late nineteenth century, the dominant philosophy of science in the United States was Baconianism. This philosophy defined proper scientific method as the careful, unbiased observation of nature, followed by the classification of data and the identification of regular patterns. In this way, science was supposed to be built upon individual facts. If these facts were clear and unquestioned, scientists believed that the generalizations based on them would be similarly authoritative. As a consequence, the use of hypotheses, imagination, and theories that relied on imperceptible causes was prohibited. The ultimate aim of scientific study was the discovery and description of natural laws, conceived of as invariable series of events that regulated nature. Once a true law was identified, it would become part of people's unchanging body of knowledge. Progress, according to this view of science, entailed either discovering new laws or broadening the application of already known laws. Scientists assumed that a finite number of natural laws would eventually account for all natural phenomena.

In the late nineteenth century, American scientists rejected Baconianism. In part as a response to the debates over evolution, American intellectuals engaged in wide-ranging discussions about the nature of science. Although they did not reach a philosophical consensus, a new image emerged that emphasized the uncertainty of science, the importance of hypotheses and causal explanations, and the progressive development of science. Some American intellectuals elaborated on this image and drew on evolutionary theory to develop a progressivist theory of science that rejected the notion of natural laws and emphasized the instrumental rather than descriptive character of scientific hypotheses.

This conception of science maintained that progress—the ability of science to come up with better and better theories—set it apart from other forms of knowledge. Intellectuals often compared science to theology and philosophy, which seemed for centuries to be repeating the same endless disputes over basic issues. Scientific theories, on the other hand, were tested and either improved or rejected. Proponents of this view of science, however, could not explain how scientific methods ensured that new theories improved upon the old. In absence of other measures of progress, they assumed that scientific progress could be identified by agreement. They believed that scientists studying the same problem would eventually come to the same solution. William James explained that the "only safeguard" for the fallibility of science is "in the final *consensus* of our farther knowledge about the thing in question, later views correcting earlier ones until at last the harmony of a consistent system is reached." Although progressivist views of science allowed for some disagreement, in the form of challenging old theories with new, science was distinguished from less reliable forms of knowledge because it moved consistently forward—beyond controversy to agreement.[2]

Agreement among scientists came to be viewed as proof of the validity of a theory and the main mark of scientific success. This value placed on consensus played an important rhetorical role in early twentieth century debates about the social sciences. Social scientists, who advocated methodological changes that would eliminate moralism from their disciplines, used disciplinary disputes as proof of the inadequacies of current practices. For example, Frank Fetter maintained that disagreements among economists indicated that economics was not yet a science. The "diversity of opinion in the fundamentals among leading exponents of the subject argues strongly that economics is still a philosophy—a general attitude of mind and system of opinion—rather than a positive science."[3] These social scientists used consensus as evidence of the scientific status of research. A decade later, Wesley Clair Mitchell presented the "slackening of doctrinal controversy" among economists as proof that the discipline was becoming scientific. "I think that we debate broad issues less, because increasing concern with factual observation is breeding in us a more scientific and a less dialectical temper."[4] Younger social scientists argued that adopting more rigorous scientific methods would end disciplinary discord and that consensus could serve as proof of the superiority of their methods.

This circular reasoning encouraged scholars to look for ways to eliminate disagreement. Many of the younger generation of scholars thought that eradicating ethical concerns was the key to achieving intellectual consensus. These scholars viewed morality as a matter of personal preference. They argued that ethics contaminated scientific research by confusing subjective values with objective facts. "Nothing," maintained A. Gordon Dewey, "is more liable to lead astray than the injection of moral considerations into an essentially non-moral, factual investigation."[5] According to this view, one of the main reasons that social scientists did not agree on the results of their research was that moral concerns colored their interpretation of facts. Moral aims, these social scientists believed, had undermined the research of their predecessors. Based on this criticism, some social scientists insisted that ethical neutrality was an essential condition of scientific research.

These academics associated disagreements and controversy with unscientific, unscholarly methods. This attitude was reinforced in contemporary discussions about academic freedom. In the early twentieth century, much of the writing about academic freedom was devoted to defining what constituted an illegitimate use of a faculty position. University leaders wanted a policy that apparently left faculty free to say and teach what they wanted, while still discouraging faculty from engaging in public controversy. In order to preserve the sanctity of the content of ideas, writers focused their attention not on *what* professors said but on *how* they expressed it. Academics believed that the mode of expression had an effect separate from the content of the ideas. "The manner of conveying the truth," wrote John Dewey, "may cause an irritation quite foreign to its own substance." Dewey warned that faculty could present their views in a way that "is disintegrating instead of constructive; and [these] methods inevitably breed distrust and antagonism."[6] This kind of analysis implicitly made faculty responsible for the reaction of their audience.

According to this view, faculty members who became embroiled in public controversy did not deserve the protection of academic freedom. Nicholas Murray Butler, president of Columbia University, wrote: "Professors of established reputation, good judgment and good sense rarely if ever find themselves under serious criticism from any source. Such men and women may hold whatever opinions they please, since they are in the habit of expressing themselves with discretion, moderation, good taste and good sense." On the other hand, there were faculty whose statements attracted public censure. Butler maintained that there was a difference between the "manner" and "matter" of intellectual expression, and he assumed that faculty who attracted public scrutiny did so by the manner, not the content of their speech. "It is a misnomer," Butler argued, "to apply the high and splendid term 'academic freedom'" to these cases. Instead, Butler viewed these as "exhibitions of bad taste and bad manners."[7] The faculty involved were irresponsible agitators, not victims of "improper attacks" on their scholarly freedom. Academic freedom, therefore, did not necessarily protect faculty who addressed controversial moral or political subjects.

Faculty leaders did not oppose the distinction between the manner and content of intellectual expression. In 1915 the American Association of University Professors (AAUP) issued its seminal report on academic freedom. The AAUP committee agreed that professors must conform to the dictates of appropriate scholarly behavior. "The liberty of the scholar within the university to set forth his conclusions, be they what they may, is conditioned by their being conclusions gained by a scholars's method and held in a scholar's spirit; that is to say, they must be the fruits of competent and patient and sincere inquiry, and they should be set forth with dignity, courtesy, and temperateness of language." In public, as well as in the academy, the AAUP believed that professors should avoid "exaggerated statements," and "intemperate or sensational modes of expression."[8]

This reasoning allowed university administrators to assert that their institutions were fully committed to academic freedom while still being able to regulate faculty speech. By defining the presentation of ideas as an act independent of the ideas expressed, by establishing normative guidelines for appropriate scholarly presentation, and by judging presentation by audience reaction, they could limit freedom of speech by labeling the provocation of controversy as a form of unprofessional behavior. This, of course, ignored the reality that, in some contexts, certain subjects will be controversial and the only way to avoid controversy is to avoid those subjects.

Academic freedom policies reflected an epistemological position that associated consensus with valid knowledge. This position encouraged scholars to avoid issues that were inherently controversial. For many social scientists this meant trying to eliminate moral concerns from their research and avoiding advocacy in their classrooms.

NOTES

1. Parts of this chapter are from my book, *The Making of the Modern University: Intellectual Transformation and the Marginalization of Morality* (Chicago, IL: University of Chicago Press, 1996).

2. William James, *Principles of Psychology* (Cambridge, MA: Harvard University Press, 1981 [1890]), 191. On the failure of the late-nineteenth-century philosophers to justify their views on progress, see Larry Lauden, "Peirce and the Trivialization of the Self-Correcting Thesis," in Ronald N. Giere and Richard S. Westfall (Eds.), *Foundations of Scientific Method: The Nineteenth Century* (Bloomington: Indiana University Press, 1973), 275-306. On the importance of consensus as a sign of scientific truth see William Earnon, "From the Secrets of Nature to Public Knowledge: The Origins of the Concept of Openness in Science," *Minerva* 23 (1985), 321.

3. Frank Albert Fetter, "The Teaching of Economics," in Paul Klapper (Ed.), *College Teaching: Studies in Methods of Teaching in College* (Yonkers-on-Hudson, NY: World Book Co., 1920), 238.

4. Wesley Clair Mitchell, "Economics," in *A Quarter Century of Learning, 1904—1929* (New York: Columbia University Press, 1931), 51.

5. A. Gordon Dewey, "On Methods in the Study of Politics, I," *Political Science Quarterly,* 38 (1923), 638.

6. John Dewey, "Academic Freedom," in Jo Ann Boydston (Ed.) *The Middle Works, 1902-1903, Vol 2* (Carbondale: Southern Illinois University Press, 1976), 58-59.

7. Nicholas Murray Butler, *Annual Report of the President to the Trustees* (New York: Columbia University, 1915), 21-22. See also N. M. Butler to James McKeen Cattell, May 15, 1916, James McKeen Cattell Papers, Columbia University.

8. American Association of University Professors, "General Report of the Committee on Academic Freedom and Academic Tenure," presented at the Annual Meeting of the Association, 1915, 19-25.

TWELVE

Academics, Advocacy, and the Public Schools: A View from the 1930s

MARK C. SMITH

WHEN I FIRST SAW THE ANNOUNCEMENT FOR THE ADVOCACY CONFER-
ENCE, I was excited for a number of reasons. First, because as a
historian writing about advocacy among social scientists in the 1920s
and '30s, I have come to feel, like many historians, that I know more
about the past than the present and I looked forward to learning
something. Second, because I did know enough about contemporary
issues to recognize that my subject of the American Historical
Association (AHA) Commission on the Social Studies was directly
relevant to a number of present-day advocacy issues.

The AHA Commission grew out of the organization's reaction
to a 1923 statistical report noting the decline in the number and
quality of history courses in the public schools. Over the next ten
years the scope of the commission grew to include all the social
sciences and 16 volumes of findings. In the commission's final report,
published in 1934, coauthors social reconstructionist George Counts
and historian and political scientist Charles Beard rejected the
possibility of value-free social science and argued for the necessary
adoption of an individual "frame of reference—. . . [meaning] the
values for which knowledge is to be used."[1] Although Counts and

Beard made clear their own frame of reference of a collectivist democracy, they argued for placing local decision-making authority in the hands of teachers who would best represent the common interests of the community. The specifics of the chosen ethical goals were relatively unimportant; what was essential was their existence and the conscious construction of educational objectives tied to their advancement. As Counts and Beard noted in the *Conclusions and Recommendations of the Commission,* "Knowledge, like method, if ineffectively related to purpose, is sterile."[2] Nor did they shy away from charges of indoctrination. In earlier works Counts had noted that the educational process always involved a culture's determination of desired social and individual behavior. The question was never whether one should impose anything but rather *what* one should impose. Altruistic educators must accept the responsibility of indoctrination for moral ends, or special interest groups would assume control and propagandize for their own selfish goals.[3]

Today many of us hear echoes of the commission's final report in the ongoing debates within our respective disciplines and professions. Certainly this is true in my field. For at least the last decade historians, both individually and institutionally, have sought to apply their knowledge and skills to the material and spiritual crises in the United States. This emphasis on applied knowledge clearly includes the improvement of history teaching in the public schools. As Henry Louis Gates recently noted, "Education in a democratic society (or one that aspires to that ideal) has particular burdens placed upon it. Few theorists of United States education in this century and the preceding one separated pedagogy from the needs of citizenship."[4] This past year the AHA's Ad Hoc Committee on Redefining Scholarly Work extended its official definition of scholarship to include application and transformation of knowledge as well as its advancement and integration.[5] Similarly, the Organization of American Historians' official publication, *The Journal of American History,* devoted the December 1994 issue to a study of the strengths, weaknesses, and normative goals of the discipline. Almost all the contributions specifically noted approvingly its practitioners' commitment to making a difference. Columbia's Alan Brinkley, who attacked the idea that history can provide "answers and lessons," nevertheless concluded his piece with "If historians choose not to play a role in that struggle [of man against power], we can be sure that others, not of our choosing, will take our place."[6] Or as Counts and Beard put it 60 years earlier, "In the sphere of moral decision and choice, the very refusal to choose . . . is itself a moral act [and] . . . a statement of policy."[7]

Still, the area in which I personally see the 1930s report having the most contemporary resonance is in the recent hysterical response to the National History Standards developed by the National Center for History in the Schools at the University of California, Los Angeles. The standards project grew out of a 1983 Carnegie Foundation Report that noted American students' far inferior knowledge of history compared to their international counterparts. The National Endowment for the Humanities (NEH) enthusiastically funded the project to establish suggested guidelines for elementary and secondary school history curricula, and the center received the endorsement of 35 professional organizations. Relying on advisory groups composed of over 6,000 teachers, school administrators, parents, university professors, and businesspeople, the project called for the inclusion of more information on minorities, women, and working people and emphasized analytical skills over rote memorization. Given the traditional local control over education in the United States and the absence of accompanying textbooks, everyone connected with the project always perceived these standards as voluntary.

Nevertheless, a week before their official announcement, Lynne Cheney, head of the NEH in the Reagan and Bush administrations during the initiation and development of the project, attacked the standards as a "warped view of history" that made "it sound as if everything in America is wrong and grim."[8] She protested that they privileged minorities over white males and ridiculed such seminal American institutions as the Constitution and free-enterprise capitalism. Numerous attacks from conservative publications and talk shows followed; most simply repeated Cheney's assertions, called the project a totalitarian imposition of radical values on a helpless citizenry, and demonstrated no knowledge of either its specifics or general purpose.

What has been most interesting to me about this conflict is its similarity to the response to the AHA Commission final report, specifically in the identity of its critics. If the standards truly represented a totalitarian threat, one would assume that one would hear outraged cries from those who actually control education in this country—local school boards dominated by businesspeople, school administrators, and teachers. Yet, at least from my reading, these groups have remained quiet. In a November 19, 1994, *New York Times* guest editorial, Carol Gluck, a Columbia professor of Japanese history and member of the consultant group National Council for History Standards, emphasized the decentralized nature of the decision-making process and local schools' request for multicultural guidelines.[9] As with the 1930s commission, the critics have been academics—and academics associated with the respective reports. While today we can only speculate on the motives of Cheney and her group, the passage of time and the centralized nature of the fight over the AHA Commission's final report allows one to see the bases of that conflict. I believe that it can also provide possible insights into the present situation.

Surely the AHA Commission's report represented more of a threat to local control than does the National History Standards. Teachers rather than local political elites would make curriculum decisions, and the report's authors freely admitted their commitment to national planning. Yet school administrators as well as teachers responded positively, due partly to anger at their traditional business allies. Throughout the 1920s school superintendents had allied themselves with businessmen to obtain financial support for the schools. Faced with shrinking resources during the Depression, business leaders sought to cut back school budgets and blamed school executives for extravagance and waste. This was especially distressing coming from individuals who, in the words of one superintendent, "were responsible for this saturnalia of ruin."[10] The academicians of the commission at least wholeheartedly believed in the central importance of public education and its essential role in a free society.

Although the commission's 16 members had unanimously agreed to emphasize social over purely technical issues in the final report, several criticized Counts's first draft for excluding the latter and presenting too radical conclusions. Even Beard remonstrated with his disciple: "you put on a red coat, jump up on the ramparts and say to the American Legion, the D.A.R. and every school board in America: 'Here I am "a good Red" shoot me.' . . . Dead men do no work."[11] While successive drafts toned down the ideology, four members refused to sign. Their reasons reflect many of the academic politics which continue to affect us today.

Two individuals refused because of the failure of the final report to offer definitive curriculum revisions. Ernest Horn, a specialist in instructional methods at the University of Iowa, wrote the commission volume on teacher training and was allied with the educational establishment and its emphasis on efficiency. The final report, however, reflected Counts's personal disdain of teachers' colleges and their lack of innovation and Beard's animus against testing as "an enemy of teaching."[12] Frank Ballou the Superintendent of Schools for Washington, D.C., joined Horn in his angry dissent, dismissing the *Conclusions* as "glittering generalities" instead of the needed specific curriculum revisions.[13] As school superintendent in the District of Columbia, Ballou faced particular political problems and intense public scrutiny. A year after the publication of *Conclusions,* a congressman from Texas called Ballou a Communist for even serving on the commission and mailed out a questionnaire to all D.C. teachers asking: "Do you believe in God?"; "Do you believe in any of the doctrines of communism?"; "Do you approve of George S. Counts' writing?"; and "Do you approve of Charles A. Beard's writings?"[14]

Commission members realized that Horn and Ballou would dissent once they decided to go beyond their strictly technical concerns to address political issues. On the other hand, the attacks of political scientist Charles Merriam and his ally Edmund Day, director of Social Sciences for the Rockefeller Foundation, were much more unexpected and of greater concern. Merriam had joined the committee at its inception in 1924 and had been second in importance only to its chairman through most of its existence. Merriam was a pivotal figure in organized social science, establishing and controlling such institutions as the Social Science Research Council through his access to foundation funding. He wrote widely on education topics, edited a series on civic education in other nations, and wrote the key volume, *Civic Education in the United States,* for the commission.

Although Merriam consistently insisted on the need for normative goals in education, he had implacably opposed the final document from the time of the first draft. Although his criticisms were extremely vague, they centered around the hated term "collectivism." Merriam was also envious of Beard's greater reputation with the general public. The two had also clashed publicly in their American Political Science Association presidential addresses and reviews of each other's books, and the commission chairman noted in exasperation that a political scientist had warned him years before of the impossibility of Beard and Merriam ever agreeing on anything.[15] One of Beard's chief complaints about Merriam was that he consciously steered away from controversial subjects. As chairman of the Social Science Research Council in its early years, Merriam refused to sponsor several studies for fear of alienating financial supporters. Throughout the 1920s and '30s the council awarded its research fellowships almost exclusively to individuals doing empirical, small-scale studies and followed Rockefeller Foundation guidelines in denying money to known Communists.[16]

Despite Merriam's personal animosity toward Beard and his political caution, he did represent an articulate position held by a considerable number of academics, both then and now. In his books on civic education, Merriam perceived educators as he did social scientists, as technicians who "should be on tap, not on top." Merriam agreed that educators could create new values and attitudes but argued that they should do so only "if it is desired to do so" by those in positions of authority.[17] Thus, Merriam argued for Tennessee's right to outlaw the teaching of evolution in its public schools and opposed Clarence Darrow's pleas for freedom of thought.[18] In *Civic Education,* Merriam went so far as to limit the educator's role to the determination of "the special methods by which there may be accomplished through political channels what it is it desired to accomplish." It didn't matter whether it was a fascistic, communist, or democratic regime since "aptitudes, skills, tricks . . . have a definite value in any organization. . . . The object is given and he proceeds on that assumption, as an engineer builds a bridge." Educators should be "servants of power" and not use their technical positions to try to impose their own views.[19]

The eminent sociologist Lewis Coser has noted that intellectuals through time have chosen from several strategies in their utilization of knowledge. Some have used it to try to attain power through political office or leadership of a mass movement. Others have advised men of power or provided them with ideological justifications for their preconceived decisions. A final group, the most common Western tradition, has followed Socrates' example and used their information to become critics and intellectual gadflies.[20] Charles Merriam and Lynne Cheney fit into the second category, while those supporting advocacy in the classroom accept the Socratic tradition. When phrased in this terminology, it seems a simple enough disagreement. I think even my cursory view of the role of academics in the public schools, then and now, demonstrates that it is not.

NOTES

1. *Conclusions and Recommendations of the Commission: Report of the Commission on Social Studies* (New York: Charles Scribner's Sons, 1934), 29.

2. *Conclusions and Recommendations,* 73.

3. George S. Counts, *Dare the School Build a New Social Order?* (New York: The John Day Co., 1932), 9-10, 25; George S. Counts, *The Social Foundations of Education* (New York: Charles Scribner's Sons, 1934), 2-3, 548-53; and George S. Counts, Committee of the Progressive Education Association on Social and Economic Problems, *A Call to Teachers of the Nation* (New York: The John Day Co., 1930), 18-22.

4. Henry Louis Gates, "The Transforming of the American Mind," *Social Education* 56 (October 1992), 328.

5. "Redefining Historical Scholarship: Report of the American Historical Association Ad Hoc Committee on Redefining Scholarly Work," *Perspectives* (March 1994), 19-23.

6. Alan Brinkley, "Historians and Their Publics," *Journal of American History* 81 (December 1994), 1030.

7. *Conclusions and Recommendations,* 28.

8. "Plan to Teach U.S. History Is Said to Slight White Males," *New York Times,* October 26, 1994, B12.

9. Carol Gluck, "History According to Whom?: Let the Debate Continue," *New York Times,* November 19, 1994, 15.

10. David Tyack, Robert Lowe, and Elizabeth Hansot, *Public Schools in Hard Times: The Great Depression and Recent Years* (Cambridge, MA: Harvard University Press, 1984), 47.

11. Charles A. Beard to George S. Counts, August 5, 1934, George S. Counts Collection, Special Collections, Morris Library, University of Southern Illinois, Carbondale, hereafter cited as *Counts.*

12. Beard to Counts, November 23, 1933, *Counts.*

13. Frank Ballou, "Statement Concerning the Report of the Commission on the Investigation of History and Other Social Studies by the American Historical Association," *School and Society* 39 (June 2, 1934), 702.

14. Tyack et al., *Public Schools,* 64.

15. A. C. Krey to Frederick Kepler, quoted in Lawrence J. Dennis, *George S. Counts and Charles A. Beard: Collaborators for Change* (Albany: State University of New York Press, 1989), 95.

16. Louis Wirth, "Report on the History, Activities, and Policies of the Social Science Research Council" (memorandum prepared for the Committee on Review of Council Policy, August 1937), 13, in the Charles E. Merriam Collection, Joseph Regenstein Library, University of Chicago, hereafter cited as *Merriam*; and Donald Fisher, "American Philanthropy and the Social Sciences: The Reproduction of a Conservative Ideology," in Robert F. Arnove (Ed.), *Philanthropy and Cultural Imperialism: The Foundations at Home and Abroad* (Bloomington: Indiana University Press, 1980), 256.

17. Charles E. Merriam, *The New Democracy and the New Despotism* (New York: McGraw-Hill, 1939), 129.

18. Merriam to John Merriam, July 10, 1925, *Merriam.*

19. Charles E. Merriam, *Civic Education in the United States* (New York: Charles Scribner's Sons, 1934), 39-42.

20. Lewis A. Coser, *Men of Ideas: A Sociologist's View* (New York: Free Press, 1965), 136-143.

THIRTEEN

A Full Circle: Advocacy and Academic Freedom in Crisis

RICHARD MULCAHY

INTRODUCTION

A SENIOR COLLEAGUE ONCE TOLD ME that his working definition for a conservative was someone who quoted a dead liberal. If this is the case, then the opposite must be true: liberalism grows out of ideas once offered by conservatives. The point is that while ideas remain the same, their significance shifts depending on the circumstances. So there's no confusion, the term "circumstances" here refers to the setting in which competing groups use ideas to justify various social agendas. Hand-in-hand with this is the belief that *everything* is political, and that professional neutrality or disinterest does not exist.[1] In its simplest form, the argument goes as follows: "Nature abhors a vacuum."

Whether such is the case remains to be seen. As a historian, I am certainly aware of the argument made by Charles A. Beard 61 years ago about an author's "frame of reference."[2] But as a scholar, I am even more concerned about the concept of academic freedom. Certainly, the idea is slippery and difficult to define. In addition, those who defend it are subject to the fallout that occurs when opinion changes.

Writing near the end of his career, Professor Sidney Hook recounted how as a young man and a member of the executive council of the American Association of University Professors he fought to "depoliticize" American universities, and the difficulties he encountered as a result.[3] The model Hook sought was for the college or university to provide a forum that allowed the faculty to search for truth, without allegiance to any social or political ideology. Radical as this may have been for the 1930s, the model was viewed as stodgy and lacking in vision by the end of the 1960s. This view was based on the belief that universities needed to be directly involved in promoting social change.[4] To fulfill such a role, institutions had to inculcate certain values.

Hook found the idea frightening. First, taxpayers should fund public universities if, and only if, they followed a doctrine of intellectual impartiality. Second, value inculcation, with its inherent assumption that certain views were to be disallowed, represented a direct threat to academic freedom. What values would be communicated? Would professors be at the mercy of student demands concerning class content?

These concerns were real, and they remain. In spite of denial, academic freedom is in crisis.[5] The purpose of this chapter is to explore that crisis by comparing the issues involved in the current debate with a famous AAUP investigation that took place at the University of Pittsburgh in 1934: the matter of Dr. Ralph E. Turner. The comparison will underscore the fact that questions confronting higher education today are not new and that the answers to those questions are just as old.

THE TURNER AFFAIR

The Turner affair ranks as one of the great academic freedom cases of the 1930s. Aside from receiving national attention, the matter resulted in the University of Pittsburgh's inclusion on the AAUP censure list and prompted an investigation of the university by the state assembly. The reason why this particular matter received so much attention lay with the fact that it was a classic example of two major concerns within the academy at the time: abuse of power by an uncollegial administration and the right of faculty to speak out on social issues.

The facts of the case were these: Ralph E. Turner had served on Pitt's faculty in the department of history for 11 years and had risen to the rank of associate professor.[6] Regarded by his students as a dynamic teacher, Turner was also an active scholar. Among his publications were a biography of James S. Buckingham issued by McGraw-Hill and a survey textbook entitled *America in Civilization* issued by Alfred A. Knopf.

These accomplishments notwithstanding, Turner was informed on June 30, 1934, two months after his contract had been renewed, that he had been dismissed by Chancellor John G. Bowman. Not having received any written notice of this action, Turner confronted Bowman about it. Although Bowman attempted to calm Turner down, he refused to give any official explanation, other than a vague statement about discontent in the wider community over Turner's activism.[7]

When news of the dismissal became public a week later, a welter of criticism was directed at the university. Turner's supporters were convinced that he was fired because of his politics, especially his work for social legislation.[8] Angered over what had happened, Governor Gifford Pinchot wrote Dr. Bowman and told him that a person did not lose his or her constitutional rights by joining Pitt's faculty.[9]

In the face of this criticism, Bowman attempted to remain silent, but Pittsburgh's newly empowered Democratic leadership insisted on an explanation. After all, Turner had been their ally. Moreover, although the university was officially a private institution, it received an annual subsidy from the state that amounted to a quarter of its operating budget.[10] Because of this, state Democratic chairman David L. Lawrence demanded an investigation.[11] In response, Bowman sent an open letter about the matter to Pittsburgh congressman Henry Ellenbogen, which said Turner's dismissal had resulted from the antireligious attitude he displayed in his classes.[12]

Turner's antipathy for religion was a matter of record. The university had no difficulty in substantiating its claim and did so by securing affidavits from students who recounted Turner's various comments. These included his comparison of baptism to hog wallow and a claim that he could turn a staunch Catholic into an atheist within two years.[13] In addition, Turner's department chair, Dr. John

Oliver, claimed that he had received complaints from students about Turner's antireligious commentary four to five years prior to the dismissal.[14] It should also be noted that Turner's attitudes on the subject did not soften with the passage of time. After leaving Pittsburgh, Turner was eventually appointed to Yale's faculty, where he continued to express his opinions on religion as part of his teaching. He was criticized for this later by William F. Buckley, who characterized what Turner had to say as "bigoted atheism."[15]

Despite this, however, Bowman's explanation for Turner's dismissal did not stand up. First, at no time in the previous 11 years was Turner ever reprimanded, or even approached, about his behavior. Second, during the course of the state and AAUP investigations, the bulk of the evidence showed Turner's dismissal was politically motivated. This was made especially clear when Dr. Bowman's record as chancellor of the university was examined.

Having assumed the office in 1921, Dr. Bowman immediately ended the tenure program initiated by his predecessor, Dr. Samuel B. McCormick, replacing it with single-year contracts. At the same time, Bowman acted with impunity against anyone whose opinion he did not like.[16] This was clearly demonstrated by the fact that between 1929 and 1934, no less than 84 full-time faculty members, ranked at instructor or higher, left the university either as a result of dismissal or resignation.[17] Under these conditions, an atmosphere of "acute anxiety, worry, and fear" pervaded the institution.[18]

Over and above this, Dr. Bowman himself provided evidence when questioned about his educational philosophy during the state investigation. According to him, parents who sent their children to the university expected the faculty to advance certain values, including patriotism and respect for authority. It was a professor's duty, therefore, to avoid any subject matters that negated these or similar beliefs.[19]

Considering all that happened, as well as Dr. Bowman's expressed views, it is little wonder that the University of Pittsburgh was placed on the AAUP's censure list in 1936. Even more interesting, however, is the similarity between the Turner affair and more recent cases. Today, under our current ethos, Turner would have been accused of "insensitivity." As part of this, it should be noted how

Pitt's administration, in striking similarity to what has been done today, sought out student commentary about Turner's transgressions. Taking all of this into account, the question must be asked whether Turner overstepped the bounds. In other words, were Turner's comments inappropriate, and if he was dismissed for them, was his academic freedom violated? The answer is as vitally important today as it was in 1934.

ACADEMIC FREEDOM AND VALUE INCULCATION

When asked about Pitt's censure by the AAUP, Bowman presented a picture of calm by responding "What of it?"[20] But, privately, he was livid over the association's decision and what its report said about the university.[21] Nevertheless, Bowman refused to change how the university was managed, and it was left to his successor, Dr. Rufus Fitzgerald, to win Pitt's removal from the censure list.[22] Although no evidence exists to prove it, Bowman's intransigence may have been fueled by a realization that he represented a losing side. Whereas university administrations had once been omniscient and dismissed faculty at will, the situation began to change by the middle 1930s.

For its part, the AAUP had been founded 20 years earlier by some of the leading lights of the American professoriate, most notably John Dewey and Arther O. Lovejoy.[23] Although the association appeared elitist in terms of who it first allowed to join, eventually it opened its membership to all who held an instructor's position at a college or university. Seen broadly, its goals were to win autonomy and professional respect for all college and university faculty.[24] While such efforts met opposition in the beginning, college presidents began listening by the early 1920s.[25] This culminated in 1934 with the first of a series of joint conferences between the AAUP and the Association of American Colleges (AAC) in an effort to find a common ground on academic freedom and tenure.[26]

While these events were happening, the Hearst press had launched a campaign to unseat Professor Sidney Hook from his position at New York University (NYU). His crime: joining with several labor leaders in organizing the American Workers' Party.

Despite pressure from the Hearst press, NYU refused to dismiss Hook. According to Roger Baldwin, a turning point had been reached: academic freedom was now a reality, especially since other institutions were moving in the same direction. For Hook, the importance of this event was that it marked the arrival of the "non-political university."[27]

This concept fit neatly with the association's goals and provided the basis for what could be referred to as the AAUP's "classic program" for American higher education. The university as an institution would be thoroughly depoliticized and avoid aligning itself with any particular ideology. This would allow the faculty the freedom it needed to pursue its work.[28] For Hook, having achieved that goal was a major victory. After all, the purpose of American universities had been to inculcate traditional values, and anyone out of step with the program simply did not work.[29]

At the center of this victory was the belief that the American professorate needed to pursue its goals in a free environment, without the confines of any given orthodoxy. There is no question but that Dewey, Lovejoy, and Hook subscribed to this view. Unfortunately, in one way or another, each man failed to practice fully what he preached. The most flagrant example was Dewey, who persuaded the editors of *The New Republic* to close their magazine to submissions from Randolph Bourne. A former student of Dewey's, Bourne disagreed with Dewey over America's entry into World War I.[30]

Lovejoy's and Hook's failures were more subtle. Dewey acted out of ego, but Lovejoy and Hook were concerned about preserving hard-won gains from a major threat: the fear of Communist subversion. The danger this presented to academic freedom cannot be exaggerated. For example, in 1948 a loyalty oath was imposed on the University of California system that was so thorough, private misgivings about American foreign policy could be seen as subversion.[31]

To head off any problems, Lovejoy and Hook took a stand as anti-Communist liberals. The academic freedom movement was thereby placed squarely within the bounds of American patriotism. Writing in *American Scholar* in 1949, Lovejoy presented the case in this way: freedom of thought and inquiry was the basis of academic freedom. Communism denied such freedom and was thereby antagonistic to the association's goals. Thus, any college or university had the right to dismiss Communists or "fellow travelers" from its faculty. At the same time, those who were dismissed had no right to the protections offered by academic due process, since they were a part of a group whose aim was to destroy freedom.[32]

Presumably Hook agreed with Lovejoy's reasoning. Beyond that, however, Hook added that institutions had to guard against Communist faculty, since these people were troublemakers who would destroy staff morale and sustain institutional turmoil. Such an environment would hinder teaching and learning.[33]

While this reasoning may have been understandable, even defensible, it had the unfortunate side effect of creating an orthodoxy. It was here that William F. Buckley found the basis to level a well-reasoned assault on the association's goals in his book *God and Man at Yale*. Extrapolating from his experiences as an undergraduate, Buckley posited that the American professoriate was teaching values, specifically socialism and secularism, despite claims of impartially searching for "the truth." If "truth" was the goal, and no one set path existed, it stood to reason, therefore, that all ideas would be welcome. Yet Yale subscribed to the anti-Communist ethos articulated by Hook and Lovejoy. From Buckley's perspective, this was an orthodoxy with very definite limits. Taking this to its logical conclusion, Buckley wrote: "My task becomes, then, not so much to argue that limits be *imposed*, but that existing limits should be *narrowed*" (emphasis in original).[34]

Arguing a point of view similar to Bowman's, Buckley went on to say that since values were already being taught, any university should communicate those beliefs to which the students' parents subscribed: capitalism and Christian individualism. After all, the parents were paying for their children's education. As such, they were consumers, and it was a hallmark of a free society that consumers pay for something they want. Therefore, requiring faculty to adhere to a conservative orthodoxy violated no freedom, and if it meant dismissing radical professors, so be it. When *God and Man at Yale* appeared in 1951, Buckley intended it to be more than just a philosophical statement. He wanted to expose Yale's course content, and by extension that of other schools, for the alumni's inspection. By so doing, he hoped to turn higher education around and away from communicating those ideas that he regarded as radical. His method of achieving this goal was encouraging alumni to withhold their financial support until changes were made.[35]

Although Buckley's conservative program did not take hold, the reasoning behind it was the important thing. First, it denied the existence of the nonpolitical university and went on to say that the model was undesirable. Second, it introduced consumerism to the classroom. Since parents, and by extension students, were consumers of educational services, they had the right to determine the curriculum. In this setting, faculty would lose all professional autonomy and discretion, and simply provide the public with what it wanted.

Ironically, while such reasoning was originally intended to advance a conservative program, eventually it was adopted by the radicals of the 1960s. A good example was Students for a Democratic Society (SDS) and its demand that universities become vehicles for social change.[36] As part of this movement, efforts were made to silence professors who expressed contradictory views as well as those seen as "unwitting tools" of the "establishment." These efforts included the disruption of courses via sit-ins, called "classroom interventions."[37] In other cases students demanded the addition of courses to the curriculum, or insisted professors apologize for certain statements, all in the name of student rights and participatory democracy. Rather than fighting this infringement of faculty rights, university administrations backed down and sought to address so-called student grievances.[38]

In the time since, the student rebellion may have quieted, but it left a legacy in American higher education inimical to academic freedom. This legacy includes the institutionalization of protecting the group over the individual, the use of direct action tactics by students to silence people, and an administrative apparatus designed to combat "insensitivity" in its various forms.[39]

Concern about this legacy has surfaced over the last several years with the debate over "political correctness." On the one side, people have warned about a "thought police" out to repress any and all ideas contrary to the program just outlined.[40] On the other, critics deny that "P.C." actually exists. While they admit that there have been instances of the abridgement of individual rights and academic freedom, they insist these events are rare and do not represent a trend. The stories have simply been blown out of proportion.[41] Turning the issue back on their opponents, these critics maintain that the movement against "political correctness" is in fact a conservative-inspired reaction against inclusiveness and diversity in higher education.[42]

Yet the evidence shows that political correctness is, and continues to be, a real concern, not only for conservatives but liberals as well.[43] Going further, even if the critics were correct in their contention that there have only been a few "horror stories," the fact that they happened at all should be a matter of concern. As has already been shown, attitudes change. An idea regarded as progressive today could be seen as reactionary tomorrow, throwing the offender who articulated it into a situation that only George Orwell could devise. This will be illustrated in the next section.

VALUE INCULCATION AND POLITICAL CORRECTNESS

Of all the recent cases cited about whether a crisis of academic freedom exists, the one most discussed is the Thernstrom affair at Harvard. This is not surprising since Dinesh D'Souza covered it in his book *Illiberal Education*.[44] However, even if D'Souza had not picked up on it, the story would have gotten out of its own accord. The reason: Steven Thernstrom is not an obscure member of the professoriate teaching at a small college. He is one of the leaders of what has been dubbed the new social history, teaching at a premier institution. In addition, two of his monographs—*Poverty and Progress* and *The Other Bostonians*—are considered classics in the field. On top of this, Thernstrom considered himself to be a liberal. But, as is well known, he was accused of "racial insensitivity."[45]

According to Thernstrom, the charge was made by four students who attended a course he taught on ethnic and racial groups in America. For six weeks, the charge was front-page news in the *Harvard Crimson*, which ran stories questioning Thernstrom's concern for racial matters. In the meantime, he was not allowed to discover who his accusers were, presumably to prevent any retaliation by him.[46] Thernstrom also states that when he finally saw something in writing, it was a document prepared by two of the four students listing his offenses. Among these were the following: use of the term "American Indians" as opposed to "Native Americans," use of the term "Oriental," and agreeing with Daniel Patrick Moynihan that the cause of black poverty was the disintegration of the black family.[47]

For their part, critics writing about this affair vociferously deny that anything serious happened and insist there was no such thing as the "Thernstrom case." It is interesting to note, however, that at least two of these writers present entirely different accounts of what happened.[48] Leaving that issue aside, if we look at the facts of the case, not as presented by D'Souza but by Jon Wiener, one of the critics, it is obvious that an attempt was made to limit Thernstrom's academic freedom.

The matter centered around the fact that some of the students did not like Thernstrom's presentation on the black family because it did not mirror their experience. They supposedly approached Thernstrom on this, and he cited an authority in support of his contentions. Also, the students concerned did not like the source materials Thernstrom used for his lectures. According to Wiener, the students believed the sources presented an "inadequate" picture.[49] If Wiener is correct, we had students attempting to "peer review" Thernstrom's course and demanding that he include sources that met with *their* approval. The interesting thing is that Wiener, who is an academician himself, sees nothing wrong with this.

Just as interesting are the various side issues in the matter. First, while Thernstrom angrily denied he was a racist, one of the complaining students responded that no such charge was made. Thernstrom was only accused of "racial insensitivity." Just what constitutes this crime was not made clear.

Second, there was the attitude of the administration. According to Hilda Hernandez-Gravelle, then assistant dean of Racial and Minority Affairs, Thernstrom's expressed antipathy for her office was an "uncollegial" attitude. In saying this, Hernandez-Gravelle ignored what Thernstrom had just gone through and refused to comment about any possible complicity her office had in assisting the students making the charges. In defending herself, Hernandez-Gravelle maintained that her office was about creating "dialogue," and to pursue this goal she would assist students when "appropriate."[50] At no time, however, did she express any regret to Wiener about the possibility of a misunderstanding having taken place.

Finally, Thernstrom's colleagues reacted as if nothing at all had happened. For instance, Wiener quotes Professor Martin Kilson as flatly saying "There was no Thernstrom case." In a similar vein, Professor John Womack, who chaired the history department at the time of the incident, expressed the opinion that Thernstrom had overreacted, since he had only been accused of being insensitive.[51]

Nowhere in the available sources is there one statement of concern about students attempting to determine course content or the lack of definition for the term "racial insensitivity." Collectively, as part of their denial, Thernstrom's colleagues appeared to be advising him not to be so "thin-skinned."

Although the overtones of the Thernstrom affair are disturbing, they are dwarfed by what happened to Christie Farnham Pope at Iowa State. A professor of Afro-American history, Dr. Pope had taught in the Department of Afro-American Studies at Indiana University for eight years and the University of Oregon prior to that without any problems. But before her first year with Iowa State was finished, *Uhuru*, the newsletter for the university's Black Cultural Center, was taking issue with her being white, her course content, and her choice of textbooks.[52]

This was just the beginning. The following year Pope was accused by a student who styled himself as "Dangelo X" of attempting to "brainwash" his associates. Her crime: presenting facts that contradicted the teachings of the Nation of Islam. After threatening Pope with what she characterized as a "jihad," the young man was removed from the class, on the advice of the administration. This sparked a flurry of protest, including silent sit-ins of Pope's class by both black students and university employees. Instead of standing by the professor, however, the administration backed down and allowed Mr. X to return to the class.[53]

Still, the protests continued because the Black Student Alliance did not care for how Pope presented her course. Specifically, Pope was not an Afro-centrist. Clearly, students and other interested parties were attempting to dictate course content. The university administration, when confronted with these demands, did everything in its power to appease the critics, including offering shadow sections of Pope's course. At the same time, the administration told Pope that she was overreacting to the situation. Only as a last resort did the administration finally give her the support she needed.[54]

Despite this, there were those who refused to consider that Pope had been wronged. Using Buckley's reasoning, one graduate student had this to say: "[Students] as *consumers* of higher education have the right, nay, the *obligation* to be critical of the 'product' we receive" (emphasis added). Moreover, this student adds that such criticism is good. America's (spelled Amerikkka's) educational system lags behind the rest of the world, and such controversy assures quality. In conclusion, the student hinted the matter was not finished, and that he and his associates stood ready to continue the debate with Pope.[55]

Aside from his obvious anger and vituperative attitude, this student displayed a thorough contempt for professional authority. The message is clear: "Teach what we want, or do not teach!" Sadder still is the fact that the administration, representing the university as an institution, was willing to try to accommodate such a demand.

This sort of behavior is a direct outcome of the politicization of the American university, and there is no indication that the situation is improving. For example, in 1990 the University of Delaware, on the recommendation of its Faculty Senate Committee on Research, decided to disallow funding for faculty research from any organization deemed at odds with the university's "diversity" goals.[56] The premise behind this decision was the belief that whenever a faculty member received external funding, the university became a "partner" with the funding agency. As a result of this thinking, Professor Linda Gottfredson was disallowed from receiving a grant she had secured through the Pioneer Fund.

Commenting about the situation, the president of Delaware's board of trustees wrote that the Pioneer Fund was perceived as a group that subsidized research that could be seen as racist. Whether this actually was the case was immaterial. The perception existed, and allowing monies from the fund to be used by a faculty member could possibly hamper the university's efforts to achieve an increased minority presence.[57]

Such a ban was unprecedented and amounted to a de facto squelching of Gottfredson's research. Technically, if Gottfredson moved her research off campus, she was free to receive the funding. However, under these circumstances, her research would no longer count toward her expected workload as a university employee, and she would be allowed only bare access to Delaware's resources, especially its library.[58]

As unfortunate as these, and similar, incidents have been, higher education in America may suffer the most. If these events come to be viewed as part of a general trend in which individual rights are ignored, there will be a true right-wing reaction. Thus, to protect social change, especially "inclusiveness," academic freedom must not be abridged but defended and expanded.

ACADEMIC FREEDOM AND ACADEMIC OBLIGATION

In order to defend academic freedom, the concept must be defined. This has been done many times. Essentially, it is a libertarianism within the academy that allows the professor the freedom to inquire, teach, and research what he or she sees fit. The only limitation imposed is that the professor in doing this work be dedicated to seeking "the truth." If truth cannot be defined, the professor would be expected to show a healthy respect for fact.

According to Professor Edward Shils, when the AAUP was founded, two committees were created: Committee A on Academic Freedom and Tenure and Committee B on Academic Obligation. Whereas Committee A met frequently, Committee B never met at all. Presumably, the reason was that the members of the American professoriate in 1915 had a clear understanding of their professional obligations.[59]

Today Committee B still exists, although its title has been changed from "Academic Obligation" to "Professional Ethics."[60] Although the new title is more comprehensive in its concerns than the old, the two do overlap. In the "1940 Statement of Principles on

Academic Freedom and Tenure," it is written that "Freedom . . . is fundamental to the advancement of Truth."[61] Thus, there is an assumption that an academic in pursuing his or her work is seeking truth. It therefore holds that anyone who knowingly offers anything specious or false is behaving unethically. In such an instance, the protections of academic freedom would not apply.

But in the cases that have been presented in the previous sections, no such unethical behavior took place. Rather, each of the people covered somehow transgressed against the virtue of "sensitivity." Of all of them, the Turner affair was the most salient on this point, since Turner was antireligious. But all that Turner did was to express an *opinion*. Even Buckley admitted that Turner was a capable academic.[62] And, Turner probably made the distinction between fact and opinion. Thus, even if Bowman was telling the truth and did in fact dismiss Turner for his antireligious commentary, Turner's academic freedom was violated.

In the other cases presented, the question of sensitivity also appeared. In those cases, however, the matter concerned limiting what a professor could say or do for the sake of diversity. Despite arguments to the contrary, the actions taken against the faculty involved were flagrantly improper and amounted to attempted thought control. In instances where students disagree with professors, the professor is presumed to be the authority. Students are in the classroom to learn, and certainly asking questions is part of the learning process. But *students are not peers*; because of this, they are not entitled to demand that a professor change his or her presentation, or to determine what source materials are allowable. If this happens, for whatever reason, the educational process ends. The same is true when an institution places limits on where a professor can seek funding.

Taking all of this into account, how can academic freedom and professional ethics be protected? The answer is simple: the use of a rigorous tenure review system as well as a program of continuing peer review. Having gone through both, I realize they are inconvenient for all concerned, especially the person being reviewed. But they are necessary.

Outside the academy, and within some colleges and universities, "tenure" is almost a dirty word. It is seen as protecting the incompetent as well as providing others with absolute job security in the face of an uncertain economy.[63] It is also blamed as an obstacle to institutional flexibility. For many people, tenure amounts to an unearned free ride and thereby contributes to a lack of respect for academicians. What makes matters worse is that academicians themselves, in many cases, do not point to tenure as necessary to protecting academic freedom but stress the economic security it affords.[64]

The only thing that can counteract these impressions is a rigorous tenure review system that is well publicized. It should be uniform within a given institution, with the stated purpose of weeding out unethical and incompetent instructors, and applied equally to all. Failure to do so can have disastrous consequences.[65] It reflects badly not only on the institution but on the profession as a whole.

Continuing peer review also serves this purpose. It helps professors remain current within their fields, while guarding against unethical behavior. In judging peers and in tenure review, a professor's politics and opinions are to have no bearing. Rather, the issue would be whether the person under review actively promoted falsehood or taught unsubstantiated opinion as fact. In such reviews, an ethic of impartiality is vital, and this can be achieved only if the university itself as an institution subscribes to such an ethic.

CONCLUSIONS

It has been 35 years since Sidney Hook defended the nonpolitical university. There are many within academe today, both administrators and faculty, who view the concept with contempt. But the fact is, despite what the critics say, Hook was correct: the nonpolitical university is the foundation of academic freedom. However, the possible reaction mentioned earlier is already beginning.

Alumni groups are now organizing to fight political correctness and to promote their own values at their alma maters. Although these groups deny having a set agenda, there is no question but that many are conservative. Their tactics are simple. Following Buckley's recommendation, they are withholding contributions and demanding change. It is true that Yale recently returned a $20 million contribution that came with too many strings attached, but how many schools can afford to do such a thing?[66] Just as ominous, taxpayers are beginning to question why they should support public universities.

This trend can be reversed only by the assurance that institutions of higher learning, both private and public, are impartial and provide an environment open to all views. If not, academic freedom, and liberal education with it, will suffer the greatest assault made upon it since the beginning of the century.

NOTES

1. Louis Menand, "The Trashing of Professionalism," *Academe: Bulletin of the American Association of University Professors* 81, no. 3 (May-June 1995), 19.

2. Charles A. Beard, "Written History as an Act of Faith," *The American Historical Review* 39 (1934), 228.

3. Sidney Hook, "From the Platitudinous to the Absurd," in Sidney Hook (Ed.), *In Defense of Academic Freedom* (New York: Bobbs-Merrill/Pegasus, 1971), 257.

4. Ibid., 15.

5. Elizabeth Fox-Genovese, "Debating Political Correctness: A Kafkaesque Trap," *Academe: Bulletin of the American Association of University Professors* 81, no. 3 (May-June 1995), 8, 10.

6. Proceedings Before a Committee of the House of Representatives [of Pennsylvania] to Investigate the University of Pittsburgh, Hillman Library, University of Pittsburgh, 3, 377; "University of Pittsburgh," *Bulletin of the American Association of University Professors*, (March 1935), 224-26.

7. Unedited copy of report of Committee A on Academic Freedom and Tenure of the American Association of University Professors on the University of Pittsburgh pertaining to the Turner case, 1935, 14-15, F.F. "Turner Affair," Bowman Files, University Archives, Hillman Library. The Bowman Files are open without restriction for scholarly research.

8. "Liberal Fired by Pitt," *Pittsburgh Sun-Telegraph*, July 5, 1934; "Sweatshops' Foe Fired as Pitt Teacher," *Pittsburgh Press*, July 5, 1934;

"Storm Rising Over Firing of Pitt Teacher," *Pittsburgh Post-Gazette,* July 7, 1934; *New York Times,* July 8, 1934; *Proceedings,* vol. 3, 406-10.

9. Letter to Chancellor John G. Bowman from Governor Gifford Pinchot, dated July 11, 1934, F.F. 135, Bowman Files.

10. "[Pitt Chancellor Bowman] Ignores [Governor] Earle's Demands," *New York Times,* December 9, 1936.

11. "Pitt Ouster Fought by Labor," *Pittsburgh Sun-Telegraph,* July 7, 1934.

12. "Open Letter to Pittsburgh Congressman Henry Ellenbogen from Pitt Chancellor John G. Bowman," *New York Times,* July 22, 1934.

13. Affidavit of Charles A. Rucks, F.F. 137, Bowman Files.

14. Handwritten extract from Dr. Oliver's Testimony from the *Proceedings,* 1.

15. William F. Buckley, *God and Man at Yale: The Superstitions of Academic Freedom* (Chicago, IL: Henry Regnary Co., 1951), 13.

16. C. Hartley Gratton, "The Fight for Academic Freedom," *Survey Graphic,* March 1936, 147.

17. "University of Pittsburgh," 250.

18. Ibid., 255.

19. *Proceedings,* vol. 5, 858-59.

20. "Professors' Group Votes Ban on Pitt," *New York Times,* January 1, 1936.

21. Letter from Chancellor Bowman to National office of the AAUP, dated February 29, 1935.

22. "Thirty-Third Annual Meeting [of the AAUP]," *Bulletin of the American Association of University Professors* 33 (1947), 7.

23. Walter Metzger, *Academic Freedom in the Age of the University* (New York: Columbia University Press, 1955; reprinted 1964), 194, 202.

24. "Honoring Fifty Year Members," *Academe: Bulletin of the American Association of University Professors* 78, no. 40 (July-August 1992), 39.

25. Metzger, *Academic Freedom,* 210-11.

26. *AAUP Policy Documents & Reports* (Washington, DC: American Association of University Professors, 1990), 3.

27. Hook, "From the Platitudinous to the Absurd," in Hook (Ed.), *In Defense of Academic Freedom,* 257.

28. Ibid.

29. Ibid., 250-57.

30. Alan Ryan, "Pragmatism Rides Again," *New York Review of Books,* February 16, 1995, 33.

31. Richard Mulcahy, "Robert Colodny and the Pittsburgh Renaissance: A Study in Local McCarthyism," *Mid-America: An Historical Review* 74, no. 2 (April/July 1992), 172-73.

32. Arther O. Lovejoy, "Communism vs. Academic Freedom," *American Scholar* 18 (Summer 1949), 332-33.

33. Michael McDonald, "A Lawyer's Brief Against Litigating Academic Disputes," *Academic Questions* 5, no.4 (Fall 1992), 18.

34. Buckley, *God and Man at Yale,* 12-13, 46-47.

35. Ibid., 149-151, xiv, 185, 186-87, 194.

36. Hook, "The Long View," 14-15.

37. Arnold Beichman, "Academic Freedom and the Failure of Nerve," in Hook (Ed.), *In Defense of Academic Freedom,* 191-92.

38. Hook, "The Long View," 17.

39. Benno C. Schmidt, "False Harmony: The Debate over Freedom of Expression on America's Campuses," *Vital Speeches of the Day,* November 1, 1991, 46.

40. Heather MacDonald, "D'Souza's Critics: P. C. Fights Back," *Academic Questions* 5, no. 3 (Summer 1992), 17-19.

41. Cathy H. Davidson, "'P.H.' Stands for Political Hypocrisy," *Academe: Bulletin of the American Association of University Professors* 77, no. 5 (September-October 1991), 9-10.

42. Ibid., 11; "Statement on 'Political Correctness' Controversy," *Academe: Bulletin of the American Association of University Professors* 77, no. 5 (September-October 1991), 48; "The P.C. Monster," *The Progressive* (May 1991), 9.

43. Barbara Dority, "Civil Liberties Watch: The P.C. Speech Police," *The Humanist* 52, no. 2 (March-April 1992), 31-33; Fox-Genovese, "Debating Political Correctness," 8, 10, 12, 14; Schmidt, "False Harmony," 45-48.

44. See Dinesh D'Souza, *Illiberal Education: The Politics of Race and Sex on Campus* (New York: Free Press, 1991); Jon Wiener, "What Happened at Harvard," *The Nation,* September 30, 1991, 384-88.

45. Steven Thernstrom, "McCarthyism Then and Now," *Academic Questions* 4, no. 1 (Winter 1990-1991), 14.

46. Ibid.; Rosa Ehrenreich, "What Campus Radicals?" *Harper's Magazine* 283, no. 1699 (December 1991), 57-59.

47. Thernstrom, "McCarthyism Then and Now," 15.

48. Compare the accounts of Ehrenreich, "What Campus Radicals?" with that of Wiener, "What Happened at Harvard."

49. Wiener, "What Happened at Harvard," 384-386.

50. Ibid., 386.

51. Ibid., 388.

52. Christie Farnham Pope, "The Challenges Posed by Radical Afro-Centrism: When a White Professor Teaches Black History," *Chronicle of Higher Education,* March 30, 1994, B1.

53. Ibid.

54. Ibid., B2-B3.

55. Letter to the Editor from Michael Boulden, *Chronicle of Higher Education,* April 27, 1994.

56. Jan H. Blits, "The Silenced Partner: Linda Gottfredson and the University of Delaware," *Academic Questions* 4, no. 3 (Summer 1991), 41.

57. Ibid., 42.

58. Ibid., 4, 43

59. Edwards Shils, "Do We Still Need Academic Freedom?" *American Scholar* 62, no. 20 (Spring 1993), 187.

60. "Committees of the Association," *Academe: Bulletin of the American Association of University Professors* 77, no. 6 (December 1991), 42.

61. "1940 Statement of Principles on Academic Freedom and Tenure, with 1970 Interpretive Comments," *AAUP Policy and Documents* (Washington, DC: American Association of University Professors, 1990), 3.

62. Buckley, *God and Man at Yale,* 12-13.

63. James E. Perley, "Tenure, Academic Freedom, and Governance," *Academe: Bulletin of the American Association of University Professors* 81, no. 1 (January-February 1995), 43-45.

64. Shils, "Do We Still Need Academic Freedom?" 188-189.

65. See John Taylor "He's Back!" *New York,* May 24, 1993, 10-11.

66. Joyce Mercer, "Alumni Activism," *Chronicle of Higher Education,* March 31, 1995, A29-A30.

FOURTEEN

"Judge" or "Advocate"? Scholars, War, and Protest in the Anti-Vietnam War Teach-Ins of 1965

TOM JEHN

WHEN COMMENTATORS ON HIGHER EDUCATION consider "the role of advocacy in the classroom," the word "advocacy" attracts much of their attention. I want to explore not only how an earlier generation of professors and students in the 1965 anti–Vietnam War teach-ins understood "advocacy" but also what it meant that in struggling to define their roles, professors and students pressed on two other words that coincidentally came to make up today's vexed phrase: those words are "in" and "classroom." "In" and "classroom" suggest the significances of context, place, and spatial boundaries, themes I believe increasingly inform and trouble the politics of pedagogy, and ones I will return to.

But, first, why do I think that the teach-ins can give us a perspective on our arguments over "advocacy in the classroom"? To return to those all-night marathons of speeches, heated discussions, folk songs, and the occasional bomb threat is to find in our past a moment when higher education became riven by conflicts over its aims and its relationship to society and to structures of power, a moment when the university classroom became a controversial site of counterhegemonic activity as faculty and students disturbed the university culture, the political establishment, and the media. It also was a moment when academic activists recontained their potentially subversive energies by ultimately privileging the educational apparatus. I see the advocacy of 1965 as offering a lesson about the problems of making the classroom the *exclusive* agent of social change.

To be sure, the 1965 teach-ins were not the first time that faculty had become activistic. But it was in the 1960s that activistic professors increasingly agitated for social change from *within* the classroom, from *inside* the institution, rather than from outside, through political parties, union organizing, the media, or rallies. The teach-in's components were not new, but its combinative zeal was; more important, its sense of the classroom as a highly charged political space was new. For the teach-in was a mix of seminar, lecture, strike, and mass demonstration deliberately enacted as educational experience inside the university.

The intellectuals who planned the first teach-in in the spring of 1965 were aware of the dangerous direction they were charting as they imagined new responsibilities for themselves as pedagogues. By following the trajectory of their early organizing efforts, we can see how these activists struggled to reshape the roles that the dominant culture expected the professoriat to inhabit.

As the Johnson administration ordered the bombing of North Vietnam and sent more U.S. troops into battle, a research psychologist at the University of Michigan called a meeting of concerned faculty on March 11, 1965, to discuss how they might express their opposition to the war. More than 25 professors heeded the call. Their previous political commitments had varied from participating in the civil rights and test-ban treaty movements to writing letters to newspaper editors on Johnson's behalf.

Not surprisingly, from the start the group was divided over how radical their protest should be. Some first suggested that the group should sign their names to an antiwar advertisement that they would place in local papers. But one sociologist called for a more contentious one-day faculty strike. According to a memorandum on the Michigan teach-in distributed by organizer and biology professor

Anatol Rapoport, classes would be canceled for a day and students invited to attend the "Free University of Michigan" where they would participate in a day-long analysis of the historical, political, military, and moral aspects of the Vietnam War in university classrooms during the scheduled class periods.[1]

In discussing their philosophy of protest, organizers wished to recall the sit-down strikes of the 1930s and their most recent manifestation, the civil rights sit-ins. The Michigan professors decided to adopt the strategy of the sit-down strike because, as Rapoport explained, it had "move[d] the picket line from outside the premises, where it [could] be ignored, to inside, where it [could not] be ignored."[2] Since faculty and students felt that the Johnson administration and the media were failing to provide adequate information to the public, that the public had been betrayed by Johnson's peace candidacy, and that there was no public discussion of the war, it would be necessary to initiate and situate discussion where citizens, the government, and the media could not ignore it: in the university itself.

When the professors declared that the strike would take place on March 24, the announcement was met with outrage both on and off campus, making manifest how the dominant culture conceived of academic activity as properly uncritical. The university's president, Harlan Hatcher, Michigan's governor George Romney, and the Michigan State Senate joined in condemning the plan. The Senate introduced a resolution calling the professors "un-American" and their proposed action "illegal."[3] University department heads and other professors subsequently pressured their colleagues to alter the plan.

The impasse was broken when at an all-night meeting of organizers six days before the scheduled strike, anthropologist Marshall Sahlins is reported to have shouted in the middle of the debate: "They say we're neglecting our responsibilities as teachers. Let's show them how responsible we feel. Instead of teaching out, we'll teach in—all night."[4] Sahlins's definition of teach-in, which stuck, underscored the group's disagreement over what difference the context of activism made. According to Sahlins, to teach inside the classroom in the middle of the workday was to teach "out," but to teach outside the normal classroom at night—outside the normal class schedule—

was to teach "in." Yet what was "out" for Sahlins, what was "too political," was "in" for a "militant" faction of organizers, as Rapoport described the supporters of the strike.

Sahlins's proposal, which was conceived as more moderate than the strike, finally won out but not without an exhaustive debate by organizers. This debate showed that although the teach-in would early on recontain the strike's potentially more radical energies, the militants understood more clearly than the moderates that *where* professors articulated their politics was just as important as *what* those politics were.

The "militants" felt that the all-night teach-in would be, as Rapoport described,

> a compromise . . . a fixation on the constraints of the academic tradition. . . . In the eyes of the militants, the time for polite academic discussion of the issues was past. Speaking out was no longer enough; it seemed useless to speak out and to be told that you had a perfect right to speak out, while the people who held the whole of humanity as hostages proceeded with their genocidal plans. Therefore . . . it was actually necessary . . . that the protest be imbued with some aspect of questionable legality.[5]

Moreover, the militants believed that a strike would show that "all issues were relevant—civil rights, the investments of the Chase Manhattan Bank in South Africa, Latin America, and academic freedom."[6] Teaching-in during class periods would attempt to make *explicit* to the dominant culture the politics of knowledge production at the university. By criticizing government policy during class time, the militants hoped to subvert the expectations of a public and a power structure used to thinking of the university as a place committed to business as usual.

The militants were drawing out connections that had been slowly surfacing for some time, most recently articulated in the attack on the multiversity by the Berkeley Free Speech Movement. During and since World War II, there had developed a direct liaison between American universities and the capitalist state. Inscribed in the educational apparatus was the fact that the university's production of knowledge was not disinterested but rather intimately tied to illegitimate power relations that pervaded the capitalist state and the world system. Thus, for the militants to call the university into question was to pierce the ideological veil thrown over the university and the classroom as space that could ever be apolitical. In fact, the militants would argue, all classrooms were political; all instructors were political; all intellection was political.

The moderates, however, early on prevented the teach-ins from more critically interrogating the politics of education. They believed that rather than target the Johnson administration, the militants would wrongly raise issues entirely irrelevant to the war. When the proponents of the all-night format contended that by shifting from regular working hours to night hours, they could, in Rapoport's words, "undercut all the talk about . . . 'propaganda in the classroom,'" they creatively shifted but then reinscribed the conventional spatial boundaries of political activity, suggesting even as they opened up the classroom to political discussion that a discussion of the politics of the classroom was not acceptable inside the classroom.[7]

Yet for all the moderates' fears that the militants' strike would have become an imbroglio over academic freedom, the moderates' version of the teach-in was nonetheless exposed by its critics as a contested political space. The media, academic, and political establishments savagely attacked faculty who participated in the more than 50 teach-ins that spring for violating their duties. *New York Times* columnist James Reston wrote that the demonstrations were "disguised as teaching and backed by propaganda of the most vicious nature. . . . [The administration's effort to negotiate a settlement] is a serious moment justifying serious discussion and debate, but this is not what it is getting from many university campuses, where the tradition of responsible inquiry is supposed to be strongest."[8]

As for the academic response, it generally followed the line of reasoning voiced by Dr. Grayson Kirk, president of Columbia University, who stated that a professor "should hesitate before [making a ringing public declaration on a controversial subject] simply because . . . he can never entirely shed his scholar's gown. . . . He cannot escape a certain popular presumption of intellectual authority. . . . A scholar has an implied professional commitment to approach all issues in the spirit of a judge rather than as an advocate."[9] According to this logic, "judges" are curiously drained of the force of their opinions, leaving intellectuals sentenced to silence. Unlike those who argued that the academic sphere was a priori apolitical, Kirk nightmarishly acknowledged that politics permeated all realms of human activity, including the academic, but then moved to deny the intellectual her or his right to be political. For the unlucky professor, there was nothing outside the academy and its disciplinary injunctions against political expression.

The rebukes from Washington were less polite. Secretary of State Dean Rusk intoned, "I sometimes wonder at the gullibility of educated men and the stubborn disregard of plain facts by men who are supposed to be helping our young to learn—especially to learn how to think."[10] The capitalist state used less subtle methods to delegitimate the professors' forays into politics. The State Department sent "truth squads" to campuses to counter the "propaganda" of the teach-ins, but by doing so, they further supported the teach-in participants' contention that "truth" and consent were being engineered in Washington.

While the teach-in participants proclaimed that they were forced by government recalcitrance to provide the other version of Defense Secretary Robert McNamara's and Presidential Adviser McGeorge Bundy's "truth," they were always nervous about carrying on what they called "a monologue," or one-sided demonstrations. Organizers frequently stated that they would prefer dialogues with administration officials, believing that a discussion with the State Department could lead to a reconsidered Vietnam policy. What increasingly made organizers—and not coincidentally politicians, university presidents, and *New York Times* columnists—more comfortable was any teach-in that moved away from a protest and instead rigidly followed rules of academic decorum and enshrined consensus between opposing parties.

Indeed, in many ways the teach-ins attempted to situate themselves firmly within the discourse of institutional and capitalist state power. This was no better shown than by the National Teach-In that Michigan organizers conducted in Washington, D.C., two months after the Ann Arbor event. Organizers proudly hailed the National

Teach-In as the culmination of the teach-in movement, but the love affair that the political and media establishments suddenly had with the event and its much-vaunted academic high seriousness suggested that any transgressive political force the teach-in once had had now been screened out. Held in the Sheraton Park Hotel Ballroom on a Saturday, the teach-in convened 500 professors from across the country and an audience of 5,000 people and was televised live on the networks. Politicians and newspaper columnists now celebrated the teach-in as an American tradition and as a tribute to the ability of the nation's brain trust to help solve problems. The event's main attraction and critic of the teach-ins, McGeorge Bundy, who suspiciously canceled at the last minute, sent a telegram that effusively praised the participants for convening what promised to be a fair and open discussion between citizens and their government. The scholarly debate, moderated by distinguished philosophy professor Ernest Nagel, did not disappoint. Panelists no longer spoke of moral outrage at the war but instead cautiously discussed Vietnam within the existing context of foreign policy. The one protester at the event, a West German who wanted to burn his citizenship papers on stage, was promptly hauled away by security guards.

The National Teach-In, then, indicated how ardent was the academic activists' belief in the primacy of the educational apparatus to affairs of the capitalist state. One organizer said that the academy "could contribute to a political awakening in America by mobilizing the knowledge and skills concentrated in that sector of society."[11] Organizers, of course, knew that the burgeoning postindustrial state valued the services of higher education; they seemed only too happy to be courted by the political and media elites. They did not, however, sense how schools were ideological, how universities had become a dominant ideological state apparatus, and thus how easy it was for the activists' dissidence to become co-opted.

Joan Scott noted in an article she wrote as a graduate student on the National Teach-In that the event saw professors desiring to compete with policymakers.[12] The participants' impulse to become equals with the ruling elite speaks volumes. Ironically, the National Teach-In blithely made the spheres of the academy and of the capitalist state bleed into one another, collapsing boundaries between educational and political spaces. The only trouble was that the "classroom" now looked and acted much like a policy meeting at a think tank, unaware of its complicity with power and so inhospitable to citizens. And the politics were those of Cold War consensus thinking, disdainful of alternative visions and so beloved by those in power. The classroom was political, as always, but it was once again free of the kind of politics that truly criticizes the dominant ideology and that the dominant ideology speedily attempts to recontain. If the teach-ins taught us anything, it is that, because the university is so inscribed with the ideology of the capitalist state, all instructors are advocates in the classroom.

NOTES

1. Anatol Rapoport, "Dialogue or Monologue? Parts One and Two," in Louis Menashe and Ronald Radosh (Eds.), *Teach-ins: U.S.A.: Reports, Opinions, Documents* (New York: Frederick A. Praeger, 1967), 5.

2. Ibid., 5.

3. "Michigan Faculty Created Teach-In," *New York Times,* May 9, 1965, 43.

4. Mitchel Levitas, "Vietnam Comes to Oregon U," *New York Times Magazine,* May 9, 1965, 24.

5. Rapoport, "Dialogue," 6.

6. Ibid., 6.

7. Ibid., 6.

8. James Reston, "Washington: The Decline of Serious Debate [Editorial]," *New York Times,* April 21, 1965, 44.

9. Grayson Kirk, "A Sanctuary of Concern: The University in Contemporary Society," *Columbia University Forum* 8, no. 2 (1965), 36-37.

10. Dean Rusk, address at meeting of American Society of International Law, Washington, D. C., April 23, 1965, quoted in Max Frankel, "Cambodian Talks Gaining Support as Asia Peace Key," *New York Times,* April 24, 1965, 1.

11. Rapoport, "Dialogue," 173.

12. Joan Wallach Scott, "The Teach-In: A National Movement or the End of the Affair," in Menashe and Radosh (Eds.), *Teach-ins,* 192.

PART III

PRINCIPLES

FIFTEEN

Advocacy and Explanation: The Problems of Explaining Adversaries

JOHN O. VOLL

TEACHERS OF MIDDLE EASTERN STUDIES are acutely aware of the issues of advocacy in the classroom and in the broader arena of providing information for the general public. Accusations of advocacy have long been a basic charge brought against teachers discussing the Middle East as a way of imposing control over materials presented to students and the interested public. This is an area of debate not simply in terms of the specifics of the content being presented but also in terms of the very structures of intellectual analysis.

"Truth squads" for years have visited American classrooms and scholarly conferences on the Middle East in order to determine whether people are involved in advocacy. Most of these so-called truth squads are active not to ensure that there is no advocacy but, rather, that there *is only* advocacy of the position supported by the organizers of the visits. They represent a form of pressure and an effort of censorship rather than an effort to ensure that all views are fairly presented. In this way, these truth squads represent a tacit recognition that all teaching is in some ways a form of advocacy.

The effort to check coverage is not, however, simply harassment. There are bigots who teach and by their teaching reinforce dangerous prejudices. In dealing with Middle Eastern subjects, a number of distinguished groups have sought to discover prejudicial advocacy as well as just simple advocacy. Groups such as the Anti-Defamation League of the B'nai B'rith, which was formed already in 1913, and the more recent Arab-American Anti-Defamation Committee have distinguished histories of opposition to prejudicial advocacy in schools and media.

This sensitivity to advocacy in presenting materials about the Middle East is the result of teaching content that is of great importance to different groups of people. This is one of the major reasons why people undertake the study of the Middle East and why people want to teach about it: the content of the study has real significance in a way that involves people emotionally as well as intellectually. Much of the content of Middle Eastern studies involves what W. B. Gallie called, in terms of philosophical and political ideas, "essentially contested concepts." He noted that "there are disputes, centred on [such concepts] . . . which are perfectly genuine: which, although not resolvable by argument of any kind, are nevertheless sustained by perfectly respectable arguments and evidence. This is what I mean by saying that there are concepts which are essentially contested, concepts the proper use of which inevitably involves endless disputes about their proper use on the part of their users."[1] In an "essentially contested concept," people see their definition as being the only rational perception and any other usage is dangerously irrational and needs to be opposed actively. While Gallie is dealing with terminological usage and concept definition, his idea is helpful in thinking about advocacy in Middle Eastern studies.

In Middle Eastern studies, many of the basic interpretations of human experience have this character of being "essentially con-tested." Historical accounts can be fully and rationally coherent but absolutely contradictory, with the difference depending not on the actual available information but rather on the starting personal commitments of the narrator or analyst. "Essentially contested" content is at the heart of all Middle Eastern studies. A high proportion of the content of any course on modern Middle Eastern studies will, by definition, be controversial. Any Middle Eastern course that does not teach *something* that is a controversial subject is not teaching about the Middle East that anybody in the world cares about.

As a result, teachers have a long experience of sensitivity to the need for being aware of advocacy and the necessity of some kind of balance in presentation. In other chapters in this volume, a number of authors suggested that the appropriate way for dealing with the problems of advocacy in the classroom is to present a balance of perspectives and positions. This is, of course, almost by definition true. Teachers can avoid at least some of the charges of advocacy by presenting a variety of viewpoints in a way that can be described as balanced. However, it is important to remember the dangers of what John Esposito informally calls the "zoo theory" of presenting a controversial subject, that is, making sure that "one of every species" is represented in the presentation. I have, on occasion, spoken of this as the "Noah theory" of course-organization wherein you make sure that each species is preserved in the materials and presentations of the course.

Such an approach is practical if you are dealing with binary dispute situations or relatively simple contested narratives. However, a balanced presentation is less possible if the situation is complex and there are many different antagonists. How many positions would you choose to present if you were, for example, teaching a course on the Lebanese civil war in 1981? One news report at that time noted that there were more than 24 militias, as well as the Syrian, Israeli, and Lebanese armies and a United Nations peacekeeping force that had "cut the country up into de facto enclaves."[2] Would "balance" require that all of these voices be presented? If you are teaching about modern Islamic "fundamentalism," you have a choice that itself represents advocacy. If you opt for binary "balance," you present the views of the "fundamentalists" and the "nonfundamentalists." This already involves an advocacy position because you have made the prejudicial judgement that all fundamentalists are essentially alike and all nonfundamentalists are alike. However, to present an adequately balanced discussion of Islamic fundamentalism in the contemporary world, one might need to show at least 15 or 20 different "fundamentalist" positions and possibly even more "non-fundamentalist" positions. The very choice of type of balanced approach, in other words, becomes advocacy for a position: a binary balanced presentation advocates the view that Islamic fundamentalism is a monolithic force, while presenting many voices advocates the position that Islamic fundamentalism is *not* monolithic. Situations like this mean that using "balance" as a way of countering the problems of advocacy is not an effective or efficient solution if you are attempting to teach about the Middle East.

This situation creates major problems for teachers dealing with many Middle Eastern subjects. Few people accept the "objectivity" of someone who disagrees with them on an "essentially contested concept." If the escape from such debates is to present a "balanced" approach, then such an escape is not viable in dealing with most Middle Eastern subjects, which leaves the teacher of Middle Eastern studies in an impossible situation. The situation becomes even more difficult if the new understanding of the nature of discourse and narrative itself is recognized. A fundamental issue rises to the surface as a result of contemporary understanding of the nature of discourse: the very structure of analysis, or the nature of the discourse, shapes the coverage and presentation, so that advocacy is inherent in the analysis and presentation itself. This situation involves more than choice of coverage or mode of approach. It involves inherent advocacy on specific content issues that are contested by adversaries. To resolve this problem, we must go far beyond the simple search for "balance" in presentation. We must be aware of the inherent advocacy in the modes of analysis and the very subject matter itself.

This leads to three basic generalizations that need to be examined in more detail:

First, as he or she deals with "advocacy, explanation, and adversaries" in Middle Eastern studies, the teacher may appear to be acting as an advocate rather than an explainer. Effective explanations of positions may be mistaken for advocacy.

Second, this is especially true in explaining adversaries when the learning audience or the students may see one of the adversaries as a "repugnant cultural other." Susan Harding utilizes this term when she discusses the difficulty of representing a "repugnant cultural other" in analyzing Christian fundamentalism in the United States.[3]

Third, the problem of explanation and advocacy is reinforced by the basic structures of the disciplines that are used to create our explanations. The discipline that we use may itself represent a form of advocacy.

EXPLANATION SEEN AS ADVOCACY

Teachers and scholars tend to be identified by the fields and the subjects that they cover. One frequently hears a historian talk about "my period" or an anthropologist talk about "my people," or we speak of colleagues using such terms as "our Middle East historian" or "our Russian historian." Because they are experts, because they have spent so much time with the people being explained, teachers and scholars are the ones who are best able to present the words of the people of the subject matter.

Sometimes familiarity can produce sympathy: and sometimes, as was common among American scholars studying the Communist movement from a more conservative perspective, it can produce antipathy. Whether sympathy or antipathy is produced by familiarity, the teacher should be able to answer such questions as "How could people believe that Khomeini was a man of God?" or "How could a person drive a suicide car-bomb?" in a manner that has integrity with the subject matter.

In Chapter 2 Professor Troy Duster wrote of the experience of giving a presentation on Kwakiutl culture and being challenged by a student who was Kwakiutl. It is difficult to accept the integrity of an explanation or a description of a group of people or a culture if someone from that group finds nothing familiar in the explanation. If a teacher presents a description of Shi'i Islam that is not recognizable in some way to a Shi'i Muslim, that explanation is inadequate or lacks integrity. Such descriptions have the same lack of credibility that can be found in descriptions of life in the United States presented by doctrinaire Soviet scholars in the 1950s and 1960s. Explanations that lack credible contact with the subject matter are a form of prejudicial advocacy.

Descriptions that have integrity with the subject matter may also be subject to the accusation of advocacy. In a situation where authentic portrayals of different groups and their views are being presented, the presenters may themselves become involved in the disputes. Advocacy is too often simply a charge made against someone who has sufficient expertise to be able to present the words and positions of the subjects of study. This is a matter of "presentation," not "representation" in the political sense of being an agent for a group.

Historically, scholars in area studies have been especially vulnerable to having explanation be seen as advocacy. The "old China hands" in the 1940s suffered because they knew too much about China. They provided accurate descriptions of the corruption of the Nationalist regime and the strength of the Communist movement—and, for their accuracy, they were charged with being Communists themselves.[4]

One of the most widely accepted stereotypes involving the belief that expertise will create advocacy is in the field of Middle Eastern studies involving the concept of an "Arabist." In journalistic usage, there is the frequent implication that an "Arabist" is pro-Arab. Stated in the most simple terms, this is the belief that a person who has studied Arabic and, therefore, is able to read Arabic sources is by that very fact disqualified from being able to analyze Arab politics in an effective and nonadvocacy way. The identification of "the Arabists" in the U.S. Department of State usually means *both* that the persons know the Arabic language and that they are pro-Arab. Such a stereotype is distinctive and rare outside of discussions of Middle Eastern policy. In the days of the Cold War, for example, one seldom accused Soviet diplomats who could read Shakespeare of being pro-American simply for that reason.

Informed explainers often are perceived as advocates because they can explain positions in ways that authentically reflect the realities being described. This issue is especially visible when scholars try to explain controversies and conflicts in the Middle East.

EXPLAINING "REPUGNANT CULTURAL OTHERS"

The charge of advocacy is possibly most frequently made when someone is explaining the position of a person or group that for some reason is viewed by the audience as a "repugnant cultural other." Sometimes teaching in this context can be hazardous. Truth squads and zealots can make a variety of accusations, and emotional responses can, on occasion, be dangerous. A scholar at the University of California, Los Angeles, who was trying to explain Ottoman policy in the late nineteenth century had his car firebombed by Armenian activists who thought that the explanation represented advocacy of the Ottoman policies toward Armenians.

Part of the dynamics of this process involves the creation of images of cultural "others." Through a variety of mechanisms, people—students, scholars, the learning public—develop concepts of significant social categories with which they interact in different ways. In modern, contemporary discourse, there are some categories of "others" that are essentially repugnant. As mentioned, Susan Harding has discussed how the representation of "Christian fundamentalist" has been developed by "modern discursive practices" as a "repugnant cultural other."[5] In this context, attempting to explain "fundamentalists" in any way other than portraying them in terms of the prevailing repugnant image results in charges of supporting them or advocating their position.[6] People resist explanation of a repugnant cultural other in terms that have integrity with the subject matter and would be fully credible to the people being described. Explainers are involved in a process of trying to answer, rationally and logically and factually, questions for which people want and expect a different answer.

"How could people believe that the Ayatollah Khomeini was a man of God?" Most people who ask that question expect a certain type of answer. They assume that the answer will involve a description of the Ayatollah Khomeini's followers as ignorant people who are deluded or in some other way mentally deranged. If, in fact, an answer is given that shows that many of his followers were intelligent and rational human beings with modern educations, and if such examples include people like Mustafa Chamran, who has a Ph.D. from the University of California, Berkeley in civil engineering and was the leader of the Revolutionary Guard, the person providing that answer is likely to be accused of justifying the excesses of the revolution or advocating the ideology of Khomeini.

Although people have gone beyond that kind of simple response to an unexpected answer in many areas, it remains a major problem in presenting most important subjects in modern Middle Eastern and Islamic history. It is difficult to explain the activities of terrorists who blow up buses in Tel Aviv or individuals who shoot worshipers who are praying in a mosque in Hebron without being accused of advocacy or at least showing sympathy for a reprehensible act. Even broader subjects such as the history of Zionism, the rise of Arab nationalism, the development of British imperial control in the Middle East, or the policy of the United States in the Persian Gulf emerge as essentially contested subjects rather than topics for scholarly study and explanation. Possibly the best example of these difficulties is the case of Salman Rushdie, where an explanation of the issues involved will arouse charges of advocacy from virtually any literate audience anyplace in the world.

The incorrect identification of the explainer as an advocate is most common and most vitriolic when the phenomenon being explained represents a repugnant cultural other. In many older cases, the general public has gone beyond this simple response. In the days of the Cold War and strong feelings of anticommunism, there were strong pressures in the academic world against the teaching of Marxism, and teachers who taught the subject were often charged with being Communists themselves. However, in the classroom, it is important to explain even groups that may be repugnant to the teacher as well as the students; if that explanation is to have integrity and veracity, the teacher has to be able to present the voice of the group being explained. An inaccurate explanation is worse than no explanation.

THE DISCIPLINES AS ADVOCATES

A final aspect raises the fundamental issue of the nature of the explanation itself. The basic structures of the intellectual disciplines used in Middle Eastern studies create explanations that may themselves represent advocacy. Edward Said, in his important book *Orientalism,* raised this issue clearly with regard to the old academic approach to the Middle East and the Islamic world. This older academic discipline is Orientalism, the discipline for studying "the Orient." Said examined the whole process of creating "the Orient" as a mental construct: The "Orient is an idea that has a history and a tradition of thought, imagery, and vocabulary that have given it reality and presence in and for the West." In this analysis, Said argues that the Orient "is itself a constituted entity, and that the notion that there are geographical spaces with indigenous, radically 'different' inhabitants who can be defined on the basis of some religion, culture, or racial essence proper to that geographical space is . . . a highly debatable idea."[7] In this conceptual framework of Orientalism, analysis starts from the assumption that the Orient and the people in it are radically different rather than allowing the knowledge of radical difference to arise as a result of empirical research. The construct of "the Orient" as a radically different and exotic "other" was and remains a powerful conceptual tool both in shaping Western images of the Middle East and in advocating and determining appropriate attitudes and policies toward the exotic "other." Accepting the concept itself was an important form of advocacy.

Replacing Orientalism with interdisciplinary area studies reduced the exotic dimensions of the construct at the heart of the discipline. However, the emergence of area studies also involved important basic assumptions that represent another advocacy. Post-Orientalist scholarship did not remove the concept of a radically different other as the object of study. It tended to keep that basic framework, simply changing the description of the other from "exotic" and "mysterious" to an object that could be studied with the developing research tools of the social sciences and interdisciplinary studies.

In these disciplines there are some specific assumptions and moods that involve important advocacy positions. Social sciences and interdisciplinary studies established and maintain a commitment to an "objectivity" that makes it possible for some to claim that these disciplines are "value-free" and that this stance is desirable. In most disciplines and in most fields scholars have recognized that the social sciences are not simple analogs to the natural sciences or that social scientists cannot discover and then present the "objective truth" in a value-free way. However, scholars who in principle accept the critiques of the old-style, absolutist positivism will in dealing with certain specific subjects in Middle Eastern studies continue to assert the value-free nature of their analysis and their ability to find Truth as a result of their researches.

Such discussions arise especially in the examination of contemporary Islamic movements and thought. Ernestine Friedl reminded us in Chapter 4 that linguists refer to "marked" and "unmarked" categories in discourse. In discussions of academic disciplines, the old advocacy for belief in value-free disciplines arises out of the use of terms for academic disciplines that are, in some sense, "unmarked" categories, despite the fact that they have very specific identities. In the past, people used to speak of teaching "economics" and then might discuss the desirability or dangers of teaching "Marxist economics." This latter was a "marked" category while "capitalist economics" is an unmarked category. This situation is similar for most disciplines in the social sciences, where there is a tacit acceptance of the "unmarked" category being the contemporary Western form. The "unmarked" discipline then can be viewed as somehow value-free, while the marked versions of the discipline represent a form of advocacy.

The existence of this situation in Middle Eastern studies was illustrated by a discussion between some Western-trained social scientists and an economist from Pakistan. In the terminology of the discussion, the Western scholars assumed "economics" as an unmarked category. A sociologist argued:

> I remember being involved, a few years ago, with a number of
> colleagues who were trying to define an "Arab sociology." They
> spent two days in a very wonderful isolated Italian mansion and
> produced a book on it. I still do not know whether science has
> a nationality, neither do I understand how sociology could have
> a nationality any more than economics have a religion. . . . Is
> there really an Islamic science of economics? . . . The discipline
> of economics or sociology or any of these empirical sciences is a

system of statements that are subject to being true or false. Religion, on the other hand, is . . . a system of normative statements, that is not subject to being true or false.[8]

The response by the "Islamic economist" was:

We, who have been brought up in the tradition of the social sciences as they have grown over the last 200 years, have become prisoner[s] to our methodology . . . In certain cases unthinkingly, the methodology of natural sciences has been extended to social sciences. . . . We have to stop here and reflect on the nature of the social sciences. In social science, we deal with human behavior. . . . The human model is different from that of physics of the mid-19th century. . . . We do not say that the empirical method is wrong; we regard it to be an important method. But it is only one method, not *the* method. We believe that one must take both the positive and normative aspects of the social sciences into account.[9]

The point of noting this exchange in the context of advocacy in the classroom is not to agree or disagree with either of the positions presented. Instead, it is to note that the very structure of the Western disciplines, in this case "economics," represents an advocacy position in terms of examining Middle Eastern and Islamic affairs. If "economics" is an unmarked discipline, a value-free empirical science, by the very definition of the discipline, "Islamic economics" is not possible. The rejection of the possibility of Islamic economics is a major position of advocacy, which is the result of the conceptual structure of the discipline itself rather than any empirical study.

The area where the advocacy of the post-Orientalist disciplines may be strongest is in the area of teaching about and explaining religion. Religion is generally treated as a subject to be examined or explained, but it is not one of the disciplines that is utilized in order to undertake the examinations. In this context, the post-Orientalist social scientists tend to create discourses and explanation narratives in which "religious believers," like the "Orient" of old, are defined as somehow radically different from the people who are doing the explaining.

The analytical framework of post-Orientalist area studies involves the self-assumption of being value-free and also accepts the basic assumptions of secular perspectives. When examining religious movements and experiences, this can lead to some difficulties in the contexts of the religious revivals of the late twentieth century. Stephen Warner noted that sociologists of religion in the 1970s tended not to see major developments of religious revival in the United States and presented an analysis of the "theoretical barriers to understanding Evangelical Christianity."[10] Many of these barriers reflect the current difficulties that social scientists have had with perceiving and then explaining the Islamic revival of the 1980s and 1990s.

Warner sees the perception of a radical difference between the social scientist and the Evangelical as an important obstacle to effective analysis. "Sociologists who speak of mainline, liberal lay believers with respect and fellow feeling treat evangelicalism as if they were witnesses to a bizarre spectacle. It is as if evangelicals were denizens of the zoo." In this context, the problems may arise because of the "evaluative bias" of the scholars who "are repelled by the perceived conservatism, supernaturalism and emotionalism of the evangelicals." However, Warner notes that there are also some basic preconceptions that prevent clear analysis. These preconceptions—that evangelical believers are lower class, politically conservative, and historically retrogressive—are based on appropriate studies and respectible empirical correlations. "However, these empirical generalizations have been hypostacized to the status of theoretical constructs so that the correlations have come to take on the appearance of identities."[11]

Much the same process appears to have taken place in post-Orientalist area studies. Radical revolutionaries such as the Ayatollah Khomeini are regularly identified as "conservatives," and the fact that a high proportion of members in the Islamist movements are modern-educated professionals rather than illiterate, lower-class people still elicits surprise after more than a decade of familiarity with the movements. Older images of fanatic holy warriors of Islam have been revitalized by characterizations of Muslims as terrorists. "Experts" on Middle East terrorism could instantly identify the bombing of the federal building in Oklahoma City in the spring of 1995 as the characteristic work of Middle Eastern terrorists, even though it soon became clear that it was, in fact, the work of people of non–Middle Eastern origins. In general terms, post-Orientalist scholarship has frequently replaced the exotic, mysterious "other" of Orientalism with a violent repugnant cultural "other." In this latter type of scholarship, advocacy continues to be inherent in the structure of analysis itself.

In disciplines where secular perspectives are accepted as a natural part of the analytical framework, religion will inevitably be viewed only as a subject to be studied. In this context, the analyst by the act of analysis becomes an advocate for a secular worldview.

In the fields of Middle Eastern studies, Susan Harding's observations about the study of Christian fundamentalists also apply. She noted that the methodologies of critical self-examination of explanatory concepts have now become routine in most studies except in those dealing with religious cultural others.

> It seems that antiorientalizing tools of cultural criticism are better suited for some "others" and not other "others"—specifically, for cultural "others" constituted by discourses of race/sex/class/ethnicity/colonialism but not religion. . . . Many modernist presuppositions still operate uncritically within contemporary studies of politics and culture, thwarting scrupulous interpretation and re-representation of some cultural "others," specifically those deemed inappropriately religious or otherwise problematic or repugnant.[12]

In Middle Eastern studies, issues of advocacy in the classroom and presentations to a learning audience present critical problems. In general terms, the teacher may appear to be acting as an advocate when presenting explanations of adversaries' positions. This situation may be almost inevitable when the explanations deal with essentially contested narratives. A special problem exists when the position being explained is that of a person or group occupying the position of a repugnant cultural other in the view of the audience. All of these difficulties are made especially complex by the evolution of the academic disciplines dealing with the Middle East. It is widely recognized that the older disciplines of Orientalism were culturally committed and involved unconscious advocacy. However, the disciplines of post-Orientalist area studies also involve some forms of inherent advocacy.

In the face of these conditions, the teacher in Middle Eastern studies must go beyond the simple attempt to be "more objective" or solve the problem by presenting more voices in order to give a "balanced" presentation. The situation in Middle Eastern studies reminds us that as we attempt to teach about controversial subjects, militant adversaries, and repugnant cultural others, we must look at the very structure of our analysis.

The basic recognition of the essentially contested nature of the content of Middle Eastern studies can itself be constructive. W. B. Gallie suggests that "recognition of a given concept as essentially contested implies recognition of rival uses of it (such as oneself repudiates) as not only logically possible and humanly 'likely,' but as of permanent potential critical value to one's own use or interpretation of the concept in question." Although Gallie is referring to contested concepts and definitions, similarly positive results can be gained from the recognition of the essentially contested nature of many of the important explanatory narratives in Middle Eastern studies. In fact, adversaries have much to learn from each other, even in the context of advocacy. Perhaps even more important, Gallie suggests that this may help limit the influence of the extremists: "One can well imagine cases in which moderate and sane representatives of two or more contestant parties could express agreement as to where the *real* issue between them lies, and agreeing that this issue is simply obscured or debased by the intrusion of lunatic voices, from whichever side. . . . [In this way] a given contest can at least be identified with the best elements that take part in it."[13] Advocacy, which would seem to be unavoidable, can, in other words, be put to useful service.

In the long run, what is needed are new approaches that are more conceptually inclusive and that avoid relying on binary perspectives that create images of radically different others. Simply exchanging images of exotic or repugnant others for some new type of "other" will continue to make advocacy a problem, not just in Middle Eastern studies but in all areas of study dealing with human culture and interactions.

NOTES

1. W. B. Gallie, *Philosophy and the Historical Understanding* (London: Chatto and Windus, 1964), 158.
2. John Yemma, "Lebanon: Too Many Guns, Too Many Feuds," *Christian Science Monitor,* April 3, 1981.
3. Susan Harding, "Representing Fundamentalism: The Problem of the Repugnant Cultural Other," *Social Research* 58, no. 2 (Summer 1991), 373-93.
4. See, for example, the discussion in Jerald A. Combs, *The History of American Foreign Policy: Volume II Since 1900* (New York: Knopf, 1986), 338-39.
5. Harding, "Representing Fundamentalism," 374-75.
6. Ibid., 375.
7. Edward W. Said, *Orientalism* (New York: Random House, 1978), 5, 322.
8. Statement by Iliya Harik quoted in Ibrahim M. Abu-Rabi' (Ed.) *Islamic Resurgence: Challenges, Directions & Future Perspectives—A Round Table with Khurshid Ahmad* (Tampa, FL: World & Islam Studies Enterprise, 1994), 76.
9. Khurshid Ahmad quoted in ibid., 77-78.
10. Stephen Warner, "Theoretical Barriers to the Understanding of Evangelical Christianity," *Sociological Analysis* 40, no. 1 (Spring 1979), 1-9.
11. Ibid., 3, 4.
12. Harding, "Representing Fundamentalism," 375-76.
13. Gallie, *Philosophy,* 187-88.

SIXTEEN

Professional Advocates: When Is "Advocacy" Part of One's Vocation?

MICHAEL BÉRUBÉ

I RECENTLY RECEIVED TWO STUDENT RESPONSES to my teaching that, I thought, shed some interesting light on my classroom practices and my students' expectations. The first was from a student who wrote on one of my evaluation forms that he or she was glad that I had discussed the question of whether gay or lesbian sexuality was an issue in the work of Willa Cather, Hart Crane, and Nella Larsen. The student was pleased that my class even broached the subject, and praised me for being unlike "those politically correct professors who never bring up controversial topics for fear of offending someone." I admit I was not merely happy but actually amused by this evaluation, since, of course, it is much more common to hear the term "politically correct" hurled at precisely those professors who *do* bring up the subject of gay or lesbian sexuality in the literature classroom. Then again, I thought, it's also quite common to hear the term applied in the culture at large to people who seem dominated by the imperative not to offend—as when "politically correct" is used more or less as a synonym for liberal hypersensitivity to words such as "handicapped," "Indian," or "woman." So here, I decided, I inhabited a nice conundrum: in asking my students whether they thought a writer's sexuality does or does not have any influence on their work or on the way we read it, I was certainly politically correct, in the pejorative sense used by the Right, and, better still, I was also politically correct in avoiding politically correct squeamishness about offending my students.

The second student response got back to me only indirectly. One of the graduate students told me that he had assigned my essay, "Public Image Limited," to his class in introductory composition, whereupon one of his students asked him whether the Michael Bérubé who'd written that essay was the same Michael Bérubé who taught English at the University of Illinois. Upon learning that the two of us were indeed one and the same, the student was mildly astonished; apparently, he or she had taken a class of mine in the recent past and would never have guessed my political orientation. At first I was entirely pleased with this report, thinking, Well, if there's one thing I'm not guilty of, it's advocacy in the classroom. But then I began to wonder whether in fact I was doing such students a disservice by *not* making it clear to them that I have a stake in American cultural politics and something of a record of weighing in publicly on various issues of concern to my profession. Not that I should wear my politics on my sleeve or announce my various positions on the National Endowment for the Humanities (NEH), NAFTA, and NATO in the hopes of converting my students to my causes; but perhaps students would be better served if I did not pretend to a form of political "objectivity" I cannot profess and do not even believe in.

I should note that I am skeptical of claims to epistemological objectivity not because I believe that everything is political (on the contrary, I believe that many things are *a*political) but because I believe, with Hans-Robert Jauss and Hans-Georg Gadamer, that "interest" is a precondition for knowledge and that the surest way to trap yourself inside a narrow, parochial, "subjective" view of the world is to believe that you have transcended all merely subjective worldviews.[1] Indeed, the reason hermeneutics demands of us that we theorize our own historical and epistemological positions is that if we *fail* to do so, if we attribute to ourselves the Archimedean point beyond history and mere "interest," we will almost certainly lapse into dogmatism and intransigence. When Gadamer critiqued the "Enlightenment prejudice against prejudice," therefore, he did so not to defend parochialism but precisely to guard against it—as any responsible teacher and scholar should do.

Still, the question remains: Even if I eschew claims to "objectivity" on hermeneutic grounds, does that mean I am entitled to say anything at all in the classroom, or even to address any topic I desire? In the past, when I have strayed from the syllabus and addressed contemporary politics directly, I have largely confined myself to mentioning or describing various issues, policies, figures, or statements; the only social activity I have ever directly advocated is that of voting. (Of course, I have no doubt that assiduously paranoid conservatives could find systemic bias in my courses merely because I address some issues and not others, and because I do not condemn communism with every other breath. But my courses try to tackle serious subjects in a 15-week semester, and therefore I have no time for placating the demands of assiduously paranoid conservatives.) But what about current Republican plans to cut student aid? Is it not within my ambit as a college teacher to inform students of such measures and to urge them to write their elected representatives so as to make their feelings known on the subject? I cannot consider that an illegitimate form of "advocacy," since federal student aid policies directly and materially affect the classrooms in which I teach, and I am certainly within my rights as a citizen to advise students that they should participate in the political process, especially insofar as their interests *as students* may be at stake.

But here's where things get tricky. As a limit case, let's take the hypothetical example of an astronomy professor who uses his or her introductory cosmology course as a vehicle for recruiting students to support the Strategic Defense Initiative or Phil Gramm in 1996, on the grounds that Gramm's candidacy and SDI—or, if you like, Clinton and his national service program—are materially relevant to the future of introductory courses in cosmology. It might be possible to argue that that kind of political advocacy is clearly illegitimate, since it violates the boundaries of a discipline whose object is the study of phenomena that predate any human social organization; this is, in rough form, the rationale most people rely on when they distinguish the "objectivity" of the natural sciences from the inevitable "fuzziness" of the human sciences. (I myself would not consider it proper to advise students to write their representatives about proposed cuts in the NEH or the National Endowment for the Arts [NEA], since public policy concerning those agencies does not materially *and immediately* affect the students in my classroom, however much it may affect teaching and learning in the arts and humanities in the long run.) But then let's consider the position of a teacher whose job it is precisely to make judgments about various forms of human social organization: How indeed can such a person eschew "advocacy" and remain a responsible member of his or her profession?

The difficulty of this quandary was brought home to me once my second child, James, entered the public school system in Illinois, which he did at the age of three, because he has Down syndrome. For the purposes of the Individuals with Disabilities Education Act of 1975, I am legally Jamie's advocate; this poses few ethical problems either for me or for my classroom, of course, but it has introduced me to the possibility that if I were a professor of education whose work concerned the disposition of what's currently known as "special education," I could not possibly carry out my professional and pedagogical duties without advocating one form of social organization over another. Not merely because my job depended on it, so to speak, but because I could not responsibly represent current research in my field without simultaneously attending to the ramifications of that research for public policy. Indeed, among the public policies I would be called on to adjudicate is the very question of whether "special education" should exist at all, or whether the policy of "full inclusion" offers superior educational programs and potential for people with disabilities.[2]

Now, as it happens, the study of literature, the way I practice it, rarely bumps up against controversies in public policy or political disputes over the reauthorization of acts of Congress. Literature is, after all, one of the fine arts and not an explicitly social discipline like, say, anthropology, history, political science, or law; and it is on these grounds that cultural conservatives have criticized teachers like myself, who stress the social ramifications of literary works, for underemphasizing aesthetic considerations at the expense of political considerations. But literature cannot avoid being a *representational* art, which is why the ancients, in their wisdom, spoke not merely of its capacity to delight but of its potential to instruct, as well. Literature, more than music and dance, tends to be propositional, and on occasion it even contains specific propositions about the disposition of human social organization. I therefore find it impossible, in ordinary classroom practice, to discuss literature in ways that do not involve worldviews, even when I am trying to make the simplest case about authorial intentionality.

Let me take an example from a novel I teach fairly regularly. The great black critic Darwin Turner once wrote of Zora Neale Hurston's *Their Eyes Were Watching God* that the scene in which Janie speaks her mind to her second husband, Joe Starks, on his deathbed, is a profoundly disturbing exchange, since, as Turner put it, nothing about Starks's treatment of Janie merits the cruelty with which she treats him on his dying day. Turner's judgment reads as follows:

> Either personal insensitivity or an inability to recognize aesthetic inappropriateness caused Miss Hurston to besmirch *Their Eyes Were Watching God* with one of the crudest scenes which she ever wrote. While Joe Starks is dying, Janie deliberately provokes a quarrel so that, for the first time, she can tell him how he has destroyed her love. During the early years of their twenty-year relationship, Joe Starks jealously sheltered her excessively; during the later years he often abused her because he resented her remaining young and attractive while he aged rapidly. But in a quarrel or two Janie repaid him in good measure by puncturing his vanity before the fellow townsmen whose respect and envy he wished to command. Never was his conduct so cruel as to deserve the vindictive attack which Janie unleashes while he is dying.[3]

Not a single one of my students, male or female, agreed with this assessment; most of them disagreed even with Turner's characterization of Janie and her "attack" and, far from being sympathetic to Joe, were outraged that Janie had failed to speak her mind in 20 years of marriage. But that's not the point. The point is that you cannot even begin to broach discussion of that scene, regardless of what you think of Turner's critical judgment *and* regardless of Turner's invocation of "*aesthetic* inappropriateness" (my emphasis), without reference to some notion of what constitutes normative behavior between a husband and a wife—any more than you can teach *Huckleberry Finn* without engaging the meaning of various representations of race, or *Measure for Measure* without engaging students' understanding of social phenomena such as justice or gender. Nor is it possible, as I have argued elsewhere, to broach a book like James Weldon Johnson's *Autobiography of an Ex-Colored Man* without delivering yourself of propositions concerning unpleasant things like the Atlanta race riot of 1906 and the inconceivable ubiquity of the practice of lynching at the turn of the century.[4]

Indeed, in her now-classic essay "Vesuvius at Home: The Power of Emily Dickinson," Adrienne Rich wrote of literary criticism as a form of advocacy, whereby she tried to retrieve and revivify Dickinson's claims upon our attention—or, as Rich puts it, "I have come to understand her necessities, could have been witness in her defense."[5] And as Rich is to Dickinson and Alice Walker is to Hurston, so, once, was T. S. Eliot to John Donne and Irving Howe to Henry Roth: The critic seeking to engage with the writers of the past, if he or she is a responsible critic, will at least want to make those writers intelligible to an audience of our contemporaries, to tell us why those writers are important enough to be considered integral to the history of human expression. And in my teaching, this principle holds true regardless of the writer I am trying to ventriloquize, whether that writer is a black quasi-feminist conservative Republican like Hurston, a gay Midwestern visionary like Hart Crane, or a devout Catholic Southerner like Flannery O'Connor.

This is a principle that, under ordinary circumstances, would go without saying: of course a responsible teacher is expected to be an "advocate" of various writers and their worldviews, even if only heuristically. But in these troubled times this principle does not, actually, go without saying—which is why most criticism of so-called advocacy in the classroom is so slippery and protean. When I have seen professorial advocacy come under attack in recent years, I have found that critics sometimes define "advocacy" to mean a specific classroom practice or pedagogical theory; sometimes the term refers to individual texts whose mere presence in the classroom is thought to entail unacceptable political ramifications, such as *I, Rigoberta Menchú* or *Their Eyes Were Watching God;* and sometimes the term applies to entire disciplines or subfields. I suggested earlier that if I were a professor of "special education," my job might well depend on whether there continues to be such a thing as special education; likewise, professors in programs of women's studies or African American studies are routinely charged with unscholarly advocacy simply insofar as they advocate the existence—and, on bold days, the growth—of their programs, in a way that no professor of economics would be accused of "advocacy" if he or she advocated the continued existence of departments of economics (or, for that matter, even if he or she advocated the continued dominance of so-called classical free-market models of economics in their field).

For a particularly slippery example of how ordinary scholarship can be refigured as "advocacy," let us turn to a recent *Wall Street Journal* op-ed by Catholic University history professor Jerry Muller, who cautions conservatives to think, before they defund the NEH and the NEA, about how those much-maligned federal agencies may have actually *slowed* the spread of feminism and multiculturalism— "advocacy" movements fostered by radical organizations such as the Ford and Rockefeller foundations. According to Muller, apparently it is acceptable for women's studies programs to study women but not to advance feminist theory (he refers to "*ever more abstruse* varieties of feminist theory," but I submit that there are those who look upon even garden-variety brands of feminist theory as forms of "advocacy," and that Muller may in fact be among them).

> As those who follow these matters know, the two philanthropies most active in supporting the humanities, the Ford Foundation and the Rockefeller Foundation, have for over a decade funneled their considerable largess into promoting multiculturalism, programs in women's studies (the institutional incentives of which have diverted scholarly attention from the laudable aim of the

study of women to the lamentable pursuit of ever more abstruse varieties of feminist theory), and the burgeoning field of lesbian and gay studies. Conservatives must keep these in mind when making policy recommendations regarding the NEH.[6]

I am not sure, given Muller's terms, what I would do if I were in women's studies and the women I were studying were themselves feminists; I surmise from this formulation that it is all right to advocate the study of women so long as the women in question don't sound like Mary Wollstonecraft, Virginia Woolf, or (heaven forbid) Adrienne Rich, who are, of course, advocates of varieties of feminist theory—advocates who attract the most fire from conservatives when they're at their *least* abstruse.

And as I've suggested, matters become thornier yet when "advocacy" is an integral part of one's field. In a recent issue of the *Chronicle of Higher Education,* Stephen Meyer, a professor of political science at the Massachusetts Institute of Technology and a conservation commissioner in Massachusetts, writes in reference to proposed revisions of the Clean Water Act: "Any study that holds the potential to shift policy, redistribute resources, and influence the relative power of advocates and opponents of environmental protection is *fundamentally political.* . . . For scientists to pretend to be above the political fray is to consign science to irrelevance in policy making." Since the study in question, released in May 1995 by the National Academy of Sciences, touched on matters at once scientific and political, and since the House Committee on Transportation and Public Works deliberately rushed the bill to a vote in order to beat the release of the study, Meyer charges scientists with having acting unethically because, as he writes, "the panel of the academy working on the report had refused to discuss its details ahead of the official release, for fear of appearing 'political.'"[7]

Meyer's point, and mine, is that some forms of advocacy are not merely *permitted* but positively *mandated* by certain fields of study. Interestingly, Meyer blames narrow professionalism for this state of affairs: professionalism substituting for public-mindedness, academic scientists overly concerned with "publishing an article in *Science* or *Nature,* or giving presentations at professional conferences."[8] But I would say that the problem with academic scientists who pay no attention to the social ramifications of their work is that they're unprofessional. And what I want to suggest by saying this is that we should rethink what we mean by professionalism when we talk about issues of advocacy and professional responsibility.

In the work of cultural critics influenced by Russell Jacoby, "professionalism" is usually a synonym for mere careerism, an attitude of hermetic self-enclosure that leads academics to think in terms of padding their résumés and accumulating perks rather than advancing the public good.[9] I want to suggest, however, that professionals are supposed to serve clients and that a professional who does not do so is, strictly speaking, unprofessional. In Meyers's example, scientists whose professional domain touches on the disposition of public funds and natural resources have an obligation to serve the public good as they see it—and, I would want to add, that obligation to one's potential clients and constituencies should not be presumed to end at the threshold of the classroom door.

My argument, then, is that we must recognize that there are innumerable disciplines and subfields in which political "advocacy" for one form of social organization or another is an integral part of one's professional protocols. Conversely, there is another sense in which "advocacy" is simply the name for whatever practice seems to *violate* the professional protocols: as Lawrence Levine has pointed out, teachers of evolution were once considered practitioners of political advocacy.[10] Therefore, just as there is a sense in which professors of special education or women's studies are compelled to be advocates, so, too, is there a sense that in astrophysics as practiced in the 1940s and 1950s, advocates of the Big Bang theory were seen as engaged in a form of special pleading that violated the range of reasonable inferences that could be drawn from the available data. As Sidney Hook suggested 25 years ago, then, the question of advocacy is always and everywhere a question of professional legitimation:

> The qualified teacher, whose qualifications may be inferred from his [*sic*] acquisition of tenure, has the right honestly to reach, and hold, and proclaim any conclusion in the field of his competence. In other words, academic freedom carries with it the *right to*

heresy as well as the right to restate and defend the traditional views. This takes in considerable ground. If a teacher in honest pursuit of an inquiry or argument comes to a conclusion that appears fascist or communist or racist or what-not in the eyes of others, once he has been certified as professionally competent in the eyes of his peers, then those who believe in academic freedom must defend his right to be wrong—if they consider him wrong—whatever their orthodoxy may be.[11]

There's much to admire in Hook's formulation, not least of which is the fact that so few academic or nonacademic conservatives would dare to second it today. What's all the more remarkable about it, however, is that Hook used this rationale to defend a young, impolitic Marxist named Eugene Genovese, who had recently made public his support of the Viet Cong—and, as Hook notes, became immediately infamous for doing so: because New Jersey's Democratic governor rightly refused to fire Genovese from Rutgers on the grounds of aiding and abetting the enemy, the Republican gubernatorial candidate "focused his entire campaign on the issue of Genovese's right to teach."[12] I suggest we will wait in vain for the day when Genovese extends a similar professional courtesy to those "politically correct" scholars with whom he disagrees. Nonetheless, Genovese should have learned an important lesson from this episode, and so should we: our task here is not to ask whether "advocacy" constitutes an acceptable classroom practice, of what, for whom, and by whom; rather, our task is to ask each other across the disciplines, from the natural sciences to the human sciences to the professional schools, what kinds of "advocacy" are legitimate—and, in fact, required—by the standards of responsible professional behavior.

NOTES

1. See Hans-Georg Gadamer, *Truth and Method*, 2nd ed., trans. Garrett Barden and John Cumming (New York: Continuum, 1975); Hans-Robert Jauss, *Toward an Aesthetic of Reception*, trans. Timothy Bahti (Minneapolis: University of Minnesota Press, 1982), and *Question and*

Answer: Forms of Dialogic Understanding, trans. Michael Hays (Minneapolis: University of Minnesota Press, 1989).

2. Villa, Stainback, Stainback, and Thousand have been among the most energetic of scholarly advocates for "full inclusion" policies, arguing that separate educational facilities are always unequal and therefore always stigmatizing; see Richard A. Villa, Susan Stainback, William Stainback, and Jacqueline Thousand, (Eds.), *Restructuring for Caring and Effective Education: An Administrative Guide to Creating Heterogeneous Schools* (Brookline, MA: Paul H. Brookes, 1992). Carlberg and Kavale, by contrast, advocate "inclusion" in some cases and not others, on the basis of their review of 50 independent studies of special classrooms, which found that "special classes were . . . significantly inferior to regular class placement for behaviorally disordered, emotionally disturbed and learning disabled children" (Conrad Carlberg and Kenneth Kavale, "The Efficacy of Special Versus Regular Class Placements for Exceptional Children: A Meta-Analysis," *Journal of Special Education* 14 [1980], 295-309, quoted in Douglas Fuchs and Lynn S. Fuchs, "What's 'Special' About Special Education?," *Phi Delta Kappan* [March 1995], 522-30; quote on p. 526). Needless to say, the very categories "behaviorally disordered," "emotionally disturbed," and "learning disabled" are themselves open to contestation, and there's often no clear line between the constituency of such categories and the constituency designated by "below average IQ": the constitution of those categories depends radically on our social and professional construction of them. The difference between Villa et al. and Carlberg and Kavale, in other words, cannot simply be attributed to different "subjective" readings of "objective" data. Nonetheless, the point remains that I could not, as a professor of special education, take any stand whatsoever on this set of issues without "advocating" one form of study—and, consequently, one set of findings, and one form of social organization—over another.

3. Darwin Turner, *In a Minor Chord: Three Afro-American Writers and Their Search for Identity* (Carbondale: Southern Illinois University Press, 1971), 108.

4. Michael Bérubé, *Public Access: Literary Theory and American Cultural Politics* (New York: Verso, 1994), 253-62.

5. Adrienne Rich, "Vesuvius at Home: The Power of Emily Dickinson," in *On Lies, Secrets, and Silence: Selected Prose 1966-78* (New York: Norton, 1979), 157-83. Quote from p. 158.

6. Jerry Z. Muller, "A Conservative Defense of the Humanities Endowment," *Wall Street Journal,* April 12, 1995, A14.

7. Stephen Meyer, "The Role of Scientists in the 'New Politics,'" *Chronicle of Higher Education,* May 26, 1995, B1-B2. Quote from p. B2.

8. Meyer, "Role of Scientists," B2.

9. See Russell Jacoby, *The Last Intellectuals: American Culture in the Age of Academe* (New York: Basic Books, 1987); Carl Boggs, *Intellectuals and the Crisis of Modernity* (Albany: SUNY Press, 1993); Christopher Lasch, *The Revolt of the Elites and the Betrayal of Democracy* (New York: Norton, 1994).

10. Lawrence Levine, "A Historian in Wonderland." Conference on the Role of Advocacy in the Classroom, Pittsburgh, PA, June, 1995. For Levine's more general assessment of "advocacy" in American higher education, see his *The Opening of the American Mind: Canons, Culture, and the Search for National Identity* (Boston, MA: Beacon Press, 1996).

11. Sidney Hook, *Academic Freedom and Academic Anarchy* (New York: Cowles, 1970), 36.

12. Ibid., 42.

SEVENTEEN

Feminism: A Long Memory

CAROLYN G. HEILBRUN

LIKE MOST MARRIAGES, whether they end in divorce or continuing companionship, the marriage between women and the study of literature began as a romance. Women, in love with reading, dreamed of themselves as valued members of a community of literary scholars. James Atlas in a recent book remembered with passion the sense of empowerment he encountered in the depths of Harvard's library, empowerment flowing from the sacred words of Plato through Milton and beyond.[1] Women, too, have felt the romance of that empowerment. I have memories of such fervent encounters, not in Harvard's library, which did not, in my youth, admit women, but in public libraries and those of Wellesley and Columbia. I, too, can wax nostalgic about that early romance. The joyful past, of course, is always remembered with an aura of enchantment and, for women, innocence.

But it has only been in the last 25 years that I and other women have come to understand how one-sided was that romance and the marriage that followed. Maud Bodkin, whose book *Archetypal Patterns in Poetry* was widely studied when I was a graduate student, noted in the 1940s that any gifted woman's "imaginative life has been largely shaped by the thought and adventure of men."[2] We women, roaming the stacks in the days before paperbacks, reserving the assigned books and reading them intensely in the hours they were allotted to us, transposed our adventurous and literary selves into male minds and experiences. If it occurred to us that this was in any way an odd undertaking, we did not allow so outrageous a thought to rise into consciousness. Just as I would eventually discover the difficulty of making graduate students in the late 1970s and '80s grasp the sexual mores of an earlier time, so they could hardly understand that women in my youth, particularly in the terrible 1950s, did not question their allotted roles as readers, students, and assumers of a male persona. We dreamed we might become an equal among equals, hardly daring to wonder how.

Lionel Trilling, at whose feet I all unnoticed sat, could write, with no fear of contradiction, this paragraph about Jane Austen's *Emma*:

> The extraordinary thing about Emma is that she has a moral life as a man has a moral life. Women in fiction only rarely have the peculiar reality of the moral life that self-love bestows. Most commonly they exist in a moon-like way, shining by the reflected moral life of men. . . . They seldom exist as men exist—as genuine moral destinies. . . . Nor can we say that novels are deficient in realism when they present women as they do: it is the presumption of our society that women's moral life is not as men's. No change in the modern theory of the sexes, no advances in the status that women have made, can contradict this. The self-love that we do countenance in women is of a limited and passive kind, and we are troubled if their self-love is as assertive as man's is permitted and expected to be. Not men alone, but women as well insist on this limitation. . . .[3]

Trilling published that in 1957, nor was he wholly inaccurate for the time; thus had we been taught, in graduate school, to see ourselves. By 1976, when Ellen Moers would remark upon "the disgrace of that paragraph," she would imply also the disgrace of women's earlier collusion in the belief that we did not exist as genuine moral destinies.[4] That was the change feminism brought about in the classroom. In 1951 when, still in the romantic mode, I earned my

M.A. at Columbia, Trilling published *The Liberal Imagination*. In the preface to that collection of essays, he wrote the following sentences, amazing to us today: "In the United States at this time liberalism is not only the dominant but even the sole intellectual tradition. For it is the plain fact that nowadays there are no conservative or reactionary ideas in general circulation." He added that "this does not mean, of course, that there is no impulse to conservatism or to reaction. Such impulses are certainly very strong, perhaps even stronger than some of us know."[5] But, he assures us, these conservative and reactionary impulses "do not express themselves in ideas but only in action or in irritable mental gestures which seek to resemble ideas." He warned us that when a movement is bankrupt of ideas, we are terribly mistaken to assume it is at the end of its powers. He then refers us to the history of the last quarter of a century in Europe. It is important to notice that while Trilling did not recognize his own ideas about women as conservative or reactionary, he understood very well the danger in which what he most treasured, the liberal imagination, stood. It is ironic, indeed almost comic, that the single movement—the Women's Movement—that first and most emphatically brought about the battle regarding advocacy in the classroom was the one movement he failed to recognize as "liberal."

To us women, back in those days of Trilling-like heroes in the academy, the revelation that we, too, were entitled to self-love, that we, too, had moral destinies, and that, as students of literature, we could read, in texts and subtexts by men and women, accounts of that female moral destiny came upon us like a heavenly gift. It was only later, perhaps a decade later, that the realization that the masterpieces of Western culture are not the only, let alone the most consequential, literary accomplishments in the world became palpable. Many feminists joined in that so-called multicultural campaign, but academic feminism in the United States was itself less concerned with reading different non-European texts than with finding new questions to ask of those texts we had read, with the passion James Atlas describes, in the libraries that let us in. For myself, I am unalterably Euro-centered, even English language–centered, and while I welcome into my field of knowledge works from other cultures, my life, my past, my present destiny, rests in the great works from Plato to today that I have read and loved and pondered over in English. My job as a feminist—speaking only for myself—is to read the ancient and modern authors of the Western world, including, of course, women authors, and to ask new questions of them.

For what are we feminists advocating in the classroom? That we, too, may claim there a moral destiny and the right to discuss the implications of that destiny in the classroom. Why is that so frightening a demand to those like James Atlas who ask only to preserve the glories they remember from their student days? Is it feared that in asking questions of these great texts, we will somehow harm them? Literature is the most innocent of studies, for, unless censorship prevails, the text remains, ultimately unchanged by our interpretations, our questions, our theories. As to the argument that the major texts are being pushed aside by intruders hitherto unknown to the canon, my answer to that fear is twofold: first, that the canon, as an extensive Modern Language Association study recently demonstrated, is still what is mainly taught in college literature courses in the United States[6]; second, that every body of literature requires the intrusion of new ideas and new texts. The English language is the richest in the world, we might recall, because, unlike, for example, the French, it has always welcomed into its vocabulary words from other languages expressing nuances hitherto not present in English. A study of the *Oxford Dictionary of the English Language* offers the amazing number of words used for the first time by Shakespeare, a great incorporator of hitherto alien expressions.

We believe that the academy, like the English language, can only be enriched by the new expressions and new vantage points that feminism can bring. We feminists wish to claim full citizenship in the academy, a citizenship that will allow us to study what has been written by women in the past, and to live a life that is written and that continues to be written. We wish, moreover, to assert the privilege of expressing what we know and question those who, like Trilling, presume to know with certainty what limitations for themselves women are supposed to insist upon.

The aim of feminism in the academy, as I understand it, is that women's point of view, women's sense of entitlement to a place in the cultural heritage, be understood and sympathetically included in the teachings of professors, men as well as women. Those men in the academy who observe with discomfort the teachings and writings of open-minded, feminist men may marvel, with Hamlet, that such a man could, in a fiction, in a dream of passion, suit his whole function to this liberal conceit. "And all for nothing," Hamlet cries, "for Hecuba. What's Hecuba to him or he to Hecuba / That he should weep for her?"[7] Alas, those who want to ban feminist advocacy from the classroom believe, with Hamlet, that only they, in their masculine hearts, have "the motive and the cue for passion."

We women who, like men, encountered Shakespeare and Milton and the Greeks (in translation) with all the fervency of youth, we, also, have our motives and our cues for passion, even as we find in the very works men cherish questions too long unasked, of Penelope, Antigone, Andromache, Iphigenia. We need to remember that when Wayne Booth years ago recognized the insult to women in some of Rabelais's jokes and mockeries, he did not suggest that we do not read Rabelais, but rather that we allow those injured and insulted to challenge the text and that we read not only Rabelais but works by women as well, works that question the ideological assumptions underlying our social thought and practice.[8]

We need to know, as Euripides understood, what Hecuba is to us and we to Hecuba. And so, when with perhaps the longest memory of volume contributors, I recall the passion of reading literature in libraries all those years ago, I bring to mind words written a century and a half ago by the young Margaret Fuller, a woman unmentioned in my college and graduate classes, whose name I scarcely knew and whose agony I could not then have recognized as my own:

> I felt within myself great power, and generosity, and tenderness; but it seemed to me as if they were all unrecognized, and as if it was impossible that they should be used in life. I was only one-and-twenty; the past was worthless, the future hopeless, yet

I could not remember ever voluntarily to have done a wrong thing, and my aspiration seemed very high.[9]

My hope is that eventually feminism will need to advocate nothing special because the passions of women like Margaret Fuller, and all the young women whose frustrations she has named for them, will find themselves and their questions of the texts they read naturally and continually present in all the classrooms of the academic community.

NOTES

1. James Atlas, *Battle of the Books: The Curriculum Debate in America* (New York: W. W. Norton, 1992).

2. Maud Bodkin, *Archetypal Patterns in Poetry* (London: Oxford University Press, 1948), 300.

3. Lionel Trilling, *Introduction to* Emma, Riverside Edition (1957). Quoted in Ellen Moers, *Literary Women* (Garden City, NY: Doubleday, 1976), 157-58.

4. Moers, *Literary Women,* 158.

5. Lionel Trilling, *The Liberal Imagination* (New York: Viking, 1951), ix-x.

6. Bettina Huber, "Today's Literature Classroom: Findings from the MLA's 1990 Survey of Upper-Division Courses," *ADE Bulletin,* no. 101 (Spring 1992), 52.

7. William Shakespeare, *Hamlet,* Act II, Scene 2, line 559.

8. Wayne Booth, "Bakhtin and the Challenge of Feminist Criticism," *Critical Inquiry* (September 1982).

9. Margaret Fuller, *Memoirs of Margaret Fuller Ossoli,* Vol. 1, eds. James Freeman Clark, Ralph Waldo Emerson, and William Henry Channing (Boston, MA: Phillips, Sampson, 1852), 139.

EIGHTEEN

Unveiling the Myth of Neutrality: Advocacy in the Feminist Classroom

---

HELENE MOGLEN

I WAS INVITED to write a chapter as a feminist literary critic on the subject of advocacy in the classroom. For most readers, the link between feminism and advocacy will speak for itself: to be a feminist (literary or not) is to support and practice classroom advocacy. For those on the Right who have initiated and sustained the political correctness debates, a further deduction will appear appropriate: to be a feminist advocate is to participate in the politicization of the university by fomenting identity politics, subverting traditional canons, and preaching a form of dogmatism that undermines students' personal, familial, and social values. Perceived as a threat to free speech, advocacy is rejected by this group as antidemocratic. Those on the Left who have accepted the terms delivered to them by the Right have defended advocacy strongly—often on the grounds that intellectual neutrality is obviously a myth and that pedagogical partisanship is dangerous not when practiced in the open but in its pernicious invisibility. While I agree with this position, I think that it surrenders too much ground. In my judgment, progressives should refuse altogether the false and harmful dichotomy between advocacy and responsible teaching and should demonstrate how the two, while inevitably existing in some tension, are also crucially and productively interdependent. My point is that teachers, *as* advocates, are responsible for modeling the difficult skills of advocacy for their students, enabling them to express their own commitments and to evaluate the competing advocacies of others. To advocate as a teacher and to enable advocacy are not, of course, the same activities, and there is often a disconcerting strain between the two. Further, to teach advocacy when one does not oneself embody it is to project a hollow image that students will recognize as cynicism, incompetence, or cowardice. These are the tensions that we, as teachers, need to acknowledge and struggle to make productive.

Feminist advocacy in literary studies provides a particularly rich and complex example of advocacy's possibilities and pitfalls, and I would like to begin by exploring some of the ways in which it has developed over the last decades. Certainly—whoever the feminists and whatever the forms of feminist criticism they practice—it seems self-evident that to be a feminist in the academy is inevitably to be an advocate: an advocate for women. It is also to be an advocate for women-centered knowledges that are capable of interrogating masculine perspectives and male-authored texts that have traditionally been centered within humanistic and social science disciplines. The compensatory movement that emerged within literature in the 1970s represented a reaction against the interpretive assumptions and curricular suppressions of an academic establishment that had long been white, middle-class, and male. The collective project of that generation—my generation—was to redefine the canon by adding to it excluded women's texts, to conceptualize traditions of women writers where none had been conceptualized before, to center women in our readings, and to problematize the gender relations of writers, readers, and characters. In those years, feminism was rooted in the material cultures of women and was unabashedly committed to institutional and social change. The theories that we phrased were shaped experientially by the emotionally charged but still analytic practices of consciousness-raising. Identity politics suffused and integrated personal, professional, and pedagogical relations, even as those identities multiplied, challenging each other—not least of all, in classrooms—as they competed for primacy. And while many of us subsequently came to see identity politics as part of a transitional, if necessary, phase in an increasingly complex intellectual, academic, and social movement, the value of that transitional moment for ourselves, our students, and our institutions seemed and still seems incontrovertible. Affirmative action hiring practices—from which I and most women of my generation benefited—brought women into the university, at all levels, in unprecedented numbers. With members of other marginal groups, we participated in an affirmative action movement of the mind that centered texts, perspectives, and experiences that permanently changed the discipline of literature.

Of course, even this first compensatory moment of academic feminism was an evolving rather than a static phenomenon. In literature departments, courses first emerged in "women's writing" (the writing, as it usually turned out, of middle-class white women); classes in the literatures of black women, lesbians, Asian and Mexican American women followed—all mapping new areas of the curricular terrain while designating, implicitly, the groups that would be primary and those that were peripheral. The general tone was celebratory and militant, and advocacy was unabashed. The power relations of the traditional classroom, while replicated, were increasingly reversed: members of habitually dominant groups became marginalized, and many who had previously experienced themselves as peripheral now felt that they were authorized to speak. Because they emphasized the significance of material culture and the integrity of experience, many teachers shared authority with students, attempting to enable more collaborative environments. Of course, as the power dynamic within the classroom shifted, some of the newly marginal felt aggrieved, while others profited from the explicit questioning of their assumed entitlement. Similarly, some teachers who had been accustomed to authority were discomforted, while others were exhilarated by the innovations made possible by the change. An important but limiting aspect of this initial phase was, and still remains, its separatisms: its refusal—at intellectual, institutional, and pedagogical levels—of interactive engagement with multiple and conflictual forms of difference.

Partially as a response to this refusal, identity politics was increasingly open to internal critique, even as the compensatory project that depended on it continued to vitalize curriculum and scholarship. It was seen that to make oppositional the essentialized categories "male" and "female" was merely to reverse while reproducing the hierarchicalized binary against which feminism had defined itself. Further, the category of "women"—which had initially been the cornerstone of feminism—fractured and split under the pressure of historical, socioeconomic, sexual, and national differences, at the same time that the relational dynamic which that category had created dissolved in the changing perceptions of margin and center. Many feminists grounded in literature (as well as in other humanistic and interpretive social science disciplines) looked to poststructuralist and psychoanalytic theory to help them move beyond the separatist, empiricist, and essentialist modes of analysis that were increasingly associated with women's studies. Constructed as a naive sister (or, perhaps, a wife) of theoretical feminism, women's studies was assigned responsibility for the basic emotional and intellectual upkeep of students as well as for pedagogical experimentation. It was a division of labor that freed many feminist theorists for another revisionary project: the interrogation and appropriation of the powerful male-authored paradigms that have come to dominate critical and cultural theory. Often drawing on social history to ground the analyses of ideology, and diverse theories of discourse, representation, and subjectivity, these scholars significantly helped to shape current theoretical debates at the same time that they tended to surrender political activism and local institutional loyalties to the enhancement of professional careers.

As critical, cultural, and psychoanalytic theory came to provide the catalytic impulse for feminist literary criticism in the 1980s and '90s, the relevance of personal experience was shunted aside—in the classroom as in scholarship. Feminist theorists wrote for other theorists, seeking to modify the intellectual rather than the social landscape. And while the move to poststructuralist and psychoanalytic theory did express an urge to expand and usefully complicate the terms of feminist analysis, the conceptual abstractions and linguistic jargon that it produced tended to mystify experience and to depoliticize its analysis. It also depoliticized the classroom, ironically reinstating many of the pedagogical, epistemological, and social hierarchies that feminism had vehemently protested. The teacher was the one who "knew," and her authority could be contested only with difficulty. It is not uncommon now for feminist critical theory to be seen as another sexy discourse that aspiring literary scholars would be well advised to master but toward which they need not, and often do not, feel any real commitment. Feminism has not only helped to construct—and been constructed by—a range of discourses about culture, sexuality, and gender; it has also increasingly been subordinated to them. As the category "woman" vaporizes and disappears, the sense of women's materiality is also threatened with erasure. For this reason, the problem in many feminist classrooms is not too much but too little advocacy on behalf of embodied women who occupy real worlds in which discrimination, injustice, and inequality remain, at all levels, hard facts of daily life. In the feminist classroom, where the assumption shared by faculty and students is that gender is socioculturally constructed under conditions that are historically specific, the feminist project should be to analyze collaboratively the material and symbolic terms of those constructions in ways that will enable advocacy for a society that is more equitable and just.

As I have tried to suggest in this brief and admittedly subjective history, many forms of feminism and many forms of feminist advocacy have emerged in the academy over the last 30 years, and their varied and frequently conflicting practices have been influential in many different ways. In my field, there is scarcely a literature course that has not been overtly or covertly influenced by feminism and other contemporary, compensatory movements that are identified with specific constituencies. The fact is that, however course descriptions in current catalogs might resemble those in university catalogs of the past, the study of literature has been decisively changed by the addition of texts and cultural traditions that had previously been ignored. It has been changed as well by the awareness—however mocked, resisted, and reduced—that identity categories and power relations are relevant to textual analysis and that textual analysis is relevant to the ways in which we conceptualize and live our lives. Literature students (whether on the Left or on the Right) have come in recent years to understand that there are real social, personal, and political stakes involved in the choice of curricular materials and reading strategies, and many believe, as I do, that self-conscious reading helps to enable personal and social change.

It is this prevalent and quite radical shift in consciousness that has brought the issue of classroom advocacy to the surface, establishing a visible and, for some, a disturbing connection between the classroom presumed to be political—the women's studies classroom, for example—and the classroom of traditional humanistic study, which presented itself in the past as politically neutral. The Left has emphasized the incontrovertible nature of that connection while the Right has categorically rejected it. What has been lost in the melee is the fact that the crucial distinction that needs to be made is not one between a politically neutral classroom and the classroom that is political, but rather one between classrooms that are political and those that are politicized. In politicized classrooms, teachers deploy their institutional authority in order to impose their own intellectual agendas on students whom they perceive to be passive and incapable of intellectual reciprocity. This is a practice of advocacy that turns readily into an effort of indoctrination. In the political classroom, teachers self-consciously play the advocate role while encouraging students to advocate thoughtfully for themselves. This does not mean that the two pedagogical approaches can always be maintained as separate. However we might fear and even loathe indoctrination, institutionalized relations of power make it difficult for us to avoid politicization altogether. The tension, while troubling, can also be productive—forcing us continually to assess and modify our teaching practices. Most of us who are committed to the political classroom recognize the responsibility we have to help our students to become effective advocates by modeling for them skills of advocacy—which can also be the skills of attentive, respectful, and self-reflective reading. It is in this spirit that, at the beginning of every literature class I teach—of whatever size, with whatever emphasis, and at whatever level—I start by explaining to my students how I define myself as a reader, and I urge them to define themselves, as well: the social, intellectual, moral, and political (as well as aesthetic) presuppositions that we bring to texts; the systems of belief that inform our thought; the theoretical assumptions and methodological strategies that guide our interpretations; the ways in which we seek to have our opinions reinforced; whether and where we are open to influence and change. I see all classrooms as sites of advocacy (as many forms of advocacy, potentially, as there are students) and of contesting advocacies, as well.

Perspective is inescapable in human vision after all: physical bodies are always situated somewhere. We read and write out of who we are and whom we wish also to become. We read and write out of our own personal and intellectual histories, and in the context of our social and cultural positionings. It is necessary for us, as self-conscious readers, to be mindful of those positionings: to understand the ways in which we represent them and the ways in which they represent themselves through us. Classrooms offer us—both teachers and students—spaces in which we can articulate and test our values, summoning evidence to support our views even as we learn alternative ways in which our evidence can be read. Classrooms offer us opportunities to project ourselves into the intellectual and experiential situations of our colleagues and our texts so that we can comprehend the ways in which their perspectives have been formed and reinforced. These projective strategies, which are so central to the act of literary interpretation, are crucial to acts of informed advocacy, as well.

To acknowledge a multiplicity of values and perspectives is not to embrace nihilistic relativism; it is to honor the intellectual and personal struggles through which commitment is achieved. To speak for advocacy is not to endorse indoctrination but to foster communication. To teach the skills of advocacy—difficult skills to teach and learn—is not to hinder but to promote free speech. Heterogeneity is the condition rather than the enemy of our democracy. Because of our investments in the outcome of those struggles, we have an obligation to speak—and to help our students to speak—as knowledgeably and articulately as we can on behalf of commitments that are deeply rooted in our personal and cultural experiences. In the openly political, as distinguished from the politicized, classroom, students are prepared for the practice of democracy by learning how, respectfully, to disagree. It is not surprising to me—although it may be surprising to others—that the explicitly feminist classroom is the most contentious of the classrooms in which I teach. There, women who have found their voices use them not to reify some mythical shared identity but to question everything from the instructor's ideologies, to her curricular choices, to her pedagogical style: everything from one another's interpretive assumptions to their projected goals. Neutral? Of course not. Unanimous? Never. Pleasant? Not always. Committed, self-reflective, serious, articulate? You bet!

The real threat to democracy in the classroom is posed today by the right-wing insistence that advocacy is opposed to responsible teaching and that the self-reflective articulation of personal experience and belief are somehow opposed to freedom of speech. These oppositions, once constructed, then deploy an ideology of neutrality to silence advocacies and block communication under the guise of consensual agreement. Although many of us recognized that the stakes in the political correctness debates were high, few of us could have anticipated how devastating the costs would be. As usual, it is the poor, the marginal, the vulnerable, once-again alien others who will be forced to pay the price. Rampant anti-intellectualism has been armed in the domestic war fought now against education, against the humanities, against the arts, even against students themselves. The effort, one feels, is to make the university a mirror image of the culture's urge to agnosis: the terrifying desire not to know. Indeed, those who condemn advocacy and diversity are precisely the ones who refuse to know the experiences, the needs, the longings, and the deprivations of those who have been excluded in the past from the illusory consensus that has often been cynically projected. Some will find it ironic that as I survey the implications of the current scene, the words that I, a left-wing, feminist literary critic, find most applicable, are the tragic lines with which Alexander Pope, a conservative misogynist, concluded *The Dunciad,* a powerful indictment of the hazardous and deepening anti-intellectualism of his time:

> Thy Hand, great Anarch! lets the curtain fall;
> And Universal Darkness buries All.

The hand that threatens to bring down this curtain of darkness is indeed the hand of agnosis—the hand of those who fear to know the multiple and conflicting realities of our complex society. If we are to resist this tide of anti-intellectualism, we must, I believe, insist upon a difficult truth that is rooted, for most of us, in our years of practical experience in the classroom: to be good teachers—which is to say, to enable students to become informed and articulate advocates for themselves—is not incompatible with our own acts of advocacy. The two are, in truth, indispensable to one another, although they are always in some tension; to abandon either is to lose them both. And a democratic society can simply not afford this loss.

NOTE

I am grateful to Wendy Brown for the lively discussions and quite vehement disagreements we had about issues related to this topic. I am grateful also to Lynda Marin and Pamela Karlan for their careful readings of the chapter and—as always and particularly—to Seth Moglen for his insightful comments, provocative questions, and generous support.

NINETEEN

Academic Skepticism and the Contexts of Belief

C. JAN SWEARINGEN

MY THESIS IS SIMPLE, but expressed in deliberately unfamiliar language, for which I ask your patience and invite your tolerance. I propose that it is impossible to understand the impetus behind the American civil rights movement, behind Gandhi's leadership in India, behind Paolo Freire's liberatory pedagogy of the oppressed, behind Frederick Douglass's oratory—indeed, behind the phenomenon of the subaltern who wishes to speak and whose voice always renews the academy—without understanding the deeply spiritual and religious values and beliefs that have led and inspired so many subalterns. However, since the Enlightenment, the belief system of the academy has eschewed the languages of belief and the phenomenology of the spiritual, much to its own disadvantage. The result: an erosion in the ability of the academy to speak to political, cultural, and even academic constituencies increasingly defensive about mandatory multiculturalism, doctrinaire cultural relativism, and what they regard, rightly or wrongly, as secular humanism hostile to religion and spiritual values.

Growing discord surrounds the cultural, ethical, and epistemological values assigned to programmatic skepticism, adversarial argumentation, and deconstructive hermeneutics as methods for reading and discussing texts. Yet the very tradition that produced these methods carries within it its own dialectical antidotes. The dispute is as old as Plato's defense of Socrates' dialectic as an analytic method designed to test and perfect true belief. It is taken up again by Cicero, who quipped that although the Stoic philosophers are very good at dissecting arguments, they provide no tools for the construction of proofs and arguments. The Stoic academicians, Cicero charged, propound a purely negative dialectic. They can state what is not but not what is or what should be. Like many of today's doctrinaire theoreticians, the Stoics were ethical and epistemological minimalists. Augustine found the teachers and teaching of literature and rhetoric in his time so repugnant in their celebrations of obscenity and amorality that he resigned from the teaching profession when he converted to Christianity. Introducing the *Metalogicon,* a defense of the study of grammar, rhetoric, and logic in the twelfth century, John of Salisbury writes, "I have purposefully incorporated into this treatise some observations concerning morals, since I am convinced that all things read or written are useless except insofar as they have a good influence on one's manner of life."[1] The nineteenth-century philosopher Søren Kierkegaard chastised his fellow Danes for practicing "mere Christianity": a smug, hypocritical businessman's comfort that bore little relationship to the social reforms that were the goals of the earliest Christians.[2] His diverse range of literary and philosophical works challenged both the academy and the churches of his day to revive and teach the ability to feel, to restore the ability to be affected by human suffering, and to address the human—all too human— failings that they professed to care about.

Once again we find ourselves in what Stephen Carter has termed a "culture of disbelief."[3] A hermeneutics of suspicion dominates academic models of textual analysis and interpretation. Reading is directed at unmasking and dismantling hidden and illusory meanings; the best, as Yeats observed in "The Second Coming" in a similar period, seem to lack all conviction.[4] In the current academic climate of programmatic doubt, the relationship between the life of the mind and the resources of belief, values, and convictions receives little attention or affirmation. How can we, or should we, reform the current academic methods, pedagogies, and scholarly goals that focus so relentlessly on skepticism and debate? As writers and readers, as teachers of writing and ways of reading, how should we expand the repertoire of analytic methods and practices that we employ? How can we reintegrate the valuable rigors of the life of the mind with the ability to read with the eyes of faith, such as those of Fiorenza, Frymer-Kensky, and Trible, and not solely with an unquestioning faith in disbelief?[5]

Gerald Graff and others defend "the culture wars" as edifying strife and propound "teaching the conflicts."[6] Others, such as Thurow and Torgovnick, ask whether recent critical theories—the hermeneutics of suspicion, deconstruction, and postmodernism— mean that the discovery and articulation of truth and meaning is no longer a valid aim of interpretation.[7] Should criticism and interpretation be devoted exclusively to questioning all bases of judgment, with that analysis the final product of academic inquiry? Have we accepted a hermeneutics guided solely by suspicion of discovered or constructed meaning? To these reigning canons of abstract, analytic thought challenges have been advanced by critics from unexpectedly different camps. Feminist language scholars, some postmodern theorists, and proponents of multicultural curricula have converged on one point. For very different reasons, they warn that outside of carefully defined goals, such as criticism directed at understanding, and the reasoned examination of belief, the practices of skepticism, debate, and negative dialectic as they are conducted today can lead scholars and students alike to become "expressionless, pitiless, unteachable . . . incapable of belief."[8] Others ask whether in an increasingly multicultural academic environment, the goals and tacit traditions of argumentation, dialectic, and criticism are simply too narrowly European to be sustained as models for thought and language in a global intellectual culture.

As it recurrently has in the past, academia today responds to the demands of new multicultural student demographics and shifting canons. We expand and realign our repertoire, and diversify our models of thought, identity, ways of thinking, knowing, interpreting, meaning, and writing.[9] Jerome Bruner proposes that our global cultural context once again reminds us—as it did in the heyday of Buckminster Fuller and Marshall McLuhan's global village—that the

Western-educated self is only one among many possible "canonical images of selfhood" within as well as outside of the academy.[10] Individualist models of self and voice contrast sharply with collective phenomenologies of speech and knowing. Individuals accustomed to learning and acquiring knowledge in groups implicitly understand—indeed believe in—the individual's voice as willingly and consciously partaking of collective consciousness and as drawing on the shared common beliefs of a people. Where Socrates' axiom "know thyself" came to mean "separate yourself from the Other,"[11] Epictetus understood the same enjoinder in an irreducibly collective sense: "Bid a singer in the Chorus 'know thyself' and will he not turn for knowledge to the others, his fellows in the chorus, and to his harmony with them?"[12]

Despite its reputation for spawning culture wars, the current multicultural academic setting is proving particularly hospitable to dialogue and dialogical hermeneutics, ways of knowing and ways of learning in the academy that have long provided alternatives and complements to skepticism, analytic dialectic, adversarial debate, and doctrines of linguistic contingency.[13] Truth-building, knowledge-constructing modes of discourse have always informed academic models; they provide ample illustrations that faith need not, indeed should not, be regarded reductively, as an enemy of reason.[14] Reading with the eyes of faith is an activity that secular Romantic aesthetics borrowed from Protestant hermeneutics in the late eighteenth century. Contemporary advocates of the ability to read *with,* and *as,* such as Elbow, promote a believing game that is firmly grounded in Romantic literary aesthetics:[15] Reading directed at understanding and interpretation requires a willing suspension of disbelief, an edifying suspension of skepticism. Dialogue, thus understood, has long functioned as a classroom paradigm without diminishing or impeding the complementary merits of skepticism and analysis. The current climate of conflict within academia makes the task of rehabilitating dialogue, and the belief in understanding that it implies, particularly urgent.

Academic theorists have become dogmatically anarchic in their practices of skepticism. Too often they appear as theatrical exponents of warring theoretical and political orthodoxies locked in ideological debates with each other and with the culture at large.[16] We need not, however, overcorrect the intellectual and public image problems created by warring theorists by retreating to timidity and practicing deliberately "weak prophecy"[17] simply to avoid dogmatism. Instead, I propose that a dialectical understanding of the relationship between committed belief and dialogue, on the one hand, and the discourses of analysis and debate, on the other, is badly in need of rehabilitation. Academia's models can and should be reshaped as less hostile to the worlds of belief, conviction, and reasoned action where most people spend most of their time.

Where in our academic tradition is there room for both forging and discovering the common beliefs on which goals, such as mutuality and creative interaction, can be pursued? I hope we can begin to ask this question without apology. What does it mean to read with the eyes of faith—in this sense—in academia, and what can academia teach the eyes of faith? It is encouraging to see questions raised concerning defenses of teaching difference and conflict, defenses that have perhaps once too often seemed to conflate culture with particular theories of culture, confused the political with partisan, and failed to distinguish between teaching students theories and teaching them to theorize with specific purposes.[18] Liberal arts humanism and a civic-minded academia often have manifested a certain tension between the roles of paragon and gadfly, between the aspirations to teach creativity and original-ity and the responsibility to define standards of taste and cultural value.[19] Similarly, academia and culture alike have tolerated a commendable range of styles and goals among writers, artists, and critics, some of whom define themselves as makers and readers of literary art and others who define themselves as exponents of political agendas. I advocate a continuation of the practice of encouraging the study and production of literary and critical writing that directly addresses social issues as well as that which does not.

A larger, dialectical understanding of the relationships among the different modes and purposes of academic discourse can be resuscitated to help redefine such oppositions, to sustain a double vision[20] of their nature and value that can guard against the formation of the doctrinaire master narratives propounded by fundamentalist theories and theorists.[21] But a new, improved, dialectical understanding should also define constraints on unlimited, unguided self-questioning and on the ethical and political quietism that tends to result. An eminent exponent of just such an expanded larger dialectic, and one not at all unfamiliar with the question of the relationship of the life of the mind to the life of faith, was Søren Kierkegaard.

Always professor-advocate, Kierkegaard is vividly didactic; in a number of confessional modes he repeatedly asserts that "the concept" must, and seeks to, take form in "the phenomenon." According to Kierkegaard's model of indwelling, "the concept," for better or worse, will like a heat-seeking missile find life and affect it. Hence, the warning: beware what you theorize and what you advocate, for it *will* find its home in you. He applies this proviso to academic and nonacademic methods of inquiry alike. The use of confessional and polemic images and characters in Kierkegaard's work both requires and models a participatory hermeneutic.[22] Not only is the reader in the text; the reader completes the text and is measured by the form of the completion. It takes only a small leap of interpretive faith to see parallels between the academic and cultural environment of Kierkegaard's day and that of our own. In a double rebuke of the academy and the religion of his day, he assigns to them joint responsibility for a cultural malaise that found its most graphic expressions in limp but doctrinaire practices of religion and in philosophical methods and movements bent on undermining conviction.

We can recover from many earlier cultural periods like Kierkegaard's models of reading, interpretation, and discussion that rehabilitate belief and faith-sustaining aspects of knowledge, learning, and classrooms and thereby temper overly psychologized, skepticism-based notions of writing and textual interpretation as fragmentary, eternally incomplete, merely personal, and exclusively therapeutic. Belief-oriented intellectual practices can and should be employed to enhance the ability to comprehend diversity as a unity. Even dispassionate analysis, Kierkegaard and for that matter Plato long ago taught, is always directed by interests and purposes, passions and beliefs however well masked these may be by rationalizations and self-denial. Kierkegaard's deliberately personal forms of philosophizing were designed to provide instructive, edifying examples of philosophy as comprising multiple genres and fostering tolerance for many varieties of self while still retaining a common language and common goals. The belief popular today—that objectivity is impossible and even undesirable—may be advanced in either a gleeful or a deeply human spirit. In either case, the defense is guided by beliefs: that we should look for division or for commonality. Why not, along with the diverse and multicultural group of Greek thinkers who originated so much of our intellectual equipment, look for the harmonic dialectic that yokes permanence and change, sameness and difference, the One and the Many, self and Other?

Julia Kristeva's recent thought is an attempt to rehabilitate Kant's dialectical alternatives of pure practical reason and idealized utopia while still giving full emphasis to more recent psychological understandings of the paranoid projections that blind us to the element of strangeness in ourselves and locate such strangeness in the feared and hated other.[23] From the Greek and Roman Stoics to the late metapsychological Freud there has existed a tradition that has striven to reconcile this harsh knowledge of individual pathology with a sense of how it might be transformed into a source of renewed self-knowledge and tolerant regard for the variety of human values, beliefs, and social organizations.[24] What might be involved in such an undertaking, Kristeva suggests, is extending the notion of foreigner internally, to the right of respecting our own foreignness and thereby redefining the nature of privacy that ensures freedom in democracies. The many warring strangers and feared foreigners within agree to be One under democratic canons of contract and covenant. But this cannot be achieved, she warns, if we continue to fetishize difference as a *ne plus ultra* of radical theory, a term whose indiscriminate usage very often brings it close to the active false logic of persecution mania and a rhetoric of cultural apartheid.[25]

It is a welcome wonder that Kristeva, like Edward Said, Henry Louis Gates, Ashis Nandy, and other reappraisers of poststructural thought, has undergone a sharp conversion from alterity-driven theory as she confronts the testimony of recent events—Yugoslavia, Palestine, Hindu-Muslim strife in India alongside the looser and looser canons of our academic debates. These events demonstrate with chilling regularity the peril—the potential for human catastrophe—in the slide from an ethic of shared humanity across cultural differences to a notion of "otherness" that all too easily translates into the rampant xenophobia exemplified in hate speech. The concept— Kierkegaard notes—*will* find an embodiment in life. In recent comments on the revised edition of *Orientalism,* Said has asserted the need for recuperating a notion of universal human values, an adaptation of enlightenment utopianism; like Kristeva's proposed brakes on fetishizing alterity, this alone can balance recent excesses in theorizing difference.[26] Said proposes that the principle of cultural relativism is acceptable only to the extent that it accepts the universalism of some core values of humankind. Along similar lines, Nandy argues that diversity-driven anthropologism is no cure for ethnocentrism; it merely pluralizes it. Absolute relativism can become absolute justification of oppression in the name of ethnic tolerance, as it becomes in the ostensibly and often fastidiously apolitical anthropologist's field report.[27] The currently popular theoretical refusal to accept history and one's part in its legacy is a refusal to chain the future deterministically to the past. But it is also a refusal that marks a hyperindividualist attitude to human potentialities, an alternative form of utopianism that has survived until now as a language alien to and subversive of every theory that in the name of liberation circumscribes and makes predictable the spirit of human rebelliousness.[28] Post-Renaissance, Cartesian preoccupations with clean divisions and oppositions, such as aggressor and victim, victor and defeated, master and slave, are part of a central dichotomy between subject and object that Nandy styles "the central cancer of all Western psychology."[29] According to this reasoning, the languages of recent theory—"dismantle, oppose, subvert"—far from being reformist, are languages of binarist resistance and opposition that only extend traditional skeptical and analytic modes of academic thought. Taken into the political arena, Said suggests, nationalism is the philosophy of differential identity made into a collectively organized passion. Similarly, Kristeva's position now amounts to a point-for-point rebuttal of the entire poststructuralist *doxa* on Enlightenment and its supposed evil legacy.[30] The Nazis, she writes, did not lose their humanity because of the "abstraction" that may have existed in the notion of "man." Rather, they replaced the lofty, symbolic notion of shared humanity with a local, national, and ideological membership that was considered superior to the lesser Others. Her line of argument directly opposes the genealogy established in recent postmodern doctrine that traces a direct line of descent from the tenets and terms of Enlightenment rationality. It is not the assertion of universal values of humankind that leads to Satanizing the Other but rather the localizing of alterity-driven thinking. Saying "I can know myself, and only myself, and not very well at that" may seem a timid form of skepticism. In the political world—these recent appraisals suggest—such skepticism leads all too easily to genocide. We should examine alterity-driven identity politics in the academy along similar lines. Finding reasons to believe in recuperated and redefined universals of the human life and spirit could be one of the most important tasks the academy has set for itself in several decades.

NOTES

1. John of Salisbury, *Metalogicon,* trans. Daniel D. McGarry (Gloucester, MA: Peter Smith, 1971), 6.
2. Søren Kierkegaard, *The Concept of Irony, With Constant Reference to Socrates* (New York: Harper & Row, 1966).
3. Stephen L. Carter, *The Culture of Disbelief* (New York: Basic Books, 1992).
4. William Butler Yeats, *Selected Poems and Three Plays,* ed. M. L. Rosenthal (New York: Macmillan, 1986).
5. Elisabeth Schussler Fiorenza, *But She Said; Feminist Practices of Biblical Interpretation* (Boston, MA: Beacon Press, 1992); Tikva Frymer-Kensky, *In the Wake of the Goddesses. Women, Culture, and the Biblical Transformation of Pagan Myth* (New York: Free Press, 1992); Phyllis Trible, *God and the Rhetoric of Sexuality* (Philadelphia, PA: Fortress Press, 1978).
6. Gerald Graff, *Beyond the Culture Wars: How Teaching the Conflicts Can Revitalize American Education* (New York: Norton, 1990).

7. Sarah Baumgartner Thurow, "Illusory Compromise." Review of Gerald Graff, *Beyond the Culture Wars: How Teaching the Conflicts Can Revitalize American Education* in *First Things* (1993), 50-52; Marianna Torgovnick, "Hartman's Dilemma: *Minor Prophecies: The Literary Essay in the Culture Wars,* by Geoffrey H. Hartman," *ADE Bulletin,* no. 104 (Spring 1993).

8. Christa Wolf, *Cassandra,* trans. Jean Van Huerck (New York: Farrar Strauss Giroux, 1984), 136.

9. Henry Louis Gates, "Beyond the Culture Wars: Identities in Dialogue," *Profession 93* (New York: MLA, 1993), 6-11.

10. Jerome Bruner, *Actual Minds, Possible Worlds* (Cambridge, MA: Harvard University Press, 1986).

11. Kierkegaard, *The Concept of Irony,* 202.

12. Epictetus, *Meditations,* 3.14. Trans. A. Lawrence Lowell. Reprinted in Charles P. Curtis, Jr. and Ferris Greensleet (Eds.), *The Practical Cogitator* (Boston, MA: Houghton Mifflin, 1962).

13. Henry Louis Gates, "Pluralism and Its Discontents," *Profession 92* (New York: MLA, 1992), 35-38.

14. Walter J. Ong, S.J., "God's Known Universe," *Thought* 66 (1991) 241-258; Carter, *Culture of Disbelief.*

15. Peter Elbow, *Embracing Contraries in the Teaching Process* (New York: Oxford University Press, 1986).

16. Christopher Norris, *Truth and the Ethics of Criticism* (Manchester, UK: Manchester University Press, 1994); Torgovnick, "Hartman's Dilemma."

17. Geoffrey H. Hartman, *Minor Prophecies: The Literary Essay in the Culture Wars* (Cambridge, MA: Harvard University Press, 1991).

18. Thurow, "Illusory Compromise," 50-52; Louise Wetherbee Phelps, "A Constrained Version of the Writing Classroom," *ADE Bulletin,* no. 103 (Winter 1992), 13-20.

19. Edward M. White, *Teaching and Assessing Writing* (New York: Jossey Bass, 1985).

20. Northrop Frye, *The Double Vision. Language and Meaning in Religion* (Toronto: University of Toronto Press, 1991).

21. Hartman, *Minor Prophecies.*

22. Louis Mackey, *Kierkegaard, A Kind of Poet* (Philadelphia: University of Pennsylvania Press, 1971).

23. Julia Kristeva, *Strangers to Ourselves,* trans. Leon S. Roudiez (Hemel Hempstead, UK: Harvester Wheatsheaf, 1991). See Norris, *Truth and the Ethics of Criticism,* 76-92.

24. Norris, *Truth and the Ethics of Criticism,* 97.

25. Ibid., 76-92.

26. Edward W. Said, "East Isn't East. The Impending End of the Age of Orientalism," *Times Literary Supplement,* February 3, 1995, 3-6.

27. Ashis Nandy, *Traditions, Tyranny, and Utopias* (Bombay: Oxford University Press, 1987), 34.

28. Ibid., 49.

29. Ibid., 33.

30. Norris, *Truth and the Ethics of Criticism,* 98-100.

TWENTY

Teachers, Not Advocates: Toward an Open Classroom

JEFFREY WALLEN

I WANT TO ARGUE AGAINST ADVOCACY IN THE CLASSROOM, but because I have only a very limited space, I won't present a fully developed argument about why I think advocacy—and by this term I mean espousing our political viewpoints in the classroom and attempting to persuade students to share these views—is a bad idea on both moral and pedagogical grounds. Nor will I analyze the arguments of others, such as Edward Said's remarks about why we should not bring our own political involvements into the classroom.[1] Instead, I will discuss only some of the effects of advocacy and will use just a few examples from personal experience: from my own college and my own field of literary studies.

One of the main claims for advocacy in the classroom is that it helps spark debate. By asserting one's views about issues that have real importance and are hotly contested outside the university, so the argument goes, one engages students in a debate about questions that are central to contemporary intellectual controversies and social conflicts. And the corollary is that since interpretation always takes place within a specific sociopolitical context and always proceeds from a particular perspective, putting one's own views on the table and revealing the politics that shape one's own interpretations helps students in turn to become more self-aware, more critically astute, and better interpreters of what they read.

I don't want to take issue with the goal of generating a critical, self-reflective, and vigorous dialogue in the classroom—I think that this is an essential component of teaching. I will contend, however, that advocacy hampers more than it fosters such a dialogue. In the second half of my chapter, I will go on to argue that the current forms of "politicized" literary criticism also fail to generate the productive dialogues that they claim to promote. These forms of criticism, rather than opening a debate on the social theory, moral judgments, historical understanding, and agenda for political change that structure their interpretive framework, largely confine debate to a few questions about the interpretation of literary texts. Even when there is a heated discussion about the contentious issues that underlie the interpretative framework, the driving impulse in literary studies is still to shape the notions that will be most effective for literary criticism rather than to achieve the broader task of producing the soundest ideas about equality or about a better political system. Advocacy in literary criticism displaces debate away from the issues it claims to engage.

In most colleges and universities, the people who call for "advocacy in the classroom" are a small minority, and their political views are usually outside the mainstream. Advocacy is sometimes justified as a small window of resistance to the dominant discourse and, therefore, an opportunity to generate new perspectives for the students. The contention here is that advocacy will widen and enrich the spectrum of thought. It is further assumed that advocacy and tolerance for opposing views go hand in hand: When we encourage openly espousing our own political positions, we of course support the right of other professors (and students) to do the same thing and hope that the real sources of conflict, often repressed and misunderstood, will thereby be brought into the open.

But tolerance and advocacy do not go hand in hand. The viewpoint of the professor in the classroom is not simply one view among many. It is allied with the educational mission: imparting knowledge, teaching students to think, evaluating and certifying their performance. Once a professor sets up one set of political views as the ground for critical insight and the basis for knowledge—and this always proceeds from advocacy—then the tendency is to discredit and eliminate opposing views as the product of hegemony, as uncritical and uninformed, ignorant of the latest academic knowledge, subservient to ruling class ideology, and so on, and therefore outside the realm of legitimate academic practice. At most institutions, this tendency is kept in check, as those who push for or practice advocacy, being in the minority, are so busy defending their own right to speak that they still embrace academic freedom and have less opportunity to silence others. At Hampshire College, an alternative, progressive institution, where almost everyone—faculty and students—is on the political Left, advocacy by professors works instead to shut down opposing viewpoints and to insulate the students from any examination of their presuppositions and convictions.

At Hampshire, advocacy is encouraged, if not required. In his inaugural speech to the college, the president declared that Hampshire's mission was "to educate for social justice." He aligned education with spurring people to engage in activities that will produce a more "just" society. This doesn't sound too bad. But any classes that do not have "social justice" as their endpoint, or that even may employ a different notion of "social justice" (not egalitarian redistribution of income, abortion rights, championing the empowerment of racial and sexual minorities), are ipso facto deemed to be poor teaching and a failure to fulfill the educational mission. One might think that a starting point would be an open inquiry into the idea of social justice, perhaps even beginning, God forbid, with a reading of Plato. But this isn't what happens. Any too wide-ranging or too speculative an inquiry would only be a distraction from the task at hand, which is bringing about social change in American society, not meditating on the good or the just. Thus the topic for an introductory science class is breast-feeding in the Third World and the bad effects that multinational producers of infant formula have on public health.

What evidence do I have for any detrimental effects arising from linking pedagogy to advocacy? And how are such strictures enforced? If I had more space, I would describe the failures of thought, the missed opportunities, and the superficial education that result from what is finally an instrumental as much as a political view of education: turning students in the appropriate direction, training them to give the appropriate responses. And I could supply many examples directly tied to the classroom, both from what students have told me about their classes and especially from the papers they have written for these classes.[2] But here I will only briefly describe the attempt to shut me up, to deny me reappointment a few years ago, when a few people felt that I was failing to conform to their idea of the educational mission of the college.

When I came up for reappointment in my third year of teaching at Hampshire, a few people voted against me, and in explaining their votes to the dean, they offered such justifications as: "Jeff failed to provide any Third World challenge to the canon or to the theoretical priorities in his teaching." Another person wrote: "I don't think Jeff is addressing the Third World Expectation adequately in his courses." And someone else wrote: "I seriously question his understanding of the Third World Expectation except on the most superficial, perfunctory basis. His is a conventional attitude of privilege *[sic]*, inappropriate in a faculty member at a time when Hampshire is moving is *[sic]* such a different direction."

I don't want to go through the whole nonsense and describe the year-and-a-half-long battle to finally win back my job. Nor do I want to explore the set of arguments around having a "Third World Expectation," something that exists in similar form at many schools: the idea of looking at things from a foreign perspective is certainly not bad and does not in itself lead to intolerance.[3] But something else was going on. The operative logic in the votes against me was that most education ignores Third World perspectives and thereby condones the oppression of Third World peoples. We therefore need to embrace a political position from which we can challenge most things Western as racist, sexist, and imperialistic. Any different outlook only perpetuates social injustice and passes on the dominant ideology. This version of Third World studies is fostered by an administration that each semester tallies the number of courses having a "Third World component."[4] If one fails to teach the proper Third World writers (such as making the mistake of teaching Jorge Luis Borges), or to teach them in the right context (Richard Wright's *Black Boy* in a course on autobiography rather than as part of the African American literary tradition), or to draw the correct lessons, one is accused of having only a "superficial, perfunctory" understanding and therefore judged professionally incompetent. If good teaching is linked to adopting a "challenging," "subversive," "transgressive" or "transformative" perspective,[5] then anyone who does not share this perspective is a bad teacher and ought to be dismissed. After all, the school "is moving in such a different direction."

Championing advocacy in the classroom does not lead to everyone joyfully advocating highly diverse opinions but results instead in getting rid of those who don't advocate whatever views are deemed most "productive" for contemporary pedagogy, and it also discourages dissent by students.[6] Advocacy in teaching restricts rather than opens or broadens the dialogue, and it undercuts the ground on which a wide range of opinions can prosper. The result is finally much greater insularity—everyone mouthing the accepted views, the ones required for advancement—and also a high degree of silliness. The main reason why what happens at Hampshire is more extreme than elsewhere is that few other institutions have so widely promulgated "advocacy in the classroom."

I am going to present only the barest outlines of my second argument: that while practitioners of "advocacy" in contemporary literary criticism usually claim that their goal is a broad, public dialogue and a frank, critical exchange, current critical practices often work instead to undermine the grounds on which such interchanges might take place and to displace debate away from the real sources of disagreement. My point is that advocacy in our professional work also does not lead to the desired results.

For example, race is now one of the most popular categories in literary criticism. Race is used as a tool for performing a critical analysis, for arguing for social change, for providing the leverage to attack "ideological formations"; but what is to go in the place of the discredited "formations"? What alternative vision is offered? What policies are advocated? What vision of equality is being promoted? How might it be implemented? What views are to be contested by this privileging of race? All these questions remain largely unaddressed in literary criticism. Although such analyses are motivated by a desire to be socially significant and politically effective, they add little to any debate when the sources of disagreement with others—the political premises—are not subject to scrutiny. And in contrast to earlier forms of literary criticism, where the "reading" worked to illustrate or "prove" the theoretical framework (or, in the case of deconstruction, to complicate it), the readings that focus on race or on forms of inequality, and the debates that ensue, do little to prove or disprove the overall theory that shapes the interpretation.

Instead of an open debate on the possibilities of equality, we get instead a *reading for evil,* in which the critic always finds and condemns inequality in the "cultural text." Such literary criticism performs the function of certifying that one is not complicit in processes of domination; criticism is now often akin to a rite of purification. Yet if literary criticism discredits in advance any position other than "resistance" to those forms of "domination" that it seeks to dispel, there is little possibility of a dialogue in which competing ideas can be scrutinized and contested. Moreover, the attempts to stage debates over the politics of literature usually result in poor literary analysis and bad political debate. For instance, the question of whether a particular theory of economic exploitation does or does not illuminate the complexities of Wordsworth's poem "Michael" has little to do with whether the vision of economic equality that motivates the analysis would in fact help to ameliorate the inequities of our contemporary world.

In conclusion, I do not want to suggest that literature professors should ignore the "political" dimensions of literary works—quite the contrary; such prescribed ignorance is ridiculous at a university—but rather that advocacy in literary criticism cannot stand in for philosophical and political dialogue. We need to draw distinctions—between analysis and advocacy, between the classroom and the public sphere, and between literary study and political debate—even though such distinctions are never absolute and need constant reexamination. Also, we need to question the repercussions of our positions: advocacy in the classroom may sound like an improvement over past or current practices, but the actual consequences are rarely those that are envisioned by those who promote it.

NOTES

1. In a talk at the MLA convention in December 1992, Edward Said made the following remarks:

> Neither the classroom, nor the academy as a whole, however, should be the site for political discussion [that isn't taking place elsewhere].
>
> Being a better reader of *Wuthering Heights* does *not* mean having a better head for politics.
>
> I have never brought into the classroom the politics I am involved in. But my teaching has been greatly informed by my educational experience, and issues of exile, imperialism . . .
>
> Can an experience help in literary studies? Yes, but only if one remembers that the politics of the classroom are not the politics of the outside world.
>
> Politicization is more salutary than de-politicization.
>
> To use the academy as the place to instill new orthodoxies and to replace old ones is to abuse academic freedom. Critiques of society have to be addressed in the public sphere. To use the literary text as an ersatz object on which to perform a political critique instead of a real critique is an abuse of the classroom. The classroom is *not* the sphere for politics; the public sphere is the place.
>
> [There is] a need to keep a *distinctness* of the classroom. To think of the university classroom as the place where the problems of the world "out there" are to be solved is a mistake.
>
> The idea that a university career is de-politicized is not right, but neither is the notion of "everything is political," because everything is not political in the same way.

   I note these remarks since Said is the most prominent Leftist critic in literary studies, and I take these comments to at least put into question an easy acceptance of "advocacy in the classroom."

2. At Hampshire, we have a portfolio system of evaluation, so I often end up reading the papers that students have written for a dozen different courses.

3. As an undergraduate at Stanford in the mid-1970s, I was required to take a course in non-Western literature as part of my comparative literature major. The course, on Native American literature (taught by N. Scott Momaday), was one of the best classes I had at Stanford. I have no disagreement with such "diversity" requirements, nor with distribution requirements (e.g., having to take some math or science courses).

   Hampshire adopted a Third World "Expectation" in 1985, shortly before I arrived. During the course of their education, students are "expected" "to present tangible evidence, prior to graduation," that they have had "an intellectually substantive engagement with the experience of the peoples of Asia, Africa, and Latin America (including North America's own domestic 'third world')." This has been translated into a *demand* that almost every course address the Third World and offer the "proper" Third World perspective: challenging the "dominant ideology" of Europe and the United States.

4. When I was on the Faculty Senate, the Dean of Faculty presented statistics about the percentage of courses that contained a "Third World component," and her stated goal was that the percentage would someday reach 100. (My recollection is that the current percentage was in the 70s.)

5. Any study of "advocacy" in academia would need to pay attention to the ubiquitous and myriad uses of these words.

6. When students feel that there is a party line in the class to which they are supposed to adhere, the range of their discussion is limited. This is often the case at Hampshire. Despite whatever attempts to encourage disagreement (and many professors do not attempt to do this), the fear of saying something that will be challenged by someone else as aiding oppression, or racist, sexist, imperialist, and the like, silences many students. These students do not want to be, and are not, racist, but such critical epithets work to dismiss and disqualify, rather than engage, the views of others.

TWENTY-ONE

The Politics of Aesthetic Distance

LAMBERT ZUIDERVAART

THERE WAS A TIME earlier in this century when a title like "The Politics of Aesthetic Distance" would have been greeted with puzzled stares or hoots of derision. In Edward Bullough's 1912 essay on the concept of distance, perhaps the most widely anthologized piece on the topic, aesthetic distance seems to have little connection with politics, other than its avoidance.[1] At the same time, traditional conceptions of politics, ones that tie it to governance and the nation-state, seem to have little connection with a topic so esoteric as aesthetic distance. It is a testimony to the cultural and political impact of the civil rights and student protest movements of the 1960s and of the new social movements of subsequent decades that such appearances have dramatically and irrevocably changed. Today it makes sense to inquire into the politics of aesthetic distance.

Before going further, let me define my terms. When I speak of politics, I refer to all the various groups, practices, and institutions that participate in struggles for liberation, recognition, and social justice. Although party politics and state governance constitute an important aspect of such struggles, there is much more to politics than what occurs via parties and governments. Hence to inquire into the politics of aesthetic distance is not simply to look for connections, usually forced, between aesthetics and party politics or government policies.

Similarly, when I speak of aesthetic distance I do not mean to restrict my attention to a certain normative concept whose roots lie in eighteenth-century notions of disinterestedness and whose flowering occurs within modernist aesthetics. Certainly the normative concept of aesthetic distance is a crucial aspect of what I have in mind. But I also wish to address those practices and institutions that simultaneously give rise to the concept and take their guidance from it. Although such practices and institutions, like the concept itself, have mainly to do with the arts as a relatively autonomous sector of Western societies, they also pertain to less formalized matters such as the enjoyment of urban environments or participation in games and rituals.

Interestingly enough, Bullough's first illustration of what he calls "psychical distance" comes neither from the arts nor from participation in other human constructs. Instead he asks us to imagine "a fog at sea." Abstracting from the fog's "danger and practical unpleasantness," we are to direct our attention to the opaqueness of the misty veil, the "carrying-power of the air," the "curious creamy smoothness of the water," and, "above all, the strange solitude and remoteness from the world"—with the possible result that "the experience may acquire, in its uncanny mingling of repose and terror, a flavour of such concentrated poignancy and delight as to contrast sharply with the blind and distempered anxiety of its other aspects."[2]

What this illustrates, says Bullough, is an ability to insert distance "between our own self and its affections" or, alternatively, "between our own self and such objects as are the sources or vehicles of such affections." The phenomenon, in this case the fog at sea, is put "out of gear with our practical, actual self" and is allowed "to stand outside the context of our personal needs and ends. . . ."[3] Hence aesthetic distance involves the operations of a divided self, one that not only can exist over against its affections but also can insert distance between itself as a creature of desire and the phenomena that normally fulfill its desires. On this model, aesthetic distance is a function of what Theodor Adorno would later label "castrated hedonism."[4]

My immediate concern, however, is not with Bullough's problematic psychology but with the implications he draws for the arts and the aesthetic dimension. Let me mention several.

1. Aesthetic distance provides an abnormal and revelatory outlook.
2. Aesthetic distance is a fundamental principle serving to distinguish the beautiful, the artistic temperament, and aesthetic consciousness.
3. People who are expert in the arts, whether as critics or as artists, must maintain a minimum of aesthetic distance, despite the practical and personal character of their involvements in the arts.
4. Because of the danger of "under-distancing," sexual references and social criticism require "special precautions" in the arts.
5. Because art requires a certain degree of distance in order to be aesthetically appreciated, all art is "anti-realistic" in the sense that it "never pretends to be nature and strongly resists any confusion with nature."[5]

One discovers in Bullough's account of aesthetic distance, as in Clive Bell's book *Art* from around the same time, a transition from a Victorian emphasis on *moral* elevation and the repression of physical desires to an early modernist emphasis on *aesthetic* elevation and practical abstraction, into which Bullough has folded a rather Victorian suspicion of sex and the body.[6] For a time, this dual emphasis on aesthetic elevation and practical abstraction fit rather nicely with an Anglo-American paradigm in philosophy that stressed analytical rigor and attention to formal problems, whether in the arts or in the sciences or in language. Perhaps this fit helps explain the number of times Bullough's article has been anthologized, reproduced, and cited.

I find, however, that it has become increasingly difficult to help students understand Bullough's essay. Pure exegesis and discussion do not work. And the reason for this is not simply the old chestnut, often false, that today's students don't know how to read. Rather, the politics of aesthetic distance has shifted so dramatically in the past few decades that neither the instructor nor the students can readily accept the intuitions that inform Bullough's discussion. Let me mention three such intuitions.

One is that the arts are unique and special by virtue of their relation to the principle of aesthetic distance. Although Bullough might regard a fog at sea as an aesthetic phenomenon, his essay assumes that the *arts* are the primary field of aesthetic experience, particularly in their distinction from nature.

A second intuition is that art proper, to use R. G. Collingwood's term, maintains appropriate distance from all practical matters, whether those be sexual, social, economic, political, moral, or religious.[7] Bullough is particularly concerned about appropriate distance from explicit sexuality and pointed social criticism.

The third intuition is that the proper experience of art—experience that takes the right amount of aesthetic distance—is characteristically the experience of a discrete individual who can disregard, at least on occasion, all "personal needs and ends." The proper experience of art is neither intersubjective nor sociohistorically situated.

As I have said, the current politics of aesthetic distance makes it difficult to adopt any one of these intuitions. Not only do most of us experience the arts via a mass-mediated culture that challenges both the autonomy of the arts and the discreetness of the individual self, but also many recent forms of artistic practice and academic discourse specifically and deliberately challenge the aestheticism and individualism built into Bullough's account of aesthetic distance.

Hence the study of Bullough's essay quickly and properly becomes an exercise in contextual and dialectical inquiry. On the one hand, efforts must be made to uncover the essay's political subtext. What gender and class positions does it tacitly occupy? What social and cultural conditions have framed its production and reception? What implications, if any, might Bullough's account of aesthetic distance hold in current struggles for liberation, recognition, and justice? In the absence of such questions, made more precise and provocative in a classroom setting, Bullough's account will remain cordoned off from contemporary concerns and its meaning will become either thin or inaccessible.

On the other hand, Bullough's essay must be allowed to speak for itself and to expose and challenge contemporary predilections. Which of his insights are valid, and how might they be reformulated for a contemporary context? Are there significant aspects of the arts and aesthetic discourse to which Bullough calls attention that contemporary artistic practices and academic approaches would tend to ignore or reject? Are there limits to what can be uncovered by questioning the essay's political subtext? If such questions are not raised, readers will remain locked into their own culture-political prejudices, unable or unwilling to relativize their own positions and struggles.

Much has been written in recent years about "the ideology of the aesthetic," to borrow the title of Terry Eagleton's important book on this topic.[8] Aesthetic distance is central to that ideology. What has hampered the discussion, however, as Eagleton repeatedly points out, is too simple and cynical a view of ideology, a view that reduces the complexity and ambiguity of ideology to the mere machinations of oppressive power. Commenting on the avant-garde, but clearly eyeing postmodernism as "the latest iconoclastic upsurge of the avant garde," Eagleton writes:

> The avant garde's response to the cognitive, ethical and aesthetic is quite unequivocal. Truth is a lie; morality stinks; beauty is shit. And of course they are absolutely right. Truth is a White House communique; morality is the moral Majority; beauty is a naked woman advertising perfume. Equally, of course, they are wrong. Truth, morality and beauty are too important to be handed contemptuously over to the political enemy.[9]

Something similar can be said about aesthetic distance. As conceived by authors such as Bullough and institutionalized in modernist concert halls, museums, and arts curricula, aesthetic distance amounts to a complex and ambiguous matter. While it may have served to strip the arts of social content, reduce their social relevance, and shore up the cultural power of a mostly male, white, and upper-class elite, aesthetic distance may also have provided a counterweight to ideologies such as nationalism and consumerism and, in a sense, may have democratized participation in the arts by reducing the necessary qualifications to a bare minimum.

Moreover, as Rita Felski argues in *Beyond Feminist Aesthetics,* the context of reception is crucial for assessing the political significance of artistic practices. More specifically, the assessment must be made with regard to what Felski calls the "feminist public sphere."[10] Along these lines, one might add that aesthetic distance may have different political functions in different contexts of reception. Yet it may also generally be the case that in contemporary Western societies, where public spaces and public discourses face a double threat from downsizing governments and globalizing corporations, the rearticulation and institutional transformation of aesthetic distance can have a progressive political purpose. For such rearticulation and transformation, it will be important that scholars and their students reconsider the politics of aesthetic distance.

NOTES

1. Edward Bullough, "'Psychical Distance' as a Factor in Art and as an Aesthetic Principle." In Stephen David Ross (Ed.), *Art and Its Significance: An Anthology of Aesthetic Theory* (Albany: State University of New York Press, 1994), 458-67.
2. Ibid., 459.
3. Ibid., 459-60.
4. T. W. Adorno, *Aesthetic Theory,* trans. C. Lenhardt (London: Routledge & Kegan Paul, 1984), 16.
5. Bullough, "'Psychical Distance,'" 460, 461, 463, 464, 467.
6. Clive Bell, *Art* (London: Chatto and Windus, 1914).
7. R. G. Collingwood, *The Principles of Art* (New York: Oxford University Press, Galaxy Book, 1958), 105.
8. Terry Eagleton, *The Ideology of the Aesthetic* (Oxford: Blackwell, 1990).
9. Ibid., 373, 372.
10. Rita Felski, *Beyond Feminist Aesthetics* (Cambridge, MA: Harvard University Press, 1989), 154.

TWENTY-TWO

The Internalization of Disinterestedness

HILDE HEIN

TO ADVOCATE IS TO ARGUE in favor of or to recommend a position and thus to take a point of view. Traditionally this is understood as "having an interest in" a particular outcome; however, it must be emphasized that personal advantage is not necessarily entailed. It is quite possible to promote a cause with no particular first-order benefit to oneself; the success of the cause would still be a ground for pleasure, or second-order satisfaction. The confusion of these first- and second-order satisfactions is regrettably widespread, but I will assume that readers are capable of discerning the difference between the two. There is such a thing as disinterested pleasure, which has long been a matter of concern (or interest) to philosophers. I am discussing it because it appears to be at odds with advocacy, the topic of this volume, and there are strong arguments that not only support advocacy in the classroom but even cast doubt on the very possibility of doing anything else. Disinterestedness seems to be a lost cause— neither desirable nor achievable. But before we give up on it entirely, I would like to take a closer look at it.[1]

The concept of disinterestedness has played a major role in European philosophy since the beginning of the eighteenth century, especially in the areas of epistemology, ethics, social philosophy, and law, and, I believe most fundamentally, aesthetics. To its proponents, disinterest has never meant a disinclination or a negative withdrawal of concern, but it does convey a privative sense of self-removal. One who is disinterested is self*lessly* (as distinct from selfishly) engaged. (The term "indifferent," similarly ambiguous to our modern ears, likewise conveys an initial neutrality—as a well-aligned balance measures only the comparative masses of the contents of its pans, remaining indifferent to their substance.)

Modern philosophy has advanced disinterestedness as a condition of effectiveness, in most instances as a means to an end. Only in aesthetics—and this is the point that I mean to emphasize—is it constitutive of the enterprise. The aesthetic, on some accounts, is confined within the domain of the disinterested.[2] The concept of disinterestedness is often conflated with the notion of *distance* (although they are not identical) and in that form turns up in unexpected places. Take, for example, Charles Taylor's excellent essay "The Politics of Recognition" in which he overtly advances the cause of *interestedness.* Notice, however, what he says: "In order to examine some of the issues that have arisen here, I'd like to take a step back, achieve a little distance, and look first at how this discourse of recognition and identity came to seem familiar. . . ."[3]

He is asking us to "step back"—to assume a disinterested stance as a condition of better understanding— the impartial, detached observer being well positioned to see his subject clearly (gender identification intentional). And thus Taylor achieves a very convincing and authoritative overview of the bifurcated history of liberal identity theory.

My object here is not to discuss Taylor's beautifully articulated reasoning but only to note that to realize it, he believes he is compelled to position himself as the distanced, disinterested (omniscient) observer who displays the object of his scrutiny for judgment. As Susan Wolf objects in her commentary, in the end, however, Taylor's advocacy of cultural diversity is contingent on the "worthiness" of the cultures' contribution to some kind of universal good— and presumably *he* is the judge of that.[4]

Apparently this good as well must be assessed by some disinterested, ideal judge who has no particular ax to grind, no personal investment, no prior conviction or private agenda. Who then might he be—the proverbial detached "man of reason" of the Western legal tradition (or *l'homme moyen sensuel* of its more libertarian counterpart)? Probably that is not what Taylor has in mind, but it is what the celebration of disinterestedness has historically validated. And it is what brings us to the cultural and political impasse that now confronts us.

Post-Enlightenment secular European philosophy decrees a posture of selflessness in the quest for the good and the true, and this appears to be mirrored in the pursuit of the beautiful. Is not the judgment of taste a quasi-cognitive apperception in which the perceiver comes to the object with no prior claims? That seems to be Kant's reasoning in the First Moment of the Judgment of Taste, which grounds the universal validity of the aesthetic judgment in the disinterestedness of the observer.[5] I think there is no doubt that there is a merging of discourses here and that the validation of *all* judgments, cognitive and evaluative alike, is taken to follow a similar model. But there is an important difference between the aesthetic and other domains to which philosophy applies that is lost in that assimilation—namely, that aesthetics is not confined to discerning and judging beauty.

As Jerome Stolnitz argues in "Of the Origins of 'Aesthetic Disinterestedness,'" disinterestedness marks a historical watershed in aesthetic theory. This is the idea of a philosophical discipline that embraces not only all the arts but also Nature and anything else that can be approached in a unique and particular state of mind.[6] Beginning with the writings of the Third Earl of Shaftesbury addressed against Hobbesian egoism, disinterestedness is characterized as motivation unguided by anticipation of consequences. Disinterestedness is lodged in an appreciative apprehension of quality and form uncolored by choice or action. It is chiefly a mode of attention indifferent to possession or even (as Kant was later to stress) to existence. Aesthetic interest (or appreciation) attends perception alone and terminates with the object perceived. It is disinterested in any other good or value that is to be realized thereby. Stolnitz maintains that as the Hobbesian moral and religious associations are left behind, aesthetics comes into its own as a distinct subject matter—later characterized along with a paramount object of its concern, Art—as autonomous.[7]

In the wake of a century of development of disinterestedness theory, aesthetics shifted its ground away from the nature of beauty or of the objects that merit aesthetic veneration toward examination of the aesthetic experience. This is a wholly concentrated, focused state of mind, attentive to its object even to the exclusion of the concerns of the philosopher, the critic, or the art historian. In its later usage, it barely harks back to the anti-Hobbesian privative connotation of selflessness. The self becomes merely irrelevant.

Now, how does this sense of "disinterestedness" depart meaningfully from the disinterest mandated to scientific observation and to responsible ethical and social judgment? As a well-trained liberal inquirer I was certainly taught the gospel of objective impartiality—one must hang one's opinions at the door of the laboratory along with one's hat and coat. I began to have some quivering doubts when I read André Gide and Jean-Paul Sartre and other philosophers of engagement in the 1950s; but only in the '60s (that much-maligned moment of intellectual ferment) did I truly question the merit, let alone the feasibility, of noncommitment. The notion began to take shape that, without conviction, one could not truly enter into one's subject, know it from within. One could have only a superficial, analytic sense of it. I began to think of conviction (or interest, if you like) not simply as a *result* of understanding, but neither as a condition prior to understanding. Instead, conviction appeared to be partially constitutive of knowledge—and thus I also had to doubt the positivistic distinction that had been made between fact and value.

This was hardly original. We did know about Nietzsche and, more importantly, about Dewey's continuum of valuation, the mutual modification of distant and proximate ends.[8] Closer at hand for me was C. L. Stevenson's unique form of emotivism that emphasized the imperative, expressive, and *persuasive* function of value judgment.[9] Stevenson sought to fuse these with *good* reasons for bringing about agreement in belief and attitude. There was, we understood, a difference between reasons and mere causes for likes and dislikes, approvals and disapprovals; and the effort to identify these engendered a whole industry that persists today in analytic philosophy to validate, vindicate, and valorize appreciative and critical judgments.

Of course we were respectful of the ideal, impartial, disinterested (epistemic) observer, but he had grown behavioristically bound to "satisfactions" and the "gratification of interests"—no longer a blank slate or the rational cipher at the center but a seething mass of raw nerve endings. In fact, reason itself had become a passion—perhaps a terrible one. "Good reasons," in their turn, might advert to pleasure enhancement or to human well-being. They enlisted agreement but did not insist upon universality. Again, under the influence of behaviorism, we quickly gave up the aesthetic "state of mind" (the "myth of the Aesthetic Attitude")—no need to increase the clutter of the universe—but we did not abandon the secular concept of human flourishing which that aesthetic state promised to enlarge.

Meanwhile, on the epistemological front, the claim to disinterestedness had also been compromised. Knowledge is power; theory is value-laden; observation is theory-driven; judgment is imbued with gender-, race-, and class-consciousness; gender, race, and class are forms of domination; and the objective gaze is an example of prurient scopophilia. As Laurie Anderson says, it's all about Control and the loss of it![10]

What remains then of disinterestedness, and should it be defended? My answer is qualified as a result of abuses that have been rightly noted. As an instrument of dominance and objectification it has produced great harms, and, in its more familiar and ordinary sense, it has permitted colossal indifference to injuries committed in the name of fairness, objectivity, and the advance of knowledge. But as a liberation from the "proprietary self," disinterestedness augments attentiveness and sharpens sensitivity. It holds prescribed (or proscribed) judgment in abeyance and opens the mind to the unexpected and the uncertain. Aesthetic disinterestedness deepens the capacity to care. These are surely good reasons for its cultivation and good reasons "to search the world over, with patience and with care, to find and learn to appreciate great human achievements, wherever they may be."[11] They are also good reasons, as Susan Wolf points out, to treasure the small and trivial things of this world that matter to and differentiate us, such that, when one child encounters another, "she neither expects him to be the same as she nor sees him as alien or foreign."[12]

I would like to end with an observation taken from Iris Murdoch, who in turn borrows it from Simone Weil. She refers to a kind of attention that is loving and just yet knowing. Unlike the "quasi-scientific" knowledge of the ordinary world, it is "a refined and honest perception of what is really the case, a patient and just discernment and exploration of what confronts one, which is the result not simply of opening one's eyes, but of a certainly perfectly familiar kind of moral discipline."[13] There are innumerable such acts of attention—no single one that is "right" or "necessary." Yet it is not the case that we are free to choose among them; for the occurrent one comes with a certain sense of inevitability. It commends itself to the will as individual but not personal; as resolute but not immovable. We should be moved by such claims upon our capacities to think and feel—not for the sake of the advantage accrued but for their renewal of those same capacities to think and feel.

NOTES

1. Like many feminists, I have been critical of the very notion of disinterestedness, charging to it the crimes of patriarchy—from paternalistic condescension to scopophilic exploitation and opportunistic neglect. But notwithstanding the lease that power takes on disinterestedness, I think it deserves a second look.
2. This view is, of course, directly challenged by the position that declares advocacy both inevitable and unobjectionable, but historically, aesthetics as a philosophical discipline begins with the denial of that claim.
3. Charles Taylor, "The Politics of Recognition," in Amy Gutmann (Ed. and Intro.), *Multiculturalism: Examining the Politics of Recognition* (Princeton, NJ: Princeton University Press, 1994), 26.
4. Susan Wolf, "Comment," in Gutmann, *Multiculturalism*.
5. Immanuel Kant, "Analytic of the Beautiful," in *The Critique of Judgment*, trans. J. C. Meredith. (Oxford University Press, 1952). (Originally published in 1798.)

6. Jerome Stolnitz, "Of the Origins of Aesthetic Disinterestedness," *Journal of Aesthetics and Art Criticism* (Winter 1961), 131-143; reprinted in G. Dickie and R. J. Sclafani, *Aesthetics: A Critical Anthology* (New York: St. Martin's Press, 1977), 607-25.

7. An interesting alternative hypothesis is offered by Preben Mortensen in "Francis Hutcheson and the Problem of Conspicuous Consumption," *Journal of Aesthetics and Art Criticism* 53, no. 2 (Spring 1995), 155-16. Mortensen argues that the eighteenth-century defense of aesthetic sensibility was a moral vindication, meant to counteract Puritan asceticism rather than Hobbesian egoism. Its aim was to justify such hedonism as would support the bourgeois culture and promote an expanding market economy.

8. John Dewey, *Theory of Valuation,* in *International Encyclopedia of Unified Science,* vol. 2, no. 4, (Chicago: University of Chicago Press, 1939).

9. Charles L. Stevenson, *Ethics and Language* (New Haven, CT: Yale University Press, 1944).

10. Laurie Anderson concert in Dallas, TX, June 1986.

11. Wolf, "Comment," in *Multiculturalism,* 84.

12. Ibid., 82.

13. Iris Murdoch, "The Idea of Perfection," in *The Sovereignty of Good* (London, NY: Routledge, 1991), 38.

TWENTY-THREE

The Open Secret: Dilemmas of Advocacy in the Religious Studies Classroom

SUSAN E. HENKING

Scene 1: Having arrived in Macomb, Illinois, a month before, today is my first day teaching religious studies. I'm nervous because my load includes teaching a course well outside my areas of graduate work: New Testament. As I walk into the classroom for the first time, a young man stands up in the rear of the room and roars: "The Devil Incarnate—a woman cannot teach. . . . "

LIKE JUDITH BERLING in her 1991 presidential address to the American Academy of Religion, I begin with a scene from my early teaching career that haunts my reflections about advocacy in the classroom. While I never teach New Testament now and only rarely encounter fundamentalist students, each entrance into the classroom and all of my reflections on religious studies pedagogy are informed by those first shocking moments when who I am—my gender—immediately and significantly shaped the pedagogical possibilities in my classroom. In Berling's case, the scene revolves around the question of whether she, a young teacher of Taoism, was—or was not—a Christian. Here the central issue was not gender (or the intersection of gender and religion) but religious identification per se.[1] Yet implicit in both tales are dilemmas commonly encountered in discussions of religious studies pedagogy: *Who* can teach religious studies (and who can teach *which* subdisciplines that reside under the umbrella of the academic study of religion)? What is the relation of religion (religious belief, religious practice, religious identity, theology) to religious studies? Can a secular person teach religious studies? Should she? Is "methodological atheism"[2] the most appropriate pedagogical stance? Must religious studies education be "value-free" in order to avoid the trap of proselytizing? If not, which "value positions" are legitimate and which are not legitimate?

Read alongside each other the two stories I have offered—Berling's and my own—require that we consider issues about identity and identities, about what counts as "neutrality" or "objectivity" and what counts as "advocacy," about religion and religions and secularity. Interwoven in complex and contradictory ways, these issues shape the dilemmas and difficulties, the ambivalences and enigmas of teaching (religious studies) in the 1990s. To take up such concerns is to join with Stephen H. Webb, who asks:

> How should each participant in a discussion reveal her own personal narrative in regard to the substance of the discussion? More broadly, how can the significance of tradition be both raised and resolved in the classroom? Even more sweeping, how can the question of truth be introduced once the particularity and the passion of religion are given their due weight? These problems are simultaneously practical and theoretical. . . . [3]

Indeed, these questions are simultaneously about our daily enactments in the classroom and constitutive of our field. They point to concerns lying at the very intersection of religious studies scholarship and teaching.

THE ILLUSORY COMFORT OF NEUTRALITY AND THE PLACE OF CRITICAL DISTANCE

Scene 2: I am team teaching a required senior-level general education course with three other faculty—one anthropologist, one poet, and one literary critic. On the first day of class, a religious studies major argues that homosexuality is unnatural. Two of the faculty are lesbians. Somewhat later a group of women students complain to a dean that the course is too "uniform." Everyone says the same things; all four faculty are women, are feminists. At least one student argues that since the course is a requirement, four women ought not be permitted to teach together. At my own lecture, a student argues that my views are specious because "You can't discuss religion without discussing—and acknowledging—God."

This student's reaction takes us into yet another, no less labyrinthine, issue. The special status of religious studies in American higher education is rooted in—and is an expression of—lengthy historical interactions between religion and education. Constitutional protections of religious freedom and limitations on the establishment of religion form part of that history.[4] Early close relations between American college education and Protestantism as well as the complex processes of secularization impinging upon the organization of higher education in the years since the Civil War also leave traces in contemporary religious studies.[5] In today's peculiarly religious and peculiarly secular social order,

> Our culture and the academy are both skittish about religion as a topic of public conversation. The discomfort is created and sustained by a number of widely held cultural assumptions: 1) that all statements about religion are statements for a particular religious position (that they amount to a form of evangelism); 2) that hearing about a position other than one's own might undermine faith, challenge belief, and seduce one away from certainty; 3) that the legal separation of church and state relegates religion to the private realm, unfit for public discourse; 4) that statements about religion, since they are suited only for a particular and discrete religious community, cannot contribute to the public good; 5) that different religious positions can meet only as competing systems in a one-up, one-down winner-take-all encounter.[6]

Out of such skittishness emerges such oppositions as the Schemp dicta differentiating between teaching religion and teaching *about* religion[7] as well as heated squabbles between advocates of theology and advocates of religious studies, often equated (oddly enough) with the very opposition between advocacy and objectivity. Out of such skittishness, too, comes the emphasis on differentiating religious studies from religion in many of our introductory textbooks and, for me at least, the parallel strong temptation to devote the opening lecture of religious studies courses to distinguishing between our religious education and the liberal arts endeavor.

It is such oppositions that undergird the presumption, as well, that *feminist* scholarship, because it is positioned scholarship, is somehow theological, somehow illegitimate as religious studies per se. Likewise, such oppositions serve to legitimize particular enactments of knowledge/power relations, including the "scientific" study of religion with its claims to "objectivity." These oppositions have, indeed, been central to the establishment of religious studies as a legitimate part of contemporary secular academia; they have also, as Wilken notes, shaped the boundaries and character of both our field and our professional experience:

> . . . the phrases "study of religion" and "teaching about religion" signify more than the adoption of a new vocabulary to designate a traditional area of inquiry. The prepositions "of" and "about" portend a profound redefinition of the subject matter that requires in turn a new relation between the scholar and the thing studied. . . . I am sure that some of you have had the experience . . . of stepping into a taxi with a chatty cabdriver. When the cabdriver heard what we do, he said: "So you are religion teachers?" There was an embarrassed silence and in chorus the group answered: "Oh, no, we are teachers of religion."[8]

Yet these are oppositions that are *simple* and, we increasingly recognize, *simplified*. As Burkhalter notes: ". . . scholars in the field recognized early on the ambiguities confronted in taking the 'of/about' differentiation into the classroom: What pedagogical design rightfully merits the designation of 'teaching *about* religion' as distinct from 'teaching *of* religion'"?[9] she asks.

It is the impossibility—and indeed, the undesirability—of such distinctions that the fundamentalist student in the senior forum pointed out. Religion, for her, was simply incomprehensible as a (purely) human endeavor, and a nontheological (indeed, nontheistic) study of religion was unreasonable. Her worldview axiomatically ruled mine out of court; likewise, my arguments for what Berger calls "methodological atheism" ruled hers out as an acceptable mode of "religious studies." (That this may have a serious effect for her is hinted at by Stephen Carter in his controversial book, *The Culture of Disbelief,* where he wrote: "I think the legal theorist Michael Perry has it right when he argues that forcing religious arguments to be restated in other terms asks a citizen to 'bracket' religious convictions from the rest of her personality, essentially demanding that she split off a part of herself. Says Perry: 'To bracket them would be to bracket—indeed, to annihilate—herself. And doing that would preclude her—the particular person she is—from engaging in moral discourse with other members of society.)'"[10]

Here perhaps is the crux of the issue of advocacy in the classroom. As a person who came to religious studies through a process of secularization—however traumatic—and was happy to find an intellectual home where, as Wendy Doniger noted "it is deemed wrong to *care for* religion, [but] it is not wrong to *care against* religion . . . [where] hatred of religion has been a more respectable scholarly emotion than love, particularly hatred of one's own religion,"[11] the impasse illustrated by this interaction is more than merely conceptual. Indeed, it runs deep. Here, also, is the crux of the issue for a feminist who is a true believer in liberal arts education: How *can* we converse across such a divide, and how can we accept the validity of feminist and other critical work on epistemology without agreeing with that student and reintroducing God into religious studies?

The strategy of linking theology to advocacy was, of course, historically central to the establishment of religious studies as a distinct academic enterprise. (As I have noted, it was also central to my own arrival in the religious studies fold.) Yet

> Connecting theology with subjectivity and other teaching professions with objectivity is neither fair nor realistic. After all, most professors profess; if teachers were not enthusiastic about their subject matter, they would be held in suspicion, not esteem. . . . As Edward Farley remarks: "Both advocacy and historical specificity are well-entrenched principles of university teaching."[12]

Rather than arguing for a "neutral," "objective," disengaged religious studies that views any incorporation of values as "cryptotheology"[13]—something I might once have done and remain tempted to do on occasion—my experience as a woman teacher and scholar leads me to argue now that all scholarship and teaching involves positioned epistemologies. In doing so, I reject the appropriateness (in this context) of a wide, functionalist definition of religion (as courts have rejected use of such definitions to define secular humanism as a form of religion) and affirm my own ambivalent commitment to critical distance and, indeed, secularization. I maintain, as well, with figures such as Gail Griffin, a particular view of teaching and of teachers. In her words:

> Teachers have always been voices *for* culture passing on accumulated knowledge. Academe thus amounts to oral history. If in thinking of oneself as a voice a teacher has in mind a sort of funnel through which culture transmits itself into the waiting student-shaped bottle—or, conversely as a megaphone through which culture spreads to the little pitchers with big ears—then one's task is relatively simple. If, however, one sees oneself (or, I would add, if one is seen) as inescapably changing the story one passes on; if one sees oneself (or, again, is seen as) in a problematic, ironic relation to that story as its narrator; if one cannot tell (or others see one as unable to tell) the story without disrupting it—then in that case, one's

vocation is at once more difficult, more dangerous, and much more interesting.[14]

Whether self-consciously so or not, many teachers are thrown into the latter position by virtue of their students' understanding of them. That is, if one is a woman teaching, a black or Asian or gay or Native American male, a Jew or a Muslim or other religious believer in a secular department, if one is, more broadly, a member of a marked rather than unmarked category of professor, one's teaching may be assumed to always be problematic and one's vocation always dangerous. (The issue, for religious studies, is the multiple—and shifting—nature of such marked categories: Is Protestant Christian marked or unmarked in American culture? Believer or unbeliever in American higher education? Answers to such questions, I would argue, are most often local.)

The *open secret*, thus, is the role of teaching as cultural formation—whether instantiating the status quo, offering resistance to it, or some complex mix of the two. (We know this is the place of education even when we pretend it is not.) This is not a new problematic in higher education; particular forms of such concerns appear whether discussing the pedagogical and curricular changes associated with the emergence of the American university of the late nineteenth and early twentieth centuries[15] or a century later as I walked into the classroom as "the devil incarnate." The *dilemma*, as I would pose it, is about accepting epistemologies (and pedagogies) rejecting a *simplified* opposition between advocacy and objectivity without falling into the equally (to my mind) problematic position of the student who argued that "You can't discuss religion without discussing—and acknowledging—God." The dilemma is, also, our ambivalence about distanciation.[16] It is the struggle to enact a feminist religious studies that is nontheological.

To address these, I would argue, is to work against the culturally powerful opposition between advocacy and objectivity (an opposition intertwined with other equally problematic dualisms: private/public, women/men, religious/secular). To do so involves recognizing the opposition's rootedness in history and culture and the ways one pole of this dualism is normalized. It also involves efforts to reexamine and rethink reflexively links between forms of knowledge and knowers. Our questions must become questions about power, about legitimation of forms of knowledge, and of particular knowers. We must ask, that is, not whether (or even where) there is advocacy in the classroom, but what advocacy patterns have been powerful. Which advocacy positions have been (more or less) marginalized? How does one adjudicate among the various (sometimes competing, sometimes contradictory) advocacy positions?

PASSING AND OUTING: THE "ETHOS OF DISCLOSURE" IN (RELIGIOUS STUDIES/LIBERAL ARTS) PEDAGOGIES

> Scene 3: I am at the School for Criticism and Theory, enrolled in a class with well-known feminist scholar and psychoanalyst Juliet Mitchell. One day Mitchell reminded her seminar that an analyst is doing her job only if she is "using herself" and, she commented, she suspected that the same was true of teaching.

What did Mitchell mean by her comment? That one needs, qua analyst, to reflect on one's own experience within the analytic dyad in order to attend responsibly to the other. And, within teaching, that one needs to attend responsibly to one's own involvement in the classroom in order to respond appropriately to the student. That, as Miller, Patton and Webb note, "In the classroom, faces matter"[17] and, I would add, not just the faces of students. That the academy's endeavors intersect with concerns regarding the identity of teachers and students—with the question Judith Berling faced, with the student so certain that women ought not to teach the New Testament and others equally sure that four women could not be dissimilar teachers together. To address these matters, I need first to make what may appear to be an oblique turn. And that is to the matter of disclosure in the academy.

In a 1988 article on introductory courses, Jonathan Z. Smith argues for a view of the academy as a site characterized by an "ethos of disclosure." In his discussion, Smith asserts that students ought to be "in the know." What should they know and what is involved in such an ethic? Smith argues, most specifically, for student awareness of the choices involved in the construction of courses and syllabi, for the need for students to "negotiate difference, evaluate, compare, and make judgments," for the need to turn "narratives into problems."[18] He argues, as well, for such presuppositions as the following:

> . . . a central goal of liberal learning is the acceptance of (and training in) *the requirement to bring private percept into public discourse and, therefore, the requirement to negotiate difference with civility.*

> . . . that *argument exists for the purpose of clarifying choices* and . . . choices are always consequential.[19]

Such an ethos is not unfamiliar; it resonates well with such well-worn historical constructs as "academic freedom" and American individualism. Yet this ethos raises as many questions as it seeks to answer. What private percepts are at stake? What are we to disclose? Is disclosure itself advocacy? What counts as civility and who determines this? Is there ever a place or time for "uncivil" discourse, for civil disobedience, in the academy? Are any "differences" ruled out? How are "choices" and their absence enactments of power, authority, legitimacy, and identity? In what ways is the academy's "ethos of disclosure" enacted? What remains undisclosed? Who controls the limits of disclosure?

While not, of course, the only way to examine such questions, depictions of our era as both "the age of testimony" and the time of a crisis in witnessing[20] lead me to turn my attention toward the conflation of disclosure with identity.

Discussions of identity politics are filled with assertions of the crucial importance of identity and identities in the contemporary world. Much political work, for example, rests upon specifying identities that have been oppressed or marginalized and working to obtain rights for such groups and such individuals. (Much political work moves, as well, toward identification of the responsibilities of those of us whose identity positions permit more rather than less access to privilege.) These endeavors are complicated, of course, by the historical and social construction of our world(s) and our identities, including alignments of power and knowledge/power relations. This can be illustrated by considering debates regarding census categories (and the use of such categories politically), debates regarding when HIV-positive folk become persons with AIDS and, thus, count as disabled, as well as debates regarding the efforts of gays and lesbians to obtain civil rights. Such debates are a reminder that the search for rights often risks rigidification and elaboration of category distinctions. In the very effort to attain equality, difference is reinstantiated. In the effort to establish "lesbian," for example, heterosexual is created, recreated and, often unwittingly reinforced; just as unwittingly, the establishment of lesbian serves to destabilize heterosexuality as the only form of sexuality. Likewise, the reminders that males are gendered, that whites are raced, are both salutary —and risky—moves. These moves, that is, reinstantiate categories while pressing beyond category identification and analysis to ask whose identity is at stake and at what cost. Identity as destiny? as resistance? as choice? as "historically contingent but seemingly inevitable; potentially limiting—but apparently politically essential"?[21]

How might these dilemmas be related to advocacy in the classroom? Is there such a thing as "identity scholarship" or "identity pedagogy"? Are they subject to the same limitations and do they offer the same promise as identity politics? Is the effort to legitimate advocacy something that risks relegitimizing its opposite? What strategies would help avoid such risks? How are such risks particularly important for religious studies as it has defined itself historically?

A variety of solutions to such dilemmas have been posited within the context of debate regarding identity politics. Perhaps we might consider analogies to Gayatri Spivak's notion of "strategic essentialism,"[22] to bell hooks's refusal of feminist as an identity category in favor of an understanding of it as a specific advocacy position.[23] Perhaps we can negotiate the need for local knowledges and local pedagogies within a global context[24] or work toward unlikely coalitions in the pursuit of justice. Perhaps we might think about drag, about parody,[25] and about passing. Perhaps we need to

think about the nature of the "advocacy" closet, the possibi.
outing ourselves and others, the performance of disclosure.

As we do so, we will need to consider the consequences of ea
strategy—remembering both (analogous) truisms: that people's support of gay and lesbian rights is frequently based on knowing a gay
person personally and that emerging from the closet, in some ways, is
impossible, remembering the ways in which hegemonic culture
constantly reinscribes power and delegitimizes those who "flaunt"
their sexuality while punishing those who hide. (Or, in different
ways, delegitimates and punishes both the open and the closeted.) By
analogy, we must place ourselves at the site of contradiction and
ambivalence (in the Freudian sense), for religious studies is simultaneously the site of hatred and love for our object, distance and close
relations, closeted religion and its opposite.

RESPONSIBLE ADVOCACY:
DEFINING DILEMMAS AND CONCLUDING STRATEGIES

Having hinted at these possibilities and raised a seemingly endless
array of questions that, I would argue, we must face each time we
enter the classroom responsibly, let me also warn us of the immobiliz-
ing potential of the questions themselves. The dilemma of advocacy
seems, in part, to be about steering between what I have in other
contexts called naïveté and paranoia and what we might also call the
Scylla of lofty principles and the Charybdis of local circumstances.
Put in the terms of Paul Tillich, we need to steer between the twin
abysses of annihilating openness and annihilating narrowness.[26]

On the one hand, religious studies faculty seem to agree with
emphasizing the role of religious studies in understanding religious
pluralism in contemporary culture. Judith Berling advocates, for
example, a view of religious studies as the enactment of a "broadening conversation" that "enables us to understand each other better
with our differences."[27] In making such arguments, many call for a
reappraisal of the ways in which the study of religion is enacted—
urging us to return to a more engaged approach, to move toward
confidence and criticism, as Robin Lovin has put it, or a passionate

scholarship, as Carol Christ has argued. They remind us, as well, that as Berling has said, "We religionists know how to live with what Geertz termed the loss of 'inward ease' that comes from encountering a profoundly different religious sensibility, and have learned that from dis-ease there can be considerable growth not only in insight, but in self-understanding."[28] And feminists in religious studies—both scholars and pedagogues—remind us to adopt a perspective that attends carefully to the potential for our work to reinscribe sexism, racism, imperialism. In doing so, feminists within religious studies urge us not to rest on our laurels but to widen the circle of our dis-ease.

Perhaps our role as teachers, then, is to create structures that support our students—and ourselves—in encountering the ongoing dis-ease which is learning. Perhaps our role is not to create a safe haven but to confront—and advocate—the value of struggle. Perhaps, that is, our role is to remain uncomfortable ourselves and to advocate, among other things, for our students.

In thinking this through and in enacting it, let us recall, as Gail Griffin writes, that "the truth does not immediately set you free after all. It sometimes leaves you speechless. Education can be unspeakable."[29] Let us turn, then, with both epistemological and pedagogical humility[30] to the struggle that is teaching and learning. Let us move back to the local—and I hope readers will think about their own teaching (and learning) experiences as we do so:

Scene 4: I wonder sometimes, about the student in Macomb, Illinois, who wrote an extremely articulate and one-sided exegesis of why women should not teach. Should I have given him the A I gave him, or was that an effort to hide the unhideable—that I am a woman who teaches and, indeed, a woman who teaches religion?

Scene 5: I wonder about the student in the senior forum—and, indeed, about the religious studies majors who replied to her assertion that you cannot discuss religion without acknowledging God by emphasizing the need to "bracket" God. Have they brought together confidence and criticism in their lives?

Scene 6: I think about Juliet Mitchell's advocacy of "using oneself," wondering if she finds it difficult or dangerous. I think about my own move from religiosity to religious studies, about the struggles, the students, the learning. And I admit, I advocate religious studies (and liberal arts education) with the passionate ambivalence of a secular lesbian feminist scholar with tenure.

NOTES

1. See also Judith A. Berling, "Is Conversation About Religion Possible? (And What Can Religionists Do to Promote It?)," *Journal of the American Academy of Religion* 61, no. 1 (1993), 1-22.

2. Peter Berger, *The Sacred Canopy* (New York: Doubleday, 1967).

3. Richard B. Miller, Laurie L. Patton, and Stephen H. Webb, "Rhetoric, Pedagogy, and the Study of Religion," *Journal of the American Academy of Religion* 62, no. 3(1994), 819-50, quoted on 837.

4. Stephen L. Carter, *The Culture of Disbelief* (New York: Doubleday, 1993); W. Royce Clark, "The Legal Status of Religious Studies in Public Higher Education," in Frank E. Reynolds and Sheryl L. Burkhalter (Eds.), *Beyond the Classics? Essays in Religious Studies and Liberal Education,* 109-39 (Atlanta: Scholars Press, 1990).

5. Conrad Cherry, "Boundaries and Frontiers for the Study of Religion: The Heritage of the Age of the University," *Journal of the American Academy of Religion* 57, no. 4 (1989), 807-28; Richard Hofstadter and C. DeWitt Hardy (Eds.), *The Development of Higher Education in the United States* (New York: Columbia University Press, 1952), 3.

6. Berling, "Is Conversation About Religion Possible?," 1-2.

7. See Carter, *The Culture of Disbelief;* Clark, "The Legal Status of Religious Studies"; Robert L. Wilken, "Who Will Speak *for* the Religious Traditions?," *Journal of the American Academy of Religion* 57, no. 4 (1989), 699-718.

8. See Wilken, "Who Will Speak *for* the Religious Traditions?," 700.

9. Sheryl Burkhalter, "Four Modes of Discourse: Blurred Genres in the Study of Religion," in Reynolds and Burkhalter (Eds.), *Beyond the Classics?,* 141-62. Quoted on 145.

10. Carter, *The Culture of Disbelief,* 56.

11. Cited by Wilken, "Who Will Speak *for* the Religious Traditions?," 701, from O'Flaherty; see also Susan E. Henking, "From Fundamentalism to Religious Studies: Notes Toward a Narration of Selves and Discourses," Presented at the American Academy of Religion meeting, Washington, DC, 1993.

12. Miller, Patton, and Webb, "Rhetoric, Pedagogy, and the Study of Relegion," 839. Cited from Edward Farley, *The Fragility of Knowledge* (Philadelphia: Fortress Press, 1988).

13. Cited in Benson Saler, *Studies in the History of Religions,* vol. 56, *Conceptualizing Religion: Immanent Anthropologists, Transcendent Natives and Unbounded Categories* (New York: E.J. Brill, 1993), 3.

14. Gail B. Griffin, *Calling: Essays on Teaching in the Mother Tongue* (Pasadena, CA: Trilogy Books, 1992), 180.

15. Cherry, "Boundaries and Frontiers for the Study of Religion"; Lawrence R. Veysey, *The Emergence of the American University* (Chicago: University of Chicago Press, 1965).

16. Compare Saler, *Conceptualizing Religion,* 251.

17. Miller, Patton, and Webb, "Rhetoric, Pedagogy, and the Study of Religion," 821.

18. Jonathan Z. Smith, "'Narratives into Problems: The College Introductory Course and the Study of Religion," *Journal of the American Academy of Religion* 56, no. 4 (1988), 727-40, Quotes from 737, 735.

19. Ibid., 733.

20. Shoshana Felman and Dori Laub, *Testimonies: Crises of Witnessing in Literature and Psychoanalysis* (New York: Routledge, 1992).

21. Jeffrey Weeks, "Questions of Identity," in Pat Caplan (Ed.), *The Cultural Construction of Sexuality* (New York: Tavistock Publications, 1987), 31-51, passim and 47.

22. See, in this regard G. C. Spivak, *In Other Worlds: Essays in Cultural Politics* (New York: Methuen, 1987).

23. bell hooks, *Feminist Theory: From Margin to Center* (Boston, MA: South End Press, 1984).

24. Cf. Miller, Patton, and Webb, "Rhetoric, Pedagogy, and the Study of Religion," 845.

25. As an example, see Martin E. Marty and Jerald Brauer (Eds.), *Unrelieved Paradox: Studies in the Theology of Franz Bibfeldt* (Grand Rapids, MI: Eerdmans, 1994).

26. Paul Tillich, *The Courage to Be* (New Haven, CT: Yale University Press, 1952).

27. Berling, "Is Conversation About Religion Possible?," 9; see also William Scott Green, "The Difference Religion Makes," *Journal of the American Academy of Religion* 62, no. 4 (1995), 1191-1206; Frank E. Reynolds, "Reconstructing Liberal Education: A Religious Studies Perspective," in Reynolds and Burkhalter (Eds.), *Beyond the Classics?*

28. Berling, "Is Conversation About Religion Possible?," 18.

29. Griffin, *Calling*, 179.

30. Compare Berling, "Is Conversation About Religion Possible?," 131.

TWENTY-FOUR

"A Teacher Is Either a Witness or a Stranger"

PENNY S. GOLD

WITHIN THE WIDE RANGE OF COURSES I TEACH—from Western Civilization to an introduction to women's studies, from a course on
friendship, love, and marriage in historical perspective to a course on
the Holocaust—the courses that I enjoy the most, the ones in which
I feel I come closest to fulfilling my mission as a teacher, are those in
which the relationship between learning and life, between knowledge
and action, comes to the surface—sometimes by plan and sometimes
by surprise, but naturally, from the heart of the material being
discussed. These are courses that have a message, that have moral
lessons in them, courses that have the potential of changing students'
lives. It was in the midst of teaching one of these courses last year, a
course on the Holocaust, that I came across the statement by
Abraham Joshua Heschel that I have used as my title: "A teacher is
either a witness or a stranger."[1] I found this statement provocative
and perplexing, but also helpful to me as I tried to think about my
role in the classroom, as someone helping students to think through
the complexities of motivation for historical action and as someone
inviting them to apply their understanding of past action to an
analysis of contemporary behavior—both their own and that of
others. I kept the quote posted on a wall near my desk, but I wasn't

quite sure what it meant. Preparing a paper on "Advocacy in the Classroom" gave me an opportunity to think through the implications of "witnessing" in the classroom.

The call for papers invited us to think about "advocacy" in the classroom. My own position is that the teacher should not so much be an advocate of a position but rather a model of a person who takes a position, which, of course, necessitates voicing that position. This essay explores why one might want to be such a model, what the risks are, and how such risks might be managed.

My thoughts on this subject come out of my own experience as a teacher, from reading, and, most recently, from an extended conversation with teachers and students at Knox, facilitated by an in-house e-mail discussion group on teaching.[2] My own college education, on the other hand, superb as it was, provides me no model of what I seek to accomplish in this sphere. I learned methods of interpreting a wide variety of texts, of analyzing different sorts of evidence. I am deeply grateful for this training, and use such critical skills every day. But I saw no models in the classroom of applying these skills to contemporary moral and political issues.[3]

So why do otherwise? Why not make an effort to be neutral in the classroom, or to put forward a variety of positions with equal force? It is because neutrality on issues of deep moral and political import is not something I want to encourage in my students. Why, then, attempt (or pretend) to be neutral myself? But having a position, and voicing that position, does not necessarily mean trying to convince others of it. This is where the term "witness" helps me. I see it as part of my role in the classroom to express, from time to time, simply and straightforwardly, what are core truths for me—to witness to the viability, for me, of a particular path, of particular choices. But I do not see it as my task to convince people to adopt my position. To continue in the religious language implied by "witnessing," I am not out to proselytize.[4] If a "conversion" occurs, it will be because of the long-term impact of thinking about and responding to the variety of positions expressed in the class (through the readings as well as through discussions), not because I have actively gone out to convince someone. An analogy that helps me visualize this process is that of conversion to Christianity in the early Middle Ages, in particular, the contrast of royal and monastic methods of conversion. The royal method was the quickest but most superficial in its results. A king's own conversion often spawned the immediate conversion of thousands of followers (Constantine, Clovis), or a king such as Charlemagne forced conversion through military conquest. Another method, however, was to send a small group of monks and sometimes nuns out to a frontier area and to have them live their lives, available to people who became interested in this strange but committed lifestyle. Every classroom seems a frontier to me—full of the new and unknown—in which I try to live my life, available to those who are interested in learning whatever it is I might have to offer. As part of our encounter, and in the course of our grappling together with texts from the past, I open windows, from time to time, on pieces of my life, on decisions I've struggled with.

In her recent book called *Teaching to Transgress,* bell hooks criticizes what she calls the "banking system of education" where teachers endeavor to fill students up with information, which they are supposed to then draw on at a later time. She advocates instead a vision of teaching—which is appealing to me—as a vocation that is "sacred," that aims "not merely to share information, but to share in the intellectual and spiritual growth of our students." It is essential, she says, "to teach in a manner that respects and cares for the souls of our students."[5] My college teachers also had nothing to do with the "banking system of education"; they pushed on process and asking questions, training me to ask questions to get to what I wanted to know. Their questions have served me well, but to get to a level that engages souls, I take those questions one step further: not asking only "What does this text mean?" or "Why did people behave in this way?" but also "What does this text mean to me?" "What can I learn for myself from this behavior?"[6]

Parallel questions, a colleague has convinced me, are possible in the teaching of poetry, though the judgments being nurtured are aesthetic ones rather than moral or political: Which poets are good and which are bad, and on what kinds of bases does one make this assessment?[7] In both arenas, there is a strong student current to row against: that all "opinions" are equally valid. Our task is to make clear that we're not in the business of exchanging opinions but of developing understanding and, eventually, of making judgments. To make judgments we need sharply focused questions, and we need evidence on which to base our answers. It's not just a matter of taste.

Which is not to say there can't be more than one answer, even if there is one that makes the most sense to me. I have thought especially about how to present multiple goods, or multiple truths, in the context of teaching a comparative religion class on Judaism, Christianity, and Islam. I am Jewish myself, an identity I do not attempt to hide from the students. I have a commitment to Judaism that does not extend to the other religions, and I have struggled with how to present the three religions evenly, given my own inclinations.[8] I have been helped in this by Lee Yearley, who has written recently about the question of how to understand multiple "goods" in religious traditions. Yearley, a Catholic, gives an account of spending two hours in Korea in front of an ancient statue of the Buddha, a statue that drew his attention "with a magnetic power [that] generate[d] a mysterious kind of peace or at least stillness." He concludes from this experience: "The spiritual vision presented there was as powerful and as tempting as any I have ever seen. Yet I wanted it neither for myself nor for those about whom I care most. I wanted the religious goods expressed in the Sokkurum Buddha to exist, and even to be incarnated by many people, and yet did not want the people I cared about most to possess them."[9] This is, indeed, the way I feel about many aspects of Christianity and Islam, and Yearley's formulation of goods that one wants present in the world, even while not wanting them for oneself or one's loved ones, has given me more confidence in my exercise of sometimes speaking in the first person as I discuss each of the three religious traditions. I use first-person speech ("we Muslims") in order to attempt an insider perspective, weighing the attractions and problems of a particular religious tradition from the special position of an insider, while also, on other occasions, stepping back outside.

There can be multiple religious goods, just as there can be many good poets. But that still leaves us with the issue of those positions about which one *cannot* say: "I want this position incarnated by many people, even if not myself." In teaching about the Holocaust, for example, I don't allow to flourish a pro-Nazi, anti-Semitic position on the place of Jews in the modern world, even though I spend much of the course helping students understand why that sort of position could, indeed, flourish in the 1930s and '40s, and we spend time reading and discussing Hitler's *Mein Kampf* and other anti-Semitic writings of the period. Another example: In my introductory women's studies course, which I describe on the syllabus as "an introduction to the analysis of human life using feminist perspectives," an avowed antifeminist will probably not hear his or her positions embodied by me, in contrast to a Muslim student in the religious studies class. Is this bad? Would it be better to play out a neutral stance?

When I asked students to comment (anonymously) on an abstract of this essay, only four out of the forty or so respondents thought it best that the teacher take a neutral position in the classroom. Several students commented that the teacher could be figured out anyway and that a stance of neutrality is a pretension or a fraud. One said, "To me, it shows that the teacher doesn't care about what is being taught." They liked teachers to make their positions explicit for a number of reasons: to give students something clear to react to; to help make the teacher part of the class, participating like the students; to give the students the benefit of their insights; to model a process of coming to a position.

But much as students wanted their teachers to make their own positions clear, they had serious concerns about how those positions were expressed and about consequences for students who disagreed with the teacher's position. Many talked about the strong influence that teachers have on students—"the most influential people outside the family," said one. "Students are always affected by the stance of the teacher," said another, and "Getting that effect to be a positive one is difficult . . . if the views between the teacher and student differ." The teacher knows more; the students are impressionable. And the teacher has power over the students, which enters into a concern expressed by several that a student's grade might be affected by a difference in view.

The answer some students and colleagues came up with to this problem is that a teacher can perhaps be *both* a witness and a stranger—a stranger in the sense of maintaining a distance from, or a lack of emotional involvement in, the positions students come to. I had stated in my abstract that I wanted to nurture in students the courage to take a stand on issues that matter but that I also cared what stand they took, and I asked if that was bad. Students answered that it was good to care about the views of students but that I should "never condemn or look down upon someone who views things differently for a good reason," that I should never make a student "feel threatened or alienated." Another warned me to "do what you can to get people talking, but don't care too much to pass judgment," don't "get emotionally involved." "Be sensitive to the students' attachments," another said. I think this is all good advice, and the longer I teach, the easier it is for me to maintain this delicate balance of caring deeply for my students and yet remaining distant from them, leaving them a large space to stake their claims.

The risk, then, of witnessing to one's own beliefs in the classroom is that students will feel dictated to, forced, stifled. But I was impressed with how many of my colleagues and students felt that risk was important to take, in order to gain the benefits of an engaged stance. The challenge, thus, is to create a classroom environment in which the witnessing of the teacher opens up the possibility for the witnessing of the students rather than closing it off. How to do this? It must be through establishing a web of mutual respect, concern, and careful listening.

bell hooks has much to say about this kind of classroom, a classroom that becomes a community of people "hearing one another's voices, . . . recognizing one another's presence." To make this happen, she says, "the professor must genuinely *value* everyone's presence" and there must be "an ongoing recognition that everyone influences the classroom dynamic, that everyone contributes."[10] A colleague of mine at Knox, for example, justifies his mandatory attendance policy to each class by explaining his belief that "we cannot possibly know who is going to do the most effective teaching on any given day, and none of us wants to be cheated out of what the absent person might have been able to add had he or she been there."[11] It has to be a classroom where many voices are heard and where each voice is listened to carefully and with respect. But this does not mean that voices go unchallenged. And much will be gained if the teacher can model changing his or her own position as a result of a considered challenge from a student. Or when, in the gift of team teaching, teachers can model vehement but respectful argument. Such a classroom will not always be comfortable, but it can, when everything is working, provide the safety of a community, forged by a shared commitment to work together to reach understanding of the issues at hand. I want students to love the excitement of rising voices, not be scared by them.

I cannot claim to achieve this kind of classroom community in every course I teach or throughout the term in any one class. But with the hope of eliciting examples from others, here are some specific strategies that, in my experience, can contribute to such a classroom. These strategies include assigned readings, discussion strategies, and writing assignments.

An assigned reading that explicitly challenges the status quo, or what passes for common sense or sensibility in our culture, can have the effect of cracking open responses in students. They can produce "moments of misunderstanding and anger," which Geraldine Casey calls "a great, untapped resource for our teaching praxis."[12] In a class on "Gay and Lesbian Identities," for example, I've used Gayle Rubin's article on "Thinking Sex," which calls into question our culture's standing assumptions on what is appropriate and inappropriate sexual behavior, going so far as to make one think about sadomasochism and sex with children.[13] In the Holocaust class, I've used Elie Wiesel's "A Plea for Survivors," which speaks with pain and anger about the treatment of Holocaust survivors in contemporary culture; his deep anger at even well-meaning people disturbs many students.[14] If things work well, readings like these will generate an emotional rejection in some students, which is responded to by other students, with a heated conversation resulting. In such a discussion, I try to manage the heat with questions, but at some point, as the discussion is either winding down or spinning out of control, I may give students my own response to the piece, witnessing to the ways in which it made me rethink my own assumptions and to the questions it leaves unsettled in my mind.

To accomplish the goal of connecting thought and action, of applying learning to life, I look for moments in class discussion when examples of such connections can be played out. This is only a very small part of what we do, but it can have a large impact. A few years ago, for example, when David Duke was campaigning with significant success in Louisiana, a student in my Holocaust class (where we discuss, at the end of the term, neo-Nazi movements in the United States) suggested that we should invite David Duke to speak on campus. Here was a question, "Should we invite him?" to which the only possible answers were "yes" or "no," but the reasons to decide one way or another were multiple. After the class had debated this question at length, I offered my own position on the question—not as an attempt to settle the issue with the one right answer but to model for them one answer, the considerations I brought to that answer, and—most important—to model the importance of reaching an answer and not just leaving the matter as an interesting debate. Another year we had a similarly productive discussion on the issue of whether the campus newspaper should run an ad for a "revisionist" journal that promotes the nonoccurrence of the Holocaust. On this occasion I had assigned readings on the issue (a selection from the journal itself as well as Deborah Lipstadt's description of it) and then structured a debate, with half the class assigned to argue for running the ad and half against.[15] Again, after a lively debate in which all positions were examined and challenged, I talked to the students about my own stand on this issue. I don't think this closed off students' thinking but rather, I hope, confirmed the importance of, eventually, taking a stand.

Finally, through specific written and oral projects, students can be encouraged to bring their own experience to bear on the subject and material of a course. In an introductory women's studies course, for example, I have students apply theories from the course to material around them—to a children's book, to an advertisement, to a social interaction—and when they bring the papers in, I have them share their analyses in small groups. I also require all students to make brief oral presentations to the class—to tell the class about something they've read or experienced that would be of interest to us (with recent students analyzing, for example, video games, beauty contests, experiences in foreign countries). And sprinkled lightly through the course are examples from me, in which I try to model how experience and academic material can illuminate each other.[16] One story I sometimes use, for example, tells of the moment I finally figured out that my perennial discomfort in high-heeled shoes was not due to my inability to find just the right pair but was rather one part of a whole system of body control for women designed to keep them uncomfortable and constrained.

Self-disclosure is risky for the teacher, and small doses go a long way. But such disclosure—which is one form of witnessing—is a powerful act of permission to the students—permission to bring their life to the classroom and the classroom to their life. The teacher shouldn't tell students what to do, but through a balance of setting an example and of giving students permission to go out on their own, a teacher can help a student cut a path in life.

One student wrote to me, "It's okay to tell younger students where you stand, but not college-aged students—they need to find their own way." But I really don't think it's a question of age. I still need teachers and am grateful for those who occasionally enter my life. Yes, a teacher is an influence on students! And from the many different teachers a student has, let us hope that there are one or two who provide a beacon for the path that student becomes determined to follow.

NOTES

1. Abraham Joshua Heschel, *The Insecurity of Freedom* (New York: Noonday Press, 1967), p. 237.
2. I would like to thank the many people without whose help this essay would have been much diminished: Thanks to Sheryl St. Germain, who set up the e-mail teaching list at Knox, and who, along with Harley Knosher, Ivan Davidson, Elena Glasberg, Frank McAndrew, and David Amor, helped me work out the ideas presented here. Thanks also to the students in my classes on "Judaism, Christianity, and Islam" and "Gay and Lesbian Identities," and to the students on the modern poetry discussion list, who told me what "advocacy" feels like from the student perspective. Most wrote anonymously, but I'd

like to acknowledge by name those who signed their remarks: Paul Benson, Michael Calomese, Christy Durall, Jason Eisner, Christine Glover, Sarah Hartz, Terez Ivy, Jen Katz, Heather Lorance, Dan Polley, Larry Reifler, Eric Swegle, Kydalla Young.

3. I can recall only two moments in my undergraduate years when some sort of personal conviction—or even just personal emotion—entered the classroom. Once was when a teacher explained that he had missed the previous class because his wife had had a baby; the other was when a teacher, in the wake of a controversial tenure decision, took class time to talk to us about what tenure meant. These moments made an impression on me because of the strange inclusion of the personal in the classroom—yet still in neither case were the remarks linked in any way to the substantive project of the class. Even more important to me were a couple of occasions in which I saw a teacher take a considered political stand. The first was a teacher who stood on a picket line, protesting a negative tenure decision. The second, in graduate school, was a teacher who, during the period of the Cambodian invasion, talked to me about his own antiwar stance, showed me a letter he had written to the president, and did community education work against the war. Yet these incidents were both outside the classroom, and no connection was made between being a medieval historian (as both teachers were) and contemporary political action.

4. Other volume contributors make a similar point, with Myles Brand also arguing against "proselytizing," Nadine Strossen against "indoctrination," and Louis Menand against "hammering."

5. bell hooks, *Teaching to Transgress: Education as the Practice of Freedom* (New York: Routledge, 1994), 13.

6. I have been helped here by the source analysis questions presented by Mark A. Kishlansky in his Western Civilization anthology, the last of which is "What does this document mean to me?" (*Sources of the West*, 2nd ed. [New York: HarperCollins, 1995], 1:xxi). Similarly, bell hooks speaks of students' rightful expectations that their teachers "will not offer them information without addressing the connection between what they are learning and their overall life experiences" (*Teaching to Transgress*, 19).

7. Thanks to Sheryl St. Germain for discussion of this analogy.

8. See Penny S. Gold, "Teaching Judaism in Three Weeks: Selectivity and the Position of the Instructor," *Shofar: An Interdisciplinary Journal of Jewish Studies* 13 (1995), 58-80.

9. Lee H. Yearley, "New Religious Virtues and the Study of Religion," paper presented at the Fifteenth Annual University Lecture in Religion at Arizona State University, February 10, 1994.

10. hooks, *Teaching to Transgress*, 8.

11. Thanks to Harley Knosher for this comment and for the fruitful discussion between us that it engendered.

12. Geraldine Casey, "Racism, Anger, and Empowerment: Teaching Anthropology in a Multi-Racial, Working-Class Environment," *Transforming Anthropology* 2, no. 1 (1991), 9, 12-13. Thanks to Sharyn Kasmir for sharing this article with me.

13. Gayle S. Rubin, "Thinking Sex: Notes for a Radical Theory of the Politics of Sexuality," in Henry Abelove, Michèle Aina Barale, and David M. Halperin (Eds.), *The Lesbian and Gay Studies Reader* (New York: Routledge, 1993), 3-44.

14. Elie Wiesel, "A Plea for Survivors," in *A Jew Today* (New York: Vintage, 1979), 218-47.

15. David Cole, "A Jewish Revisionist's Visit to Auschwitz," *Journal of Historical Review* 13, no. 2 (1993), 11-13; Deborah Lipstadt, *Denying the Holocaust: The Growing Assault on Truth and Memory* (New York: Free Press, 1993), 137-56.

16. "It is often productive if professors take the first risk, linking confessional narratives to academic discussions so as to show how experience can illuminate and enhance our understanding of academic material" (hooks, *Teaching to Transgress*, 21).

TWENTY-FIVE

Theory and Politics of Art History

KEITH MOXEY

HOW DO THE TITLE AND THEME OF THIS VOLUME, "Advocacy in the Classroom," intersect with the disciplinary work of art history? How do we understand the concept of advocacy? Is art historical instruction necessarily identified with a notion of advocacy? Does it inescapably involve the advocacy of certain cultural values or political attitudes? If so, with what kinds of values is the history of art identified? Can they be changed? Is there a role for agency in the production of art historical knowledge? What can the individual art historian contribute to the cultural agenda of our discipline?

This chapter is not intended as a descriptive account of the art historical situation, but an account of what kinds of advocacy art history is currently concerned with. This is not a sociological survey of past and present historical trends, something I am not competent to write. It is a comparison, rather, of what seem to me to be some of the social implications, some of the attitudes advocated, by both the traditional and what has come to be known as the "new" history of art. What, in other words, was and is advocated by those who subscribe to a traditional vision of the history of art's social function, and what is advocated by those who subscribe to a new vision of what that function should be?

One way to understand the phrase "Advocacy in the Classroom" is descriptively, as a recognition of what actually goes on when any form of instruction takes place. In this view, there could be no instruction without the projection of a specific ideological agenda; no instruction that did not involve a particular point of view. My interpretation of the title clearly subscribes to a poststructuralist understanding of the nature of knowledge. Far from regarding knowledge as fixed and constant, this perspective would view it as transitional and evolving, something that is inflected and colored by the processes of its articulation and production.[1] It is no doubt this view of knowledge, and the ways it transforms our notions of education, that challenges some of the fundamental assumptions of traditional art historical studies, for it denies that the methodological models that the discipline has so carefully and patiently evolved are capable of producing lasting analyses of works of art. It suggests that rather than working in concert toward some institutionally sanctioned goal of enlightenment, art historians inevitably produce accounts of the past that are marked by their own idiosyncratic concerns in the present. Far from basing our production of knowledge on some firm epistemological foundation, we actually work according to certain paradigms of meaning production, paradigms that have more to do with the sociology of the discipline than with the nature of art or reality. These ideas, which have been widely disseminated throughout other humanities disciplines, still have the power to shock certain members of our profession. The scientific model of meaning production, according to which empirical observation and deductive reasoning are considered essential, is too deeply entrenched to be easily overthrown. The self-appointed guardians of art historical truth have objected to this new conception of disciplinary practice and indeed have worked to alter the nature of the College Art Association's annual meetings as well as to found an organization of their own, one that, unlike the CAA, would have no place for the newer forms of art historical interpretation.

While most of us might agree that all forms of art historical instruction involve the advocacy of a particular cultural agenda, how can we define that with which art history has been traditionally associated? What, in other words, has the transmission of art historical knowledge entailed in the past? What values were woven into the presentation of art historical information, and how do those values relate to the ideological structure of our society?

As one of the genres of higher education, art history is closely identified with an institution, the university, which functions to produce cultural meaning that in turn serves to acculturate and socialize the subjectivities of those who come in contact with it. The university as well as the museum disseminate social attitudes regarding the raced, classed, and gendered roles of those with whom they come in contact. One of the most important aspects of art history's social message is the way it inculcates a knowledge of and respect for a canon of great works of art. According to Ernst Gombrich, the canon:

> . . . offers points of reference, standards of excellence which we cannot level down without losing direction. Which particular peaks, or which individual achievements we select for this role may be a matter of choice, but we could not make such a choice if there were really no peaks but only shifting dunes. . . . the values of the canon are too deeply embedded in the totality of our civilization for them to be discussed in isolation. . . . Our attitude to the peaks of art can be conveyed through the way we speak about them, perhaps through our very reluctance to spoil the experience with too much talk. What we call civilization may be interpreted as a web of value judgment that are implicit rather than explicit.[2]

Gombrich's statement is representative of attitudes that have wide currency within our discipline. As a consequence, it may be worth deconstructing its contradictions and exposing its hidden assumptions. While we are allegedly free to choose which peaks of achievement we want to recognize, this choice is, in fact, vitiated by the fact that there are already peaks there to be recognized. Instead of being subjective and relative, the judgment of quality involves the recognition of differences that are already inscribed in the order of things. According to Gombrich, "the values of the canon are too deeply embedded in the totality of our civilization for them to be discussed in isolation."[3]

The canon is self-evident, part and parcel of the culture we belong to, an aspect of a value system that is too deeply naturalized to be scrutinized. The notion that the civilization of which he speaks—Gombrich's Austrian and British educated bourgeois culture—might be relativized by a recognition of the values of other cultural worlds, the possibility that his values might not be those of all human beings, is never raised. Finally, the qualities that make the canon canonical cannot be openly discussed. The attitude that Gombrich urges us to adopt is that of a reverential silence. Nothing must disturb our appreciation of the peaks because rough analysis might tear the apparently fragile fabric of the civilization to which they belong. Evaluation and discussion are not part of the civilization Gombrich asks us to subscribe to, for its values are specifically described as implicit rather than explicit. This civilization depends, like all ideologies, on what is unsaid. To articulate its values might be to subject them to debate and even criticism. More important perhaps, such a process would suggest that the values of this civilization were relative, that not only might they not be universal but that they might be completely incomprehensible to others. The extent to which the canon is considered part of the order of things, something that cannot and therefore should not be questioned, means that art history's ideological function becomes part of the social unconscious.

Art historical methodologies operate on the assumption that the canon is simply there and that all sensate individuals acknowledge its existence without questioning its cultural validity. Starting with the work of art, art historical approaches, from formalism to Marxism, do not find it necessary to argue why the works they address are worthy of the kind of analysis to which they are subjected. The formalist, for example, locates the work in a history of style; the iconographer explains its subject matter by reference to literary texts; the social historian provides it with a social context; and the Marxist clarifies its relation to the class struggle. None of these perspectives regards it as necessary or even desirable to attempt to articulate what it is that distinguishes this particular work of art from those produced in the same period, or what it is that separates it from other cultural artifacts, because they have already been canonized by tradition. Its status as a legitimate object of study is simply assumed. That most subjective of judgments, the judgment of quality, has been naturalized to such an extent that the question as to why art historians study the objects they do would probably be answered with looks of incomprehension or incredulity.

If we were, for example, to subscribe to Gombrich's account of the universality of the notion of quality, then those who do not respond to works of art in the way a universalist aesthetic predicts they should are marginalized, their opinions discounted on the grounds that they are uneducated and thus fail to appreciate what is obvious to those who are. In these circumstances, art history operates as a mechanism of class distinction, supporting and maintaining class identities on the basis of an unequal access to knowledge. A discipline built on the notion that an important aspect of human knowledge depends on the recognition of a canon of great works of art and that this canon can be recognized only by those with the education to do so excludes those who do not have the means, the ability, or the inclination to obtain that education. The result is that art history becomes an agent in what Pierre Bourdieu has called the transfer of "cultural capital."[4] The discipline is implicated in the process by which a class society perpetuates itself; it ensures that future generations of the elite will have access to what are regarded as civilization's masterpieces, that they will appreciate not only the works themselves but the process by which they came to believe that these works were valuable. Art history thus serves the elite by instructing them in the cultural values that are thought to define the concept of quality. The role of art history might be said to interpellate those who would share the dominant ideology by serving as a means by which they can identify themselves as card-carrying members of the social elite.

The irony involved in subscribing to a universal theory of aesthetic appeal and simultaneously believing that aesthetic value can be perceived only by the educated is overlooked. Far from recognizing the contradiction as one that disables this enlightenment theory of aesthetics, the protagonists of a universal concept of quality, art historians, connoisseurs, museum curators, and the like simply ignore it. They appear to believe that education serves to uncover truth rather than to create it. It is as if there were some bedrock of human nature that was always and forever the same in all human beings, regardless of their race, nationality, class, or gender. They believe that if all members of a culture had access to education, then they, too, would be able to make discriminations based on the concept of quality, not because they had learned to do so, not as the product of class acculturation, but because education had somehow allowed them to know something about themselves, about art and their responses to it, that they did not know before.

Art history's role in supporting the ideology of the status quo takes many forms. While the theoretical difficulties of its promotion of a canon of primarily Western art has been widely discussed, most notably by Norman Bryson, it is worth dwelling upon the canon's social implications.[5] Since European art is mainly naturalistic in character, that is, its representations tend to bear some relation to our perceptual experience of the world, Bryson has argued that the art historical canon promotes naturalistic art, an art based on the principle of mimesis, over artistic traditions based on abstraction. This bias leads not only, as he points out, to a reductive approach to pictorial representation—works of art being evaluated on the basis of their relation to the circumstances they appear to depict rather than their capacity to make cultural meaning—but to the marginalization of many non-Western traditions. The Eurocentric quality of the canon and the representational values associated with it serve to distinguish art history from other disciplines by making it less sensitive as well as less capable of dealing with the concept of difference in its approach to and evaluation of other cultures. Art history in this country is often a discipline whose values continue to promote the artistic preoccupations of the Western tradition. An analysis of recent introductory survey books for the history of art suggests that while authors are anxious to incorporate other cultures into their art historical narrative, these often depend on extending to alien cultures homegrown concepts such as "art" and "quality" that are ultimately irrelevant to the conditions in which those traditions were generated.

As was the case in literary studies, art history has attempted to come to terms with the notion that its romantic definition of the artist as a transcendental genius merely justifies the canon of great works of art without affording much insight into the nature of artistic production. The social consequences of the myth of the artist as an extraordinary individual serve to promote the idea that works of art do not belong to conventional systems for creating pictorial meaning so much as they are manifestations of forces that are by definition unintelligible (or sublime). This heroic account of human subjectivity serves as a moral allegory of the status of the individual. It suggests that the individual has the power to overcome the circumstances to which a raced, classed, and gendered society has assigned it. It serves as a parable of the way in which "natural" talent, that which once again defies analysis and is incomprehensible, can receive the social recognition it deserves. It is, indeed, the exception that proves the rule. It is, for example, the myth that Vasari promoted of the peasant status of the likes of Giotto that serves to support the naturalized system of social privilege.[6] A system that would ordinarily work to ensure that a peasant (or a woman) never got anywhere near the conditions necessary for effective intervention in the processes of artistic production is validated by those allegedly extraordinary individuals, dubbed geniuses, who managed to defy its protocols and discredit its assumptions.

So far, this has been an unmitigated indictment of art history's role as a support of the status quo. The equation of the concept of quality with the values that have been sanctioned by tradition means that art history has often been complicit in perpetuating an unreflective attitude toward which works of art and which artists merit its disciplinary attention. The fact that the list of works and artists regarded as outstanding has varied in the course of time is only rarely brought disciplinary consciousness. (One thinks here of the exemplary but isolated work of Francis Haskell.)[7] Quasi-scientific objectivity has been pursued at the expense of a recognition that subjective evaluation must inevitably register in the process of historical interpretation. Unlike other disciplines in the humanities in which the attack on foundationalist epistemology has been listened to and acted upon, art history remains largely untouched by poststructuralist critique. Does this serve to consign it to what Bryson has called "the leisure sector of intellectual life"[8] forever, or is it possible that transformation and change are likely in this youthful yet strangely venerable institution? How, in other words, can its current role in support of the established social hierarchy be overturned?

First and foremost, it seems to me that it will be necessary to abandon a universalist theory of aesthetics in favor of theories that are specific and local. If art history is to become an innovative discipline, one that is in the forefront of theoretical and methodological development in the humanities, the aesthetic power of works of art can no longer be taken for granted. It will be necessary, rather, to articulate the qualities that serve to distinguish certain objects from the cultural artifacts that surround them, in order to subject them to special attention. This special status will have to be argued case by case so that the need to make it the object of intense scrutiny and speculation, the focus of an intellectual and cultural ritual, becomes apparent. There will be, of course, nothing self-evident about such arguments. In place of an appeal to universal response, it will be necessary to articulate the peculiar values that serve to make certain objects exceptional for us. What is it that we attribute to such objects? What is it that prompts us to bestow upon them the status "works of art"?

In the absence of universalist aesthetics, the cultural artifact becomes a work of art because of the meaning projected into it by particular individuals in particular cultures at particular moments in time. The work neither calls forth a universal response, nor is it possessed of the intrinsic significance such a response implies. The aesthetic importance of any work will hinge on the meaning ascribed to it by those who seek to make it the object of a ritualized fascination. It is at this point that it will be possible to discern the cultural and political agendas on which such discriminations are made. In these circumstances it will be the claims made about the object, rather than the object itself, that articulate the ideological work that the object is being called upon to perform.

It is clear that in the past decade, art history has begun to address the types of issues raised in this chapter. Art historians are now confronted with an array of politically motivated forms of interpretation that seek to transform the discipline's traditional identification with the status quo. Feminism first challenged the validity of the art historical canon on the grounds that it was the product of masculinist values, and feminists pointed out that the canon of great works to which art history was dedicated was the result of cultural processes that had excluded women from the ranks of artistic producers.[9] To extol this canon as the achievement of Western civilization and to acculturate the members of the elite in the appreciation of its qualities was to ignore the fact that it existed only as a consequence of the systematic exclusion of women. By insisting that it recognize that the Western canon depended on the marginalization and subordination of the interests of an important sector of the population, namely women, feminists challenged art history's involvement in the dominant ideology, effectively asking art history and art historians to become aware of the discipline's ideological agenda, its commitment to the support of the values of a male elite. Art historical narratives written from this perspective have taken a variety of forms. Some scholars have argued, for example, that canonical status be extended to certain women artists whose importance has been over-looked because, far from being universal, the concept of quality had long been linked to specifically male characteristics. Others have analyzed the historical context in which the canon was produced in order to indicate that rather than there being an absence of female "geniuses," cultural values have prevented the involvement of women in the processes of artistic production. In doing so, they argued that there was nothing obvious about the canon, nothing self-evident, but rather that the canon is a cultural creation that inevitably bears the marks of the social circumstances in which it is produced.

The feminist challenge to traditional art history has been followed by other forms of political criticism, among them African American studies, gay and lesbian studies, and postcolonialism. It is in the midst of these new conditions that the issue of advocacy takes on new meaning. The plethora of different voices that advocate the interests of one particular group or another constitute an important countercultural discourse, one that has the potential of transforming our discipline. What has happened is that the canon of Western art has been adapted to serve the interests of these new political agendas. Feminists, for example, not only teach courses that point out the patriarchal values that dominate the traditional canon, but they also pay special attention to historical moments in which those values appear particularly incoherent and trite. They also teach courses that promote the qualities of contemporary women artists whose work explicitly engages the way in which gender relations are characterized by the dominant ideology.

These politically inspired forms of art historical criticism are clearly responsible for the gradual transformation of our discipline and its function as an ideological discourse. They have dramatized the way in which traditional art history has been implicated in the ideological support of the social elite, and in doing so, they have relativized the narratives with which this work had been achieved. Rather than accept that there is an established canon of artists and works that art historians are meant to address, these new perspectives question the respect that has been accorded them in the past by spinning new narratives about their historical significance. The subversion of the master narratives of art history that these new points of view represent means that the social function of the discipline is more varied and heterogeneous than it was before. It is possible to study art history now as a discipline that advocates an equal position for women in the distribution of social power, or as a discipline that advocates that there is no place for homophobia in our culture's dominant ideology, or as a discipline that advocates a recognition of the ways in which the colonial experience was a two-way street, one in which European cultures were manipulated and transformed by Europeans as well as one in which the European ideologies of domination and control were subjected to scrutiny and criticism they could not survive.

In contrast to the situation in higher education, however, the art market and the museum continue—with a few notable exceptions—to be deeply involved in disseminating received ideas. Depending for their existence on a universalist aesthetic that fails to recognize racial, class, or gendered difference, these institutions are currently farther from academic art history than they have ever been. The gulf that separates critical history from museum practice could be used as an index of the extent to which the discipline has changed in recent years. Whereas, for the most part, the market and the museum remain wedded to a conception of art history that depends on its continued identification with a canon of Western art and with the dissemination of a knowledge of that canon by means of the educational process, the educational process itself has changed so that it is no longer concerned to reproduce the attitudes on which they depend. The laments of connoisseurs and curators are all too familiar. One is continually regaled with stories about recent graduates who do not know enough to distinguish the works of one artist from another and who no longer possess a sense of "quality." All of this indicates that in higher education, art history is beginning to stand for a broader engagement with cultural issues than was previously the case.

In conclusion, I believe it is important to remember that the types of change that have been all too inadequately sketched in this chapter could not have been brought about without the appropriation or incorporation of a variety of theoretical impulses that had their origins outside of art history. The very concept of art history as advocacy of one political agenda or another is unthinkable without the revision of the concept of epistemology that became possible as a result of theoretical developments that took place in psychoanalysis, linguistics, and anthropology. Without a relativization of the theory of knowledge, without a recognition of the fact that all knowledge is local knowledge, it would have been difficult to challenge the universalist claims of the aesthetic on which our discipline was founded and on which its claims to legitimacy have rested ever since. Disciplinary change is thus a product of the intersection of theory and politics. If art history is reaping the benefits of the introduction of politically animated forms of historical interpretation, and if it recognizes that art historians are always committed to advocacy in the classroom, it is because our entire understanding of the relation between subjectivity and objectivity has been transformed by poststructuralist theory.

NOTES

1. See, for example, Thomas Kuhn, *The Structure of Scientific Revolutions* (Chicago: University of Chicago Press, 1970); Donna Haraway, "Situated Knowledge: The Science Question in Feminism and the Privilege of Partial Perspective," *Feminist Studies* 14 (1988), 575-599; Edward Said, *Orientalism* (New York: Vintage Books, 1979); Johannes

Fabian, *Time and the Other: How Anthropology Makes Its Object* (New York: Columbia University Press, 1983).

2. Ernst Gombrich, *Art History and the Social Sciences: The Romanes Lecture for 1973* (Oxford: Clarendon Press, 1975), 54.

3. Ibid., 54.

4. See Pierre Bourdieu, *Distinction. A Social Critique of the Judgment of Taste,* trans. Richard Nice (London: Routledge, 1989); Pierre Bourdieu and Jean-Claude Passeron, *Perspective in Education, Society, and Culture,* trans. Richard Nice (London: Sage, 1990); Pierre Bourdieu, *The Field of Cultural Production* (New York: New York University Press, 1993).

5. Norman Bryson, *Vision and Painting. The Logic of the Gaze* (London: Macmillan, 1983).

6. See Ernst Kris and Otto Kurz, *Legend, Myth, and Magic in the Image of the Artist* (New Haven, CT: Yale University Press, 1979), 25.

7. Francis Haskell, *Taste and the Antique. The Lure of Classical Sculpture, 1500-1900* (New Haven, CT: Yale University Press, 1981).

8. Bryson, *Vision and Painting,* 11.

9. Linda Nochlin, "Why Have There Been No Great Women Artists," *Artnews* 69 (1971), 23-39, 67-69.

TWENTY-SIX

Be Reasonable and Do It My Way: Advocacy in the College Classroom

FELICIA ACKERMAN

You mean they think professors ought to advocate for their political views? In the *classroom*?

THIS RHETORICAL QUESTION from Donna Harvey, a nonacademic friend whom I told about some material I was reading in preparation for writing this chapter, illustrates one outsider's reaction to the question of professorial advocacy in the classroom—the very idea strikes her as preposterous and presumptuous. Is my friend right? The answer requires distinguishing different kinds of advocacy.

When I was a Cornell undergraduate in the 1960s, I sometimes heard about professors who spent all or part of class sessions discussing the Vietnam War rather than the course's official subject matter. My recollections are hazy, but I'm pretty sure this included courses where Vietnam discussions could not have plausibly been said to improve students' understanding of the course material. This never happened in a course I took, and I don't know how often it happened at all. But such cases are a useful starting point for my chapter, because—at least where the Vietnam material had no bearing on the official subject matter of the course—they are a prime candidate for the category of improper use of advocacy by a professor.

Why? Because these professors were reneging on their jobs while still drawing their salaries. If they considered antiwar activity important, they could have devoted many out-of-class hours to it. If they considered antiwar activity important enough to override their professional responsibilities, they could have taken a term's unpaid leave to do political work full time. Some professors did do these honorable things. Reneging on one's job while still expecting to be paid, however, is difficult to defend as a moral position. It may also show arrogance and inegalitarianism. How many of these professors would have paid their garage mechanic for a tune-up if the mechanic had instead given them a political lecture, or would have paid for a full hour's piano lesson for their child if the piano teacher had spent half the time trying to engage the child in political discussion instead?

Several objections can be made to what I have said here. First, as I have acknowledged, the foregoing extreme version of my thesis applies only to courses on which the Vietnam War had no plausible bearing, such as Old English grammar or music theory. In fact, there is a continuum here, ranging from such courses, through courses where Vietnam could be worked in with various degrees of stretching, to courses where it would have been inappropriate *not* to discuss Vietnam, such as a course on contemporary American politics. Second, anyone who has endured professors' classroom jokes or anecdotes about their graduate training or travels abroad knows well that a fair amount of what goes on in many classrooms is irrelevant to the subject matter of the course. So it can be argued that antiwar digressers should not be singled out for reneging on the job. This is true, although I think it calls for a dimmer view of long-winded anecdotal digressers rather than a brighter view of long-winded political digressers. But I want to stress that no view about what constitutes proper or improper classroom behavior for professors entails anything about the separate issue of how, if at all, rules for proper behavior should be codified and violations monitored—a point made by Peter Markie in his book *A Professor's Duties.*[1] In fact, I think that (except in cases of the most egregious violations) such monitoring is apt to do more harm than good. Finally, I want to refute two bad arguments against my view of this particular case. One is that going about one's classroom business as usual during what one takes to be a political atrocity constitutes tacit approval of the status quo. But of course it doesn't; one can wear a political button in the classroom and do whatever political work one feels impelled to do outside. The other bad argument is that it is appropriate even for professors in courses on music theory or algebraic number theory to use class time to discuss political issues, because their mandate is to educate students and they are entitled to use their own judgment about how best to do so. Well, their mandate isn't that broad. The mandate of algebraic number theory instructors is to teach algebraic number theory. They have considerable leeway about how to do this, but they are not entitled to take it upon themselves to teach some other subject in an algebraic number theory class instead.[2]

That's one kind of advocacy. Here's a different sort of case. A few years ago, I saw a syllabus for a course called "Ecofeminism" at a state university. The syllabus contained this stricture: "ALL WRITTEN WORK MUST BE TURNED IN ON THE BACK OF USED PAPER".[3]

Although the professor in this course cannot be said to be reneging on her job by using class time for something else, I think this requirement is clearly improper. First, it requires students to act in accord with their professor's particular political views about the importance of recycling. Second, it gets students to act in accord with these views not by convincing them, through evidence and reasoned arguments, of the correctness of these views, but simply by a direct order—a naked exercise of professorial authority. Third, this order is not in an area where it is legitimate for a professor to exercise authority, such as requiring that students do what is designed either to make them learn and think or to measure how effectively they have learned and thought. Fourth, a professor who requires that students act in conformity with her political views is hardly creating a climate where students will feel free to engage in classroom discussion that is critical of these views.

This case may sound bizarre—it certainly does to me—but the issue it reflects is more widespread. This issue also arises with professors who require "inclusive" language (spurning the generic "he") in student papers, a matter about which I have only anecdotal evidence, and would of course arise in exactly the same way with professors who required "traditional" language (spurning the generic "she" or "he or she"), if there are any nowadays, as there may be, but not in cases I have heard about.

Of course, there are possible objections to my arguments here, as well. One is that it is intellectually valuable for students in courses dealing with environmental issues to learn firsthand how easy (or hard) it is to turn in their work on the back of used paper, and that eschewing the generic "he" enables students to see social and political issues in a new way.[4] But this would at most call for having students in an ecofeminism course turn in *one* assignment (not all assignments) on used paper and would call for students in courses dealing with social and political issues to do one paper in inclusive language and one in traditional language, to see for themselves whether these different linguistic forms really do encourage different perspectives on the material. Professors should avoid making unsubstantiated assumptions about students' backgrounds and prior beliefs—a point I will return to later—such as, in the present context, the assumption that recycling or inclusive language will be new ideas to one's students. Colleges and universities vary enormously, as do the sorts of students they attract. Most students seem to come to Brown, for example, already inclined to eschew the generic "he." This may or may not be true of the students in your classes, but it is obviously better to try to find out than to base your teaching on unsubstantiated assumptions about the influence that the great patriarchical hegemony has had on your particular students.

Another possible case provides an interesting wrinkle here. Orthodox Jews write the word "God" as "G-d"; now imagine an Orthodox Jewish professor who requires students to do this in their philosophy of religion papers. This would be obviously improper at a secular university, but the interesting wrinkle is what we should say if it occurred at a college that is officially Orthodox Jewish. Many of my objections to the ecofeminism course would not apply in such a case, as students at such a college would presumably not be required to act in conformity with views they do not all hold. Their very choice to attend an officially religious institution can be construed as consent to that religion's restrictions. But now a new question arises.

If religious colleges have a legitimate place in higher education, then can't there be a case for officially rightist and leftist ones, as well, where particular political and social principles would officially underlie and guide their programs in a way parallel to the way Catholicism guides Notre Dame or Calvinism guides Calvin College? I will only raise this question, rather than discuss it in detail, because I have some difficulty appreciating the point of officially religious or partisan higher education at all, at least at the undergraduate level. Catholic theology Ph.D. candidates may well gain intellectually from working out the refinements of their views with other Catholic scholars who share their basic assumptions. But 17-year-olds who are fresh out of a conservative Catholic background and 12 years of parochial school are unlikely to have a maximally broadening experience at a conservative Catholic college, just as 17-year-olds from secular liberal-leftist backgrounds are unlikely to have maximally broadening experiences at colleges that are overwhelmingly liberal-leftist. Frankly, I think one thing colleges could do for true intellectual growth and real diversity would be to offer student and faculty exchange programs between such schools as Hillsdale College and Thomas Aquinas College, on the one hand, and Oberlin and UC Santa Cruz on the other. But I'm not holding my breath waiting for this to happen. At any rate, for the rest of this talk, my remarks are directed only at institutions that are officially secular and nonpartisan.

The cases I have discussed so far may make it sound as though I think advocacy in the classroom is categorically bad. But I don't. For one thing, many different activities can come under the heading of "advocacy"; so we have to get clear about just what the concept of advocacy is. *The American Heritage Dictionary of the English Language* defines "advocate" as "to speak, plead, or argue in favor of." Several aspects of this definition should be noted. First, it does not entail that one believes in the position one is advocating, and thus allows for the familiar idea of playing devil's advocate. Second, it allows that a professor can advocate different and even incompatible positions at different times in a course; perhaps we should introduce the notion of advocating on balance for cases where the balance of speaking and arguing is for a particular position. Third, it allows that advocacy can be done either through appeal to rational faculties (e.g., by giving evidence and reasoned arguments for a position) or through appeal to irrational faculties (e.g., by intimidation or appeal to authority) and, within the rational category, can be done either intellectually dishonestly, such as by withholding relevant evidence and arguments that one believes could raise reasonable doubts about the position one is advocating, or honestly.

There are some philosophical niceties about this definition that I will not go into here. But what I want to stress is that it allows for what seems to be a perfectly intellectually respectable way of advocating in the classroom—teaching in a way that is designed to get students to accept the controversial views one believes to be true, and to accept them purely on the basis of reasoned arguments and evidence,[5] including reasoned arguments and evidence against the strongest known contenders among opposing positions. The possibility of this sort of advocacy is not limited to moral, social, and political issues. It can apply to any scholarly controversy, such as the debate between epistemological skepticism and antiskepticism in philosophy.

Is this sort of advocacy advisable in the classroom? This question itself is a hot topic in philosophy nowadays. In fact, there is a growing literature by philosophers, often arguing either that professors in the classroom should take a neutral position on controversial issues[6] or that they should *not* be neutral on such issues.[7] But why suppose that professors have to be all alike? Why not allow for some *real* diversity? Of course, excellent teaching can be as "neutral" as possible, in the sense of having students read and discuss works on various sides of a controversial issue, with the professor taking no official position about which is correct, either because he is unsure or because she thinks such an approach reflects the genuine lack of consensus in the field and best stimulates students to develop their own reasoned arguments. I say "as neutral as possible" rather than just "neutral" because of the familiar point that judgment is bound to be involved in the very formulation of a controversy and in the selection of which sides are worth presenting. Even if the course readings and assignments are centered around positions taken by respected members of the field, judgment is obviously involved in deciding who is a respected member, which ones to include, whether to include promising positions that have not (yet?) gained prominence, and so forth.

But just as this sort of teaching can be done well or badly, so can teaching that involves advocacy on balance, although to be done well, it should follow Peter Markie's stricture that "To teach [at least, to teach philosophy; this is obviously not true of teaching creative writing] is to guide students to justified true beliefs. Students cannot form justified beliefs without examining all the reasonable sides of a controversial issue";[8] and, of course, these sides should be examined in what their own proponents consider the strongest formulations. Obviously, just what such examination should amount to will vary with the course level. Students who are new to a subject need to be made aware of alternatives to any view a professor is advocating; more advanced students often can be assumed already to have this background. Such advocacy on balance can promote learning just as well as maximal neutrality can. Fortunate students will have professors of both sorts and, within the advocacy category, will have advocates on balance of various views, and thus will have the benefit of exposure to a variety of approaches to teaching and to the life of the mind.

Certainly, fortunate students will not have teachers who all advocate the same thing. Yet some professors seem to endorse a kind of ideological uniformity, at least for particular fields. For example, Alison Jaggar holds that all women's studies instructors should be feminists and advocate feminism. Of course, what counts as advocating "the same thing" depends on the tightness of one's grid for measuring differences. There is an obvious sense in which feminists do not all believe the same thing, as there are different varieties of feminism. But the requirement that all women's studies instructors be feminists and advocate feminism does impose a restrictive ideological slant on the field, just as, despite the many varieties of Christianity and conservatism, it would impose a restrictive ideological slant on a field to require that all its instructors be Christians or conservatives. Of course, it can be replied that no one takes only women's studies courses and that part of the rationale for women's studies is to counteract what Jaggar takes to be the fact that "male perspectives already dominate overwhelmingly most other courses that students will take."[9] But her article gives no evidence for this claim of hers. Is it really true nowadays? Even at the sorts of schools that are apt to have strong women's studies departments? Similarly, her claim that "feminist theories, like a few others, are special in that they challenge some deeply embedded features of our common sense world-view"[10] overlooks such questions as: *Whose* commonsense worldview? To what extent have feminist ideas already been incorporated into many students' commonsense worldviews? What sorts of backgrounds and ideas have students who take women's studies courses actually been exposed to elsewhere? Surely, these backgrounds and ideas will be distributed differently at different colleges. And mightn't the students in women's studies courses (especially in advanced courses) be a self-selected group already inclined more toward a feminist worldview than against it? If no instructor in women's studies is supposed to be negative or even neutral about certain core feminist claims, where will students hear these claims discussed by instructors other than their adherents? Are they discussed much in non–women's studies courses at all? These are not rhetorical questions. I really do not know the answers. But I hope that people who insist that all women's studies instructors should be feminists do.

A similar objection applies to Harry Brod's view that philosophers should teach critical thinking and applied ethics "from the left and from feminist perspectives" as "a kind of counter-pedagogy, a pedagogy aimed against received wisdom."[11] The obvious question is: *Whose* received wisdom? Growing up during the Eisenhower years without knowing anyone who voted for Eisenhower has made me permanently wary of blanket application of generalizations about some entity called "our society"[12] to any particular segment of it. My students at Brown seem generally much more sympathetic to feminists and the Left than to antifeminists and the Right. Whether this is true of your students is, as I've said, an empirical question you should try to answer via empirical information about students at your particular school before you make any pedagogical decisions based on any particular answer to this question. And you should take into account empirical information about your colleagues, too. After all, if you are planning to teach from the Left and from feminist perspectives (or, for that matter, from the Right and from antifeminist perspectives) as a means of challenging what you take to be your students' deeply held preconceptions, it is certainly worth trying to find out how many other professors at your school are likely to be duplicating your efforts. Of course, professors should not all be ideologically similar. When you think of the best teachers you had, weren't some of them advocates—for various positions—and some as neutral as possible? Didn't it enrich your education to have professors of these different kinds? It did mine. Let's keep it that way. And how about an exchange program between Hillsdale College and Oberlin?[13]

NOTES

1. Peter Markie (Ed.), *A Professor's Duties* (Rowman and Littlefield, 1994), 11.
2. See ibid., 19
3. *American Philosophical Association Newsletter on Feminism and Philosophy* (Spring 1992), 96, capitals in original.
4. Sara Ann Ketchum, in discussion, made this suggestion about inclusive language.
5. Michael Goldman suggests this in "On Moral Relativism, Advocacy, and Teaching Normative Ethics," *Teaching Philosophy* 4, no. 1 (1981), 1-11, as does Alison Jaggar in "Male Instructors, Feminism, and Women's Studies," *Teaching Philosophy* 2, nos. 3-4 (1977-8), 247-55, although I take issue with Jaggar's application of this principle.
6. See E. Baumgarten, "Ethics in the Academic Profession: A Socratic View," in Markie (Ed.), *A Professor's Duties*, 155-69.
7. See H. Wilder, "The Philosopher as Teacher: Tolerance and Teaching Philosophy" in Markie (Ed.), *A Professor's Duties*, 129-41; A. Jaggar, "Male Instructors, Feminism, and Women's Studies"; H. Brod, "Philosophy Teaching as Intellectual Affirmative Action," *Teaching Philosophy* 9, no. 1 (1986), 5-13; and H. Brod, "Critical Thinking and Advocative Pedagogy: When Neutrality Isn't Neutral," *American Philosophical Association Newsletter on Teaching Philosophy* (Fall 1991), 68-71.
8. Markie (Ed.), *A Professor's Duties*, 33.
9. Jaggar, "Male Instructors, Feminism, and Women's Studies," 248.
10. Ibid., 253.

11. H. Brod, "Critical Thinking and Advocative Pedagogy," 69. See also his "Philosophy Teaching as Intellectual Affirmative Action."

12. See ibid.

13. I thank Heather Gert, Donna Harvey, Harrison Heil, Sara Ann Ketchum, Lucie Marsden, Jack Meiland, Alvin Plantinga, Claudia Strauss, and James Van Cleve for helpful discussion of this material.

TWENTY-SEVEN

The Limits of Appropriate Advocacy

PETER MARKIE

WHAT ARE THE LIMITS of appropriate advocacy in teaching? To put the question another way, under what conditions, if any, is it appropriate—permitted relative to our professional obligations—to advocate our own view on a particular topic in the course of our teaching? What must be true about the topic, about our position on the topic, about our class, and about our way of advocating our position, for such advocacy to be permissible?

I want to outline an answer to this question by giving a series of necessary conditions for appropriate advocacy, and I'll link each condition to more general obligations we have as teachers. I am fairly confident that the conditions are also jointly sufficient for appropriate advocacy and that it is possible to meet all their demands at once. Appropriate advocacy in teaching is possible. Nonetheless, it is not easy to meet all the conditions at once. The opportunities for appropriate advocacy in teaching are quite limited.

PRELIMINARY POINTS

Let me start with some preliminary points. First, I understand advocacy as follows. When we advocate a position in our teaching, we sincerely present that view to our students as being our own and as being correct, we encourage our students to join us in adopting the view, and we employ techniques that we believe will influence them in that direction. Advocacy thus involves more than simply identifying where we personally stand on an issue. It also differs from mere "devil's advocacy" in which our promotion of a particular view is only "for the sake of argument" and often intended simply to get our students to take seriously a view they might otherwise inappropriately dismiss. We can use lots of different techniques in advocating a position. We can present the major arguments for and against our view, as well as the competing options, in the hope that our students, as rational inquirers, will see the strength of our position. We can present only our own view and the major arguments for it, ignoring the other options and what can be said for them. We can present considerations designed to play on students' emotions and prejudice, such as those routinely cataloged in the "Informal Fallacies" sections of elementary logic texts. Some of these techniques are clearly more intellectually reputable than others.[1]

Second, note that my present concern is fairly narrow. I am interested in what is appropriate for an individual instructor rather than an entire department or college. These situations are quite different. If I advocate a particular view in my teaching, I do not preclude the advocacy of an alternative view elsewhere in the curriculum, but if my entire department or college so designs its curriculum as to advocate a particular position, it may well do so.[2] I am also concerned with the limits of appropriate advocacy in teaching rather than such other activities as research publications, invited talks to student groups, and casual conversations with students outside of the class. The boundaries between some of these activities and teaching are quite difficult to draw, but they are surely relevant. The limits of appropriate advocacy are likely to be different if a student group invites us to address them about a controversial topic than if we are teaching a course with little relation to the topic.

Third, I assume that my question is not adequately answered by the claim that our right to academic freedom makes it appropriate for us to advocate whatever we want in our teaching. Our right to academic freedom does not imply this, any more than our right of free speech implies that we may tell others whatever we want, including lies. As John Searle has put the point: "Any healthy human institution—family, state, university, or ski team—grants its members rights that far exceed the bounds of morally acceptable behavior."[3] To determine the limits of appropriate advocacy in teaching, we must look to our general professional obligations. Advocacy is inappropriate just insofar as it violates some general obligation(s) we have as professors.

Let us now consider what some of these general obligations are and how they limit appropriate advocacy in teaching.

COURSE CONTENT

Certainly one of our general obligations as professors is to teach the prescribed content of our course so that the course plays its assigned role in the curriculum. Our courses generally have a prescribed subject matter we are obligated to teach, and, as Alan Gewirth has put it, if "hired to teach quantum mechanics or molecular biology, the academic may not spend all her or his class time discussing the novels of Jane Austin."[4] I suggest, then, the following necessary condition on the permissibility of advocacy in teaching: *We may advocate a position only if our doing so does not prevent us from covering the course's assigned content.*

We can certainly meet this demand. An examination of the view we advocate may be part of the prescribed content for the course. Alternatively, if the view we advocate is not covered in the course content, we may be able to work our advocacy into the course without losing the ability to cover the prescribed content. This will be most easy to do when the course content is broadly defined—for example, the twentieth-century novel—or the course is devoted to mastering a particular skill—for example, good reasoning or writing.

Some may object that this first condition is not strong enough. They may prefer: *We may advocate a position only if a consideration of that position is part of the course's prescribed content.* Yet this stronger condition has no basis in our general obligations as professors. When we teach a particular course, we take on a duty to teach its prescribed content, but we don't take on a duty to teach/discuss nothing but that content.[5]

AN ENVIRONMENT CONDUCIVE TO LEARNING

A second general obligation we have as professors is the obligation to teach in such a way as to create an environment conducive to intellectual inquiry. Students won't take the risks necessary to gain knowledge—ask questions, try on different positions, challenge one another and us—unless the classroom environment makes them comfortable in doing so. Here then is another condition on the permissibility of advocacy in teaching: *We may advocate a position only if our advocacy does not prevent us from maintaining for students a class environment conducive to intellectual inquiry.* We may not advocate our position in a way that encourages students to unquestioningly accept our view. We may not advocate our position in such an overbearing and offensive manner as to shut down intellectual discussion and/or alienate students from the class.

This is also a condition we can meet. Suppose I am teaching a graduate seminar in the history of philosophy and I advocate a particular position on an issue of historical interpretation. I can argue for my view and against others in such a way as to maintain an environment in which the students are still comfortable in asking questions, trying on different views, and challenging themselves and me.

Note that our ability to meet this necessary condition depends on more than what we do. It depends in large measure on the intellectual maturity of our students. They must be able to maintain their intellectual independence in the face of our advocacy.

COMPETENCY

A third necessary condition concerns the need to confine our teaching to the limits of our expertise. We have an obligation to try to guide students to correct beliefs rather than incorrect ones; for it is only insofar as they have correct beliefs that they have anything approaching knowledge. We are, therefore, obligated to limit our attempts to instill beliefs in students to the cases where we are justified in thinking that those beliefs are correct. Here then is a third necessary condition: *We may advocate a position only if we have good reason to believe that that position is correct.*

We must carefully study our own position and the alternatives to it in order to be justified in our belief that we are correct. We can meet this condition, however. Consider the case in which I teach an advanced seminar in my area of research specialization and advocate a particular position on a topic I have carefully researched.

RATIONAL ADVOCACY

A final necessary condition on appropriate advocacy stems from our obligation to respect and promote students' autonomy and rationality. Students are capable of determining what they will believe, and they have an intellectual obligation to strive to attain true beliefs and avoid false ones by assessing the evidence for and against each claim that comes before them. To respect their autonomy and rationality, we must give them reasons for what we ask them to believe and we must ensure that they have the ability to assess those reasons for themselves. Kenneth Strike has put the point as follows.

> The teacher must see the student as more than a novice who is ignorant of the context and principles of the subject matter. The teacher must also see the student as a responsible moral agent who, because he is responsible for what he will believe and what he will do, must ask for and be given reasons for what he is asked to believe. The teacher must also see the student as one whose capacity for understanding reasons must be expanded.[6]

Here then is one more necessary condition on appropriate advocacy: *We may advocate a position only if our advocacy takes the form of giving students adequate evidence for what we encourage them to believe, where students are capable of assessing that evidence for themselves.*

What must we do to give students adequate evidence for what we encourage them to believe? We must give them evidence such that, should they adopt our position on the basis of that evidence, their belief will be epistemically justified. This requires, in part, that where our position is controversial, we must guide them through a detailed examination of the various options, including the arguments for and against each. Our students must be capable of making that examination.

Once again, this is something we can do. Consider the case in which I teach an advanced course in my area of specialization, and I advocate a particular position on a central topic in the course. I can take students through a detailed examination of all the various options with the arguments for and against each. The students are at a level where they can make their own reasoned evaluation.[7]

CONCLUSION

So here are four necessary conditions on appropriate advocacy in teaching: Our advocacy of any position must (1) allow us to teach the prescribed course content; (2) allow us to create and maintain an environment conducive to intellectual inquiry; (3) remain within the limits of our expertise; and (4) take the form of giving students, for their own assessment, adequate evidence for our position. I have indicated how it is possible to meet each of these conditions separately from the others. No internal contradiction seems to make it impossible to meet them all at once. Assuming that they are jointly sufficient, appropriate advocacy is certainly possible.

Nonetheless, these conditions are quite limiting. To meet the second condition of confining our advocacy to areas where we have appropriate expertise as well as the fourth condition of providing students with adequate evidence, we generally must limit our advocacy to views in our own discipline or closely related areas. Those who have never studied ethics or social and political philosophy should not advocate a particular view on the justice of affirmative action. To meet the third condition of maintaining an environment conducive to intellectual inquiry and the fourth condition of providing students with good reasons for their own assessment, we will often have to limit our advocacy to courses in which students have enough intellectual independence and adequate intellectual skills to make an independent evaluation of the reasons we present. Advocacy will seldom be appropriate in introductory courses. To meet the first condition of respecting the prescribed course content while meeting the fourth of providing students with good reasons for what we advocate, we will often have to limit our advocacy to courses in which the view we advocate is itself a major part of the prescribed course content, so we can present a detailed examination of our view and its alternatives while still teaching the course content. The advocacy of a particular position on a social problem will often have to be confined to courses explicitly intended to study that problem.

In short, while I suggest that advocacy in teaching is certainly permissible, the limits on its permissibility are severe.[8]

NOTES

1. My understanding of advocacy is fairly broad in that it includes the sort of proselytizing others sometimes distinguish from advocacy and regard as clearly impermissible. I think it is best for strategic purposes to begin with a broad definition; we can then use our necessary conditions for permissible advocacy to distinguish between appropriate and inappropriate forms, with proselytizing likely to fall in the latter category. My understanding of advocacy is also a bit narrow in that it does not include the activity of simply requiring students to act in accord with a certain view, rather than actively trying to get them to accept the view as correct, e.g. simply requiring all students to use gender neutral language as opposed to attempting to get them to believe that the use of gender neutral language is best. Requirements on students' behavior are often employed in an attempt to change students' beliefs and attitudes, but they need not be.

2. In distinguishing between these situations, I do not intend to suggest that they are unrelated. An individual instructor's obligations may, in part, be determined by the actions of his or her department or college. If, for example, my department contains an advocate for each of the

alternative positions on a particular topic, we each agree to advocate our own position in our teaching and we require students to study the topic with every one of us, then each of us can engage in advocacy without depriving students of a balanced presentation of the available options.

3. John Searle, "Reply to Gerald Graff," *New York Review of Books,* May 16, 1991, 63.

4. Alan Gewirth, "Human Rights and Academic Freedom," in S. M. Cahn (Ed.), *Morality, Responsibility and the University* (Philadelphia, PA: Temple University Press, 1990), 16.

5. I suggest that the cases of impermissible advocacy which motivate this stronger requirement can be explained in terms of one or more of the necessary conditions to follow. Suppose, for example, that an instructor takes fifteen minutes of class time from teaching Calculus to advocate a particular position on a state tax initiative. The instructor still covers the required material in Calculus and so meets the weaker condition I have presented. We are, therefore, tempted to explain what is wrong by appealing to the stronger condition: the instructor should talk about Calculus and nothing but Calculus. I think a better analysis is that the instructor has violated one or more of the conditions to come, e.g. that requiring a balanced presentation of the issues, and the instructor can only avoid violating those conditions at the cost of no longer giving adequate attention to the course material and so violating the first condition after all.

6. Kenneth Strike, "The Authority of Ideas and the Students' Right to Autonomy," in *Liberty and Learning* (New York: St. Martin's Press).

7. The application of this last condition can be extremely controversial and difficult. We must take our students through an examination of the various options. What options are those? They are whatever ones students must consider in order to arrive at a justified belief on the topic, and they are generally identified with the options taken seriously by experts in the field. Yet, a field may be based on assumptions that exclude some options from consideration from the start so that experts in the field never take them seriously, although those outside the field regard them as important alternatives. Thus, Creationism may not be taken seriously by some scientists because it does not count as a scientific theory and so, they may decide that they have no obligation

to present it to students under this last condition. Nonetheless, those outside the field may regard Creationism as an important alternative and decide that when scientists fail to examine it in their courses, they fail to meet this last condition for permissible advocacy. Such debates ultimately force us to consider the assumption that the options students need to examine to arrive at a justified belief are identical with those taken seriously by experts in the field. To determine whether this assumption is correct, we need, in part, to consider the nature of epistemic justification more fully.

8. Some of the points contained in this essay are developed in greater detail in my book, *A Professor's Duties: Ethical Issues in College Teaching* (Lanham, MD: Rowman and Littlefield, 1994).

TWENTY-EIGHT

Some Implications of the Faculty's Obligation to Encourage Student Academic Freedom for Faculty Advocacy in the Classroom

ERNST BENJAMIN

THE FACULTY RIGHT TO ACADEMIC FREEDOM, as currently understood, entails an obligation to encourage student academic freedom. In the words of the "Joint Statement on Rights and Freedoms of Students": "The professor in the classroom and in conference should encourage free discussion, inquiry and expression."[1] In this chapter I explore how this responsibility limits the professor's own academic freedom. I also outline the reasons why I believe that classroom advocacy, properly understood, is consistent with the faculty responsibility to foster student academic freedom. Indeed, it would, in my view, make little sense to require faculty to encourage students to express their views while denying faculty the right to promote or defend their own.

Classroom indoctrination, on the other hand, is certainly inconsistent with student academic freedom. Indoctrination, in the sense of compelled agreement, is specifically barred: "Student performance should be evaluated solely on an academic basis, not on opinions or conduct in matters unrelated to academic standards." More subtle forms of indoctrination, such as through dishonesty or deception, are also improper. Such indoctrination would violate the provisions in the statement on student rights assuring students freedom from exploitation and promising them an opportunity for free inquiry.[2] It contradicts the fundamental purpose of academic freedom advanced in the 1940 Statement of Principles on Academic Freedom and Tenure: "the free search for truth."[3] Moreover, the obligations of faculty, as teachers, to avoid coercion and present a model of intellectual integrity are among those considered basic faculty responsibilities in widely recognized professional guidelines, such as the American Association of University Professors Statement on Professional Ethics.[4]

LIMITS ON FACULTY FREEDOM IN THE CLASSROOM

Faculty academic freedom has not always been limited by a requirement to respect student academic freedom in the classroom. In the nineteenth-century German university, *Lernfreiheit* referred primarily to student freedom from administrative control. Students could move freely between institutions, curricula, and classes and could live off campus without class attendance requirements or periodic exams. In the United States, student academic freedom initially applied only to the elective system and voluntary chapel attendance.[5] The extension of student academic freedom into the classroom presupposed a shift in philosophic and social assumptions.

Until the mid-nineteenth century, religious restrictions on faculty and students remained the rule not only in the denominational colleges of the United States but also in many state universities. Abroad, even such distinguished universities as Oxford and Cambridge maintained religious tests.[6] The natural and social sciences were still entwined with theology and ethics, and most other subjects were taught by rote instruction. Institutions expected faculty to instruct and students to learn in conformity with established teaching to ensure both proper character development and correct understanding.

The contrary notion, that faculty are obliged to "encourage free discussion, inquiry and expression" by students, extends the idea of free inquiry from research to the classroom. At its inception, this extension was not considered inconsistent with faculty advocacy in the classroom. Professor Walter Metzger observes that in nineteenth-century Germany, most theorists of academic freedom asserted the right not only to express their views but to do so with the "aggressive finality of deep subjective convictions." They believed that "the only alternative to the presentation of personal convictions was the prescription of authoritative dogma, and the only alternative to polemical controversy was the stoppage of academic inquiry." They found the essential assurance that advocacy would not degenerate into indoctrination "in the freedom and maturity of the student, who was neither captive nor unprimed."[7]

In the United States, however, student academic freedom in the classroom emerged as a faculty responsibility and a constraint on faculty advocacy rather than as an independent student right. AAUP's "General Declaration of Principles" of 1915 called on faculty to avoid indoctrinating students through imposition of the teacher's own opinions and "to arouse in them a keen desire to reach personally verified conclusions upon all questions of general concernment to mankind."[8] Metzger emphasizes that the American view rejected the "German idea of 'convincing' one's students, of winning them over to the personal system and philosophic views of the professor."[9]

The 1915 Declaration certainly maintained that faculty should be "of fair and judicial mind"; that, although not obliged to "hide their opinion under a mountain of verbiage," they should acquaint students with divergent opinions; and "above all, remember . . . not to provide . . . students with ready-made conclusions, but to train them to think for themselves, and to provide them access to those materials which they need if they are to think intelligently." But even this liberal credo precluded indoctrination, not advocacy. It warned that students could not respect teachers who were prevented from expressing themselves "fully or frankly" and objected to "uncritical and intemperate partisanship" but not partisanship itself. Moreover, its key admonition against faculty imposition of views upon their students rests on a concern regarding "the instruction of immature students . . . especially in the first two years."[10]

The "1940 Statement of Principles on Academic Freedom and Tenure," jointly authored in that year by the AAUP and the Association of American Colleges and subsequently endorsed by more than 150 learned societies, implicitly abandons the notion of faculty responsibility for immature students by expressing faculty and student academic freedom as parallel rights: "Academic freedom in its teaching aspect is fundamental for the rights of the teacher in teaching and of the student to freedom in learning."[11] Classroom inquiry has rules and limits, but these do not preclude advocacy.

We have already noted that faculty should not be dishonest or deceptive. Professor Edward Shils also circumscribes faculty advocacy by citing the well-established provision against faculty introduction of material extraneous to the curriculum into the classroom. Shils argues that the AAUP never intended to offer the protection of academic freedom "for the attempt to persuade students in classrooms to accept the teacher's own point of view on political or parochial topics which were not germane to the subject matter of the courses being taught."[12] This is true, but the denial of protection proceeds not from the effort to persuade but from the fact that the material is "not germane to the subject matter of the courses."

The effort to persuade students to a point of view, save for such restrictions on religious advocacy stemming from the Establishment Clause as may affect professors in public institutions, is encompassed within the ordinary protections of academic freedom. As Matthew Finkin observes:

> subject to a professional obligation to state opposing views fairly (analogous to the requirement in research that the evidence not be distorted) and to treat with respect the students who disagree, the teacher is free passionately to espouse controversial views that are germane to the subject. I do not, therefore, understand freedom of teaching to be limited by any obligation of "balance" or "objectivity"; the freedom is accorded equally to dispassionate dissection and to committed partisanship.[13]

Nothing in the 1940 statement denies protection to teaching that is impassioned and partisan, provided it is not irrelevant, dishonest, or oblivious to opposing views.

UNCERTAINTY AND ACADEMIC FREEDOM

Academic freedom in the classroom, student as well as faculty, presupposes not only the liberal view that the experience of free expression is important to student learning but also the epistemological assumption that the classroom, like the laboratory and the study, is the locus of investigation into matters regarding which our knowledge is incomplete, conditional, and provisional.[14] Some might argue that only "values" or opinions are subject to dispute and that the "facts" or general course content are beyond dispute. As Metzger observes, such empiricism contributed substantially to the American emphasis on dispassion and balance in place of the German endorsement of passionate advocacy based on philosophic idealism.[15]

The "Statement on Rights and Freedoms of Students," properly in my view, encompasses both facts and values in authorizing students to "take reasoned exception to the data or views offered in any course of study and to reserve judgment about matters of opinion." Accordingly, such disagreement may be appropriate in any discipline. One may, after all, dispute such questions of natural science as the cause of the extinction of the dinosaurs, the age of the universe, the etiology of AIDS, or the reality of "global warming," just as one may dispute issues in the social sciences and the humanities.

Indeed, the greatest danger of indoctrination may arise, as Max Weber noted in his vigorous critique of classroom advocacy, from seeming factuality: "To let the facts speak for themselves is the most unfair way of putting over a political position to the student." Suppose, for example, one were to join with the many social scientists who accept Weber's own implicit view that the "fact-value" distinction is itself fact; that is, "to *see* that it is one thing to state facts, . . . while it is another to answer questions of . . . value."[16] If, then, one did not merely advocate the distinction but required that students accept it as an obvious matter of fact, one would engage in the very indoctrination the fact-value distinction purports to avoid.

Weber also argued that faculty advocacy in the classroom is inappropriate because students are not free to respond. This argument goes more to indoctrination than advocacy, because it depends on the premise, or practice, that students are not free to disagree. Moreover, this argument applies as well to "scientific" as it does to "value" disputes. But it is in "scientific" disputes that the danger of subtle indoctrination through "letting the facts speak for themselves" is greatest. Open advocacy may better safeguard a student's right to form an independent judgment than the implicit bias inherent in the presumption that the faculty member's presentation is simply factual. Even "balanced" presentations depend on a particular formulation of the dispute and the alternatives.

Weber himself drew back from arguing the scientific validity of his contention that teachers should respect the fact-value distinction, since he considered that his contention was a moral obligation—although he then proceeded to "demand" recognition of the distinction as a matter of intellectual integrity. Suppose, on the other hand, one were to emulate Leo Strauss, who, as a matter of philosophic integrity, routinely attacked the "fact-value" distinction in class. In such a case one would equally, and more obviously, be an advocate.

Would one also be guilty of indoctrination, as some of Strauss's critics alleged? For example, when I sought to defend Weber's argument in class, Strauss forcefully directed me to read his own book. With uncustomary docility, and to my benefit, I deferred debate and reread *Natural Right and History*.[17] I did not and do not feel indoctrinated. For I know that, although I maintained my opinion in my subsequent master's thesis on Nietzsche's unsuccessful search for a historical foundation for values, Strauss first accepted the thesis and only then reminded me that he considered my conclusions erroneous. Neither Strauss nor most other faculty with strong views with whom I studied required agreement, however forcefully they advanced their views.

Some faculty, and not only those who engage in obvious advocacy, do reasonably insist that students temporarily defer express disagreement. Students cannot expect to grasp a complex or unusual argument on first presentation. Indeed, some reasonably argue, as did Strauss, that "docility" remains an essential precondition of learning. Others credibly assert the contrary. Eugene Genovese enthusiastically remembers the classroom at Brooklyn College as "an ideological war zone," where "professors acted as if they were paid to assault their students' sensibilities, to offend their most cherished values"; and "self-respecting students returned the blows."[18] This difference regarding the appropriate form and limits of advocacy in the classroom clearly has both pedagogical and methodological or epistemological dimensions.

FOUNDATIONS OF ADVOCACY

From a pedagogical perspective, faculty advocacy in the classroom may foster student learning and academic freedom: many students respond positively to passionate teaching, advocacy may challenge students to reconsider inadequately founded preconceptions, and students may acquire skill in advocacy and advocacy-based inquiry. These may be among the benefits of the classroom that Genovese described as an "ideological war zone," provided one emphasizes, as he does, the student's right to disagree. Indeed, Genovese is less concerned with the ideological advocacy that characterized the Brooklyn classroom than with the pedagogical benefits of challenging student presuppositions. Thus his "First Law of College Teaching": *"Any professor who, subject to the restraints of common sense and common decency, does not seize every opportunity to offend the sensibilities of his students is insulting and cheating them, and is no college professor at all."*[19]

This statement itself, however, is unacceptably exclusionary. It offers no room to the teachers who believe that students learn better in a climate of docile consideration or dispassionate deliberation; nor to its more obvious target, the nurturing teacher, who thinks that many students, even in Brooklyn, learn more from gentle encouragement than from ideological combat. Diverse students need diverse faculty, and most students benefit from a mix of styles and learning opportunities. Reading the nurturing teacher out of the profession is no more beneficial to students nor consistent with elementary principles of academic freedom than eliminating the disputatious liberal or passionate conservative or radical.

From a methodological or epistemological perspective, faculty may assert the truth of their findings and the validity of their modes of inquiry and vigorously challenge the views of students or colleagues. For example, they may debate the merits of particular scientific methods or even the adequacy of scientific method itself. To deny this would preclude philosophical reevaluation of disciplinary foundations. Faculty are enjoined "not to introduce into their teaching controversial matter which has no relation to their subject."[20] But disagreement over disciplinary methodology has a significant relation to the subject. Indeed, "disputes on substantive issues fundamental to the discipline, between and among committed partisans, are a sign of health in a department."[21] The common expectation that faculty teach in accordance with the methodology of their disciplines is, accordingly, more complex than first appears.

Recent efforts to restrict basic challenges to disciplinary presuppositions have relied on diverse arguments. "Critical Legal Theory" was anathematized by some law faculty primarily on the grounds that the presuppositions of its advocates showed a disrespect for or were morally inconsistent with the responsibilities of legal education.[22] This line of criticism was as ideologically grounded as the subject of its critique and was largely, and properly, unsuccessful. More appropriate and specific criticism based on the scholarly validity of such legal analysis has sometimes prevailed and sometimes not as one might expect in a serious disciplinary debate.

In biology, the argument that "creationism" is simply not biology has generally prevailed. But an effort by an established scholar to present creationist arguments in a manner consistent with disciplinary standards, based on a critique of the unresolved issues in evolutionary theory and philosophy of science, should not be rejected out of hand as were simple efforts to substitute the Bible for empirical investigation and faith for scientific reasoning: "What is essential is that a creation scientist must submit to the limits of academic discipline and peer review: he must set out to prove his case according to the rules of evidence, and, even if his own conviction is ultimately of faith, in the academic arena, he must set out to do so according to the rules of reason."[23] Where the presentation of creationist views becomes more sophisticated, the argument is likely to be resolved on a case-by-case assessment of whether the challenger demonstrates a competent understanding of the discipline and accords adequate consideration to mainstream views, or simply whether sufficient class time is devoted to a collegially approved curriculum.

As the assessment of challenges to disciplinary presuppositions shifts from normative or epistemological grounds to issues of competence, pertinence, and consistency with the curriculum, it is, of course, more difficult to distinguish proper academic review from improper restrictions on advocacy of dissenting views. Many mainstream economists are as certain that Marxian economists simply do not understand economics, and many mainstream political scientists are as certain that Straussians do not understand social science as most biologists are that creationists do not understand biology.

Since peer evaluation of competence is the foundation of academic excellence, it would be wrong to deny a discipline the right to criticize or reject those individuals whose work is specifically found inadequate. Nor is any department required to present every approach to the discipline. But a "university is derelict in one of its most significant responsibilities if it . . . [rejects faculty] because of their attack on approaches or doctrines that constitute the current conventional wisdom of their disciplines."[24] The protection of academic freedom entails careful case-by-case evaluation to ensure that professional assessment is not a surrogate for ideological selection. Academic freedom in the classroom requires that faculty should no more impose their views on one another than on their students. As Jaroslav Pelikan observes, "the professor's evaluation of students or colleagues must not be based on their acceptance or rejection of the professor's ideological position: critical understanding, not adherence or discipleship, whether uncritical or critical, is the criterion."[25]

Although dissent from the prevailing methodology is protected by academic freedom, indoctrination is not. We have already recognized that it is contrary to student academic freedom to insist that students believe that a specific assertion is simply factual or true; although they may, of course, be expected to learn that it is generally so considered. Similarly, it would violate student academic freedom to insist that students accept that the contention that certain of their views are the consequence of "false consciousness" and must be set aside. Certainly one may advocate that students reevaluate their preconceptions, but insistence that students actually abandon their alleged "false consciousness," or their alleged racism, sexism, and homophobia, or their alleged cynicism, disrespect, and contempt for the prevailing order, as a condition of demonstrating adequate understanding of the course material, is indoctrination not education. Students may be held "responsible for learning the content of any course of study," but, once again, student academic freedom requires that "students should be free to take reasoned exception to the data or views offered in any course of study."[26]

INSTITUTIONAL NEUTRALITY AND FACULTY ADVOCACY

Some faculty members with whom I have discussed these issues believe that objectivity and balance, however imperfectly realized, are the guiding principles of sound teaching. They express great skepticism regarding the possibility that advocacy can stop short of indoctrination. Others share my view that objectivity is, at best, based on provisional knowledge; that balance, at best, presupposes a particular view of the nature and range of disagreement; and that advocacy not only need not lead to indoctrination but also is often the antidote. These views agree that indoctrination is unacceptable, but sometimes differ in where they find the greater danger of indoctrination: passionate advocacy or dispassionate matter-of-factness. As individual faculty members, we may agree to disagree.

But what of the university as an institution? Should it be committed or balanced? Shils argues that the "civil freedom of academics does not extend to the conduct of political propaganda in teaching . . . not because academics may properly be restricted in their political beliefs and in the expression of those beliefs but because the university is not an institution for the pursuit of partisan political objectives."[27] It seems to me that propaganda, as distinguished from advocacy, is barred by the proscriptions of deception and dishonesty. But it is not clear that institutional neutrality implies faculty neutrality.

To bar honest partisanship might easily lead precisely to a restriction of all but the least controversial political expressions. Shils himself, for example, leaps lightly from criticizing faculty who "make propaganda for socialism or for revolution among the students" to faculty who "think that the necessity and desirability of the destruction of the existing society and its cultural traditions should be incorporated into the syllabuses which they prepare for their students."[28] In my experience, he had no such qualms regarding syllabi or classroom promotion of civility and respect for the Western tradition.

Pelikan, on the other hand, although he also argues cogently that the university itself should not take sides, recognizes and approves the fact that university study may inspire utopian aspirations or revolution, just as it may inspire reaction. He argues, however, that the university should provide the self-critical or analytical skills that prevent excess: "the university is rendering a grave disservice to its students when it serves only one pole of this dialectic, either by itself becoming an apologist for an unjust society or even an accomplice in the politics of repression, or by surrendering its scholarly and rational mission by being swept away in the tide of revolutionary doctrine and social change."[29]

I do find a disturbing lack of concreteness in Pelikan's otherwise admirable discussion. He treats student rebellion as a consequence of the students' comprehensive university experience without specifically addressing the role of the faculty whose social interaction with the students substantially shapes their education. There is some truth in Pelikan's abstract perspective. Students in some universities, at some times, and especially in tumultuous times, are influenced more by circumstance and by one another than by the faculty. Nonetheless, if the university is more than the sum of the faculty, it is, as Pelikan generally recognizes, deeply shaped by the faculty. A university that is not an apologist for the status quo must not have only a reflective faculty, but also a diverse faculty, some of whom are likely to advocate aggressively their diverse, heretical views.

Pelikan argues persuasively that even those of us who value, as he does, the contribution of the university to the pursuit of social justice should preserve the university as a locus of dispassionate critical reflection. I agree. I think, though, there may be an even greater need to emphasize the less frequently understood reciprocal: that genuine critical reflection is a social process as well as an intellectual one, in which the advocate's passion and the debater's partisanship inspire new insights both for individuals and for society. In this perspective, however, advocacy is part of a larger process in which the rights of rebuttal and dissent remain essential. Without these limits, advocacy ceases to be a tool of inquiry and becomes merely indoctrination. The notion that advocacy tempered by mutual respect is the antidote to, rather than the instrument of, indoctrination is not, after all, peculiar to the university. It is the foundation of any free community.

NOTES

1. "Joint Statement on Rights and Freedoms of Students," in *AAUP Policy Documents and Reports,* 228 (Washington, DC: American Association of University Professors, 1995), 227-33; see also, Ernst Benjamin, "Freedom in the Classroom," in W. A. Bryan and R. H. Mullendore (Eds.), *Rights, Freedoms and Responsibilities of Students, New Directions for Student Services,* no. 59 (San Francisco: Jossey-Bass, 1992), 37-48.
2. Ibid.
3. "1940 Statement of Principles on Academic Freedom and Tenure," in *AAUP Policy Documents and Reports,* 1995, 3.
4. "Statement on Professional Ethics," in *AAUP Policy Documents and Reports,* 1995, 75-6.
5. Walter P. Metzger, *Academic Freedom in the Age of the University* (New York: Columbia University Press, 1955), 12, 123-34.
6. Ibid., 4-9, 118-19.
7. Ibid., 114-15.
8. "General Declaration of Principles," reprinted in *Bulletin of the American Association of University Professors* (Spring 1954), 106.
9. Metzger, *Academic Freedom,* 126-129.
10. "General Declaration of Principles," 100, 104-7.
11. *AAUP Policy Documents and Reports,* 1995, 3.

12. Edward Shils, "Do We Still Need Academic Freedom?," *American Scholar* 195 (Spring 1993), 187-209.

13. Matthew W. Finkin, "The Tenure System," in A. L. Deneef, C. D. Goodwin, and E. S. McCrate (Eds.), *The Academic's Handbook*, 86-100 (Durham, NC: Duke University Press, 1988), 88.

14. Metzger, *Academic Freedom*, 90.

15. Ibid., 128-29.

16. Max Weber, "Science as a Vocation," in H. H. Gerth and C. Wright Mills (Eds.), *From Max Weber* (New York: Galaxy, 1958), 129-56, quote from p. 146, italics added.

17. Leo Strauss, *Natural Right and History* (Chicago, IL: University of Chicago Press, 1953), see especially 35-80.

18. Eugene G. Genovese, excerpt from "Heresy, Yes—Sensitivity, No," in Patricia Aufderheide (Ed.), *Beyond PC* (St. Paul, MN: Graywolf Press, 1992), 230-32.

19. Ibid., 231.

20. "1940 Statement of Principles on Academic Freedom and Tenure," 3.

21. AAUP Committee A on Academic Freedom and Tenure, "Some Observations on Ideology, Competence, and Faculty Selection," *Academe* (January-February 1986), 1a.

22. AAUP Committee A on Academic Freedom and Tenure, "Report of Committee A 1985-86," *Academe* (September-October 1986), 13a-21a.

23. Conrad Russell, *Academic Freedom* (New York: Routledge, 1993), 31.

24. AAUP Committee A, "Some Observations," 1a.

25. Jaroslav Pelikan, *The Idea of the University: A Reexamination* (New Haven, CT: Yale University Press, 1992), 161.

26. "Joint Statement," 228.

27. Shils, "Do We Still Need Academic Freedom?," 191-2.

28. Ibid., 199.

29. Pelikan, *The Idea of the University*, 163.

PART IV

PRACTICE

TWENTY-NINE

When Academic Speech Hits the Courtroom

How Lawyers Might Argue (and Judges Might Decide) —Three Semihypothetical Cases

MARTHA CHAMALLAS,
RICHARD SEEBURGER,
AND PETER M. SHANE

INTRODUCTION
BY PETER M. SHANE

IN ONE OF HIS MOST FAMOUS REMARKS, Alexis de Toqueville observed that sooner or later, all social problems in America become problems of law. The topics of free speech and academic freedom are no exception. The purpose of this chapter is to shed light on the shape that legal discourse can give to debates over free speech on campus and academic freedom generally.

In putting this chapter together, we assumed that our readers would consist mainly of nonlawyers. Therefore, we did not anticipate that the most interesting presentation would be either a comprehensive summary of existing law or a critique of legal doctrine or philosophy. Instead, we thought that our colleagues from other disciplines might find it most interesting to ponder how arguments and debates in which they may have participated as historians or philosophers or psychologists or chemists, and so on change once they are framed by the fact of a legal dispute. We thought this could best be illustrated by three very brief and somewhat improvisational one-act plays, each of which revolves around a hypothetical campus free speech or academic freedom controversy. Perhaps we should add, as they always say following the end of every televised docudrama: "Despite the fact that these hypotheticals may resemble or even describe actual incidents, they are not to be regarded as portrayals of real characters, and their resemblance to reality is, of course, merely coincidental."

By way of preface, I would share with you just two other of our ground rules. First, none of us wanted to be typecast as either the reflexive voice of unbridled libertarianism or the heavy hand of censorship. And, of course, each of us lays some claim to a judicious cast of mind. Therefore, we alternate parts in these three one-act plays, taking turns being advocates for and against regulation, and for each of us, one turn at pretending to resolve a particular dispute.

The second rule is that whoever is the judge, after summarizing the story, will give each of the two other panelists only a brief space to present a truncated version of the legal argument. The judge or other dispute resolver will then suggest how he or she would resolve the hypothetical dispute. These presentations are intended specifically to invite reflections on how the fact that we are placing these issues in a legal context may create a discourse different from the discourses more familiar to the nonlawyers reading this work.

Finally, we have somewhat simplified things by limiting the sources of law that each side can invoke. In each instance, the basis for regulating speech is some university rule. We are generally not getting into the complexities that arise when targets of discriminatory speech, for example, argue that they are legally entitled to protection under Title VII of the Civil Rights Act of 1964, Title IX of the Education Amendments of 1972, or some analogous state or local law. Similarly, each of the universities we have created is a state university. Thus, each is governed by the First Amendment—which would not apply directly to private universities—and our legal arguments to be free of regulation will all be based on the First Amendment. In real life, faculty might invoke other protections, such as rules imposed through their own contracts or through statutes or applicable regulations.

The first of our stories, however, involves students, not teachers, and will wind up not in court but in the office of a university administrator. So let us temporarily promote Professor Seeburger to the rank of university vice president for Student Affairs and have him begin our first play.

PARK V ENORMOUS STATE UNIVERSITY
RICHARD H. SEEBURGE, THE CASE

Enormous State University (ESU) has a student code of conduct on racial harassment limited to racial insults hurled at individual students, excluding classroom comments about racial issues that might arouse anger.

ESU's campus has been tense because of recent racial incidents.

Eden Park, an 18-year-old freshman, was working late in his dormitory room typing a paper. A dozen members of a black sorority were outside celebrating, singing, and generally having fun noisily. Eden shouted out his window, "Shut up, you water buffalo. If you're looking for a party, there's a zoo a mile from here."

The sorority sisters made a complaint to the campus official who investigates allegations of racial harassment, but they have refused to allow their names to be released. Eden, a Jew, admitted the comment but denied any racial intent. He said he attended a Jewish day school where the Hebrew word "behameh," meaning water oxen, was tossed around as a mild insult for a thoughtless person or a fool.

The campus official told Eden that the comment seemed a racial insult because water buffalo are "big, black animals that live in Africa." The official by letter threatened a hearing possibly leading to expulsion unless Eden wrote a letter of apology, accepted dormitory probation, would agree to keep the matter confidential, and accepted a letter in his file noting a violation of the code of conduct on racial harassment. Eden refused. ESU's vice president for Student Affairs has invited advocates on behalf of the complaining women and on behalf of Park to advise him whether to convene a disciplinary hearing.

PROFESSOR CHAMALLAS, FOR THE WOMEN STUDENTS

Vice President Seeburger, I am grateful to have this opportunity to speak on behalf of 12 African American female students who have filed a complaint of racial harassment against Eden Park. After consultation with me and with their individual attorneys, the women have decided not to make their names public. Given the volatile, racially charged climate at Enormous State University, the women fear that if their identities are known, they will be the target of even more intensified harassment and abuse.

I am sure that the vice president is aware that as a recipient of government funds, Enormous State University has a duty under Title VI and Title IX to ensure a learning environment for its students free from discriminatory harassment and intimidation. In 1992 the United States Supreme Court ruled that universities could be held liable for damages for the injuries suffered by a student who was subjected to a sexually hostile educational environment (*Franklin v Gwinnett County Public Schools*, 503 US 60 [1992]). The duty of a university is no less when the complaint involves racial harassment. The university must fully investigate the complaint, reach a conclusion as to whether the conduct amounts to harassment, and take prompt, corrective action.

Let me explain why the facts in the case are sufficient to warrant initiation of disciplinary proceedings against Park. The student code of conduct narrowly defines racial harassment to include "racial insults hurled at individual students." There is no question in this case that Park directed his anger at the women as individual students. This is a case of targeted harassment, not the expression of a general opinion or other nondirected speech. It is also clear in this case that Park wanted to annoy and insult the women in retaliation for their disturbing his typing. Even according to Park's account of his thought processes, the Hebrew word that reminded him of water buffalo is intended as an insult. Park's shouting at the women was not intended as civil discourse; it did not invite a response or merely inform the women of his situation.

The only remaining question is whether Park's insults were racial in nature. On this question, the United States Supreme Court's decisions on workplace harassment are very useful. Most recently in *Harris v Forklift Systems, Inc.,* 510 US 17 (1993), the Court has endorsed a reasonableness test to determine whether conduct of supervisors or coworkers has created a sexually hostile environment. Adapted to our case, the test is whether in the particular context, a reasonable person would regard Park's insults as racially offensive. The black women were called "water buffalo" and directed to the "zoo." They immediately recognized these angry statements as racial in nature: Park would not have called white women water buffalo, and there can be little doubt that when black people are told to go to the zoo, it implies that they are animals, inferior to others and not part of the community.

The EEOC in enforcing Title VII has stated that the "reasonable person standard should not be applied in a vacuum," that it "should consider the victim's perspective" in determining what is offensive. Thus even if we credit Park's account that his choice of water buffalo was linked in his mind to a Hebrew word—an account I find incredible, given his simultaneous reference to the zoo—the meaning Park attaches to the word is not controlling. Instead the university must apply an objective standard of reasonableness, taking into account the meaning likely to be attached to the statements by those to whom the statements are directed. Park as a member of the university community and as an adult is responsible for the reasonable meanings persons place upon his statements.

Invoking disciplinary proceedings in this case does not violate Park's First Amendment rights. The First Amendment protection of free speech, as you are well aware, is not absolute. The insults in this case—particularly because they were directed at individuals in anger—constitute fighting words, a category of speech not protected by the First Amendment. Moreover, it is entirely proper to balance the rights of the women students to nondiscriminatory treatment in this case against Park's interest in untrammeled free speech. The university campus setting is special. As commentators have recognized, while on campus during their school years, students are a captive audience. A student cannot avoid the campus and still flourish in her studies. It is thus necessary that the university take measures to ensure that the campus is free from racial hostility and harassment, conduct that we know is destructive to the central mission of the university.

PETER M. SHANE, FOR MR. PARK

Thank you, Vice President Seeburger, for meeting with us today. Mr. Park hopes we can head off what would not only be a painful experience for him but also an embarrassing blot on this university's record of commitment to free speech.

I hope that two minutes' worth of common sense and three minutes' worth of constitutional law will persuade you that this matter should drop right here. Let me start with the commonsense part. Presumably, the fundamental function of this university is student learning. In asking several of his fellow students to quiet their voices so that he could study, Mr. Park was engaged in doing the very thing that this university wants students to do. He might have done it more politely. Perhaps he could have done it more effectively, but the undisputed facts show that Mr. Park was not trying to produce a hostile environment for anyone. He was trying to preserve an environment conducive to the very activity for which this university recruits students and presumably for which their parents pay tuition.

My second commonsense point is that no one—certainly not Mr. Park—doubts the importance of the university's interest in preserving a positive atmosphere for all students. Courtesy is good. But Mr. Park thinks it odd that the atmosphere for students of color would improve if black students in his position were told don't try to quiet people down if they are preventing you from studying. If you do, you might be discriminating against them.

The third commonsense point is that finding racism in Mr. Park's reference to water buffalo is a little like seeing the ceiling of the Sistine Chapel in a Rorschach ink blot. Indeed, the Hebrew origins of his chosen epithet demonstrate that its historic targets were surely not African Americans. The epithet is no more a racial insult when directed at African Americans than it would be a racial compliment if uttered to a group whose culture happened to honor the water buffalo. If free association can turn any blunt comment into racial insult, then the university's rule is truly Orwellian. What if Mr. Park had said, in a polite, scholarly tone, "Would you kindly lower your voices? I am trying to master my studies." Would his use of the word "master" be construed as a subtle reimposition of the ideology of white supremacy? We submit that there is no standard of reasonableness under which calling these students "water buffalo" could be construed as racist.

Now for the constitutional law part. This university purports to have a rule prohibiting the utterance of a "racial insult" directed at individual students. That rule is unconstitutional under any conceivably applicable legal standard. It is overbroad. It is impermissibly vague. It regulates speech that, in general, is constitutionally exempt from regulation, and it impermissibly discriminates by regulating speech based on its viewpoint.

First, the regulation is unconstitutional because it is not narrowly tailored to a compelling governmental interest, even though the speech being regulated is uttered in what the courts call a public forum. Certainly Mr. Park was not inciting lawless action. He was not divulging national security secrets. He was, at most, expressing in blunt words his impatience with the discourtesy of his fellow students. In this context and in this setting, the remark did not portend any harm remotely serious enough to warrant any campus regulation whatsoever.

The only way the university could begin to talk about the permissibility of regulation would be to insist that its public walkways were, in fact, not a public forum for expression but some kind of limited, and, for speech, less protected forum. But there is nothing inherently nonpublic about the walkway on which the students appeared outside Mr. Park's window. If the university intended to declare this forum nonpublic, it was required to do so more explicitly. And, of course, if this was a nonpublic forum, its main purpose was presumably to facilitate the activity of Mr. Park, not the boisterous behavior of sorority sisters.

Even if we were to concede, however, that this walkway could possibly have been a free speech zone less protected than a public forum, the regulation would still have to be reasonably tailored to a legitimate purpose. This regulation is not. Indeed, it is unconstitutional precisely because the phrase "racial insult" is so vague that it does not give fair notice to any student what he or she is or is not permitted to say. For example, racial insult might be thought to include automatically any form of racial epithet. What if it is an epithet that a member of some race uses to describe his or her own race? What if one white student, referring to a particularly clumsy fellow student at a dance, says: "Oh, man, you really dance like a honky." Would that be a racial insult susceptible to discipline? On the face of the regulation, there is no reason to think that the answer is no, but regulating this insult cannot conceivably be related to any reasonable university purpose. And, but for the press of time, we could multiply these examples endlessly.

Webster's Dictionary defines insult in part as "insolent, undignified, contemptuous or offensive utterance, or a gross indignity." The scope of these words is so broad and their range of meaning so subjective that no student could plausibly imagine for what comments he or she could be regulated.

And, of course, on top of all of this, the rule is unconstitutional because it selects for regulation only objectionable speech that has a particular ideological content. The Supreme Court, in *R.A.V. v St. Paul*, 505 US 377 (1992), held that even speech lacking constitutional protection may not be regulated on an ideologically discriminatory basis. The only insults the university is concerned about seem to be insults that are demeaning of a particular race. But universities don't have the power to pick and choose among the messages they want to suppress.

It is amazing and a little depressing to have to try to persuade a university that a reasonable understanding of its mission does not include suppressing speech. Applying this regulation to students of this university is unconstitutional, and in Mr. Park's case, it is not only unconstitutional, it would be mind-blowingly silly.

Thank you.

RICHARD SEEBURGER, THE ADMINISTRATOR'S DECISION

The decision whether to convene a disciplinary hearing involves consideration of not only possibly "drop dead" constitutional issues that apply to a state university but in any event an interpretation of our own code, which does not define "harassment." That interpretation will be influenced by our own aspirations as a university.

We deal here with words that are not facially racial. Indeed, water buffaloes are native to Asia, not Africa, and so at a technical level might not necessarily be taken as a reference to the race of the complainants. Were a purely objective standard used, a case could not be made out and a hearing should not be convened. However, the purpose of our code is to protect the listener from certain insults that could have a disruptive impact on the learning atmosphere. Thus, the words must have been understood in fact in a racial sense. That seems clear here from the fact of the complaint. But were they reasonably so understood? If not, did Eden Park nonetheless subjectively intend that they be so understood? If the understanding was not reasonable or if Eden meant only to deliver an insult but not a racial one, he ought not to be found guilty of violating the code. Such liability for facially harmless words without intent is inappropriate, especially on a university campus. Perhaps Eden's intent and what the words were reasonably capable of being understood as meaning ought to be developed at a hearing. The chilling effect on speech of holding such a hearing combined with the complexity of the legal issues, however, caution against convening a hearing.

It is not clear that the words involved here were not constitutionally protected. "Fighting words," the nose-to-nose confrontation à la *Chaplinsky v New Hampshire,* 315 US 568 (1942), are not protected by the First Amendment. Given the physical distance, the *Chaplinsky* exception for words that tend to incite an immediate breach of the peace is probably not made out. Even if it were, *R.A.V. v St. Paul,* 505 US 377 (1992), strongly suggests Eden Park's insults are constitutionally protected because our code is underinclusive and discriminates on the basis of content. This sanctioning of some but not all otherwise proscribable words was at the root of *R.A.V.* and the facial invalidation of the ordinance there involved.

An argument can be made that *R.A.V.* might not be controlling. Our campus is not necessarily the equivalent of the public streets and parks. It is not a full public forum. While students cannot be criminally punished for certain words uttered on the streets, we can and do burden them when uttered in the classroom or written on an examination paper. The university regulates the content of speech in certain places and on certain occasions in furtherance of its educational mission. Further, practice in civilized discourse is a legitimate goal. *R.A.V.* itself does not preclude our closing our resources to that speech disruptive to our ends. However, to so close our campus we should be prepared to police that speech. To so monitor extra-classroom campus speech is too high a price for a university to pay, especially where our code exempts classroom speech from its coverage.

A university should not want to get into the business of monitoring protected speech on its campus even if it had the power to do so. The request to convene a disciplinary hearing is denied.

GREG KENNEDY V UNIVERSITY OF EAST DAKOTA:
THE *TAXI ZUM KLO* CASE

MARTHA CHAMALLAS, THE CASE

Over the past year, several students and their parents complained about sexually explicit films and materials used for classroom instruction at the state university in East Dakota. The state Board of Regents has recently passed a rule requiring classroom instructors to warn students about potentially offensive material in coursework. The new policy mandates that whenever a teacher is going to use any textual or visual material that depicts human sexual acts, he or she must advise the students in advance and give the students the chance to drop the class or avoid the class meeting in which the material is used.

Greg Kennedy is a teaching assistant for the introductory course on German conversation and composition offered to undergraduates at the University of East Dakota. This past semester he showed his German section the film *Taxi Zum Klo* (Taxi to the bathroom), a 1981 German erotic comedy that contains about three minutes of explicit gay sex. Kennedy stated that he chose the film because it is critically acclaimed and presents an uncloseted view of some aspects of gay male culture. Kennedy hoped that the film would generate subjects for conversation and writing assignments. Although he was aware of the new regents' policy requiring a warning, Kennedy decided not to warn the class about the film beforehand. He objects to the new policy as a violation of academic freedom, gay rights, and free speech.

Two students from Kennedy's section complained to the dean of Liberal Arts about the film, stating that they were shocked and embarrassed by a scene in *Taxi* in which two men urinate on each other's faces. As a result of their complaint, the dean discussed the matter with Kennedy and determined that Kennedy had no excuse for failing to comply with the regents' policy. As a sanction, Kennedy has been notified that he will no longer be eligible for a teaching assistantship at East Dakota.

Kennedy has filed suit against the university, claiming that the regents' warning policy violates his First Amendment rights.

RICHARD SEEBURGER, FOR THE TEACHING ASSISTANT

Greg Kennedy is a teaching assistant at a state university and as such is a public employee whose workplace speech receives protection under the First Amendment, *Connick v Myers,* 461 US 138 (1983). It is not argued that the movie is obscene and thus could be generally prohibited under *Miller v California,* 413 US 15 (1973), since while it deals in part with explicit sex it does not, when taken as a whole, lack serious literary, artistic, political, or scientific value, without regard to any contemporary community standards. This constitutional test is independent of contemporary community standards.

Where a public employee is sanctioned for otherwise protected workplace speech, *Connick* first requires a judicial determination of whether the content of the speech is of public concern. This is defined primarily as matters other than of personal concern. Where, as here, the subject matter is of public concern, a balancing test is employed and the burden shifts to the public employer to justify its sanctions.

The state university's asserted interest in protecting students from unanticipated scenes of explicit sex is not implicated in this case since the student complaints were not about sex but about urination. The government's burden is even heavier in the area of education. The state university may not act to constrict knowledge. See *Board of Education v Pico*, 457 US 853 (1982) (removing books from library shelves); and *Epperson v Arkansas*, 393 US 97 (1968) (prohibiting the teaching of evolution). Here the action by the regents was only to prohibit offensive ideas. The regulation by its own terms had nothing to do with enhancing academics or teaching effectiveness since it sought only to permit students to avoid relevant materials otherwise protected by the First Amendment.

More particularly, the action by the state university was strictly a punishment for ideas since Mr. Kennedy is forever disabled from teaching anything there again. This permanent ban has not been justified on balance with any arguable interest in protecting students from being offended by ideas about explicit sex, which in any event was not involved in this case. The university has failed to meet its burden in justifying its action.

PETER M. SHANE, FOR THE BOARD OF REGENTS

May it please the court:

My learned opponent has offered a lot of insight as to the law that applies to prohibitions on speech. But let's be clear about this case: it does not involve any such prohibition.

The question before you today is whether the University of East Dakota permissibly barred a graduate student from future teaching assistantships on the ground that he had inexcusably violated a validly promulgated Board of Regents rule. If that rule is valid, there is no dispute that the university's discipline is also valid. The only issue is whether the board could constitutionally promulgate the disputed rule.

The answer, on behalf of the board, is indisputably affirmative. It is within the authority of public universities to determine the subjects that will be taught in university-sponsored classes and, in general, how those subjects shall be taught. The regents of East Dakota have determined that sexually explicit films and materials are not appropriate for classroom instruction if the students exposed to such materials are either surprised or coerced in their use. This is an entirely reasonable pedagogical judgment and, if anything, the board deserves credit for respecting academic freedom. The board would have been empowered simply to bar these materials altogether, but deferred instead to instructor judgment. All it demanded was prior notification to the students and an option for students to avoid the sexually explicit material if they so choose.

Perhaps the case most closely in point is *Martin v Parrish*, 805 F2d 54 (5th Cir 1986), a 1986 Fifth Circuit decision in which the court upheld the discharge of a college teacher for his inveterate use of profanity in the classroom. The faculty member was warned in writing that his use of profanity would result in disciplinary action, but he continued to swear in class, using words including "bullshit," "hell," "damn," "Goddamn," and "sucks." He was consequently fired, and that decision was upheld. A panel of the Fifth Circuit in essence deferred to the dean's implicit judgment that the instructor's profanity did not have any legitimate educational function. A majority of the panel went further, giving special emphasis to the indecency of the faculty member's language. The majority found the language, in context, to be constitutionally unprotected because of its indecency and its lack of educational purpose.

In terms of First Amendment values, this case is easier. No speech whatever is barred. The Board of Regents is willing to permit individual instructors to determine the educational suitability of sexually explicit materials. At the same time, the board has adopted a pedagogical philosophy that alternative modes of instruction are appropriate for students who do not wish to be exposed to sexually explicit materials in the course of their instruction.

The board's decision is also entirely supported by the Supreme Court's decision in *Rust v Sullivan*, 500 US 173 (1991). As Your Honor will recall, the Supreme Court there held that the federal government was entitled to bar abortion counseling in federally funded family planning clinics. The Court expressly determined that a government that subsidizes a program involving expressive activity can prohibit the use of its subsidy for expressive activity that is not properly related to the purpose of the program, as the government reasonably defines it. The Board of Regents has essentially defined a program of higher education through instructional materials that shall not be sexually explicit unless the students exposed to such materials have consented to that exposure. Individual instructors do not have First Amendment rights to revise the educational program that the Board of Regents has adopted.

To be fair, this would be a more interesting case if the facts involved a course in which the students' consent to be exposed to explicit materials might have been inferred simply from the fact of their enrollment. An art department instructor teaching a course in the history of erotic painting might well have inferred that any student who signed up for such a course had necessarily consented to being exposed to sexually explicit material. This was, however, a German class. Students enrolled in that class would not have had any reason to anticipate that their curriculum would include a sexually explicit, homoerotic comedy. Indeed, I think you are entitled to take judicial notice that the distinguished history of German cinema would have provided the instructor hundreds, if not thousands, of examples of German culture that would have been more obviously suitable to his assigned instructional mission.

But it is important to recall that Mr. Kennedy was not barred from future employment because of his poor judgment; he was disciplined because of his insubordination. That act has no First Amendment protection.

Thank you.

MARTHA CHAMALLAS, THE JUDGE'S DECISION

This case involves the use of sexually explicit films in the college classroom. The State Board of Regents of UED recently passed a rule requiring classroom instructors—professors as well as teaching assistants—to warn their students before using any visual or textual material that depicts human sexual activity that some students may find objectionable. Students are then given the option under the regents policy to drop the course or avoid the particular class in which the material is used.

Gregory Kennedy, a teaching assistant for the introductory German conversation and composition course, deliberately chose to show the film *Taxi Zum Klo* to his section, without first warning that the film contained graphic sexual material. The film is an erotic German comedy that has gained critical acclaim for its uncloseted view of some aspects of gay male culture. Two students in Kennedy's class complained that they were shocked and embarrassed by a scene in *Taxi* in which two men urinate on each other's faces. As a result of the complaint and Kennedy's knowing violation of the regents' policy, the dean of the college has notified Kennedy that he will no longer be eligible for a teaching assistantship at UED. This lawsuit involves Kennedy's First Amendment challenge to the regents' policy.

This is a novel case that pits a teacher's First Amendment right to exercise professional judgment in selecting topics and materials for use in his course against the state's interest in limiting classroom speech to promote legitimate educational goals. Because each of these competing interests is of the utmost importance, a proper resolution of this case requires a fine-tuned balancing, one that considers the degree of invasion of Kennedy's academic freedom against the harm sought to be avoided by the regents' policy of warning students about sexually explicit materials. This court concludes that the balance in this case favors state regulation because the regents' policy represents only the most limited and reasonable incursion on the autonomy of a university instructor.

We start with the recognition that the German section taught by Kennedy was not a public forum but a regular classroom activity. As part of the school curriculum, the State Board of Regents is entitled to more deference in speech regulation than it would be with respect to a personal expression of a teacher that happens to occur on school premises.

If this dispute had occurred in the primary and secondary school context, there would be no question that the denial of a renewal of Kennedy's assistantship was within the discretion of the dean. Thus, courts frequently have sustained the nonrenewal of untenured high school teachers for such conduct as the showing of R-rated films to their class, even if the school had no explicit rule against the use of such films in the classroom. In *Ward v Hickey,* 996 F2d 448 (1st Cir 1993), for example, the First Circuit ruled that a proper test is whether the restriction is reasonably related to a legitimate pedagogical concern, taking into account the age and sophistication of the students, the relationship between teaching method and valid educational objectives, and the context and manner of presentation.

This court concludes that the *Hickey* test is appropriate for use in this case, despite the fact that the regents' rule governs university classrooms. The rationale for the regents' rule is a concern for creating an appropriate learning environment, a concern that persists at all levels of education. The regents' policy recognizes that many students, particularly undergraduates, who are suddenly and unexpectedly confronted with graphic sexual material will be unable to process the information dispassionately and intelligently. The two students who complained in this case did not object solely to the viewpoint or ideology of the film, but complained because they were embarrassed and shocked by the film. Their understandable reaction interferes with, rather than promotes, learning.

As adults who have voluntarily chosen to undertake higher education, college students cannot be protected from all ideas or discussion that might disturb their sensibilities or cause offense. This kind of paternalism would undermine the generation of knowledge and the development of critical thinking. Thus, the kind of state control over the content of the curriculum that is routinely exercised in junior and senior high school is not always justified in universities and colleges. However, the test of reasonableness is still appropriate, with due regard to the context of the case. Even adults need fair warning that materials that they will be asked to study, debate, and analyze may at first be shocking. The regents' policy is a reasonable accommodation of the needs of college-age students: it allows the instructor to choose even offensive material, provided the students are given advance notice and the opportunity to exercise other available options.

Kennedy's assertion that the regents' rule has a chilling effect on free inquiry in the classroom is not persuasive. Any instructor who uses material requiring a warning may, of course, be subject to criticism by students and others because of the choice of controversial materials. But the risk of disapproval from some students is a risk that all teachers face and, in the view of this court, is not significantly increased by the regents' rule.

Finally, Kennedy's claim that he has an unrestricted right to use nonobscene material in his classroom finds no support in the case law. Sexually explicit speech—even though failing the legal definition of obscenity because the material taken as a whole has serious literary, artistic, political, or scientific value—can nevertheless be channeled and regulated under appropriate circumstances. The United States Supreme Court in *FCC v Pacifica Foundation,* 438 US 726 (1978) upheld a Federal Communications Commission order barring a George Carlin monologue using vulgar and indecent speech from broadcast during the day. Because of its sexually explicit nature, the Court reasoned that the broadcast could be legitimately restricted to a time when minors would not likely be listening. The *Pacifica* Court also analogized radio listeners to a captive audience because, absent a prior warning, the listeners could not turn off their radios before hearing the offensive speech. The *Pacifica* "captive audience" rationale was cited by the Fifth Circuit in 1986 to justify the dismissal of a college faculty member who repeatedly used profanity in his classroom (*Martin v Parrish,* 805 F2d 583 [5th Cir 1986]). These precedents on sexually explicit speech add support to the reasonableness of the regents' regulation.

Finally, it must be stressed that Kennedy had ample notice that he was violating an express curricular policy and cannot claim a lack of due process. Some might admire his civil disobedience, but it does not excuse his violation of a valid educational regulation.

PÉTAIN V UNIVERSITY OF EAST DAKOTA

PETER M. SHANE, THE CASE

Henri Pétain has been employed for six years as a professor of modern European history at the University of East Dakota. His research and teaching focus almost entirely on the economic history of nineteenth-century Europe, with particular emphasis on the social impact of technological developments. By the time of his tenure review, he has written four articles in his area of research that have been published in peer-reviewed journals. They are described by all internal and external reviewers as "workmanlike," "a contribution to the field, but not path-breaking." In student evaluations and in peer reviews of his teaching, he is described as a competent, but somewhat dull, teacher. He is to be reviewed for tenure under a university standard that requires for promotion "an established record of teaching effectiveness" and "a record of scholarly achievement representing a genuine contribution to the candidate's field and evidence of likely continued productivity and excellence as a scholar."

Among Professor Pétain's off-campus activities has been regular participation in a lecture series on the Holocaust sponsored by the Institute for Historical Research, a pseudoacademic organization that, since 1978, has been active in denying the existence of the Holocaust. In his lectures, Professor Pétain has claimed that Zyklon-B gas could not have been used as a genocidal agent in the concentration camps and that, consequently, no more than 900,000 Jews could have died during the war. He also has endorsed reports by a revisionist engineer named Fred Leuchter, who claims to have determined from his own visit to Auschwitz that there could never have been homicidal gassings in that camp. Professor Pétain has never lectured at the University of East Dakota on these topics, either as part of a class discussion or otherwise. His lectures, however, have been nationally and locally publicized.

The University of East Dakota's Department of History voted to deny Professor Pétain tenure. In a report to the dean, explaining the department's vote, the chair of the History Department wrote:

> Although Professor Pétain's teaching has so far been marginally competent, his off-campus lecturing activities have so cast doubt on his credibility that he has lost all effectiveness with his students. Furthermore, his willingness to endorse baseless, even fantastic (not to mention anti-Semitic) views, assures that he will never have any real scholarly credibility.

The dean of the College of Liberal Arts, the provost, and the president of the university have all ratified the department's decision, without offering any further reasons.

Professor Pétain has sued to require the granting of tenure on the grounds that: he has clearly met his department's tenure standards and denial of tenure on the asserted grounds violates his First Amendment rights to free speech.

RICHARD SEEBURGER, FOR THE UNIVERSITY

The merits of Mr. Pétain's arguments are exposed by the relief he seeks in this court, the judicial award of tenure, that is, a lifetime seat at the public trough and countless generations of future students forced to sit at his feet. Tenure is the expectation of continued employment with a presumption in favor of the faculty member's competency. Mr. Pétain seeks to have this court preclude the university from seeking a more qualified individual for the position he held.

The untenured teacher at a state university has no constitutionally protected property interest and can be denied future employment for no reason at all. An *otherwise* qualified public employee may not be denied employment for the wrong reasons, such as race, religion, or gender, not here involved. And an *otherwise qualified* public employee is not to suffer an adverse job action for First Amendment activity unrelated to the job. Mr. Pétain is not being offered a new position at the expiration of his contract because he has not carried his burden of establishing his qualifications for tenure within the prescribed time. The only issue before this court is whether the Department of History may consider as *relevant* to his competency for tenure his publicly and formally expressed views on the happening of the Holocaust.

Mr. Pétain is described as a marginally competent teacher whose scholarship is workmanlike. If that is all there was to the case, no one would argue seriously that the History Department denied his First Amendment rights in concluding he had not carried his burden in establishing the level of competency required for the award of tenure. Yet his teaching and writing carries with it a degree of First

Amendment protection. Surely a candidate for tenure cannot complain of First Amendment violations if the material in his tenure application file is found wanting.

The Constitution, contrary to Mr. Pétain's implicit argument, does not limit the contents of his file only to those things he wishes considered. The First Amendment does not preclude the department from considering a particularly disastrous article he has written and that he wants excluded from his file. His publicly and formally stated views on the Holocaust, while arguably not relevant to an application for tenure in a department of creative writing, do bear on his competency as a member of the History Department. The only legal issue is relevancy.

Mr. Pétain turns the First Amendment on its head. It is not that he does not want to be punished for protected speech. He cannot be. Rather, he wants to be rewarded for it. The truth of the Holocaust is not the issue for this court, any more than the existence of black holes would be for this court in an application for tenure to the Astronomy Department. If First Amendment academic freedom means anything, it is that the truth of that which is relevant is not to be resolved by judicial or legislative fiat. That is the sacred trust of the academy and its accrediting associations. Here the department has no more burdened Mr. Pétain's free speech than he burdens a student's when he grades a history exam. The enforcement of relevant standards of scholarship cannot implicate the First Amendment.

MARTHA CHAMALLAS, FOR PROFESSOR PÉTAIN

As a state institution, the University of East Dakota is bound to respect the First Amendment rights of its faculty and students. At the core of the First Amendment protection is the right of faculty to speak and write on issues of public importance without fear of retaliation simply because they hold unpopular or even odious views. In this case, Professor Pétain was denied tenure solely on the basis of the content of speeches he gave off campus, in connection with activities unrelated to his position as a professor of nineteenth-century history.

Let us briefly review what is not at issue in this case. Professor Pétain has clearly met the published standards for tenure at UED. He has an established record as an effective classroom teacher. His students regard him as competent—there is certainly no requirement that he be dazzling or exciting to meet the standards. Dull teachers are routinely tenured at UED. Professor Pétain has also met the standards for scholarship: he has published a sufficient quantity of work, and the reviewers of his work have concluded that he has made a contribution to the field. This is sufficient for tenure—as the faculty and administrators at UED recognize, young scholars are not expected to reach the height of their scholarly careers before attaining tenure. The generation of pathbreaking scholarship is simply not a requirement for tenure at UED, and any suggestion that Pétain's published scholarship did not meet the actual standard does not hold up when we compare his case to similarly situated candidates.

Most important, there is no evidence in this record that Pétain's off-campus speeches have had any negative impact on his teaching or his interactions with students. There have been no complaints of discriminatory treatment of students in Pétain's classes. To the contrary, the positive nature of the student evaluations provides evidence that Pétain's personal beliefs have not infected the environment of the classroom. Pétain lectures effectively on the economic history of the nineteenth century, the area of his expertise.

This case is very similar to a lawsuit brought by Professor Michael Levin against City College of the City University of New York (*Levin v Harleston*, 966 F2d 85 [2d Cir 1992]). In that case, Levin successfully argued that his First Amendment rights had been violated when the university retaliated against him for making off-campus speeches on the intelligence and social characteristics of blacks that many found racially offensive and inaccurate. The retaliation in that case took the form of the creation of special "shadow," or parallel, sections of the required course on introductory philosophy in order to permit students who found Levin's views distasteful to take the course from a different instructor. The key holding of the court was that it is not enough to hypothesize that a professor's views will harm the students, in the absence of proof of actual disruption and actual harm to particular students. Because there was no showing that Levin discriminated against black students or foisted his views in a dogmatic or uncivil way on his classes, the creation of the shadow sections was deemed to be an unconstitutional retaliation for his off-campus views.

Pétain's case is stronger than Levin's. Here we are faced with the denial of tenure, the university equivalent of a firing, which often means the end of a person's academic career. At a minimum, the First Amendment requires that before off-campus political speech can provide the basis for such a grave decision, there must be evidence of concrete educational harm. Hypothesized fears are not enough. Because no such showing can be made in this case, the only conclusion that can be drawn is that the decision to deny tenure is retaliatory, solely in response to Pétain's exercise of his protected First Amendment rights.

It is important to point out that this case does not involve the termination of an administrative appointment but the dismissal of a professor from classroom teaching. The government has greater leeway to determine who will carry out its administrative functions. Precedents involving government lawyers, nurses, or even university administrators are not controlling in this case. Instead, the denial of tenure to Professor Pétain implicates academic freedom to a degree not present in these other contexts. The right of a professor to engage in research and speech free from government censorship and retribution is the only way to assure free inquiry in our society. In 1992 the American Association of University Professors' Committee on Academic Freedom and Tenure adopted a statement that sums up the concept of academic freedom embedded in the First Amendment: "no viewpoint or message may be deemed so hateful or disturbing that it may not be expressed."[1] Although we may find Professor Pétain's views on the Holocaust to be hateful, the First Amendment does not permit the government to make the content of his speech the basis of an adverse employment decision. Any other standard would permit the government to choose which viewpoints to endorse and which to prohibit. The chilling effect on research, learning, and the generation of knowledge would be great.

Because of the chilling effect, viewpoint discrimination endangers not only persons who espouse potentially dangerous views but all those whose ideas engender controversy and strong feelings. The university must be a place where controversy and disagreement is encouraged, not suppressed. The antidote for odious speech is, of course, more speech, a course of action in the long run far more likely to produce reason and justice than suppression.

PETER M. SHANE, THE JUDGE'S OPINION

This is a sensitive case. It is undisputed on this record that the sole reason for denying tenure to Henri Pétain is his off-campus lecturing regarding the Nazi Holocaust. This speech, although vile and despicable, is indisputably subject to the protection of the First Amendment. It is also quite obviously of public concern. And as a life-tenured Article III judge, I hasten to add that a life spent "at the public trough" is still a life shielded by the First Amendment.

On the other hand, the personnel decision here being disputed—namely, a grant of tenure—is the kind of decision that cannot be made except by judging the merits of constitutionally protected speech. Faculty members are presumably denied tenure all the time, on the grounds that their constitutionally protected speech, whether in the form of lectures, scholarly articles, or books, fails to meet standards of excellence imposed by their academic peers. Whatever the First Amendment means in an academic context, it cannot plausibly exempt faculty members from adverse decisions based on the quality of their speech.

What a case like this really comes down to, then, is an identification of a university's actual basis in making an adverse employment decision based on a faculty member's speech. Retaliation against a faculty member simply for expressing an unpopular point of view on a matter of public concern is unconstitutional, unless it could be shown that the faculty member's mode of expression so disrupts the educational process that the magnitude of disruption justifies disciplinary action. Conversely, where a faculty member's point of view is taken legitimately as evidence of the poor quality of his or her teaching or scholarship, courts must defer.

Obviously, this is not an easy line to draw. It is the easiest thing in the world to express one's disagreement with another person's point of view as a negative judgment on the quality of his or her thought or intellectual output. But a court may find this a manageable inquiry if it attends to a variety of objective factors.

The first factor, of course, is what the university actually says. In this case, the university's point of view is expressed solely in a statement that is, unfortunately, rather brief and elliptical. It is also ambiguous. On one hand, the reason for tenure denial is expressed as a lack of teaching and scholarly credibility. That lack of credibility is tied in turn to the faculty member's endorsement of "baseless, even fantastic views." On the other hand, the statement also refers to the views as "anti-Semitic," which could be read as focusing on the speaker's point of view, rather than on his teaching and scholarly skill.

Another objective factor is the venue in which the faculty member uttered the speech in question. Professor Pétain urges that it is illegitimate for the university to judge him on the basis of off-campus speech. His speeches, however, occurred in what purported to be an academic forum—a lecture series sponsored by something called the Institute for Historical Research. The nature of this forum strongly suggests that Professor Pétain intended to be understood as an academic, not merely as a mere citizen on the street, in uttering his views on the Holocaust. This tends to support the legitimacy of the university's concerns with his performance.

A third objective factor is the relevance of his utterances to his actual job description. Professor Pétain urges that his tenure decision should be judged entirely on his work concerning nineteenth-century European economic history. The record indicates, however, that he was hired as a professor to teach modern European history. The events he discussed, therefore, closely relate to the area he was charged with teaching. This case might be different if it involved a mathematician who had been disciplined for an expression of views on foreign policy, or a law professor disciplined for an incompetent public summary of quantum mechanics. The relevance of Professor Pétain's speech to his job description also strengthens the university's position.

A final objective factor concerns the plausibility, given current knowledge and professional standards, of making a reliable, objective judgment concerning the quality of the faculty member's speech. An astronomer, for example, might make what his colleagues regard as a silly prediction of the kinds of lifeforms likely to appear in the most remote corners of the galaxy. It would be difficult, however, to sustain an argument that the astronomer's views were provably false. In this case, however, the views expressed by the faculty member have been rejected as false on a virtually unanimous basis among reputable historians. Museums are filled with data disproving his assertions. It is not enough to excuse an academic's purveying of untruth to say it is merely his "point of view" that the earth is flat, the sun rises in the West, or that Joseph Stalin was actually president of the United States. In light of current knowledge, these are simply incompetent assertions.

Where the balance of objective factors renders it plausible that a university's failure to tenure a faculty member was based on the quality of his thought, and not on its unpopularity, a university's academic judgment is entitled to deference unless that judgment is expressed in an unambiguously, viewpoint-discriminatory way. That is not the case here. This court, therefore, decides to uphold the university's decision.

In doing so, we also expressly reject the *Levin* case as unpersuasive and express our relief that it is not binding in our circuit.

NOTE

1. *Academe,* July-August 1992, 30.

THIRTY

A Different Take on Advocacy in the Public School Classroom

JAYNE E. SBARBORO

I AM YOUR BASIC JOE-TEACHER, or rather Jayne-teacher, in the elementary grades. I teach at McKinley-Thatcher Elementary, which is in south Denver. To give you a picture, it is currently a racially mixed school, roughly 55 percent white, 15 percent black, 25 percent Latino, less than 1 percent American Indian or Asian. Socioeconomically it ranges from middle class to poor. Richer kids tend to go to private schools. We have students who are bused in from Five Points, one of the poorest neighborhoods of Denver.

In my district 60 percent of our students qualify for free or reduced lunch, nearly 70 percent at the elementary level. Colorado has 177,000 students who qualify for free or reduced lunch. Of those, almost 36,000 are Denver Public School students.

Of these public school students, 15,000 have limited proficiency in English. Over 80 languages and dialects are spoken in the Denver Public Schools, though not at my school. Our mobility rate—the combined number of students who withdrew from school or were admitted to a school during a given year compared to that school's total enrollment—averages 97 percent.

Our city spends about $31 a day to educate a regular education student. It spends $38 a day to educate an at-risk Chapter I student. Colorado spends $111 a day to keep a juvenile in a long-term incarceration facility.[1]

I am not presenting these statistics as problems. They are not problems. They are kids. When we talk about advocacy in the public school classroom, we are talking about kids—real, live, breathing people whose reasons for learning are as varied as their backgrounds.

Not all statistics about public education are depressing. I think it's important that the public be aware: we educate more children than ever before in our country. In 1870 the dropout rate was 93 percent. The term "dropout" was not even coined until the 1950s. By 1965 this rate had dropped to 25 percent and since then has remained steady. Contrary to popular media coverage, scores on the Scholastic Aptitude Test (SAT) are higher than ever. The "problem" is that more kids are taking the test, which means that more students are thinking about going to college than ever before, which is great news. If you compare upper and middle scores today to their counterparts 20 years ago, SAT scores have gone up. We graduate more students—about 86 percent, counting GED, general equivalency diplomas—than ever before in the history of public education. Fifty-eight percent of high school graduates go on to college. That is more than double the rate of any other nation and triple the rate of most European nations.[2]

I advocate for students best when I teach reading and writing. Although they go hand in hand, for discussion purposes I wish to focus on teaching writing as a way to advocate for the student in the public school classroom.

I passionately want each person in my class to find meaning in life, and to have ways to share that meaning. Writing is one vehicle for that search and expression.

I edit and publish schoolwide anthologies. This year I published a multischool anthology, with work from middle school as well as elementary. Anthologies have typically included poetry, narratives, biographies, and historical fiction. Generally I have tried to publish widely, and I make a strong attempt to include writing by students who don't often get published. Another of my goals is to get meaningful texts into the hands of students, so I sell the anthologies inexpensively, for a quarter or 50 cents. With the "profits" (it has never been a moneymaking proposition, and I always supplement out of my pocket and other donations), I pay students "royalties" for their work.

I want to use a student that I taught several years ago as an example. Jerome fit the above-listed statistics. He was an ethnic "minority" who had moved six times in the same year that he came to my class. He couldn't read, although he was in third grade. His scores on standardized tests were at the first percentile. I suppose that one might project the likelihood of his one day being incarcerated.

Jerome and I worked together to write a poem about his younger brother. It had strong images about the fun they had together. I was happy watching Jerome see his own words in print and for that print to have meaning for him. The print on the page was talking about something Jerome really cared about, and he literally realized that an author is a person saying something he or she really cares about on paper. It was the beginning of the realization that the difference between "author" and "authority" is just three letters.

I was happy to give Jerome his poem in a published "magazine" two weeks later. I watched him read and reread his poem, picking out words he knew and connecting meaning with text. After the magazines had been sold, I was able to pay Jerome royalties for his work. He earned $1.50. It was a significant amount of money to him, because for the first time he realized he could get paid to think. His voice was valued and he would never look at authorship the same way. To me, the lessons were priceless.

As writing process goes on, our students place well in state Anne Frank competitions and have been published in other poetry anthologies. They develop and express an incredible sophistication about their observations of the world. They are well on their way to knowing they can make a difference. This may be key to improving the statistics.

The issue of advocacy pokes its head into writing conferences. With young developing writers, I refuse to red-ink their work. I begin writing conferences with "How can I help you?" They are very specific in the kind of help they want. We talk about ways to shape our message, strengthen our verbs. It is important that they hear their own voice in the work, loud and clear. One of the real issues of advocacy is our duty to advocate for *our* students. Students who have worked on historical fiction in my class learn that historians start with bare facts and then sketch in the rest of the story. Students talk about how history has been written and begin to question the words that have colored it. Our class looked at several versions of Native Americans' migration to reservations. We read, "The government gave the Indians all the land west of the Mississippi to live on." We were able to discuss the choice of the verb, and the generosity of the government, because we were writers.

For an elementary school teacher, the issues of advocacy are so vastly different from those of the academy. I present these issues as another view.

NOTES

1. Sources include McKinley-Thatcher profile information, Denver Public Schools (DPS) Planning, Research and Program Evaluation, DPS Special Education, and Colorado Youth Services, February 1995.
2. Gerald Bracey, *Bad Schools, Good Schools—Who's Right?* (pamphlet); Richard P. McAdams, "Lessons from Abroad: How other Countries Educate their Children," *American School Board Journal* (February 1995).

THIRTY-ONE

Fight Training in the High School Classroom

RAY LINN

ONE WAY TO APPROACH A HIGH SCHOOL CLASSROOM is through an emphasis on the theme of power—focusing specifically on who gets it, why, and what the costs are, and also on who doesn't get it, why, and what the costs are. From the first day of class the teacher can make this emphasis clear, and he can also tell students that the main goal of the class is to turn them into good fighters—into people who are good at defending themselves and controlling the world they live in. This kind of an approach is in harmony with the postmodern sense that it is power relations, rather than objective truth, that explain why human beings come to believe what they do about themselves, the world, and what they should do in it. But a focus on the theme of power in high school is important for another reason: perhaps more than any other classroom focus, it helps to solve the problem of motivation, and this is especially the case for teachers faced with students from nonacademic backgrounds.

It was this second concern that convinced me that a classroom should become an arena where students study good and bad fighting. I don't want to focus on personal experience, but I began my teaching career in Watts, in Los Angeles, and what happened to me as a new teacher is what happens to most new teachers who are sent to teach in a ghetto high school: I was immediately confronted by a class that was not motivated to pay attention to what I had been trained to teach. The students just didn't have a deep interest in the standard English teacher topics that I thought were important, and they didn't even have an interest in playing the more middle-class game of pretense. But as any teacher of housing project kids soon realizes, they did have a deep interest in two major questions: "Why does the white man have the power rather than us?" and "How can we get the power?" The result was that I increasingly found myself teaching to these two questions. In other words, I began my career as a fight trainer.

The transition to trainer is pretty easy, and I began to think about it systematically when I was teaching seniors Max Weber's *The Protestant Ethic and the Spirit of Capitalism* (through secondary source materials).[1] In this book Weber himself is concerned with why the Northern Europeans and North Americans were the first to develop capitalist societies, and he traces this development back to the Reformation ideas of Luther and Calvin. He specifically emphasizes the Protestant ideas about a holy secular calling, everyday asceticism, and predestination, and he claims that, since they led to decreased consumption and increased production, the combination of these ideas inevitably gave rise to the world's first great moneymaking societies. For Weber the main issue was economic development, but in teaching Weber it is easy to shift the focus to power and the question of why the Protestant whites were able to dominate much of the world after the seventeenth and eighteenth centuries. It is also easy for the trainer to draw the moral from the story, a moral that is particularly relevant in today's American ghettos: "If you want power for yourself and your kids, start describing everyday work as a sacred duty, and start describing all play and spontaneous pleasure as 'sinful,' and start saying that a single afternoon spent at the motel rather than at work is a clear sign that you are predestined for hell fire!" Such moral fight training can be reinforced through reading some of Benjamin Franklin's "Advice to a Young Tradesman" or, even better, through a Horatio Alger novel such as *Ragged Dick*. In both cases trainees are told that the key to victory is a lifetime devoted to rational moneymaking—a lifetime of all work and no play.

Of course ghetto kids, like middle-class kids in a hedonistic, consumer-oriented society, will fight the idea that their life should be all work and no play, but that's okay because then the dialogue between trainer and novice gets started. For example, "If you want power, what is more important than rational moneymaking skills? Is Thomas Sowell right in his recent *Race and Economics* when he argues that such skills (what he calls 'cultural capital') are still the key to power in the modern world? What packs a greater punch than money?"

In working out the training schedule, there are several related topics that might be approached in the same way. First, was it the new religious beliefs that led to European power, or is Marx right when he claims that it was new material and social conditions which appeared at the end of the Middle Ages? Was it new ideas, or simply the institution of market-based production, that led to the power of nations as well as to their wealth? Or was it the Scientific Revolution and a new scientific way of thinking about the world that led to European dominance after the seventeenth and eighteenth centuries? Can any nation win a fight today without thinking scientifically? Trainers investigating these topics might also consider the Freudian view that it was the emergence of the nuclear family and stricter repression of impulse that led to the more sublimated and "civilized" fighting of the Europeans.

Since readings and discussions on these topics are abstract and often difficult, the trainer with well-developed units will still encounter student resistance, but now she has a weapon with which to beat up student apathy: "We're not playing around in this classroom, not merely pursuing truth or goodness or beauty—we are learning how to fight! Do you want to learn how to defend yourself and control things, or be another loser?" Such a line might seem directed more toward macho adolescent males than toward females, but in ghetto schools males are the greater problem. Besides, any good trainer will be quick to point out that the female liberation movement is designed to improve the fighting skills of women, for without them women get nothing but the kids and the diapers.

Of course this kind of approach to the classroom won't work for everyone—what will?—but it will work for many because it connects academic subject matter to one of the strongest desires of adolescents: the desire to come out on top. Perhaps Nietzsche and Foucault are wrong in asserting that the will to power is *everything* in human life, and let's hope they're wrong in claiming that such a will is inevitably tied to interpersonal dominance instead of the desire to create one's world—but it is hard to deny that when human beings meet and talk, they very often try to dominate each other. It is also hard to deny that most human beings hate the thought of being a weakling who is dominated by someone else. With regard to adolescent males, it might be reasonable to assume that, given the choice among truth, beauty, goodness, and power, a great many will opt first for power. God, the Creator of the universe, is, above all, power.

If a teacher plays to this desire and becomes a trainer, as a good trainer she will, of course, qualify and define her key terms. Above all, she will need to stress that major human fighting almost always differs from animal fighting in that it is symbolic—a form of fighting that takes place under the symbolic descriptions of language. This point has seemed obvious to a great many twentieth-century thinkers, but it is not obvious to high school students, especially not to ghetto males. But once they do see a connection between language and power, they have a strong motive for studying language and "boring" subjects such as semantics and logic—not merely to get to the truth, but to become a heavyweight contender! Here I think it should be emphasized that the main reason it is difficult to get high school students to think about language is that for them language is invisible. For them, what is obvious is that there are objects in the world, and also that they have thoughts and feelings about them. What is not obvious is that a collective language—a traditional way of describing the world—enters their heads first and that it shapes their thoughts and feelings about objects, including their thoughts and feelings about their "self." Perhaps the best way to point this out, the best way to make the power of language "visible" to adolescents, is to focus on specific examples where it is used to dominate how human beings think and feel about, say, dark skin, the Gulf War, or a new shampoo.

What trainers first need to stress is that, as Richard Wright said at the end of *Black Boy*,[2] words are "weapons," and also that, as

Malcolm X suggested in his *Autobiography*,[3] descriptions of the world come between two fighters and determine the outcome of the fight. Malcolm particularly emphasized that racist descriptions of American blacks as inferior and whites as superior crippled the fighting will of many "blacks," while strengthening that of many "whites." In other words, he pointed out that in fighting oppression, a fighter must keep in mind that his ultimate "enemy" is language, and that what must first be fought is not human beings but the way previous generations have described the world—especially those descriptions that shape thought about the oppressor and the oppressed. Any student who has mastered this basic training point is no longer a novice; and again, he now has a strong motive for studying and attacking language critically. He also has a strong motive for thinking about how to redescribe himself and the world in order to fight back. In teaching this point, trainers might consider going over the relevant passages from Malcolm X's *Autobiography,* and they might also consider Richard Rorty's fighting advice to women in his essay "Feminism and Pragmatism."[4]

Once the symbolic nature of human fighting is understood, students can see why a trainer insists on vocabulary development— without a strong vocabulary it is easy to get knocked down by descriptions coming from a fighter armed with a strong, persuasive vocabulary. Students should also be in a position to see why a trainer might rely on a daily Socratic dialogue—in other words, why they are constantly attacked with questions, and then, after their answers, with more attacks on their answers—for such a "negative" approach to the classroom is essential to the production of tough, highly critical verbal fighters. It should also be made clear that the Socratic method—which becomes a method of thinking as well as of talking—becomes a powerful training tool only when it is focused on abstract concepts and relevant subject matter. What gives special value to this method is that trainees will automatically use it when fighting outside the arena.

Once students realize that human fighting is almost always a symbolic activity, they are also in a position to see why note-taking and essay-writing are essential in preparation for major fights in the modern world. In establishing this connection between successful fighting and writing, trainers of high school seniors might consider a unit on Tzvetan Todorov's *The Conquest of America.*[5] In this book Todorov argues that Cortés and the Europeans were able to defeat Montezuma and the Indians because they were superior at communication—specifically, the Europeans were quicker at gaining accurate information, better at interpreting it realistically, and better at manipulating and deceiving with words and other symbols. The main point—as Todorov shows in discussing how Cortés began the fight with only 508 European soldiers and yet was able to defeat Montezuma and many thousands of Aztec warriors in Aztec territory—is that these three communication skills are especially important when different groups of people meet and struggle for dominance. For Todorov, these skills made the European Conquest of the new world inevitable, even if Cortés had lost in Mexico City. But the most important point, from a trainer's point of view, is that Todorov traces these skills and the resultant European superiority at communication back to writing and a writing-based culture—which the Aztecs lacked.

To see why this might be the case, why writing might be the key to power, we should glance at the history of Greek culture as described by Havelock in *Preface to Plato.*[6] In their early history, before they developed an alphabet, the Greeks did not think abstractly and analytically about what is real, or about knowledge, reasoning, or rhetoric. In Homer's eighth-century poems, for example, we do not find philosophical and sharply analytical thinking, but rather only a concrete narration of events, with simple-minded psychology and few abstract categories—the weak kind of thinking that limits one to a primitive, macho style of fighting, as illustrated by an idiot like Achilles. But two centuries later, after they had developed an alphabet, the Greeks started thinking in a philosophical and more powerful way, and eventually the writing-based culture that they initiated gave rise to the shrewd, well-informed, and manipulative fighting style of Cortés. The point here isn't to idealize Cortés—who was simply another cruel human being on the make—but to insist that he was one of the great heavyweights in human history.

Is Todorov right in arguing that reading and writing are the key to cultural dominance? I don't know, but after presenting his ideas about the power of the written word, the trainer has a new weapon to throw at the weakly motivated student who doesn't take essay-writing or note-taking seriously: "Yeah, Montezuma didn't take writing seriously either, but then he got his face smashed in!" Here it should be emphasized that, in evaluating the Aztecs, or other cultures in general, a trainer cannot ignore questions of power; nor should he ignore the question of whether a student should try to hang on to a culture or ethnic identity that does not promote successful fighting. Why end up like Montezuma?

At this point we can turn to what a fight trainer might add to the contemporary debate on multiculturalism. First, while he would have no argument against the multiculturalist position that Americans need to be more open to the Other, he would also emphasize that the presence of the Other very often produces fear and strengthens a Normal Fighter's will to fight, especially if the Other is seen as a member of a large group. As Sartre said in *St. Genet*, "to the normal man, to be different and to be wrong are one and the same," and what is "wrong" must be put down.[7] Those fighters who speak differently—whether through their words, dress, or behavior—are especially threatening to the Normal Fighter, and thus a fighter from a less powerful group should be particularly conscious of when to display his otherness. By covering it up, through camouflage, he can often weaken his opponent's will to fight and gain a strategic advantage. Camouflage and seduction should thus be seen as an important part of any fighting strategy. Unfortunately, retarded Macho Fighters—who think that the only way to fight is openly, through direct "man-to-man" confrontation—fail to understand this point, and thus they have sorry records. Trainers with standards will not pass them.

Trainers would add something else to the multicultural debate. It is that trainees should not be encouraged to hang on to their cultures ("culture" here means a collective, traditional way of describing the world and what to do in it). The reason trainers should avoid such advice is that, in the trainee's mind, cultures come as wholes, and there are many aspects of less-dominant cultures that prevent successful fighting with fighters from a dominant culture. For example, a fighter who hangs onto a culture that does not place a high value on literacy, economic rationality, or scientific thinking will have great difficulty when he comes up against fighters who come from cultures that do value these activities. Separatist fighting strategies, especially when accompanied by an intense hatred of a dominant group, often can weaken fighters for just this reason. The problem here is that the separatist ideology makes it difficult for a fighter to develop the fighting tools of a more dominant group. As Thomas Sowell puts it in *Race and Economics,* separatist fighters come to think it "treason" to copy more successful fighting styles.[8] And as Sowell also points out, the medieval Jews who began copying the Arab scientists and the twentieth-century Japanese who began copying the American car manufacturers have suffered less oppression because of their willingness to emulate more successful fighters. The point here isn't that fighters should turn their backs on "their own people," only that to avoid defeat, they may have to drop some aspects of their traditional cultures. In brief, trainees should be told not to idealize past styles of fighting. Rather, they must become flexible and open to new styles, like amphibians.

It is sometimes argued that, because of an obsessive focus on the suffering and defeats of the oppressed, multiculturalists tend to "victimize" students from nondominant backgrounds. But since the focus of her arena is on how to fight and gain power, this charge cannot be leveled against a fight trainer. And as a good multiculturalist fight trainer, she will emphasize that "power" is not an entity that is permanently possessed by anyone, rather that it is constantly changing hands and that disciplined fighters can always get it, regardless of the defeats of their ancestors.

A good trainer will also avoid the excesses of the "self-esteem" emphasis, which often has accompanied a multicultural approach to the classroom. In particular, while acknowledging the importance of self-esteem to successful fighting, she will not think that "low self-esteem" is primarily a problem of "self-hate" and feelings of inferiority. Rather, she will think of low self-esteem as simply a lack of confidence that one can control the future through one's own efforts. She will also think that this kind of confidence can best be gained through an arena in which there is, as Kenneth Clark said, "demonstrable achievement"—in other words through an arena in which students can see that they are able to dominate difficult subject matter. Positive stories about a trainee's ancestors and a phony "you're okay" line are poor substitutes for the trainee's knowledge that he can dominate in difficult fights. So, in passing, is the affective emphasis that has become so popular in high schools during the last few years. By "affective emphasis" I mean the tendency to think of the classroom as a talk show where students come to "express their feelings" rather than learn how to analyze, redefine, and fight. In response to this tendency, a trainer would not deny the importance of feeling in human life, but he would also emphasize that if a student doesn't learn how to fight, his emotional life will be terrible, no matter how much emoting he has done in school.

But what should a trainer do if she finds herself confronted by noble-minded students, by refined, humanities flower children who don't think their teachers should get down in the gutter with fight talk? Here trainers might begin by talking about the experience that boys may have had on the playground when the other guy kept knocking them down, and there was nothing they could do about it. At issue is whether this kind of situation is very important in life—whether the feeling of powerlessness from not being able to fight back has a major influence on how an individual comes to think of himself and his situation in the world. For a more graphic illustration of the Loser Problem, students might be asked to read *The Painted Bird* by Jerzy Kosinski.[9] It is a novel about the relation between a social group and a powerless Other, specifically, about the relation between some light-skinned Polish villagers and a homeless, dark-skinned boy who becomes their scapegoat during World War II. But it is also a novel that illustrates what happens to a human being when he cannot fight back, and what is emphasized is that he will come to idealize his oppressor and hate himself. Before the boy is finally rescued at the end of the novel, he comes to see an SS officer as God and himself as an ugly and evil "black flea." Perhaps such a psychological response in chronic losers is inevitable, and "identification with the oppressor" is a major theme in the sociology of the oppressed. Perhaps it is most dramatically revealed in the concentration camp literature. Today a great many educated people are aware of this psychological tendency in people who keep getting knocked down, and yet it often seems more difficult for privileged whites to realize that their more positive sense of self is a result of ancestors who were good at fighting and who didn't get knocked down.

Since some people might think that a fighting approach to education is immoral, I want to briefly mention a few qualifying principles that I think all trainers should follow. First, students should not be told that they should *always* be fighting. (Knowing when not to fight is important, since it saves time and energy for major bouts.) Second, as has already been mentioned, students should not be told that they should always fight openly. (In the *Tao Te Ching*, perhaps the first fight-training masterpiece, Lao Tzu pointed out that there is a great advantage in being a Closet Dominator.)[10] Third, students should not be encouraged to fight cruelly (not only because it tends to increase resistance, but also because it decreases allies—essentials in any heavyweight fight). Finally, students should not be told that winning a fight is what matters (except in those rare cases such as when we were up against the Nazis). In a postmodern world that has been created by language, truth slides into the background, but aesthetics are foregrounded—and students should be encouraged to develop a creative style of fighting rather than being macho idiots who are concerned only with winning. (Aside from lacking flexibility, macho idiocy also invites resistance, whereas a creative style disarms.) As Nietzsche, perhaps the greatest nineteenth-century fight theorist, said: trainees need to be told that their existence "can be justified only as an esthetic phenomenon."[11]

Even with these qualifying principles in mind, perhaps some teachers will resist the thought that a high school classroom should be turned into an arena designed to turn out good fighters. Many will say that a classroom can be a lot more than *that*, and I agree, but I also think that fight training should be primary. It should be primary because fights, and especially fights over how reality should be defined, will continue into the future, and also because those who cannot fight will be in worse shape than those who can. If they keep getting knocked down, the losers will continue to hate themselves, regardless of what else we teach them; and we shouldn't ignore something else: they will not be able to love. Besides, now that objective truth has become an embarrassing academic topic—now that it seems doubtful that any teacher is passing it on to the next generation—power seems to be the main issue in education. But even if Truth still made sense, an emphasis on the theme of power would continue to motivate interest in a wide range of academic topics. There are, of course, other highly motivating themes, and, as the media remind us, we should never forget sex and violence. But fight training is just as "basic," and I think it should be considered as the most promising way to take nonacademic kids into the world of abstract thought.

NOTES

1. Max Weber, *The Protestant Ethic and the Spirit of Capitalism*, trans. Talcot Parsons (New York: Scribner, 1958).
2. Richard Wright, *Black Boy: A Record of Childhood and Youth* (New York: Harper and Row, 1966).
3. Malcolm X, *The Autobiography of Malcolm X* (New York: Ballantine, 1964).
4. Richard Rorty, "Feminism and Pragmatism," *Michigan Quarterly Review* (Spring 1990).
5. Tzvetan Todorov, *The Conquest of America: The Question of the Other*, trans. Richard Howard (New York: Harper and Row, 1983).
6. Eric A. Havelock, *Preface to Plato* (Cambridge, MA: Belknap, 1963).
7. Jean-Paul Sartre, *Saint Genet: Actor and Martyr*, trans. Bernard Frechtman (New York: Braziller, 1963).
8. Thomas Sowell, *Race and Economics* (New York: Basic Books, 1994).
9. Jerry Kosinski, *The Painted Bird*, rev. ed. (New York: Bantam, 1978).
10. Lao Tzu, *Tao Te Ching*.
11. Nietzsche, *The Birth of Tragedy; and, Genealogy of Morals*, trans. Francis Golffing (New York: Anchor, 1956), 143.

THIRTY-TWO

Students Becoming Their Own Advocates

JUDITH ENTES

ADVOCACY SEEMS NATURAL IN MY CLASSROOM. Many of the students I teach must learn to be their own advocates. Often they are the first in their families to attend college, and most are labeled economically "poor." In recent years more and more of them are single teenage mothers who must learn to be advocates for both themselves and their children. Being a teacher implies being an advocate in quite a different sense. What I advocate is that students engage in critical, self-reflective thinking, and I believe that I can be most effective in achieving this goal if I am a facilitator, assisting and guiding students in discovering knowledge that encourages their personal growth.

In playing such a role, I follow an established tradition. At the Anglo-American Conference on the Teaching of English at Dartmouth College in 1966, many participants argued that personal growth, the psychosocial development of students, was a major goal of teaching English. Consequently teachers have increasingly sought ways to help students advance their knowledge of themselves and their ability to conduct day-to-day activities successfully. Interpreting the deliberations at the Dartmouth conference in *Growth through English,* John Dixon underscores this point: "from the very start of reading and writing, [the teacher] has to look beyond the minimum possibilities of a considered and extended exploration of experience, permitting . . . more individual, personal growth."[1]

Requiring students to read and write on topics of personal interest, indeed urgency, can produce positive changes in their lives, in their ability to communicate effectively, and in their capacity to be advocates for themselves. Students are empowered when they are encouraged to select topics for research and writing that address urgent concerns in their own lives. When students believe that they are in control, they are more likely to develop a genuine interest in reading and writing. Furthermore, completing a writing project that they themselves set in motion can help students recognize the importance of taking responsibility for their work and help them gain confidence.

An effective assignment for promoting this sort of personal growth uses "bibliotherapy," a procedure defined as "the use of books to help solve problems"[2] or "the use of reading to provide comfort."[3] Warner[4] and Corsini[5] broadened the definition of bibliotherapy to include "the application of all literary genres to the therapeutic process, including printed and nonprinted matter and audiovisual aids." Bibliotherapy is often practiced by teachers who read fiction with elementary school children. I believe that bibliotherapy can also be used at the college level, although I have found no literature on the subject.

To illustrate the value of bibliotherapy for college students, I highlight the work of a student I call Maria, who experienced a dramatic change when she researched and wrote about claustrophobia. I learned from our personal conferences that Maria had been walking up and down fifteen flights of stairs to get to and from class because of her fear of confined spaces, such as elevators. Maria took the elevator to class the day *after* she handed in her research paper on claustrophobia. That may not seem a striking event, but for Maria, who was then 19 years old, the act was monumental: she had not ridden in an elevator since the age of three.

I became aware of Maria's predicament when she explained to me that she was going to be absent the day the class was to visit the college library. (The course Maria was in is designed to expose students to different kinds of reading material and to introduce them to the library.) Maria had investigated the library's location and determined that the stairwells were locked for security purposes. She shared with me her fear that she would never be able to use the college library, and I arranged for her to use the library stairs. Afterward, Maria frequently initiated conferences with me to discuss personal and academic problems. In an evaluation she wrote at the end of the semester, Maria said: "I learned more about the college and about myself than I did in any of my other courses. This class really helped me with my reading strategies and with my writing. The best thing I got out of the class, with the help of my classmates and my teacher, was to get over my useless fear." Maria's case shows that students can change their lives through doing research about personally significant topics.

For research to enable students to gain the benefits of bibliotherapy, students must select and use books and materials about a topic that is of personal concern to them. Unfortunately, the importance of selecting a topic is not always recognized. In a book about undergraduate students, for example, Lutzker states that "the choice of topic is the most difficult part of [doing] a research paper" and proposes that the teacher provide a controlled list of topics.[6] Though this might be an "easy fix," providing a list of topics does not really help students address problems they care about. One day a colleague observed me helping students generate topics for their research projects and suggested that, rather than let students select such subjects as physical abuse and pregnancy, I should advise them to write about the environment or the tropical rain forest. I responded: "The subject should be of interest to the students and not necessarily reflect the teacher's interest."

Andrea Lunsford concurs that basic writers should choose their own subjects for writing. She says that assignments should:

> engage students in choosing topics for discussion and for writing. Most basic writing teachers are agreed that basic writers need to see themselves as writers, as part of the academy. To do so, they must become authors, to gain authority for their writing. Engaging students in the process of choosing and refining assignments is one good way to set them on the path toward authorship, toward owning their own voices and texts.[7]

But there are different ways of engaging students. Macrorie writes about the "I-search paper." He advises students: "Allow something to choose you that you want intensely to know or possess. Maybe it's a stereo record or tape player that's right for your desires or pocketbook. Maybe it's a motorcycle. Or the name of an occupation or technical school best for your needs. Or a spot in the United States or a foreign country you would enjoy visiting this summer."[8] Macrorie gives examples of papers that would grow out of such considerations: "A Camera Right for Me" and "Buying a House." For the most part, these topics are about ownership of material items; they are not topics that might lead students to increase their knowledge of themselves and their world.

What I've found most effective is for students to go within themselves and select topics of importance that can help them gain ownership of their lives. Our society presents students and adults with many troubling problems, which require thoughtful, informed reflection. Certainly my students confront pressing concerns that they most resolve one way or another. Failure to confront them can not only be traumatic but can prevent them from pursuing their studies. Writing about a personal dilemma can help a student deal with the problem and even find a solution. And investigating problems can be intellectually stimulating as well as personally satisfying. Most students, from elementary to graduate school, can benefit from wise and thoughtful guidance in selecting useful research topics. I outline here specific steps teachers can use in introducing students to engaging research topics.

First, teachers need to learn and understand something about the background of their students. Since many student problems are personal and confidential, private discussions are helpful. They can take place in class when the teacher meets with individual students, or after class. In addition, teachers need to be sensitive to differences among students. The National Council of Teachers of English (NCTE) Task Force on Racism and Bias in the Teaching of English adopted a policy statement that explicitly advocates addressing the needs of culturally and linguistically diverse students. The NCTE Task Force recommended "introducing classroom topics and materials that connect the students' experiences with the classroom."[9] In suggesting possible projects, teachers should use their knowledge of each student's distinctive background.

Second, in private consultations, teachers need to help a student identify which topics, given the student's background and current situation, he or she might like to investigate. Third, in class and during visits to the library, students need help in locating and using reference works that will point them to sources of information that might be useful. Fourth, students need help locating materials in the library. Fifth, they need to be guided to read productively the materials they find so they can address the important task of differentiating what is and what is not useful for their investigations. Finally, students need to meet with their instructor for guidance in writing about the materials they have found and for comments on draft papers.

Most of the students in my classes—first-year students in college developmental reading—have never written a research paper, and they are not familiar with the resources available to them for research. Those who have had experience in writing research papers often admit to consulting one source only, the encyclopedia, and copying what is printed there. In an informal survey conducted in September 1992, I asked students to define the term "bibliography." Only 14 students out of 63 provided the correct answer. In December 1992, after learning how to do a research paper, not only were 59 students able to define the word, they also demonstrated that they could produce a list of at least seven sources they had consulted in carrying out their research projects. I am arguing that engaging in bibliotherapy will promote not only students' ability to do research but also their interest in learning.

In working with students on the selection and investigation of personally significant topics, teachers should know that librarians are natural allies. Librarians are not responsible for assigning projects, but they can aid in the process. Moreover, librarians have been particularly sensitive to the needs of the developmental student. Lolley and Watkins describe the effective use of videotapes for instruction on using the library at Tarrant County Junior College.[10] Josey recommends that "the academic library must reach disadvantaged students *through* action-oriented library programs and not merely by teaching *about* the library."[11] Modern technology associated with libraries also provides advantages. Madland and Smith recommend the use of Computer-Assisted Instruction in learning about bibliographies,[12] and Lawry provides suggestions for those who are conducting on-line searches.[13] In some institutions librarians play a larger role. Koehler and Swanson report that, at Augsburg College in Minneapolis, a professional librarian collaborates with the classroom teacher in teaching research.[14]

I wish that counselors could also collaborate with teachers. Nickolai-Mays discusses how school counselors use bibliotherapy, suggesting that "allies for the school counselor interested in bibliotherapy would be an English teacher and a school librarian."[15] The alliance could be helpful to students who choose to write on sensitive subjects. Bohning cautions: "reading about a situation may even intensify a personal problem for a reader."[16] And Bishop discusses how writing may be a therapeutic process and suggests "providing new teachers and administrators with an introduction to psychoanalytic theory and the basics of counseling to support them in their necessary work."[17] Many topics, Bishop recognizes, might be extremely personal and, for some, awkward and painful. Consequently, a sensitive, knowledgeable, and skillful teacher must guide the student if bibliotherapy is to be an effective strategy and should act as a source of referrals for professional counseling if need be.

However, writing on sensitive topics can be highly instructive for students. Here are some of the topics my students selected, in consultation with me, in fall 1992: bulimia (the student's sister was suffering from this ailment), the use of mammography (the student underwent the examination), Alzheimer's disease (the student's grandmother was suffering from this illness), child abuse (the student had been a victim), and cancer (the student's mother was suffering from it). These students' papers, along with those of their classmates, demonstrated their proficiency in writing a research paper. For most, it was their first effort. And for most, not only were they proud of their final written products, but they experienced a kind of catharsis.

Reading and writing about the problems they themselves face can change students' lives. Maria not only mastered the writing of a research paper, she also mastered her fear of elevators. Teachers regularly research and write about problems of intellectual concern to them, trying to find solutions. My research and explorations of what helps students to be more successful are of great concern to me, which is why I have written this chapter. Students also need to investigate subjects that are of *personal* concern to *them*. Confronting such topics of concern is a way of learning—about themselves, about how they interact with the world, and about how to advocate for their own interests. Such learning is a kind of personal development that teachers can take pride in fostering. Not only can students' writing improve in substance, insight, and cogency as a result of such efforts, but their ability to locate important information and discover ideas on a wide range of subjects can also improve—along with the quality of their lives. And isn't that what we are all advocating, creating a better life for the student?

NOTES

1. John Dixon, *Growth through English* (Reading, England: National Association for the Teaching of English, 1967), 112.

2. Fran Lehr, "ERIC/RCS: Bibliotherapy," *Journal of Reading* 25 (1981), 76.

3. Peggy Daisey, "Three Ways to Promote the Values and Uses of Literacy at Any Age," *Journal of Reading* 36 (1993), 436.

4. Michael Warner, "Bibliotherapy: Two Sides to the Coin," *Library Media Activities Monthly* 6 (1989), 34-36.

5. Raymond J. Corsini, *Encyclopedia of Psychology* (New York: Wiley, 1984), 146.

6. Marilyn Lutzker, *Research Papers for College Students* (New York: Greenwood Press, 1988), 12.

7. Andrea A. Lunsford, "Assignments for Basic Writers: Unresolved Issues and Needed Research," *Journal of Basic Writing* 5 (1986), 97.

8. Ken Macrorie, *The I-Search Paper* (Portsmouth, NH: Boynton/Cook-Heinemann, 1988), 62.

9. NCTE Task Force on Racism and Bias in the Teaching of English. "Expanding Opportunities: Academic Success for Culturally and Linguistically Diverse Students," *College English* 49 (1987), 550.

10. John Lolley and Ruth Watkins, "Welcome to the Library," *Journal of Developmental and Remedial Education* 5 (1986), 25-26.

11. E. J. Josey, "The Role of the Academic Library in Serving the Disadvantaged Student," *Library Trends* 20 (1971), 442-43.

12. Denise Madland and Marian A. Smith, "Computer-assisted Instruction for Teaching Conceptual Library Skills to Remedial Students," *Research Strategies* 6 (1988), 52-65.

13. Martha Lawry, "Subject Access In the Online Catalog: Is the Medium Projecting the Correct Message," *Research Strategies* 4 (1986), 125-31.

14. Boyd Koehler and Kathryn Swanson, "Basic Writers and the Library: A Plan for Providing Meaningful Bibliographic Instruction," *Journal of Basic Writing* 9 (1990), 56-73.

15. Susanne Nickolai-Mays, "Bibliotherapy and the Socially Isolated Adolescent," *The School Counselor* 36 (1987), 19.

16. Gerry Bohning, "Bibliotherapy: Fitting the Resources Together," *The Elementary School Journal* 82 (1981), 166-170.

17. Wendy Bishop, "Writing Is/And Therapy?: Raising Questions about Writing Classrooms and Writing Program Administration," *Journal of Advanced Composition* 13 (1993), 512.

THIRTY-THREE

A Personal Account of a Struggle to Be Evenhanded in Teaching About Abortion

SAMUEL W. CALHOUN

IT'S A PLEASURE to be a part of this volume's effort to explore what I believe to be a very important question that faces all teachers: What is the proper role of advocacy in the classroom? The letter requesting that I submit a chapter struck an immediately responsive chord with me, because at the time I was struggling with many of the issues described in the letter. I was then teaching a seminar entitled "The Abortion Controversy." I had initially taught the seminar in the spring of 1994.

You'll note that I just used the word "struggling." The word "struggle" also appears in the title to my chapter. I highlight this to let you know at the outset that I don't claim any special expertise in the pedagogical issue that we're addressing. All I can do is share a little of my experience in teaching about abortion. I hope that it is of some benefit.

First, let me briefly describe the course. The seminar met for two hours a week, for either 14 or 15 weeks. The course didn't emphasize the laws on abortion. Rather, it looked at the abortion issue in as broad a manner as possible. This breadth is shown by the list of topics covered this past fall: (1) the pre-*Roe* history of abortion in America; (2) *Roe* and *Casey*; (3) rhetoric; (4) visual imagery; (5) religious values; (6) reasons to abort; (7) fetal personhood; (8) feminism; (9) (potential) fathers; (10) civil disobedience; (11) violence; and (12) compromise.

My goal for each seminar session can be very simply stated: I wanted the class discussion to be as informed and thoughtful as possible. The course mechanics were designed with this goal in mind. The basic mechanism consisted of my distributing, a week before our discussion, a packet of materials pertaining to the topic. The packet, drawn from a variety of sources—books, law review articles, magazines, newspapers, and the like—and maintaining a balance between pro-choice and pro-life viewpoints, served as the raw material for our discussions (supplemented by video materials that I placed on reserve in the library). To help the students focus their thinking, I usually required each student to submit, before our class discussion, one or two pages responding to the material in the packet. The format for this reaction piece frequently was as simple as "State the point of view in this packet with which you disagree the most. Explain." In addition, before our class discussion, each student had to exchange reaction pieces with a classmate and then engage in conversation.

I ended up being very pleased with the basic format I've described. Even the best mechanics, however, won't yield thoughtful discussion on a topic like abortion unless the general atmosphere of the class is healthy. We've all seen nonproductive discussions of abortion. Rather than understanding, the main by-product is anger. I wanted to avoid this result. The key to this effort, in my opinion, was to try to make the course as nonadversarial as possible. Two relationships were potential problems: student to student and my relationship with the students.

In the small law school setting at Washington and Lee, where everyone knows almost everyone else, positive intrastudent relationships seemed to occur almost naturally. The basic atmosphere was one of cordiality and mutual respect. Feelings ran high at some points, but I never sensed any real animosity. The only credit I take for all this is in my idea of having the students engage in one-on-one conversation prior to each seminar session. These conversations most often were between students who disagreed on abortion. The conversations were invaluable in combatting student-to-student hostility. It is not so easy to view as the enemy someone with whom you have talked face to face.

My relationship to the students brings me to the specific topic of this chapter: impartiality in the classroom. To promote the nonadversarial atmosphere that I believed to be essential, I decided that I needed to teach the course in as impartial a manner as possible. This would be difficult for anyone on a topic like abortion. It was particularly challenging to me: I'm an advocate of the pro-life position, who has spoken and written on the subject. More significantly, our student body knows that I am a pro-life advocate. This made me very anxious as I prepared to teach the course for the first time. I pondered the following questions:

1. Would pro-choice students even take the seminar?
2. Would pro-choice students feel free to assert themselves in class?
3. How could I avoid alienating the pro-choice students as the semester progressed? I didn't want them to become so angry at me that productive dialogue would become impossible.
4. And what about the pro-life students? Given the fact that I agreed with their basic position, would I be able to challenge their views sufficiently to make the course educationally worthwhile?

I hope by now that your curiosity has been aroused somewhat. How did things work out? Well, since I'm writing this, you know that I survived physically. I'm even still on the faculty! But what about my anxieties about relating to pro-choice and pro-life students? What steps did I take to deal with the problems I foresaw? What were my successes and failures?

I'd like briefly to mention five points.

First, my concerns about pro-choice student enrollment were so great that I decided to address the issue prior to registration for the seminar. I prepared a memorandum to our student body in which I tried to allay any fears that I would be presenting only the pro-life position. It read in part:

Some of you, knowing of my pro-life perspective, may have wondered how this would affect the manner in which the seminar is taught. I do not consider the course as a soapbox for me to proselytize about abortion. Rather, my chief goal is to challenge all students, regardless of their position on the issue, to think more deeply. This will require that the very best arguments on both sides be presented and evaluated.

The memo must have had at least some positive effect. The first time I taught the course, there were 17 students: 7 pro-choice, 7 pro-life, and 3 undecided. The second time there were 14 students: 8 pro-choice and 6 pro-life.

Second, the first time I taught the seminar, I asked a pro-choice student to give me regular feedback about how I was doing in my effort to be impartial in class. The second time a student informally assumed this role. I can't begin to tell you how important these students proved to be. They helped me correct many mistakes and prevented many others.

Third, I'll mention one of my goals for the seminar that was at least partially achieved. I had hoped to cultivate personal relationships with pro-choice students. I wanted them to feel comfortable in talking to me about abortion, not just during the class, but in the future, as well. With some of the pro-choice students, but not all, I believe I accomplished this. Two factors were key to whatever success I had: the pro-choice students had to realize that while I strenuously opposed their position on abortion, I felt no personal, moral condemnation of them as individuals; and the students needed to sense that I was not desperate to convince them to change their minds concerning abortion. While there is no result that I would rather see, I do not believe that it is my personal responsibility to bring it about. This realization has been enormously freeing. It enables me to relax around pro-choice students. It also is critical to their being able to relax around me.

My fourth point relates to what might be called basic teaching style. The first time I taught the course, in the first few seminar sessions I controlled the class rather tightly. I came into each class with a number of points that I wanted to be sure were covered. I would present the material and then solicit student comments. A student would speak to me and I would respond. Then another student would do the same. The governing principle seemed to be that all student comments should go through me.

One of my student monitors urged me to change this approach. He said that student participation would increase if I gave the students more control over each session. He said to let them decide what they wanted to talk about. Also, I should let the students talk to each other directly, without my acting as a kind of traffic director.

His idea made me nervous. I worried that the students might overlook issues of importance. I was also anxious about the unknown. What if the students brought up points that I hadn't considered?

Despite my fears, I decided to make the recommended changes. At the beginning of the fourth session—which dealt with the rhetoric of the abortion controversy—I said something like "Today our topic is rhetoric. The floor is open for discussion." Then I just sat there and waited.

I'm glad to say that the results were encouraging. The discussion was lively. All but one student spoke, many on more than one occasion. The pro-choice students spoke freely. I was very pleased with how things went and decided to continue to follow the new approach.

My last point concerns an issue that gave me the most difficulty throughout the course. I never did figure it out. You could describe the issue in this way: How could I make sure that I properly challenged both the pro-life and pro-choice students, to press them in class, to make them think carefully and force them to defend their opinions?

First, I'll discuss my problems in pressing the pro-life students. My pro-choice student monitor often stressed the importance of my doing this. The pro-choice students really needed to see me regularly hammer the pro-life students. This was key to the pro-choice students' feeling that the class was impartial.

As important as it was, I found it surprisingly difficult to press the pro-life students in class. I realize that it is the meat and potatoes of a professor's job to stimulate thought by pressing students on virtually every point, even if doing so requires teachers to challenge a position with which they agree or defend a position with which they disagree. I'm quite comfortable with this as a general proposition. But it's one thing to play devil's advocate on a question, say, of statutory interpretation and quite a different thing when it is a life-and-death issue like abortion on which my feelings run so deep.

One situation in which I failed is worth recounting. A number of pro-life students had spoken sequentially, so that there was a perceived pro-life momentum at that particular moment. I then interjected a comment offering further support for the pro-life perspective. The result was that the pro-choice students were temporarily cowed into silence. I should have exercised self-restraint and refrained from contributing to a pro-life stampede. When I sensed the scales tipping in the pro-life direction, I should have helped right them, either by a comment of my own or by inviting a pro-choice student to respond.

The word "self-restraint" recalls another area in which I sometimes failed the pro-life students. I had a very hard time keeping quiet whenever they were unable to come up with a response to a pro-choice argument. I often would jump in to bail out the pro-lifers. My pro-choice student monitor encouraged me to be silent on these occasions. If pro-life students couldn't come up with an answer, I should be willing to let them go away troubled. Doing so would force them to struggle with the issues rather than rely on me.

Following this advice about how to treat the pro-life students of course affects the pro-choice students, as well. What if a pro-choice argument is made to which I believe there is a response, but the pro-life students can't formulate it? If I keep silent, so as to force the pro-life students to think, don't I violate my responsibility to pro-choice students by not pressing them as hard as I can? But if I do press the pro-choice students zealously, won't they perceive it as a pro-life advocate's attack rather than as a professor's doing his job?

This last point should confirm what I said at the beginning about my being a long way from knowing exactly how to implement the goal of impartiality. Further confirmation that there's much room for improvement comes from the latest set of student evaluations. A few students seemed very irritated with me. They didn't think that I had been impartial in teaching the class. I can't tell you how disappointing this was. My evaluations from the first time teaching the course had been good on the impartiality issue. I'd made several changes to improve this aspect of the course. It was very frustrating to have the student evaluations be more negative. But one should not expect that impartiality can be easily achieved. In future offerings of the seminar I will continue the struggle.

NOTE

This chapter is based on the article "Impartiality in the Classroom: A Personal Account of a Struggle to Be Evenhanded in Teaching About Abortion" 45 *Journal of Legal Education* 99 (March 1995).

THIRTY-FOUR

Teaching College Students, Teaching Workers

MICHAEL D. YATES

INTRODUCTION

I TEACH TWO DISTINCT GROUPS OF STUDENTS. In my college I teach a typical cross section of undergraduates: young, white, and career-minded. But in union halls, social clubs, and community college classrooms, I teach working men and women: older, union activists, anxious to learn things that will help them in their struggles with their employers and in their struggles to understand the world around them. In this chapter I want to briefly explore how and why I teach these students so differently, why I advocate through indirection in the college classroom but with directness and passion in the worker classroom.

BEGINNINGS

In *The German Ideology,* Marx's and Engels's famous eleventh thesis on Feuerbach provided me with my teaching philosophy: "The philosophers have only interpreted the world in various ways; the point is to change it."[1] I am a son of the working class, the first in my large and extended family to attend college. I grew up with typical working-class values: a dislike of authority, especially that of employers, and the view that some people were a lot more privileged than others. The rebellions of the 1960s and the horrors of the immoral war in Vietnam, along with my first teaching experiences, moved my politics sharply to the left and toward the economics of Karl Marx. I remember teaching my first principles of economics class and being so disgusted with the aridity and lack of realism of textbook neoclassical economics that in one class I conducted a spontaneous revolt against the very things that I had been teaching. The more I read about U.S. history and about radical economics, the more I knew that I had to incorporate these materials into my classes. And the more I knew too that if I wanted to change the world, I had to advocate a radical point of view to my students.

Now the question became how to do this, how to show students the superior insights of Marxian economics in classes that had always been taught from the neoclassical perspective, indeed had been taught as if the neoclassical theory developed by Adam Smith and his progeny was the gospel truth. This proved to be a difficult endeavor. My colleagues fully expected that I would teach students that all people act selfishly and independently, that this selfishness generates socially desirable outcomes, that capitalism is the maximally efficient economic system. Had I refused to do this (which is what I wanted to do since I believe that these ideas are preposterous) and taught, say, only the labor theory of value, there is no chance that I would have been recommended for contract renewal, let alone tenure. Second, despite the fact that radical thought gained much greater legitimacy during the 1960s and 1970s, it has never had the influence that right-wingers such as Rush Limbaugh and Newt Gingrich would have us believe. In most places the power of the nation's predominant ideology, fervent anti-communism, was so strong that radical thought (Marxism in particular) was dismissed out of hand as propaganda. If I mentioned Marx in a favorable light, I was branded a Communist. Once when a guest speaker asked one of our history professors why I had criticized his remarks so strongly, my colleague just said, "Oh, don't bother about him, he's a Marxist."

Of course, nearly all of my students were hostile to radical perspectives, having been taught since birth that such views were un-American. When I canceled my classes on the day of the first war moratorium in the fall of 1969, many of my students were outraged. Sometimes I could literally feel their hostility, especially when I pointed out the many things they did not know about our unsavory relationships with the rest of the world.

A final factor that made it difficult to advocate radical ideas was my own timidity. The neoclassical paradigm has a strong hold on those who have taken the time to learn it. It is elegant, precise, mathematical. No other theory in any other social science can compare with it; the most mediocre economist feels infinitely superior to the best sociologist. For a long time I was afraid that the neoclassical theory would prove itself capable of answering the questions that its failure to answer had led me to look elsewhere. I gave it a legitimacy that made it impossible for me not to spend a lot of time explicating it in my classrooms.

Given these difficulties, I proceeded in a cautious manner. First, I focused on what economists call "market failures." A market failure occurs when the pursuit of self-interest by the participants in the marketplace does not lead to socially desirable results. An example of a market failure is the inability of a market system to prevent environmental destruction on its own. Discussions of market failures allowed me to show my students that a market system had to be regulated (by the government) if it was to satisfactorily satisfy human needs. However, this was only liberal and not radical advocacy. My growing hostility to capitalism made it necessary for me to go a lot farther than a liberal critique of the libertarian musings of Milton Friedman.

My next strategy was to pit the neoclassical and the radical theories directly against each other. I pointed out that economists did not agree on what made capitalist economies tick. First I would explain the neoclassical theory, trying to be as objective as possible. I would then use the market failures to develop a criticism of the theory, which led directly into a discussion of Marxian economics. Most students could tell that I was a radical economist, but not many of them accused me of bias in terms of how I taught and how I conducted the classes.

I grew unhappy with this comparison approach, although I still use it in my large introductory class. The neoclassical theory is difficult for students to learn, so I had to spend too much time (from my point of view) teaching it, leaving not enough time to teach the Marxian theory, which by this time I thought was far superior. Therefore, I did two things. I simply stopped teaching the core courses in economics (micro- and macroeconomics). This avoided conflict with my neoclassical colleagues and also freed me to develop new courses. I was able to do this because, fortunately for me, I now had tenure and was, in fact, the senior teacher in my entire division. I began to teach the political economy of Latin America, a subject very amenable to a radical analysis and one considered so unimportant by my colleagues that they did not complain that I taught it from a purely radical perspective with little mention of neoclassical economics. I was aided by the fact that most Latin American economists are much more open to radical theories than their North American counterparts. I also began to develop a series of courses in labor relations. I built these courses on the supposition that there is an inherent conflict between employees and their employers. This conflict is rooted in the nature of our economic system as first explained by Marx. In these classes there is no mention of neoclassical theory; the only theory that informs them is that of Marx and his modern adherents. However, while I was advocating a radical perspective and hoping that my students would adopt it as their own, I did this in such a way that I doubt that many of them knew what I was doing. In other words, I borrowed the neoclassical economist's method: I assumed that my model was correct and proceeded accordingly.

DISILLUSIONMENT

I had some success with my teaching, and until the end of the 1970s I was relatively happy. But then disillusionment began to set in. In part this was due to the sharp rightward shift in the nation's politics and the repercussions this had in the colleges and universities. The student revolt of the 1960s generated a counterattack by the leaders of business (who dominate the schools to a degree seldom examined or understood) and government. One result of this was strong pressure on academe to become more career-oriented, and it was not long before business and technical programs began to proliferate. The collapse of the great post–World War II economic boom created understandable fears among young people, and they were all too easily persuaded that they had better view their educations as investments in their "human capital" (as the neoclassical economists say) and major in something practical. When my college began a business major, I lost nearly all of my economics majors!

There were other reasons for my disillusionment, however. The neoclassical hegemony in economics had been shaken but by no means seriously challenged within higher education. For example, I could not get another radical economist hired into my department. Instead we hired mostly conservative economists, including two libertarians (in my view, extremists as far as classroom advocacy goes but seldom viewed as such). My colleagues began a campaign to marginalize my new courses; today they do not count as credits toward the major in economics. The business department has recently eliminated them from a list of acceptable courses in its management major.

The triumph of neoclassical economics was aided by the timidity of many radical academic economists. First, they adopted the tenets of postmodernism and began to reject Marx's most powerful insights, which are based on the primacy of class as a factor accounting for the main contours of capitalism. Then, instead of using the collapse of the Soviet Union as a springboard for an all-out attack upon capitalism (whose proponents could no longer use communism as a smokescreen to hide its inherent weaknesses), many radicals moved to the Right. Such luminaries as Samuel Bowles and Herbert Gintis can no longer even be called radical economists.

Finally, it began to become clear to me that advocating radical ideas in my classrooms was not very likely to help much to push the society toward greater egalitarianism and more control over the economy by ordinary people. Colleges in the United States have no heritage of radical activity comparable to their counterparts in the rest of the world. Before the 1970s it is difficult to think of a great radical professor with the exception of Thorstein Veblen. During the 1960s there was one openly radical economist in the entire nation, Stanford economist Paul Baran. Most faculty identify a lot more with the business and political elites than they do with working and poor people. They hesitate to do anything that would jeopardize their careers and future consulting work. They sometimes tell me that they are glad that I speak up, but very little will get them to act themselves. Most are comfortable with the increasingly open influence and control over the universities by corporate America, a trend hardly likely to encourage any sort of critical thinking, let alone radical advocacy.

A NEW PHILOSOPHY

So, while I continued to teach as I had before, I came to believe that if the society's class structure was to change radically, it would happen only if working people themselves saw the need for this to happen. There is no doubt that the student radicals of the 1960s opened up the universities, forcing them, for example, to end many of their racist and sexist practices. But they worked on the false assumption that social change could emanate from the colleges and universities. Years of experience taught me that this was absolutely untrue. Therefore, I turned my attention outside of the classroom. I helped the maintenance and custodial workers in the college to form a labor union. I began a campaign to unionize the teachers, a campaign that, after many years, still continues.

Most important, I began to teach working people directly in a labor studies program run by Penn State University. For 15 years now I have been teaching union members a wide variety of subjects. There are many things I enjoy about teaching workers. These students are often like the people with whom I grew up; the older students sometimes remind me of my father and his factory workmates. All of them have had a great deal of work experience and so can see what work is like a lot more than can my college students. When I talk about the labor law or about unemployment, they can bring interesting personal experiences to the discussions. What I teach has immediate practical relevance to them, and I can use this fact to get them to understand more complex and abstract economic and political ideas. For example, I once taught collective bargaining to a group of men working in a plant that made air conditioners. They had been more or less forced by their international union to make concessions to the employer during the term of their collective bargaining agreement. They videotaped every class and showed the tapes to coworkers. Then they ran a slate of new officers in their local union elections, and the new slate won. Using some of the things they learned in the class, they successfully negotiated the return of the things they had been forced to concede. One of them went on to get a master's degree in labor relations and is now teaching some of these classes. In a very real sense, these classes have been catalysts for the rebuilding of long-dormant local labor movements. They have definitely raised the class consciousness of many of the students in them.

Although most of my worker students have not graduated from college, they catch on to economic theory much more quickly than do my college students. No doubt this is because the theory has a greater practical relevance to them. And no doubt, too, they perceive the arguments through the lenses of working people. Two examples come to mind. In a class in labor economics, we were discussing the differences between the neoclassical and the Keynesian theories of unemployment. After two three-hour classes, one of the students was able to write a prize-winning essay on the subject for his local union newspaper. In a class in labor law, we were discussing the Fourth Amendment to the Constitution in the context of employee drug testing. In my college classes, most students take it for granted that an employer should have the right to randomly drug-test employees. They have been so thoroughly brainwashed that they do not even think of the issue in terms of civil liberties. The workers, on the other hand, and to a person, argued vehemently against drug testing under *any* circumstances. Most of them said that they would refuse, as a matter of principle, to be drug-tested. All of this is not to say that my worker students are perfect. Far from it. They have been subjected to the same kind of conservative advocacy from family, media, teachers, and the like to which all of us are subjected. Racism and sexism are recurring problems, although I can say without hesitation that my college students are far more racist and sexist than the working men and women I teach.

Teaching workers, then, has been teaching as I envisioned it when I became a teacher: students coming to class voluntarily (the classes run usually from 7:00 to 10:00 P.M.!), students enthusiastic to learn and to apply what they have learned to their lives, students appreciative of my commitment to teaching them (applause and gifts at the end of a course are not uncommon). And students from whom I can learn new things, as well. My labor education classes have inspired me to write three books, all of which are aimed at the general working public. Through these books, I have made contact with working-class groups around the country and have had the opportunity to give talks, conduct seminars, and help in union-organizing campaigns. I often get calls from working people asking for my help in legal or economic matters. Nothing remotely comparable has happened in my college classes.

The best thing about teaching workers, in terms of just the act of teaching, is that I do not have to abide by or feel pressured by the canons of academe. I do not have to worry that my students will not know what they will be expected to know when they take intermediate economics courses. I do not have to maintain an air of objectivity when I discuss economics. I do not have to say, for example, that economists disagree about how a capitalist economy works; instead I can say what I believe forthrightly—that neoclassical economics is the economics of the employing class and the attempt to make it into something else, a set of universal truths, is propaganda pure and simple. I can posit a radical explanation of capitalism, period. This explanation is always well received; indeed, it is usually received with great enthusiasm by the workers. This is because it fits with their actual work experiences; it helps them to understand what they are and what forces and persons are responsible for their circumstances and what they might do to alter these circumstances. In a word, in the worker classrooms, I can be the advocate I think I should be, openly and without fear.

CONCLUSION

I advocate my ideas in the college classroom in the way that I do because the college is structured in such a way that a more honest and direct advocacy is not possible. I teach workers the way I do because direct advocacy is possible. In a way, I lead a double life, and this has created great internal tension. As I see it academe, by its nature, limits, constrains, absorbs, or punishes direct radical advocacy. And even if it allows such advocacy, the colleges and universities are so far removed from the lives of working people that such advocacy is bound to have little real radical social impact. It will not help much to transform the society into the egalitarian and democratic society that radicals such as myself envision. Worker education, on the other hand, offers much greater possibilities, precisely because it is directly connected to the lives of working people, who, in the end, must be the moving force of social transformation. Right now I am at a crossroads. Honesty compels me to say that, while I still enjoy the act of teaching, the university repels me. I continue to teach there only out of economic necessity. Just as soon as that economic necessity ends, and that will be soon, I will leave the academic world and, for the first time since I was five years old, embrace the real world outside its closed doors.

NOTE

1. Karl Marx and Frederick Engels, *The German Ideology* (New York: International Publishers, 1969), 199.

THIRTY-FIVE

What Does a Black University Advocate? Student and Faculty Viewpoints

JANICE McLANE

HISTORICALLY BLACK UNIVERSITIES were specifically formed to be advocates for their students. Denied education at white institutions, black students found their opportunities for learning at black colleges. Thus, from the very beginning, black institutions have structurally functioned as advocates for both their students and the black community. Currently, African American students can attend any white institution of higher education. This might seem to indicate that the need for historically black universities has passed. However, in many ways the need for *structural* advocacy—for institutions that in their very formation politically and socially advocate for their students—remains the same.

This is true because although some mechanisms of racism have changed—for example, racial segregation of universities is no longer legal—racism is still an integral part of American society and impacts very negatively on African American students. Thus, institutions that provide structural protection against racism and strengthen African

American students in their racial identity are still strongly needed in American society.

Nevertheless, it is worthwhile to ask students if their historically black universities do function as advocates for them. This is what I did, as a teacher at Morgan State University in Baltimore. Admittedly my sample was small—about 40 to 45 students in two classes—but I believe the answers I received from them shed light on what *students* consider to be advocacy for them.

I will divide the responses I received into three groups: ways in which students said Morgan was an advocate for them, ways in which students saw Morgan itself as beset by outside political and social forces that made the university less effective than it might otherwise be, and ways in which they said it was simply not an advocate. Many of the replies covered two or three of these groups, although some were wholly positive and some entirely negative. All the students responding except one were African American (the exception was a male Pakistani); most were female.

Not surprisingly, the most positive response from students was on the issue of race. One student writes, "Just the thought of arriving on campus and seeing other African Americans helps me." Another says, "In attending Morgan State University, I have identified with my heritage, my culture, and my African American forefathers and mothers. Thus, this university will always have a special place in my memory, because it is an advocate for all African Americans in the face of racism and/or black inequality."

The response was particularly strong from many students who had attended predominantly white schools. "I was an ecstatic freshman," writes one student who had many painful experiences of racism at her white primary and secondary schools. "MSU was really a whole new world for me. I finally felt a part of something." Another woman who first attended a white university wrote, "Now I can discuss situations that affect the black community and not feel out of place." Many students praised the Afrocentric elements of Morgan's curriculum. One woman wrote, "[The African American perspective] is very important to the black community because the only true defense mechanism we will ever have against our oppression is the knowledge and understanding of what our oppression truly is. If one does not have true understanding of what he/she is fighting against, then he/she has no real reason to fight for."

Several students wrote that Morgan has high standards for its students, even higher ones than normal precisely because it is an African American university. Such preparation is seen as necessary to withstand the racist assumptions that whites will have about educated black people. Finally, some students wrote that Morgan positively deals with sexism by teaching students how to deal with sexist behavior. The class I was teaching—Power and Gender—was cited several times as an example of this concern. Another student cited the case of a female phys. ed. teacher who was sexually harassed by a male coach; she said that the university faced up to the case and dealt with it well.

The second type of response pointed out that Morgan sometimes was not an advocate for its students, but that it was not all Morgan's fault. "Do not forget that this is a minority institution," writes one student, "and that the perks that other four-year White State institutions [have] just do not float Morgan's way. That is when the political game has to be played. . . . Now, if the administration is worrying about all of the economic and the political issues that it has to dance around, when does it have time to worry about the real issue—the students? . . . The students at Morgan are suffering from racial, political, and economic stress and distress."

Finally, there are the responses that criticize Morgan for not being an advocate for its students, citing problems that are endemic to all American universities. These cover several areas: contempt for returning students, bureaucratic disregard for students, having too-low academic standards (in contrast, I'm sure readers will notice, to some other students' evaluations), and lack of consideration for students' personal difficulties.

The three issues I wish to note here are sexism, heterosexism, and an insufficient response to racism. A number of students complained about sexism—including two men who thought that women get a better break at Morgan. However, one woman pointed out that while women sometimes get higher grades from teachers who "like women," this "liking" was actually sexual harassment that teachers try to sugar-coat with higher grades.

A number of women reported that they or friends of theirs had been sexually harassed while at Morgan. As one woman says, ". . . when my friends tell me about the teacher who harasses them on a daily basis and students can walk by and know who we are talking about even though they don't hear his name, it is very obvious that this problem exists and that Morgan has not 'supported and helped to advance' . . . women."

Herein lies a problem for this chapter, and part of the reason why issues such as sexism are particularly loaded at historically black institutions. For in even in mentioning this problem in a largely white setting, and as a white professor, I have the feeling of "washing dirty linen in public"—that I should not be mentioning these things.

But African American women are often pressured to ignore or discount issues of sexism in favor of issues of racism. Sexism is no worse at Morgan than it is anywhere else, but it is also certainly no better. Approximately 70 percent of the students at Morgan are female. Thus, to be an advocate for Morgan students would seem to necessitate being an advocate for feminism. However, since a third of the papers I received cited sexism as a serious problem at Morgan in terms of students, faculty, and athletic programs, just who is being advocated for is still clearly an issue of gender as well as race politics.

The most critical student evaluation of Morgan as an advocate came from a lesbian student. She writes, "[O]ne of the main objectives of a university is to broaden the minds of its students. Well, I do not feel as though Morgan has done this for me. If anything, I feel as though Morgan has made me feel even worse about myself over the years." She writes of a friend who came out to her track coach:

> After my friend's announcement, the topic of who could possibly be a homosexual was always being brought up. Not only were the athletes having these discussions, but the administration in the athletic department were having the same discussions, and talking about how they would throw people off of their teams if they found out they were gay. This comment, was made one day, in the presence of the university president . . . and he said that if in the same position, he would do the same thing. It's a shame

that the people that are supposed to be the "adults" were acting
just as bad, if not worse, than the kids.

Finally, some students feel that the very fact that Morgan is a
historically black university leads it to not deal well with racism.
Writes one student, "As far as racism [is concerned], being at a black
college, personally, doesn't prepare African American students for the
racism that we will face. It's like we are sheltered from the rest of
America." And, writes another student, "It is understandable that
many professors would seek to encourage students by offering them
leeway but the repercussions are not worth the 'helping hand.' . . .
Educationally, Morgan lulls you into a false sense of security where
you are left unprepared for the grueling fight for the survival of the
fittest."

What are we to make of all this? That Morgan, like any human
institution, is imperfect? Certainly; but that is not enough. What I
would like to distill from all these responses is this: single-issue
advocacy cannot be sufficient for any institution, program, or even
single classroom. While historically black universities are crucial to
American society, to think of being African American as reducible to
a single concern—here, race—is to see students as having only a
single identity: something that is manifestly untrue.

However, this is true not only for historically black universities,
but of women's colleges, and Catholic, Protestant, and Jewish
colleges and universities, and their correlative departments and
programs within institutions. All of these are institutions of advocacy, whether they explicitly define themselves as such or not. A
college or university that functions as an advocate for a specific
American population cannot afford to narrowly define its mission if
it is truly to be an advocate for its students.

To end this chapter, I would like to mention one reason that this
is true. Unilinear political analyses—whether presented theoretically
in a classroom or through institutional concerns—encourage students to make reductive and oversimplified analyses of their own
lives. That is, students who are taught to think of their lives *only* in
terms of religion, race, gender, class, and so on tend to think
superficially of their lives' problems and solutions. Those students

who believe one social or political factor explains everything literally cannot perceive other factors, and will remain relatively uncritical of people who give a unilinear analysis. They are therefore more easily duped by rhetoricians and poseurs, and more easily burned out if and when they find out that a unilinear view of the world is not all it's cracked up to be.

For these reasons, I would argue that single-issue advocacy is not the best kind of advocacy that students can experience. It is oversimplified, and therefore dangerous, even to students who are in some ways empowered by it.

THIRTY-SIX

Advocacy in the Classroom: The Counseling Perspective

ANGELA ANSELMO

INTRODUCTION

AS A COUNSELOR WORKING with mostly underprepared remedial minority students in the SEEK Program at Baruch College, the City University of New York, I *consciously* advocate and proselytize, both in individual counseling sessions and in the classroom, for students' adoption of a particular set of values, attitudes, and/or behaviors. These values, attitudes, and behaviors are, I think, necessary in order for these students to graduate, to get the most out of their college experience, and to function effectively in the world of work.

I am conscious of the danger and arrogance in trying to "sell" others on ways of living life. My training in counseling and in psychology has prepared me to be objective and not to impose my values on my clients. Nevertheless, as a Puerto Rican woman working in this field for over 20 years, I have concluded that advocacy plays a crucial role if I am to be effective with students. They must be equipped with behaviors that will enable them to survive in a university culture and in a work environment.

This chapter addresses the rationale for this position; the specific values, habits, behaviors advocated; methods and approaches employed; and problems and risks to consider with this type of advocacy.

RATIONALE

SEEK (Search for Education, Elevation and Knowledge) students, who have over the years been mainly African American and Hispanic, are the most academically and economically disadvantaged of all the students attending the City University of New York. They are admitted to senior CUNY Colleges with high school averages below those required of regularly admitted students (usually under 81), and their family income is below the poverty line. Nearly 75 percent of SEEK students come from households whose net income is $10,000 or less.[1] These students score proportionately lower scores on the Math, Reading and Writing Skills Assessment Tests, placing them into remedial courses that carry no academic credit. Not surprisingly, SEEK students are the most at risk to be dismissed. A cohort study of SEEK and regularly admitted students done by Baruch College's Office of Institutional Research indicated that after six years, through spring 1994, the number of SEEK graduates was less than half that of the regularly admitted students (19 percent versus 42 percent).

Traditionally, much of counseling on the college level has been concerned with making the transition from high school to college a smooth one for students. Many campuses offer freshmen seminar classes taught by counselors who provide important information about policies, procedures, and resources of the institution. Academic rules, regulations, deadlines, curricular requirements, and course offerings are reviewed and discussed with students. In this way students learn what is expected of them and discover the various services and resources available on campus. In addition, counselors often teach skills necessary for improving academic achievement, such as how to use the library, how to manage one's time effectively, or how to get the most out of tutoring. Counselors can cut through the bureaucratic red tape of large institutions and "help negotiate the system" for students. A few phone calls often can unravel a financial or registration problem that can baffle students. Counselors also can help students with career and vocational decisions and with personal concerns.

As a SEEK counselor, I provide many of these services for students. However, in addition to this, much of my time is spent on trying to instill certain values, attitudes, and behaviors that are sometimes assumed to be automatically part of a college student's psyche. Counselors are accustomed to helping college students refine their values. The difference between what I do with students and what counselors customarily do is that I go beyond serving as a "neutral" facilitator helping students sort out their values; I become an advocate urging the internalization of particular values, attitudes, and behaviors.

For example, one technique often used by counselors working in student development groups is values clarification. Students are made to actively examine and clarify their values in a series of exercises using materials and methods that encourage alternative modes of thinking and acting. Students learn to consider the pros and cons and the consequences of the various alternatives. According to Simon, Howe and Kirschenbaum, the values-clarification technique does not aim to instill any particular set of values: "There is no sermonizing or moralizing. The goal is to involve students in practical experiences, making them aware of *their own* feelings, *their own* ideas, *their own* beliefs, so that choices and decisions they make are conscious and deliberate, based on *their own* value systems."[2]

This principle of not inculcating one's values into clients has become an important tenet in counselor training. It has gotten most attention in multicultural counseling theory and training because of the possibility of opposing values between counselors and clients who come from different racial/ethnic, gender, or socioeconomic groups. There is a general consensus among multicultural specialists that counseling in the United States is predominantly a white middle-class phenomenon. An identifiable "dominant" value system associated with the white middle-class group pervades most current counseling training programs. Because many counseling training programs neglect to give sufficient attention to the exploration of differing value systems that one might encounter in counseling, there is the danger that counselors are and can remain culturally encapsulated. This ethnocentrism can lead to counselors unconsciously advocating for client adjustment and assimilation to a dominant white culture that they think is "the best " or the "model" of mental health. According to Ponterotto and Casas this ethnocentric bias serves as a barrier to effective cross-cultural counseling. These authors conclude that counseling training programs must devote more time and training to the area of values systems: "Most counseling experts agree that to counsel effectively with any client the counselor must be very aware of his or her own value biases, second, must be knowledgeable, sensitive, and appreciative of the client's value system, and third, must be careful not to impose his or her value system onto the client."[3]

As a Hispanic who grew up in the housing projects of the South Bronx and who works with mainly Hispanic and African American of similar backgrounds, I believe that a shift in values, attitudes, and behaviors can enable the majority of SEEK students to graduate from Baruch College. Many of the values, attitudes, and behaviors that students bring with them have worked for them previously but do not serve them when they come to college. I see my role as a special programs counselor as one of optimizing the chances for students to make the most of their education. The SEEK Program and CUNY represent the student's ticket out of poverty. There is a limited window of opportunity in which students can make it. If after a few semesters they do not show significant academic progress, their financial aid is terminated and they are dismissed from the institution. Because these students enter Baruch with poor educational backgrounds, they are already playing catch-up. Time is a luxury they do not have. Besides learning basic communication and computational skills, it is equally important that students are, at the very least, aware of the values, attitudes, and behaviors that will support them in getting through the higher education system.

Because I am a Hispanic who comes from similar circumstances and made it through the system, I am in the unique position of being a role model to many students. Many of the things I say to students might be interpreted differently if I were perceived as white. I have more license to "preach" than other counselors. My goal is not necessarily to change students' existing values and attitudes but to add to their repertoire so that they can function in the "white" culture as well as their own. Most of these students will be living in two worlds. They must be bicultural to survive.

SPECIFIC VALUES, ATTITUDES, AND BEHAVIORS ADVOCATED

Some of the values, attitudes, and behaviors that I advocate include courage, open-mindedness, humility, and tenacity. I also advocate being future-oriented, organized, spiritual, and competitive as well as being careful money managers. I tell students that those students who succeed at Baruch and in most work situations possess most of these qualities, many of which are interconnected. Students already possess some of these qualities but do not recognize them as such. Many of these qualities must be adapted to a new context.

Courage

When students think of courage, they usually think of men, not of women—of warriors, heroes, machos. They also think of the accomplishment of great death-defying deeds. My goal in talking about courage is to have females (especially Hispanic females) start identifying with this value. Courage is not an attribute that is encouraged or often recognized in girls. I want them to think of themselves as today's warriors. They have the ability to greatly influence the future of their communities. I let them know that statistics show that as minority women, they will, in all likelihood, be financially responsible for their households. Being financially independent hinges on their acquiring a college education and skills.

I would like to have young minority men reexamine and redefine the notion of courage and to see heroism in the act of saying "no" to such things as hanging out. I remember a shy Dominican male student who was courageous enough to withstand the disdain of the young men and women in his neighborhood. Angel said that the guys saw him as a nerd because he carried books. He was perceived as a coward because he was not "man" enough to try drugs. Girls laughed at his inexpensive clothes. He couldn't date because he had no money to spend on women. The little money he got from a part-time job enabled him and his mother to survive. His younger brother was ashamed of him and did not want to be seen with him. I'll never forget the amazed look on Angel's face when I told him I thought he was a hero—the bravest of young men who had the courage to follow a different path. Angel graduated with a degree in computer information systems and today works for IBM. He is a great support for his mother since her younger son, Angel's brother, was jailed on drug charges.

I want students to see courage in the walking away from certain confrontations with professors and in being willing to experiment with new ways of negotiating and dealing with others. David, a very proud and tough African American student, felt that he had been disrespected in an introductory psychology class by a teaching assistant who ordered him to stop talking. David was in a crowded auditorium where other students had been talking, yet, according to him, the teaching assistant had singled him out. David had been embarrassed and felt that he had been treated unfairly. A verbal confrontation ensued, threats were hurled, and he was told not to come back to class. He arrived at my office the day before a meeting had been arranged by the chair of the Psychology Department. After a long and intense counseling session, David was willing to admit that he could have handled the incident differently. He was coura-geous enough to try a different approach in his meeting the next day that began not with an apology for his behavior but with an explanation of how he felt disrespected and picked on. The point was to allow the chair to see that the behavior of the teaching assistant was also questionable and to provide a context for David's behavior. Rather than getting physically or verbally aggressive, David was willing to take on different negotiating behavior. This leap into the unknown took courage because his self-worth was at stake.

Even when students are totally justified in getting angry with someone who has authority over them, they still have to learn to fight in a new way. Having the satisfaction of cursing someone out may feel good momentarily, but it will not solve what to do for the rest of the semester. Not showing up for class again would be self-destructive. Students have to know their rights, the lines of power, and how to follow protocol. Another student, Francisco, was told by an English instructor in front of the class that he did not belong there because he was such a poor writer. The professor wanted to know how Francisco had ever managed to pass the Writing Assessment Exam and even questioned if someone had taken it for him. Francisco was able to channel his anger in a constructive manner so that, with my assistance and that of the chair of the English Department, he was placed in a different class. As with David, Francisco's self-respect was challenged. Yet he was willing to try a different approach to solving the problem.

My goal is to connect the concept of courage to ordinary events in everyday life rather than to the extraordinary or unusual. It requires great courage for most of these students to go to college. They are usually the first members of their families to attend a university. There is great pressure on them to succeed. College also means change, and change is frightening. It can mean the unknown, new expectations, loneliness, challenge, vulnerability, risk, and failure.

Humility and Tenacity

It takes humility to be a good student. It means acknowledging that you have something to learn. No college student can learn a foreign language unless he is willing to sound and look foolish. Asking questions, admitting to not understanding something, and asking for help can be embarrassing, but they are key elements in the learning process. Humility also can mean having a certain awe and respect for knowing and learning. On the other hand, it does not mean feeling intimidated by all there is to know, nor does it mean being devastated if one gets a failing grade. Students have to develop tough skins and separate results on an exam from their self-worth. Not getting a passing grade in math does not mean that they are not meant to be in college, nor that they are stupid. It means that their math skills and training are poor. It means that they have to work harder. They must have tenacity. Not giving up is a trait of successful persons.

SEEK students come to college thinking they are better students than they really are. After all, they were among those students who managed to graduate high school. Many of the high schools that they attended have poor graduation rates, and only a small percentage of students make it through. Getting a high school diploma is quite an accomplishment for these students. Unfortunately, teacher expectations of students at these high schools can be very low. Students may have received passing grades merely because they attended on a regular basis and did not cause any problems. Students are shocked to find out that what was considered above average in high school no longer makes the grade in college. It is difficult for a student who consistently got good grades in English to receive a paper back filled with dozens of corrections and a failing grade. Some students think professors may be racist or just picking on them. Still others become so discouraged that they give up entirely. My job is to have them see failure as an opportunity—the opportunity to spot their weaknesses and to learn.

Open-Mindedness

In classrooms, numerous points of view may be expressed by many different kinds of people. Sometimes these views may go against what students have been taught. For example, many students have a difficult time with homosexuality. I have shared with them the American Psychological Association's position on homosexuality, a position with which I am in accord. It is not a disease or perversion. Students are shocked by my accepting stance. Conversations can be quite heated and graphic. Discussions revolve around what constitutes being normal or being religious. Sometimes I make comparisons between racial and ethnic hatred and homophobia. The message I try to convey is about tolerance.

Resourceful students keep an open mind and take advantage of the cultural diversity of the college. Being successful in tomorrow's workforce depends on being able to work with culturally diverse people. Initially our students have no idea of the great opportunity they have. I remember several years ago taking a group of Hispanic students to Chinatown to eat. I wanted to reward them for participating in an educational videotape that I had developed by treating them to dinner. One young lady from the Williamsburg section of Brooklyn commented, "Gee, there are certainly a lot of Chinese people here!" She had never even heard of Chinatown. We think that because students were born or raised in New York City they are sophisticated about numerous cultures. Many students are familiar with their own neighborhoods but know little else about the city. When I finally got the students inside the restaurant, everyone wanted to order fried shrimp and white rice, which seemed the closest thing to Puerto Rican food. They were unfamiliar with the splendor of Chinese food and were reluctant to try anything new. After I forced the issue, the students got to taste and enjoy food from another culture. For some students it was the first time they were in a restaurant that did not serve fast food. These students were very intimidated by the experience.

Open-mindedness also means not limiting their self-definitions or options by deciding that opera, ballet, or Shakespeare are not for them. I spend a lot of time selling students on the benefits of a liberal arts education. Joe, a 55-year-old honor student with a very colorful background including being a bookie, is typical of the prospective business students I counsel. "Hey, Doc, why do I have to take art history if I want to be an accountant? How will knowing about the metaphysical poets help me get a job?" I ask students to give liberal arts courses a chance. The things that they are learning are of great value—considered to be some of the greatest accomplishments of human history. The strange people who are their professors have spent a lifetime studying and teaching these subjects so that their students can have more to appreciate and enjoy in life. I describe how I once hated basketball and how I saw it as a waste of time—grown men running around in shorts trying to place a ball in a hoop. Because I knew nothing about it, I could not appreciate any of its beauty and skill. By learning about its rules and players and by sitting through games, I have come to appreciate it. It took effort on my part, but I was rewarded. Liberal arts classes also sharpen critical thinking skills necessary in this world. Many of the computer languages the students are learning will be obsolete in the near future, but critical thinking, reading and writing will be even more important. Knowledge of liberal arts subject matter is also part of what is considered being an educated person. The difference between a business institute diploma and a college degree is that the latter suggests that the person has a broad knowledge base and familiarity with many subjects. Furthermore, even if college graduates do not know specific information, they do know how and where to find that information.

Most SEEK students have not considered going to graduate school. Many believe it is not within the realm of possibility and have never pictured themselves as professionals. My job is to open them up to the possibilities.

Being Future Oriented

SEEK students come from families that are trying to survive economically. The focus of these families is on the present, the here and now. There is little thought about the future. Members are not accustomed to long-term planning. In addition, many of our students live in neighborhoods that can be violent and dangerous. Friends, neighbors, and relatives die at early ages. A surprising number of my students have told me that they do not expect to live very long. One of the high schools from which many SEEK students graduate houses the local police precinct. Students go through metal detectors to be allowed access to the inside of the building. As one student said, "The police officers wear bulletproof vests but the students do not." Students on my caseload get assaulted, mugged, and robbed on a regular basis. This is part of the normal life of the urban poor. Recently, one of my students lost four of his friends as a result of a shooting at a party. Baruch College represents a safe haven; it is the first educational institution in a number of years in which students are not in fear of being shot because they may speak to the wrong person or of being robbed because they are wearing an expensive pair of sneakers. One's attention to the present is crucial when living in this kind of stress.

Related to this focus on the present is the inability for students to think of long-term rewards for their present efforts. Going to school for five years seems an eternity for freshmen, especially if the future seems uncertain and vague.

Organization

This is related to not having a future orientation. Students are not accustomed to planning. They do not organize their time. Goal-setting and examining priorities is a foreign notion to many students. They may start working on a term paper late in the semester and be unable to handle both studying for finals and finishing the paper. If they have three exams in one week, they usually do poorly because they do not divide up their study time wisely.

Family obligations, personal relationships, and work can take up much time in a student's life. Many of our students have children or must work to help support their families. They must be clear in their priorities. I tell them that it has been my experience that school has to be the number-one priority for most remedial students if they expect to make up for a lack of basic skills. Only the very organized and focused student can handle all these competing forces.

Spiritual Values

Many of our students are spiritual and/or religious. They derive much support from this source. They should not feel ashamed of their beliefs or that spirituality cannot be part of their education. It can be a natural resource that can reinforce much of what I try to convey. By putting things in a spiritual context, I am more successful with counseling some students. Spiritual concerns naturally come up when students face major life events, such as the death of a parent or a serious illness. But there are other arenas, such as choosing a major or career, that can involve asking questions that I consider spiritual concerning one's purpose in life. I have found teaching students to meditate to be very beneficial not just in helping them to manage their stress levels but in having them be guided by their inner knowledge. The sharing of prayers and affirmations has been effective with other students. For certain students, courage comes from their having faith in a higher power or divine intelligence. This is an area in which I tread lightly but one that I am no longer hesitant to explore with students. I have come out of the spiritual closet by allowing students to know that I am an ordained interfaith minister.

Furthermore, because I have studied numerous religions, I acknowledge feast days and celebrations of all faiths. Students are encouraged to explain the significance of their traditions. Muslims, of whom there are a fair number at the college, are especially pleased by this because the holidays the college celebrates center around Christian and Jewish observances. There is never a day off for a Muslim feast day or for an important Asian holiday, such as Chinese New Year. Just acknowledging their occasions makes a difference to students and gives other students a lesson in cultural diversity.

Competition

Competition is a complicated concept because being too competitive can be as damaging as not being competitive at all. I want students to understand a few things about competition: (1) Competition is a core value of American society; (2) competition is not limited to sports; (3) it does not have to be against someone else—rather, it can be *with* oneself; (4) competition does not have to be a lonely process.

Money Managers

Few students handle money well because few have ever had the experience of having much of it. Only rarely do students have any savings. The PELL grant (a federal grant awarded to undergraduates who can document financial need and which averages about $1,100) may be the largest amount of money they have ever received. Students need to plan their spending. Too many students go weeks without having books because of poor planning. They need to examine where their money goes. What we spend our money on reflects what we value. Family members must not expect that student grants are for family expenses.

Friendship

It is difficult for college students if most of their friends do not go to college. They are often labeled as disloyal, stuck up, or uncaring because they do not spend the time they used to with friends.

Students have to know that true friends are committed to one's growth, that succeeding in college is not a putdown of their friends. They have to be able to make new friends. They also must be aware of the pressures of the opposite sex and get to know them as friends.

Appropriate Presentations

Students have to know that there are costumes for different roles that we play. The costume that is appropriate for their neighborhoods may not be appropriate for work or school. If they are unwilling to give up wearing a special costume, then they must be prepared to deal with the consequences of that decision. One of my students, a six-foot African American female who, because of her religious beliefs, wears Muslim garb, learned to adjust her behavior because professors were frightened by her. She has a loud and strong voice and is very bright and assertive in class. While she is a gentle person, she has been perceived as aggressive and hostile. In this case, although the problem may be with the professors who may be projecting inaccurate behavior to her, the reality is that her garb has a profound effect on people. She must know what that can be and be prepared to act appropriately. Similarly, big gold earrings and a gold tooth are not part of the corporate image.

METHODS AND APPROACHES USED TO ADVOCATE VALUES

My role is often more like a coach, social worker, cheerleader, and educator than a counselor. I spend a lot of time trying to explain the "white" world to students. I use student outreach rather than waiting for students to drop in. Social histories and transcripts are examined and discussed with students. Interestingly, this directive approach characterized by immediate solutions and concrete tangible approaches has been found to better respond to minority clients' expectations of counseling.[4] Lower-class clients expect advice and suggestions from the counselor.

No disease model of counseling is employed. Students are seen as normal individuals going through typical developmental stages. I often discuss these stages with students. One developmental theory I cover is racial/ethnic identity formation. People of color may experience anger against themselves and the "white" society. This is a normal stage in the development of a healthy racial and ethnic identity.[5]

Students are seen in classroom settings, as well as in formal individual appointments, as drop-ins, and in small informal groups. As Sue and Sue point out in *Counseling the Culturally Different,* appointments made weeks in advance with short, weekly 50-minute contacts are not consistent with the needs of lower-class clients who need to seek immediate solutions.[6] Having scheduled appointments encourages students to plan ahead. Drop-ins work for crisis intervention and for chats.

In the classroom, I like to give students tests that I have made up, such as a Success/Failure test or a Spirituality test, as a way of introducing certain topics that will lead to instilling specific values.

I give students many facts—including average income, what it takes to be a professor, typical rent in New York City, racial and ethnic composition of New York City and of the college. Many of my students do not have basic information to guide them in making decisions. For example, a student who wants to leave home to be on his own has no idea how expensive it is to rent an apartment, to buy food and clothing. Living at home can be seen as a scholarship. Likewise, students have a better understanding of why professors have high expectations of them after I explain what it takes to be a professor. Students have no idea of the years of sacrifice and hard work necessary to get a doctorate or to get tenure. I use biographical information of famous people to highlight points. For example, Thomas Edison conducted thousands of unsuccessful experiments before creating the light bulb, Lucille Ball was told by numerous agents that she had no talent, and Winston Churchill failed the exam to enter the Royal Military Academy numerous times before he was admitted.

I utilize small-group discussions in a classroom with a diverse ethnic and racial mixture, mixing English-as-a-second-language students with native born, males with females, and Asians with Hispanics and blacks. The best way for students to get to know each other is to have them work jointly on projects.

Everyone has everyone else's phone number, including my own. Students need to make friends and be able to get missed work. I encourage and help organize study groups, and networking is promoted.

Peer role models are used when possible. It is great for students to see students from similar backgrounds who are making it. It is also helpful to have these students reinforce points that I have already made in language that young people can relate to.

For discussion, I use vignettes of problems students confront. Students are asked what they would do if, for example, they are unfairly accused of cheating, are sexually harassed, are embarrassed, or given an unfair grade. Sometimes students have to learn to lose battles to ultimately win wars. Life is not always fair. They need to keep the goal of getting a degree uppermost in their minds and see that compromise is not a terrible thing.

I share my own experience not only as a student but as a counselor and faculty member. I developed an exercise that asks students to come up with the most effective way of antagonizing their professors in order to discuss effective student behavior. I let them know the student behavior that upsets me the most and why. Students get to see instructors from a different perspective.

Role-playing is common. Students rehearse conversations with professors and administrators. They learn that there are certain ways of speaking to people that may be more effective than other ways. They learn that everyone wants to save face and how to negotiate win-win solutions.

I force students to get organized. They must set long- and short-range goals of 20, 10, and 5 years, and one semester. They must buy appointment books with monthly calendars and hand in weekly priority and "to do" lists.

I employ meditations, visualizations, and guided imagery to connect students to their aspirations and dreams, to help them relax and handle stress, and to link them to their own inner guidance.

I hold family orientations so that family members and significant others can understand the pressures faced by their student and to clarify financial aid expectations.

More important than specific techniques, however, the key to all good counseling is listening and caring. Students need to be heard and need to think someone in the institution cares for them. What is different in operating from an advocacy stance is that students are being prevailed upon to adopt a repertoire of behaviors, values, and attitudes that will support them in getting through college.

The greatest resistance comes from students who think that I am trying to make them "white." Students are afraid of somehow being disloyal to their ethnic and racial groups. By adopting the ways of the dominant culture, they believe they are condemning their own ethnicity or cultural heritage as a handicap to be overcome, something to be ashamed of and to be avoided. I assure them that I am not trying to put down their groups nor am I trying to mold them into a white person. I merely want them to know the rules, norms, behavior, and values followed in the "white" world so that they are able to function in whatever world they choose to be in. I also remind them that values, attitudes, and behaviors are not fixed forever. They can change as people learn more about themselves and grow.

The other resistance comes from fear. The fear of change and of failure immobilizes many of these students. I know what that's like because I was a dropout from an Ivy League college. I left the college convinced that I was not college material.

I also think that some of these students fear white people. Many of these students have not had much real social interaction with whites. While they have had white teachers and have interacted with white store merchants, social workers, physicians, and police officers, they do not live with them nor have they sat at their homes for dinner. If they have white friends, they have not slept over in their homes. They have as many stereotypes of whites as whites have of people of color. For these students as for people in general, it is much more comfortable to stay with the known. Moving beyond one's comfort zone takes considerable effort and courage.

CONCERNS AND RISKS

Is there anything new about instilling values?

Instilling values, attitudes, and behaviors consciously or unconsciously is an inherent part of education. Education has been the natural vehicle for the assimilation of immigrants into the American culture. Therefore, what I do is not new. The difference is that we do not think of instilling values and attitudes on the college level. Another difference is that the students I work with are members of groups that may *never* assimilate because they are racially different from previous immigrants. Because they are people of color, they cannot expect to be accepted in the same way that previous immigrants have "melted" into the American pot. A successful black man in America may escape poverty but not racism. He will never be totally accepted in a racist society. I think students know this and feel that equality is not a goal worth seeking. I see my advocacy as one that will lead to biculturalism rather than assimilation. The students with whom I work should possess skills that will enable them to live in two different worlds.

What are the problems and risks with the advocacy of values in counseling?

One problem with advocacy is that it assumes that the person doing the advocating has the inside track to the "good life." The counselor is the authority who knows what is emotionally and psychologically healthy. Sometimes it appears to students that I have all the answers. This, of course, is not true. Even when I explain this to them, they still see me as the authority. Often it is difficult for students to distinguish between what works and what is good or right. This happens in part because no matter how objective I try to be, students can pick up how I feel about these values, attitudes, and behaviors. Not only do I believe that these work to get students through college, I feel that most are worthy values to live by. I do not have to say this to students; they can pick it up by my tone, enthusiasm, and other nonverbal cues.

The risk involved is that students may think that because I am advocating the adoption of values that work in white institutions, I am advocating adjustment to this dominant culture and, further, denigrating their minority culture. I am doing neither. Nor am I denigrating the dominant culture nor heralding the minority culture. I live and function in two cultures, and I see good and bad in each. For example, while I advocate being competitive to students, I personally have mixed feelings about it.

According to researchers such as Ramirez and Castaneda, Hispanic children come into the Anglo school system with a great disadvantage because they are not competitive.[7] Compared to Anglo children, Hispanic children score higher in the need for affiliation; they have a greater desire to interact with others and belong to a group. These children show greater sensitivity to the feelings of others and show a greater willingness to help others. They learn better and achieve more in an environment in which they can work cooperatively with others, while Anglo children are raised to be more independent. Autonomy and self-reliance are the most highly held goals of American parenting. Anglo children perform better when they work alone and are rewarded with a good grade or teacher attention or approval.

I greatly admire and value the willingness to help others. I have studied both in New York City and in Puerto Rico. To me, schooling in Puerto Rico was a much more enjoyable and less lonely process because students shared and helped each other. I suspect that for many Hispanics, schooling on the mainland would be more effective if there was more cooperative learning. Interestingly enough, corporations are now realizing that business education that stresses competition and self-reliance can be counterproductive. Many companies are now investing money in training their employees in the dynamics of sharing, cooperating, and being team players.

I recognize the benefits of a competitive spirit even if the competition is with oneself. The pursuit of excellence, not settling for just passing, and striving for high goals are behaviors that I want to further in my students. Therefore, I encourage students to be competitive but I also promote study groups, students' helping each other, and networking.

Another concern I have with advocating certain values and behaviors is the price students will pay by adopting them, including loneliness, stress, and alienation from family and friends. Putting school as the first priority can cause problems with friends and family members. Being future oriented can lead to stress. I fear turning students into A-type personalities who cannot relax. Stress management counselors must teach some of their clients to focus on the "here and now." These people cannot enjoy themselves because they are always on the next project; they are always in their heads. My greatest concern is creating students who are what Stonequist has termed "marginal" persons who fit in neither of the two cultures in which they live.[8]

Why continue to advocate despite these risks?

I think that the benefits of getting a college education outweigh the risks. With my students, I work on the following assumptions regarding education: (1) Education is good. (2) It is the surest ticket for most people out of the ghetto. (3) Learning is intrinsically rewarding. (4) Although education is not a panacea, it can give options, hope, and more control over one's life.

CONCLUSION

Contrary to my training in psychology and counseling. I encourage minority Special Program students to adopt certain values, attitudes, and behaviors that I think will support their successful transition into the college environment. Many SEEK students come to college without the attitudes, values, and behaviors we assume are givens if they have received high school diplomas. Twenty-five years ago, the SEEK students were considered nontraditional ones, who had special needs because of being educationally and financially disadvantaged. Today, they are not that different from regularly admitted CUNY students who are also economically and educationally disadvantaged. Nontraditional students of yesterday have become traditional students of today. According to Fernandez, 50 percent of all CUNY freshmen come from families whose family incomes are under $20,000 a year, and 50 percent of all freshmen at CUNY's senior colleges fail one or more of the basic skills assessment tests in reading, math, or writing, which forces them to take remedial courses.[9] Like the SEEK student, regularly admitted students may not come to college with the values, attitudes, and behaviors associated with traditional college students of prior years. Traditional counseling centers may want to examine and borrow from the work of Special Program counselors like myself who believe advocacy is essential for the success of their students in college.

NOTES

1. The General Plan for The Special Programs of The City University of New York (1989-90).

2. Sidney B. Simon, Leland W. Howe, and Howard Kirschenbaum, *Values Clarification* (New York: Hart Publishing Co., 1972), back cover.

3. Joseph G. Ponterotto and J. Manuel Casas, *Handbook of Racial/Ethnic Minority Counseling Research* (Springfield, IL: Charles C. Thomas, 1991), 49.

4. Derald Wing Sue and David Sue, *Counseling the Culturally Different: Theory and Practice,* 2nd ed. (New York: John Wiley & Sons, 1990).

5. Donald R. Atkinson, George Morten, and Derald Wing Sue (Eds.), *Counseling American Minorities: A Cross-Cultural Perspective,* 4th ed. (Dubuque, IA: William C. Brown, 1993); William E. Cross, "A Two-Factor Theory of Black Identity: Implications for the Study of Identity Development in Minority Children," in Jean S. Phinney and Mary Jane Rotheram (Eds.), *Children's Ethnic Socialization: Pluralism and Development* (Newbury Park, CA: Sage, 1987), 117-33; William E. Cross, "Nigrescence: A Nondiaphanous Phenomena," *Counseling Psychologist* 17 (1989), 273-76; William E. Cross, *Shades of Black: Diversity in African-American Identity* (Philadelphia: Temple University Press, 1991); James E. Marcia, "Identity in Adolescence," in Joseph Adelson (Ed.), *Handbook of Adolescent Psychology,* 159-87 (New York: John Wiley & Sons, 1980); Jean S. Phinney, Bruce T. Lochner, and Rodolfo Murphy, "Ethnic Identity Development and Psychological Adjustment in Adolescence," in Arlene Rubin Stiffman and Larry E. Davis (Eds.), *Ethnic Issues in Adolescent Mental Health,* 53-72 (Newbury Park, CA: Sage, 1990).

6. Sue and Sue, *Counseling the Culturally Different.*

7. Manuel Ramirez, and Alfredo Castaneda, *Cultural Democracy, Bicognitive Development, and Education* (New York: Academic Press, 1974).

8. Everett V. Stonequist, *The Marginal Man: A Study in Personality and Cultural Conflict* (New York: Russell & Russell, 1937).

9. Ricardo Fernandez (Ed.), *Report of the Chancellor's Advisory Committee on the Freshman Year* (New York: The City University of New York, Central Office, 1992).

THIRTY-SEVEN

Ethnography as Advocacy: Allowing the Voices of Female Prisoners to Speak

SHAWNY ANDERSON

BASED ON THE CURRENT PUBLIC HYSTERIA over crime, violence, deviance, and (perhaps most significantly) punishment, I find that my role as college professor within the context of a women's prison has taken on new dimensions in terms of advocacy; whereas many academics might interpret the controversial issue of advocacy in the classroom as a reference to advocacy *to* students, my main concern revolves around advocacy *for* my students. That is, the U.S. public seems committed to the notion that all incarcerated people are violent, greedy, and hateful, and are afforded overly luxurious conditions as they are warehoused at taxpayers' expense. Because of my personal and professional relationships with a diversity of female inmates, my reading of the situation differs markedly from that general stereotype; thus, I believe that as an educator, I have an obligation to provide students with relevant political information and methods of interpretation, while also serving as an advocate for my students to the outside world.

Indeed, in my four years of experience teaching college classes in the Indiana Women's Prison, I have become painfully aware of the crisis of identity experienced by many incarcerated women. That is, I have found that women in my classes feel abandoned by their families, their communities, the legal system, and the general public; even those who are nearing completion of college degrees seem to find little comfort in their achievements. A slight change in this perspective emerged during a critical methods class, however, while reading several texts addressing issues and methodologies of ethnography and biography; students seemed to find empowerment in their abilities to explain the concepts to each other by making reference to conditions and experiences within the prison community. They readily accepted my suggestion that they produce their own book, providing enlightenment about their everyday lives to a general readership as well as bringing empowerment to themselves.

Thus, we have embarked together on a project that attempts to explicate their lived experience while simultaneously analyzing various aspects of their lives in prison through the lens of communication theory. Ideally, the project will serve as a much-needed counterpoint to the dominant portrayals of prisoners and prison life. This chapter provides an overview of the project itself, the premises on which the project initially was based, a preview of the forthcoming insights of these talented female authors, and some preliminary observations about the unique qualities of the prison experience for women in general, and for inmates in the Indiana Women's Prison in particular. Additionally, the chapter considers the powerful potential of biography and ethnography as tools of empowerment for marginalized populations.

THE PROJECT

My experience teaching college classes in the Indiana Women's Prison (IWP) has taught me three important things: (1) women's experiences of prison life are in significant ways different from men's; (2) female prisoners are a specialized population that is often ignored by the general public; and (3) women in general, and female prisoners in particular, are less likely to see their ideas expressed meaningfully in the public realm than are men. For these reasons, 12 incarcerated female college students and I made the collective decision to produce a composite view of their life in the Indiana Women's Prison; later, ten other students also joined the project. As a practicum in speech communication, the project involved students in an attempt to express, publicize, and in some ways validate their experiences as female prisoners in Indiana.

Using a methodology we call "collaborative ethnography," the women endeavored to use narrative styles and their own familiar language practices to present in publishable form an image of what their lives are like. This atypical ethnography, then, recognizes the capacity of these women to tell their own stories rather than having them told by an "objective observer" who attempts to interpret their lives from the protected perspective of an academic anthropologist. "Objectivity," if such a thing exists, is not a goal toward which any of the book's authors (myself included) aspire. My role in the project has been to introduce students to useful reading materials to guide their thinking, edit the manuscripts that they prepare weekly, and handle all related publishing duties. The value of this project as a teaching tool is immeasurable, as it combines an enhancement of oral and written communication skills with an expansion of the creative capacities of each of the 22 student authors. Further, it is one of the first undertakings since their incarceration that does not have their punishment as its core objective.

THE PREMISES

My role as a college instructor at the Indiana Women's Prison began in January of 1991. Having heard about the experiences of several friends teaching college classes in the men's prison system, I requested assignment to IWP, believing that the prison students would be the most radical and committed students I would ever encounter. They were indeed committed, as they seemed to recognize the particular messianic value of education in their lives; surprisingly, though, they were far from "radical," as they seemed decidedly sheepish about stating any firm opinion, least of all one that challenged the status quo in any significant way. In fact, I found that they collectively held a serious lack of personal confidence and, in many cases, even seemed to lack a firm grip on their own individual identities.

When reading a somewhat ethnographic study of Milwaukee street women, they began to interpret the book by applying it to their own experiences and to interpret their experiences through reference to the book. As I heard them speak of their communication networks, flexible identities, and other areas, I proposed that they attempt to record their experiences by writing a book of their own. They at first seemed alienated from the possibility, saying such things as "We're not authors," "Nobody would care . . . ," and "We don't even exist in the public's mind." The last comment, though, became their inspiration; they seemed aware that when members of the public pictured "prisoners," they pictured men, and even if women figured into the picture, the image held by the public probably did not match the image that these particular women held of themselves and of each other. Thus, their status as unknowns came to justify the project, along with their concern about the growing hysteria over crime and criminals given constant attention and distortion in the media. So, in order to construct their own reality of life in a women's prison, they took on the project and recruited other students to become coauthors.

The conditions faced by the women at IWP are far removed from the horrific images of torture, grime, and brutality often represented in popular films or TV. Instead, the atmosphere of the prison is somewhat campuslike, as relatively clean buildings surround a neatly kept green space that often contains flowers and brightly painted outdoor furniture as well as tennis courts and other recreation areas. Although all inmates are required to hold jobs in the prison, the workday is short, lasting from 8:30 to 11:00 A.M. and from 1:00 to 3:30 P.M. Their cafeteria food is somewhat diversified and includes occasional treats, such as Ben & Jerry's ice cream. If a resident is unhappy in her job or living situation, she may request a change, with most requests eventually being met. They may have personal TVs, radios, and toiletries, and they are free to wear their own clothes rather than prison-issue uniforms. Education programs are available, including programs for general equivalency diplomas, drafting, beauty school, carpentry, computers, and college classes.

The main keys to "punishing" these inmates are complete loss of privacy and constant regulation of their activities. These controls are enough to keep the women in a constant state of subordination and consistently aware of their status in society. Even those who pursue higher education gain no special privileges, as they are expected to work a full day, maintain a full-time (12-15 credit hours) academic schedule, take only night classes (meaning that most students have classes every weeknight), and miss some of their allotted recreation time as well as special events.

Because of their recognition that the public was unaware of their existence, let alone their experiences and emotions, the students thus set out to write a book that would convey a more realistically constructed view into their everyday lives. They wanted to be sure that the book was primarily written by prisoners, at least as it attempted to describe the experiences they have. They wanted the book to be for the public, as opposed to an academic audience or correctional officials. Additionally, they hoped that their book would serve primarily as a description of their lives in prison rather than as a diatribe against prisons and incarceration.

Their rationale for writing the book was multifold: first, they hoped to portray a realistic portrait of prison life, in hopes of countering media distortions and public misperceptions. Second, they wanted to show the unique environment of a women's prison as different from men's experiences. Third, I harbored a desire to empower the women to recognize writing/description as a powerful tool of persuasion, and finally, we all shared the goal of working to allow their voices to be heard in a way that would validate their experiences and their perceptions.

CONTENT OF WRITINGS

The students chose to organize their writings by establishing topic areas and pursuing each one independently; once everyone had written on a particular area, we would compile the ideas and establish a more comprehensive view of that subject. For example, the first several writings were on very specific issues such as health care, food, and work; by combining excerpts of writings by different students, the narrative on these issues was enhanced. Later topics became more general, moving into areas such as space, power, rules, and relationships; on these issues, the range of responses was so broad that completely unforeseen insights emerged. By using these categorical organizers, we obtained a diverse set of stories and information that seemed to circulate around a number of general themes. Four primary themes included crises of reality, paradoxes of identity and desire, evolution of consciousness of the environment, and small winds of resistance.

Crises of Reality

Whether because of boredom, institutional repression, or self-suppression, it seems clear that the women of IWP seek "entertainment" through the manipulation of reality. That is, they spend large amounts of time interpreting, defining, and redefining their experience in ways that completely destabilize their ability to maintain a constant sense of what is real and what is not in the prison. The women tend to locate zones of consensus, so that a similar perception of reality is shared by certain subgroups within the community, whether it is a living area, a classroom, a worksite, a racial or religious grouping, or some other site of shared perception. Much of their construction of reality is the result of constant dependence on other inmates for information about each other, about the institution, and about the "free world." In fact, there seems to be an overt tendency to seek stimulation through interpretation and reinterpretation of their own and others' experiences, with a strong probability that the process of interpretation will result in a crisis/tragedy for the individual or for others in the individual's circle of contacts. That is, crisis/conflict seems to be a desirable product of communication, as it is apparently more interesting than avoidance of crisis. One excerpt on health care helps to demonstrate this principle:

> One of the biggest health problems in the penitentiary is determining who's sick and who isn't. When one only has oneself to dwell on, then one tends to become a bit of a hypochondriac. As

you listen to the chronic aches and pains of those around you, you begin to realize that you have similar, if not the very same, symptoms. If you figure that during the course of the day you have a minute of conversation with 50, or 60, or even 100 women, who all have something to complain about, that adds up to a lot of pain. By early evening your head is throbbing, your vision is blurred, and your ears are ringing. Surely this could only mean that you have a brain tumor. As you bend over to get a medical request slip, you feel a slight pull in your lower back; a slipped disc?

Relationships, confrontations with administrators, concerns about families, and work issues are other areas that are treated in a similar way; perceptions of reality are based in interpersonal communication and individual interpretation, but a strong tendency to create crisis emerges as communication about a particular topic increases.

Paradoxes of Identity and Desire

A second area of intrapersonal conflict involves the necessity that inmates constantly figure and refigure who they are and who they want to be in light of the multiple role expectations that the prison situation presents. For example, the women experience constant clashes of identity as they weigh their values from the "free world" against their values "inside." Likewise, they must balance their social needs within the prison against their individual needs, as in making a decision about whether to participate in a clique to gain friendships and a social identity, or to resist cliques to maintain good favor with prison administrators in hopes of personal gain. A primary example of such decisions circulates around the issue of sexuality. In the Indiana Women's Prison, lesbianism is accepted and even expected among inmates; thus, the usual social constraints against experimentation and participation in same-sex couplings are removed. Still, although certain benefits might follow sexual activity, the many paradoxes of identity problematize the decision to participate. For instance, women might fear "outside" discovery, which would serve as a clash of individual identity for outside contacts. Or women might realize that even "inside," the problem of secretive identities might surface in such a place as the visitation room, where visitors' expectations might conflict with the general practices maintained by the woman in everyday prison interaction. Further, women might weigh their individual needs against the repercussions they might experience upon breaking up with a particular partner, or if they are "discovered" by corrections officers. A writing on relationships helps to display many levels of paradox that women face:

> When and if you find someone, trust them, and fall in love, in here that is a feat in itself. Seems that everyone is just out for what material things they can get out of it. Just because you are hooked up with someone, this doesn't stop someone from trying to break you up. It's a game in here to see who can break up a couple by spreading lies, accusations of unfaithfulness, or confusing one member of the couple. If you live with your girlfriend, you won't for long—someone is soon to tell or complain. The women are jealous of these couples and soon write blueslips to your counselor saying you are having sex. After a few complaints, you are moved apart onto separate dorms. Now you must go to rec or work together in order to see her. For some, this isn't enough, so they find themselves a "cottage piece." This is someone they live with, love in secret, and they go to rec with their "real" girlfriend, the one they are hooked up with. But these relationships don't last long either. Someone always finds out, blows your cover, or tells the other woman. Nothing is a secret for long, as long as one person other than the couple knows, it's bound to get out and back to the other woman.

For some women, the identities that they maintain inside contradict their outside lives. For example, inmates create networks of extended substitute "families" that hold traditional titles, but that often do not match the roles they played in the outside world:

> More often than not, women adopt others as family members for that needed and wanted feeling that they had in the free world. You hear Grandma, Mom, Auntie, Sissy, and even a few

Granddads, Uncles, Brothers, and Dads; the latter can be confusing to a newcomer, not knowing the role playing that some women take upon themselves.

Clearly, most women did not fill roles such as "brother" and "uncle" prior to prison, but the networks solidify inside so that these labels are normal roles to fill, despite their lack of coherence to experience outside. The paradoxes extend beyond mere labeling, however, as behaviors, too, are changed:

> Most of the prisoners have extended families. The more needy you are, the more people you pretend are in your family. These extended families usually stem from a lack of real family relationships.
>
> The ladies who are studs call each other brother. The sad thing is that some of them lose their identities. They carry themselves like men and assume the role of males, some even in dress. These women are in demand by the much needy (the women who just must be in a relationship to feel worthwhile). They (studs) feel important in prison, even to the point of coming back over and over. It is the only place they feel important. Their need of being wanted is met while the lady's need of a relationship is being met. The femme side usually pays (takes care financially) for the stud's attention. Some of these studs have never lived so well. There are some I know personally from the free world who live like skid-row bums. They come to prison and clean up and look really nice.

Of course, when communicating with contacts outside of the prison, these identities must be adapted in order to maintain balance.

Evolution of Consciousness of the Environment

The experience of incarceration apparently induces a change in the understanding of such issues as space, time, and power; of course, this change is to be expected, but the level of self-reflexiveness or consciousness of the shift in perspective is particularly remarkable. In terms of space, the system manipulates individuals such that awareness of your "status" is directly related to the space you occupy. The ironic practice of the prison is to place prisoners in worse conditions the closer they get to release. For example, if a person is sentenced to a long prison term, she is initially placed in a private room, but as she gets closer to her "out date," she gets transferred to more and more crowded conditions, as explained in the following excerpt:

> After spending 3½ weeks in a cell with a woman I didn't know, I was classified to 3-6 cottage. I was sentenced with enough time to get a private room. The room was 6´ x 10´ and had a solid door with a small window in it. There I could have my TV, radio, and clothes. My mom had made me some curtains and a quilt to match. I could decorate my room and make it as comfortable as possible. The locker was huge, but I had very little property to put in it. I was allowed 30 pieces of clothing in my room at one time. Anything else had to be stored in a storage room.
>
> That cottage reminded me of a nursing home—two halls of 14 rooms on each separated by an officer's desk. In front of her desk was the cardroom and TV room to be shared by 28 women. Those rooms were 20´ x 40´ with windows overlooking the alley. After six years of living on a cottage, I was told I didn't have enough time to keep a private room. Too many women were being sentenced with 60 to 100 years, and I was considered a short-timer having 35 years. With a private room, you can find time to be alone, by yourself without 100 eyes on you.
>
> I was moved to 2-4 cottage in a semiprivate dorm, at least compared to MSC [Medium Security Complex] where I am now living. On 2-4 cottage, there was a 50" wall that separated every two bunk beds. These are called cubicles. Between each bunk bed there was a row of four lockers, giving even more privacy. There were seven cubicles to both halls. Half of the cubicle belonged to me and half to my bunkie. There was an aisle that was 24" wide from the bed to the locker where we got dressed. If I opened my locker door, it gave me the illusion of dressing in

private—only two women from across the hall could see me dressing if they looked over. My locker on 2-4 was 18" x 22" x 6'. Everything I owned had to fit in that locker, except for two pairs of shoes that I could leave under the bed. If I rolled my clothes just right, I could fit more in there. We put boxes on end and placed the rolled-up clothes in stacks. After living out of cardboard boxes and a small locker, you learn tricks on how to make more room inside the locker. One trick is to keep some of your clothes in a plastic bag in the bottom of your laundry bag.

Here on MSC, everything you own must fit in your locker. This includes your TV. Nothing but a couple of pairs of shoes can be left out. If even a pencil is left out, you will get a write-up. On MSC, the dorms are open. No walls separate the beds. When you sit up on your bed, all you see is one body after another. There isn't even an illusion of privacy over here. Even the showers are open. A shower curtain separates me from another woman showering. If I am in the back of the shower, all her rinsed soap floats past my shower shoes, and if I finish before her, I must walk past her to get out and vice versa. There is no place private on MSC. The halls have 21 women on each, and two halls share one day room that is 12' x 20'. Imagine 42 women in one room trying to hear the TV over the roar of women's voices and the humming of the ice machine. The noise can be—and is—maddening. You try to get away from the noise but you can't. People are everywhere. The only place you can go is the john and even there you have to deal with the four-inch spaces between the door and the wall. Privacy? What privacy? Space? What space? I lost both eight years ago.

Thus, women are forced to recognize and interpret space as a defining factor in their identities and to remain aware of the importance of space in their lives.

Time, too, is an issue that takes on new dimensions for incarcerated women. While many had shown little awareness of time while outside, they acknowledge the many uses of time that they have recognized on the inside, as exemplified by one woman's attempts to control her own perceptions of time:

I no longer count my time by days, I count it by seasons, for the number of days makes the year seem too long. As for seasons, there's only four—a number I can easily handle.

I do a lot of self-talk: "winter's almost over and soon it'll be spring, spring always goes fast so I can practically say that summer is right around the corner. I'd better make a list of the summer clothes I'll need and send it to my sister. . . ." In the middle of February, I find myself planning for 80-degree days. But the concept of 12 seasons left to be here is much easier to compute than 1,460 days.

Small Winds of Resistance

For many readers, the descriptions provided by the prisoners might seem maddening, and the need to fight back, resist, or revolt might seem like a driving force. Instead, most of the women in IWP seem somewhat humbled and quieted by their situation. Many argue that there will never be such a thing as a riot at this particular prison, as no one is motivated enough to unite in such a dramatic way. Apparently, the various uncertainties, clashes, paradoxes, and crises prevent unity. However, certain experiences result in collective action, although usually in a controlled and careful form, as demonstrated by the following account:

> For an inmate, power is very limited. Speaking what is on your mind is not allowed or you'll go to lock. If you talk back or question what you are being told, it could be taken as insolence, arguing, being argumentative, or maybe even disorderly conduct. Our main outlet is pen and paper.
>
> We could have power, more anyway, if the inmates exhibited any sign of unity. Since I have been here, I have witnessed this only one time. We got a new chaplain here, and it appeared that she was extremely prejudiced against couples, especially if they included individuals who did not look properly "feminine." One of these manish-looking women attended a service one day and the chaplain embarrassed her in front of everyone there,

including outside volunteers. She told her how her appearance was inappropriate and that she shouldn't come back.

News of this story spread like wildfire and everyone was outraged. It was planned that for the next service, all the couples would attend in whatever attire they chose. The look of shock on the chaplain's face was worth every bit of it. The chapel, which hadn't been full probably since the prison existed, was packed. There weren't even enough chairs; people stood. Needless to say, the problem was resolved.

We wanted the chaplain to know that she would have her hands full if she tried that again. It wasn't right and the unified front took care of the problem. Inmates together have the power but individually, there is none.

IMPLICATIONS

It is difficult to predict what the potential impact of this project might eventually be, especially in light of the current U.S. hysteria over crime and punishment and the ever-present backlash against women who break "the rules" in any way. Still, the project will help to do a number of things both for the student/authors and for the public. First, it should help to personalize the experience of imprisonment for those who have never been incarcerated or who have never known someone who has been in prison. It seems all too easy in light of current discussions to speak of prisoners as abstract deviants and to categorically dismiss them as monsters who deserve the worst treatment society can offer. Instead, by depicting the personal "normalcy" of most of the women who write for the book (their emotions and responses sound familiar to those that any reader might have), the book thereby places readers in a situation where they might be led to evaluate what their own responses to a similar situation might be ("how would I feel. . . ?"). Thus, by making connections between readers and the authors, the book argues for humane treatment of prisoners. Despite this implicit goal, the book avoids dogma and still heavily persuades. Additionally, by displaying the personal progress made by each of the students involved, the project shows the redemptive potential of rehabilitative programs, which, it is hoped, offers a strong counterargument to the "lock 'em up and throw away the key" mentality surfacing in many areas of the U.S. today. Finally, as mentioned earlier, the project allows students to acknowledge their own experiences and emotions, validate them, and assert their value as individuals with a message for us all.

PART V

RESPONSES

THIRTY-EIGHT

Advocacy in the Classroom—Or the Curriculum? A Response

GERALD GRAFF

IN CHAPTER 2, Troy Duster observes that students in Anglo-American and Hispanic schools these days often encounter dramatically clashing images of historical figures such as Sir Francis Drake. In Anglo schools, students are still likely to meet the "good" Sir Francis traditionally depicted in the history books as a hero of discovery, while in many Hispanic schools the hero has been replaced by a "bad" Sir Francis who embodies the evils of Western imperialism. Duster's observation was made only in passing, but his example of the good/bad Sir Francis reflects the divided picture of the world that the American curriculum increasingly presents to students.

In fact, in the age of the culture war, the curriculum seems to be splitting into two separate curricula representing starkly opposing views of history, literature, and the social world. My guess is it would not be unusual for a college student these days to go from a course in which Western culture is treated as an unproblematic heritage worthy of being noiselessly passed on to future generations to a class in the next hour (possibly in the same discipline) in which Western culture is assumed to be deeply compromised by racism, homophobia, and sexism. In a similar way, a student may learn in humanities courses that the concept of objective truth has been discredited, only to discover the concept alive and well in economics, political science, or physics. The chances are good, moreover, that the conflicting assumptions in these courses will not be explicitly asserted or explained but will be treated as things that go without saying among right-thinking people.

I would be surprised if the effect on students of being exposed to such disjunctions were not one of severe cognitive dissonance, accompanied by a feeling of being caught in the middle between opposing forms of disciplinary and intellectual "correctness." To be sure, some students flourish when given the opportunity to construct their own personal conversation out of conflicting course monologues. These students, however, tend to be the minority who come to college with some experience and previously formed skill at synthesizing ideas and arguments. Their less-experienced classmates probably will be able to cope only by resorting to the familiar practice of giving each of their instructors whatever they seem to "want" even though it is contradictory. These students will avoid cognitive dissonance, but only by reproducing the curriculum's compartmentalizations in themselves.

I would like to suggest that curricular cognitive dissonance, in which students become volleyballs batted back and forth in an ideological game whose rules change confusingly without notice from course to course, is at the heart of the "advocacy" problem. The modern curriculum has long made students victims of such conflicting signals, but as the conflicts across courses and fields have become more polarized and openly political, the mixed messages received by students create a new kind of inducement to give each teacher whatever he or she "wants." This is a form of "disempowerment" that cannot be addressed effectively by teaching any course differently because it occurs in the spaces between courses.

Advocacy, in short, is a problem not just of "the classroom" but of the curriculum as a whole. Reducing the problem to what goes on in "the classroom" assumes that teaching is by nature a solo activity, enacted separately in self-contained courses that are not in dialogue with each other. It is easy to accede to this assumption when as teachers (or students) we have never experienced anything but such isolated classrooms. If God had wanted courses to be connected and coordinated, why did He or She assign them to these separate rooms?

Of course, one reason why we must be screened from our colleagues' classrooms may be our fear of what we might hear in them if we were not. "The classroom" protects us from being too persistently reminded of the painful possibility that the affable colleague in the next office may well regard our most cherished assumptions as pernicious and possibly wicked nonsense. In Chapter 10 Louis Menand suggests that "disciplinarity makes us stupid." I would add that "the classroom" makes us stupid insofar as it shelters us from the criticism of our assumptions to which we would risk exposing ourselves if our courses were in dialogue. We tell our students we want them to disagree with us, yet we send them the very opposite message when we let our classroom walls protect us from the disagreements of our colleagues.

Once teaching is assumed to be a solo activity, the problem of advocacy is then seen as one with which each instructor must presumably make a separate peace. So it is not surprising that the task taken up by several of the volume contributors is to set forth guidelines for solo acts of teaching, guidelines that often come down to a distinction between advocacy and indoctrination, or between legitimate advocacy, usually identified with ideological or philosophical "balance," and illegitimate advocacy, usually associated with extremism and intolerance toward dissenting views. In Chapter 1 Myles Brand establishes what will become a familiar pattern advancing balance as the criterion for distinguishing between advocacy and indoctrination, and his argument is echoed by Nadine Strossen in Chapter 6. If any consensus emerges from the chapters in this volume, it is Advocacy, Yes, Indoctrination, No.

One of the difficulties with this view is that many who might readily agree *in theory* that advocacy is good and indoctrination is bad would disagree *in practice* over what should count as one or the other. What looks like "balance" to me may well seem outrageous "indoctrination" to you.

Once the curriculum is structured as a conversation, however, rather than as a set of monologues conducted in the isolation of "the classroom," balance becomes achievable through the clash and interaction of "advocacy" positions themselves, even when some of these positions take extremist forms. Instead of bouncing students back and forth between noncommunicating advocates (or balkanizing them in separate and contradictory courses), the curriculum could then begin helping students to take an articulate position in the conversation of advocacies, including the advocacy debate itself. I think Alan Kors takes a step in this direction in his suggestion that, in looking for ideological balance, our unit should be not the individual course or teacher, as Brand and Strossen assume, but the department or college curriculum, where balance is achieved through a conversation of diverse perspectives. Carolyn Heilbrun makes a similar point in Chapter 17. "Balance in *the classroom* is not what we should be after," she writes, "but balance in the whole curriculum."

In other words, once the curriculum rather than the course becomes the unit of analysis, lack of balance on the part of individual teachers can become a source of strength rather than a problem. And this should not seem surprising, seeing that many of the most acclaimed teachers since Plato have possessed a streak of fanaticism and inflexibility. My own best teacher, Yvor Winters of Stanford, an embattled poet, literary critic, and moralist, would never have been accused of balance. Winters believed, and frankly sought to make his students believe, that the Romantic and modernist movements had been vast and unfortunate mistakes in literary history. Keats, Wordsworth, and Shelley were greatly overrated poets, and the foggy relativism promoted by Emerson constituted a profound "betrayal of democracy." For Winters, a more balanced statement of the case on his part as a teacher would have only compounded the betrayal.

Many of Winters' judgments now seem less persuasive to me than they did when I studied with him in the early 1960s, but at the time they had a great impact on me and other Stanford students, who divided into pro- and anti-Wintersians. True, such debates can be a problem as well as a stimulus, but having myself never previously encountered a teacher who took strong positions as Winters did, I found the experience captivating and very necessary for my own education.

At the same time, what made the encounter with Winters captivating was that there was only one of him. His teaching had meaning and impact only because it contrasted sharply in content and style with that of his colleagues, who provided the resisting background that made Winters's ideas intelligible. Again, then, the job of counteracting or "balancing" the passionately committed teacher belongs not to that teacher but to his or her colleagues, that is, to the curriculum.

Dramatic as they may have seemed at the time, the ideological differences between Winters and his Stanford colleagues in 1960 appear relatively minor when compared to the much wider ideological gulf that now polarizes academic culture and the culture beyond. Though Winters's moral view of literature was at odds with the views of his New Critical and historicist colleagues (whose views in turn were at odds with each another), all these groups saw themselves as "humanists" in the traditional sense of the term. They were bound together, too, by the unspoken social values and polite manners of an academic culture overwhelmingly white and male. The shattering of this tacit social consensus has produced an academic culture today in which conflicts are far deeper and more visible than they were a generation ago.

It is this climate of deep and open conflict that has created the two separate curricula to which I referred earlier, trapping students in the middle between clashing models of intellectual correctness. As I have been trying to suggest, however, the pressure on students to conform to professorial "advocacy" is rooted not just in today's increasingly polarized cultural politics but in an insular idea of "the classroom" that leaves teachers unaccountable to the disagreements of their peers. Although we professors are routinely accountable to peer criticism when we publish articles and books or speak at conferences, this normal accountability is curiously assumed to cease once we enter "the classroom." In fact, the notion that my colleagues should know much about my teaching—much less be encouraged to enter my class and disagree with me—would often be viewed as a kind of threat to my academic freedom.

To address the advocacy problem more successfully, then, I think educational institutions will need to go beyond the kind of pluralism that is content to expose students to a diverse array of course perspectives to a pluralism that invites students into a conversation between these perspectives. In other words—and this, too, is obscured when the advocacy problem is reduced to a question of individual course strategy—teachers on the Left and the Right *need* one another in order to become intelligible to those students who are not clear on what terms such as "Left" and "Right" may mean on the academic-intellectual map. Intellectual rivals are cognitively interdependent: "non-Western" becomes a meaningful category only when put into dialogue with "Western," and if that dialogue is obscured by isolating Western and non-Western courses from one another, we can't be sure students will be able to reconstruct it on their own.

What then is to be done? My own view is that symposia such as the one this book represents provide an important model of what can be done on campus and in the curriculum. At the conference out of which the book grew, I wondered more than once what undergraduates would make of our panels and discussions were these events to take place not only on their campuses, but as a regular and continuing part of the curriculum. In fact, the conference *was* part of the educational experience of a number of graduate students who participated; why then could such conferences not serve undergraduates and even high school students as well? Periodically spaced throughout the semester and suitably adapted to different levels of schooling, such conferences could transform now disparate and often hostile course monologues into conversations.[1]

The *New York Times* of May 3, 1995 carried a report on an undergraduate course at UCLA whose aim is to create just such a conversational space.[2] The course, called The History and Politics of Affirmative Action, brings in some 20 faculty members from different disciplines inside and outside the university on a guest-appearance basis in order to engage opposing perspectives on affirmative action. It is notable, too, that, at a moment when the media has had few kind things to say about higher education, the *Times* article was highly favorable, stressing how the course gets students animatedly arguing with each other and their professors on intellectual issues, even after class. Such publicity should be welcome to institutions desperately battling to retain or attract financial support.

By organizing academic discussion around the problem, making the problem itself and the clashing perspectives on it part of our academic subject matter, symposia and courses of the kind I am discussing can not only help students sort out and enter the discussion but can clarify disputed issues for those outside the university and give them a glimpse of what is valuable about our recent controversies rather than simply what is angry and divisive. This year we will be experimenting with such cross-course symposia in the University of Chicago's new masters program in Humanities, which I am directing. Like many educational problems, then, the problem of "advocacy" is likely to be best addressed by making the problem itself part of the object of study.

This, however, means coming at times out of "the classroom" and entering into dialogues with other classrooms, where we will hear things said that we won't want to hear and therefore that we *need* to hear. The experience may be painful at first, but surely no more painful than the climate of paranoia and antagonism that surrounds all of us now and that will only worsen unless hatred can be channeled into discussion.

NOTES

1. The case for reconceiving the curriculum as a "conversation" has now been effectively outlined by Arthur N. Applebee, in *Curriculum as Conversation: Transforming Traditions of Teaching and Learning* (Chicago, IL: University of Chicago Press, 1996).
2. Seth Mydans, "Class Notes," *New York Times,* Wednesday, May 3, 1995, B8.

THIRTY-NINE

Afterthoughts on the Role of Advocacy in the Classroom

ANDREA A. LUNSFORD

GIVEN AN OPPORTUNITY TO RESPOND to chapters in earlier parts of this volume, I am reminded of the importance of perspective, of where one stands, and of the partial nature of even the broadest perspectives. Although readers are reading the same texts, they inevitably experience them in different ways.

It seems to me important that this basic rhetorical insight inform current discussions of advocacy in the classroom, for our students hear and experience what we have to say differently, as well. We may "advocate," and indeed I would argue that we inevitably advocate, that we are always already advocating. But what that advocating means to our students, what they can and choose to hear, well, there's the rub. For example, in one class I know of, a teacher attempted nonadvocacy by adopting a stance of neutrality, partly as a way of trying to raise the level of comfort in the classroom. But in doing so, she enacted one of the points made in Chapter 7 by Michael Root: a supposed neutrality can close down—rather than make a space for—the very kind of critical inquiry most teachers claim to value. In this particular case, what one of the students heard *instead* of the teacher's intended "neutral" stance was one of strong advocacy—for the mainstream or majority point of view, one that excluded both the student and his critical inquiry.

All those who take questions of advocacy seriously should take the point revealed in this teacher's classroom-based research to heart: What is presented in one way by a professor may be taken in quite another by a student. What is perceived as an attempt at openness in the classroom may be perceived by students as a closed system in which they are, ironically, coerced into being "open." In this regard, the increasing use of electronic journaling in which students and teacher engage in numerous electronic exchanges seems relevant. While the chapters in this volume do not directly address the implications of electronic media for exacerbating the difficulties surrounding issues of advocacy—for both teachers and students— these implications are abundantly clear and troubling. As every teacher who has used e-mail reflectors or local area networks or electronic dialogue journals can attest, the ethics of electronic communication, of who is allowed to speak and to advocate and of who is silenced, are far from understood or agreed upon. In fact, many have found an increase in hostility, in incivility, and in charges and countercharges of all kinds when students (and teachers) communicate electronically.

The difficulties inherent in multiple perspectives, the sine qua non of any classroom, suggest not only that teachers must assume advocacy but also, as Patricia Meyer Spacks notes in the introduction, that we understand our roles not in terms of a binary between advocacy and nonadvocacy but in relation to the both/and nature of teaching: a sense of advocacy that encompasses a teacher's rights *and* responsibilities, a teacher's advocacy *and* accountability. Indeed, on even brief reflection, it is not surprising to find the terms "professor" and "advocacy" linked, since there is much to bind them definition-ally: As a number of authors have pointed out, "advocate" is defined as one who speaks on behalf of another, as one who publicly recommends or raises a voice in behalf of a proposal or tenet. And "professor" is similarly defined as one who publicly declares, one who makes open declaration of sentiments or beliefs or allegiances to some principles.

Many contributors agree with this conjunction of professorial rights and responsibilities, of advocacy and accountability. In

Chapter 2, Troy Duster argues that advocacy should become engagement and that engagement should entail certain responsibilities to the subject of discourse, the classroom, and the students as well as to ourselves. In the same vein, in Chapter 3 Ernestine Friedl notes that advocacy in the classroom quite simply is our job, our definition, our modus operandi—and one that does not preclude what she calls "civility" or multiple points of view or critical inquiry. In Chapter 6, Nadine Strossen contributes to this exploration by demonstrating that advocacy conducted in the context of critical inquiry and analysis is entirely consistent with free inquiry and freedom of speech, while Whitney Davis's emphasis in Chapter 9 on a "new ethicism," with a focus on personal and social or "intersubjective" responsibility, helps to further illuminate the terms of discussion. So whether the term "advocacy" functions primarily today as an alarmist term or "high-octane rhetoric," as Louis Menand suggests in Chapter 10, what advocacy seems to mark for many is a complex set of rights and responsibilities professors have to subjects, to students, to themselves, and to one another.

If the contributors can agree on broad and complex definitions of advocacy, they are less in accord on how to carry out this set of rights and responsibilities in our classrooms. In retrospect, perhaps the singular focus on the term "advocacy" helps hide from view a closely related value-laden term, "authority." Who has and does not have authority, how does one get it, what knowledge systems and institutions partake in it, and which are excluded from it are questions everywhere at issue in discussions of advocacy. Duster touches on this issue when he discusses student efforts to get their own voices heard—and the divergent responses these efforts have elicited from the professoriat. Friedl also alludes to this issue when she writes of a "new harmony" now heard in scholarly as well as geographical communities and the different dynamic that such a new harmony sets in motion in regard to authority in the classroom. In Chapter 25 Keith Moxey also raises this issue in his analysis of the ways in which the process of valuation in art history has typically remained deeply hidden and unacknowledged. But from my own partial perspective, the volume does not focus clearly enough on issues of authority as one of the major causes for the amount of attention—both positive and negative—given to "advocacy" in the classroom today. After all, if the locus of authority were not disrupted, disputed, perhaps displaced; if the locus of authority remained unmarked, as it were, then we would not likely have compiled this volume. But traditional notions of authority have been unsettled, as Chapter 5 by Geoffrey Stone makes clear in its tracing of the locus of academic authority from doctrinal bodies to lay trustees. And authority has, of course, been disrupted in the last three decades, at least theoretically, on almost all fronts.

One of the ironic consequences of this dissettlement of traditional academic authority may be what Gertrude Himmelfarb, in Chapter 8, calls a "new solipsism" and what others refer to as "personalism," as a struggle for personal agency and voice, a place at the table of discourse that puts a focus on the "who" that is speaking rather than on "what is being said." I say this consequence is ironic because, in its attempts to disrupt a traditional academic authority that has been highly individualistic, devoted to the myth of autonomy, to the great teacher and his classroom, the great man and his artistic works, it manages to reify many of the radically individualist assumptions it sought to call into question.

A second consequence of the disruption of traditional academic authority, however, seems much more promising to me, and it is touched on frequently in this volume: the development of a pedagogy to nurture a differing sense and use of authority as well as a sense of advocacy that encompasses both rights and responsibilities, that enacts a "new ethicism." What is the shape of this emergent pedagogy? First, it is aware of itself as deeply embedded in the context of particular and local classrooms and universities and schools. And the doors of this pedagogy are open, not closed in the safe but ultimately isolated and unaccountable ways of many traditionalist classrooms. (It is this very openness, in part, I would argue, that invited the kind of scrutiny that led to this volume devoted to advocacy in the classroom.) If I understand the thrust of Chapter 1 by Myles Brand, this emergent pedagogy is also dialogic, based not on dogma or conversion but on the free give-and-take of ideas, on the kind of dialogism also inherent in Gerald Graff's recommendations in Chapter 38 to allow components of the curriculum to converse vigorously with one another. The goal of this pedagogy is the increasingly sophisticated practice of critical inquiry, and it focuses not on owning (as in the individual chips of intellectual property we and our students have been taught to hoard) but on owning up, on taking responsibility for words, actions, and positions in the classroom as well as in the sense of the literal ability to respond—"respond-ability" in the classroom. In addition, this emergent pedagogy values and builds on collaboration and differences. At best, it is transformative in the sense in which I believe many African American feminists use the term; it acts as an agent of change.

But in spite of the enormous efforts of feminist teachers, and especially feminist teachers of color, this emerging pedagogy is fragile at best. It will be difficult to enact (as those in this volume who write of a feminist pedagogy can attest from hard experience) because students expect and often demand that their teachers replicate traditional patterns of authority even when they seem, on the other hand, to want to challenge or eschew authority. This past year, I asked a large sample of Ohio State's 5,000+ first-year students to tell me about their associations with the word "authority." I think it is not an overstatement to say that they hated it. Out of over 1,000 responses, only a handful carried any positive connotation; none mentioned women; none identified themselves as having authority or even wanting it; none associated authority with supportive or helpful people. Instead, they reported that "Authority causes fear and is abused"; and they conjured up images of control that were overwhelmingly unfair. My own admittedly idiosyncratic favorite response out of this informal survey: "Authority: someone I would never, ever, ever date."

Nevertheless, students often expect teachers to play traditional authority roles, and they are resistant when we do not meet those expectations or challenge them with a pedagogy that arrays teacherly authority as well as the authority of knowledge in different ways. Furthermore, important institutional factors block the way of enacting the kind of pedagogy for advocacy that has been discussed in this volume. That kind of pedagogy, one that focuses on an ethic of responsibility, on the valuing of difference, on negotiation and collaboration, on inclusion, on shared attempts at critical understandings—that kind of pedagogy cannot easily occur in a 10- or 14-week parcel of time; nor can it develop easily in cramped and inhospitable and highly institutionalized, much less disembodied electronic "virtual," spaces. Even less can it develop where the system of rewards (grades) is linked thoroughly to traditional models of authority and to notions of institutional hierarchy and autonomous individualism. And finally, it cannot develop unless those of us teaching at research institutions attend to the pedagogical preparation of graduate students, a need that may call on us to develop a series of "teaching scenes" for use in our individual departments, scenes that would allow us in each particular instance to evoke a set of best practices for dealing with issues of advocacy raised in the scenes.

But these are issues of the *context* in which advocacy and accountability, student and teacherly rights and responsibilities can and must take place. Many volume contributors share large areas of agreement—on matters of professional standards, on the inevitability of advocacy, and on the limits ethical constraints raise when advocacy moves toward indoctrination. If so, we might now best turn to local contextualizations of these areas of agreement, to the questions of advocacy and freedom we address as individual teachers whenever and wherever we teach.

BIOGRAPHIES

FELICIA ACKERMAN is professor of philosophy at Brown University, as well as a writer whose short stories have appeared in ten magazines and one O. Henry Prize collection.

SHAWNY ANDERSON received her Ph.D. in 1994 from the Department of Communication at Purdue University in West Lafayette, Indiana. Currently an Assistant Professor in the Department of Communication at Loyola University of Chicago, she specializes in Cultural Studies, Rhetorical Theory and Criticism, and Qualitative Methods.

ANGELA ANSELMO, a faculty member in the Department of Counseling and Student Counseling at Baruch College, CUNY, has counseled SEEK students for over 20 years. She received her Ph.D. from Yeshiva University in developmental psychology and linguistics in 1991. Currently, she is the President of the New York State Association for Spiritual, Ethical, Religious, and Value Issues in Counseling (ASERVIC), a division of the New York Counseling Association. Dr. Anselmo's interests include bilingualism, cultural diversity, and spirituality.

ERNST BENJAMIN is a political scientist and Associate General Secretary of the American Association of University Professors. His recent publications include: *Academic Freedom: An Everyday Concern,* edited with Donald R. Wagner; "A Faculty Response to the Fiscal Crisis," in *Higher Education Under Fire,* edited by Michael Bérubé and Cary Nelson; and "Five Misconceptions About Tenure," in *Trusteeship* 3, no. 1 (January/February 1995), 16-21.

MICHAEL BÉRUBÉ is Professor of English at the University of Illinois at Urbana-Champaign. His most recent book is *Life As We Know It.*

MYLES BRAND is President of Indiana University and a Professor of Philosophy. He has published extensively in the fields of philosophy and higher education. His recent publications include *Intending and Acting: Toward a Naturalized Action Theory* and "Undergraduate Education: Seeking the Golden Mean" in *Educational Record.*

SAMUEL W. CALHOUN is Professor of Law, Washington & Lee University. A cum laude graduate of Harvard University and with a law degree from the University of Georgia, magna cum laude, he is former associate of King & Spalding, Atlanta. His areas of teaching are contracts, creditors' rights, commercial transactions, and the abortion controversy. He and his wife Jackie have three children. An elder and teacher in the Grace Presbyterian Church, he enjoys playing the guitar, tennis, golf, basketball, and American history.

MARTHA CHAMALLAS is a Professor of Law at the University of Pittsburgh where she teaches antidiscrimination law and feminist legal theory. Her writings explore racial and cultural domination, harassment, stereotyping and legal control of sexual conduct. Her recent publications include *Jean Jew's Case: Resisting Sexual Harassment in the Academy*, 6 Yale Journal of Law and Feminism (1994) and *Structuralist and Cultural Domination Theories Meet Title VII: Some Contemporary Influences*, 92 Michigan Law Review 2370 (1994).

WHITNEY DAVIS is Professor of Art History at Northwestern University. His most recent publications include *Masking the Blow: The Scene of Representation in Late Prehistoric Egyptian Art* and *Gay and Lesbian Studies in Art History* (Ed.).

TROY DUSTER is Professor of Sociology and Director of the Institute for the Study of Social Change at the University of California, Berkeley. His most recent book is *Backdoor to Eugenics*. His article "The Diversity of California at Berkeley: An Emerging Reformulation of 'Competence' in an Increasingly Multi-cultural World" appeared in *Beyond a Dream Deferred: Multicultural Education and the Politics of Excellence*.

JUDITH ENTES is an Associate Professor in the Department of English at Baruch College, The City University of New York. For over twenty years she has taught students who are labeled "remedial" in reading and/or writing. Her dissertation, completed in 1989 at Fordham University, examined time in literature. Her research interests include reader-response theory and uses of collaboration. She contributed a chapter on multiple authorship in *Writing With,* edited by Reagan, Fox, and Bleich.

ERNESTINE FRIEDL is James B. Duke Professor of Cultural Anthropology, Emeritus, at Duke University. She is a leading scholar of gender and of village life in modern Greece. Her most recent articles are "Sex the Invisible" published in the *American Anthropologist* and "The Life of an Academic" published in the *Annual Review of Anthropology*, 1995.

PENNY S. GOLD is Chair of the History Department at Knox College, where she has taught since 1976. She is the author of *The Lady and the Virgin: Image, Attitude, and Experience in Twelfth-Century France* and is now working on a book on the place of the bible in American Jewish education during the first half of the twentieth century.

GERALD GRAFF is George M. Pullman Professor of English and Education at the University of Chicago. His most recent book is *Beyond the Culture Wars: How Teaching the Conflicts Can Revitalize American Education.* He is currently directing a new Master's Program in Humanities at Chicago, in which he hopes to try some of the ideas presented in his essay.

CAROLYN HEILBRUN is the Avalon Foundation Professor in the Humanities Emerita, Columbia University, where she taught for over thirty years. Heilbrun is the author of *Writing a Woman's Life, Hamlet's Mother and Other Women, The Education of a Woman: The Life of Gloria Steinem,* and, under the name Amanda Cross, of eleven detective novels. Heilbrun was President of the MLA in 1984.

HILDE HEIN teaches Philosophy at the College of the Holy Cross, specializing in Aesthetics, Philosophy of Law, and Feminist Theory. She is the author of *The Exploratorium: The Museum as Laboratory,* and co-editor of *Aesthetics in Feminist Perspective.* She is currently at work on a book called *Changing Times in the Museum World.* A longstanding member of the American Society for Aesthetics, she serves on its Board of Trustees.

SUSAN E. HENKING is Associate Professor and Chair of Religious Studies at Hobart and William Smith Colleges. She has published on historical interactions between American sociology and Protestantism, the use of psychology by feminist theologians, and the place of religion in AIDS-related memoirs. Her work with a Lilly-endowed American Academy of Religion Teaching Workshop informs her reflections on teaching religious studies.

GERTRUDE HIMMELFARB is Professor Emeritus of History at the Graduate School of the City University of New York. She has published extensively on Victorian England and the history of ideas. She has addressed advocacy issues in *On Looking Into the Abyss: Untimely Thoughts on Culture and Society* and *The New History and the Old. The De-moralization of Society: From Victorian Virtues to Modern Values* appeared in 1995.

TOM JEHN is a graduate student in the Department of English at the University of Virginia. He is currently working on a dissertation that examines the intersections between the corporate state and public intellectuals in the postwar period.

RAY LINN is a high school teacher in Los Angeles. For several years he was an English teacher at Jordan High School in Watts, and for the past few years he has been a philosophy teacher at Cleveland Humanities High School, an integration magnet in Reseda. He has also done consulting work with the Los Angeles Educational Partnership and with both the Panasonic and Rockefeller Foundations. In August he published *A Teacher's Introduction to Postmodernism* for the National Council of Teachers of English.

ANDREA A. LUNSFORD is Distinguished Professor and Vice Chair of the Department of English at The Ohio State University. Currently a member of the MLA Executive Council, Lunsford has served as chair of the MLA Division on the Teaching of Writing and as Chair of the Conference on College Composition and Communication. Her most recent publications include *Reclaiming Rhetorica: Women in the Rhetorical Tradition;* "Representing Audience," with Lisa Ede (*CCC,* May 1996), and "Intellectual Property and Composition Studies," with Susan West (*CCC,* October 1996).

PETER J. MARKIE is a Professor of Philosophy at the University of Missouri at Columbia. His works include *A Professor's Duties: Ethical Issues in College Teaching;* "Professors, Students and Friendship," in *Morality, Responsibility and the University,* edited by S. Cahn; and "Affirmative Action and the Awarding of Tenure," *Affirmative Action and the University,* edited by S. Cahn.

JANICE MCLANE is assistant professor of philosophy at Morgan State University in Baltimore. She is currently writing a book on internalized oppression in women, and the development of women's literal and metaphoric voices as a means of combatting such oppression.

LOUIS MENAND is Professor of English at the Graduate Center of the City University of New York. He is the author of *Discovering Modernism: T. S. Eliot and His Context* (1987) and the editor of *The Future of Academic Freedom* (1997).

HELENE MOGLEN is Professor of English Literature and Women's Studies at the University of California, Santa Cruz. Her books include *The*

Philosophical Irony of Laurence Sterne and *Charlotte Bronte, The Self Conceived.* She is just completing *The Anxieties of Indeterminacy,* a feminist and psychoanalytic study of subjectivity and sexuality in the eighteenth-century, male-authored English novel.

KEITH MOXEY is currently Professor and Chair of Art History at Barnard College, Columbia University. He is author of *Peasants, Warriors, & Wives* and *The Practice of Theory.* He is coeditor with Michael Ann Holly and Norman Byrson of *Visual Theory* and *Visual Culture.*

RICHARD MULCAHY received his Ph.D. in history from West Virginia University in 1988. The author of a number of scholarly articles and papers, he has just completed a monograph on the United Mine Workers of America Welfare and Retirement Fund. He is an Associate Professor of History with the University of Pittsburgh's Titusville campus, and a Fellow of the Center For Northern Appalachian Studies, Saint Vincent College, Latrobe, Pennsylvania.

MICHAEL A. OLIVAS is William B. Bates Distinguished Professor of Law and Director of the Institute for Higher Education Law and Governance at the University of Houston. He is General Counsel to the American Association of University Professors. His books include *The Dilemma of Access: Minorities in Two Year Colleges, Latino College Students,* and *The Law and Higher Education: Cases and Materials on Colleges in Court.* He specializes in education law and immigration and nationality law.

JULIE A. REUBEN received her Ph.D. in history from Stanford University. She is an Associate Professor at the Harvard Graduate School of Education, and author of *The Making of the Modern University: Intellectual Transformation and the Marginalization of Morality.*

MICHAEL ROOT is an Associate Professor of Philosophy at the University of Minnesota and author of the book *Philosophy of Social Science: The Methods, Ideals, and Politics of Social Inquiry.* His specialties are the nature of language and the methods of the social sciences, and his articles have appeared in *American Philosophical Quarterly, Biology and Philosophy, Linguistics and Philosophy, Notre Dame Journal of Formal Logic,* and *Philosophical Studies.* He is currently writing a book on systems of classification in the natural and social sciences.

JAYNE SBARBORO has returned to teaching a fourth-fifth grade classroom full time at Park Hill Elementary, in the Denver Public Schools. She is currently a Denver Public Schools Literacy Trainer through the

Public Education and Business Coalition. She continues to be involved in multicultural studies and curriculum development through the Colorado Humanities Center, University of Colorado, Boulder.

RICHARD H. SEEBURGER is Professor of Law at the University of Pittsburgh. He received his law degrees from Harvard University. He is former Associate Dean and former Interim Dean at the University of Pittsburgh School of Law. He has served as Chair of Committee A on Academic Freedom and Tenure for the Pennsylvania AAUP and President of the University of Pittsburgh AAUP. He teaches Constitutional Law, Church and State, Remedies, Torts, Civil Rights, Conflict of Law, Evidence, and Comparative Constitutional Law.

PETER M. SHANE is dean and Professor of Law at the University of Pittsburgh School of Law. The author of numerous articles on constitutional and administrative law, he is coauthor of *Separation of Powers Law: Cases and Materials* (with Harold H. Bruff, 1996), and *Administrative Law: The American Public Law System* (3rd Edition, 1992, with J. L. Mashaw and R. A. Merrill).

MARK C. SMITH, an Assistant Professor of American Studies and History at the University of Texas at Austin, has a masters degree in social work as well as a doctorate in American Civilization. His book *Social Science in the Crucible: The American Debate Over Objectivity and Purpose, 1918-1941* (Duke: 1994) argues that a social science of advocacy existed alongside one of technical quantitative empiricism during the 1920s and '30s.

PATRICIA MEYER SPACKS, 1994 President of the Modern Language Association, is Edgar F. Shannon Professor of English and chair of the English department at the University of Virginia. Her most recent publication is *Boredom: The Literary History of a State of Mind.* She is writing a book on self-love in the seventeenth and eighteenth centuries.

GEOFFREY R. STONE is Provost of the University of Chicago and Harry Kalven, Jr. Distinguished Service Professor of Law. He is a leading scholar of constitutional law. Among his recent publications are *The Bill of Rights in the Welfare State* and *Constitutional Law.* He has written widely about freedom of speech and published "Controversial Scholarship and Faculty Appointments: A Dean's View" in the *Iowa Law Review.*

NADINE STROSSEN is Professor of Law at New York Law School and President of the American Civil Liberties Union. She specializes in constitutional law and human rights. Her most recent publications include *Defending Pornography: Free Speech, Sex, and the Fight for Women's Rights* and the coauthored *Speaking of Race, Speaking of Sex: Hate Speech, Civil Rights, and Civil Liberties.*

C. JAN SWEARINGEN is Professor of English at The University of Texas at Arlington. She is author of the award-winning book *Rhetoric and Irony, Western Literacy and Western Lies.* She is a member of the MLA Delegate Assembly Organizing Committee, the Executive Council of the Conference on College Composition and Communication, the Steering Committee of the American Society for the History of Rhetoric, and President-Elect of the Rhetoric Society of America. She is working on a book on multiculturalism in the ancient world.

JOHN O. VOLL is Professor of Islamic History in the Center for Muslim-Christian Understanding and the History Department at Georgetown University. He is a past president of the Middle East Studies Association and the New England Historical Association. He is the author of books and articles on Islamic and world history, including the coauthored book, *Islam and Democracy* (1996).

JEFFREY WALLEN is an assistant professor of comparative literature at Hampshire College. He has written widely about nineteenth-century European literature on topics such as aestheticism, literary portraiture, and biography. He has also written several essays on the problems and debates of current academic criticism, and he is finishing a book on "the poverty of conversation."

MICHAEL D. YATES is both a college teacher and a labor educator and activist. He has written several books and many articles on the topics of labor economics, labor relations, labor education, and work. His most recent book is *Power on the Job: The Legal Rights of Working People.*

LAMBERT ZUIDERVAART is Professor of Philosophy and Chairperson of the Philosophy Department at Calvin College, and President of the Urban Institute for Contemporary Arts in Grand Rapids, Michigan. He is the author of *Adorno's Aesthetic Theory: The Redemption of Illusion,* coauthor of *Dancing in the Dark: Youth, Popular Culture and the Electronic Media,* and coeditor of *Pledges of Jubilee: Essays on the Arts and Culture* and *The Semblance of Subjectivity: Essays in Adorno's Aesthetic Theory.*